# JOHN SOMERSET PAKINGTON

## HIS FIRST 50 YEARS

A Biography

by

Andrew Harris

First Published 2011


Set in Sabon
Body text 10.5pt on 13.5pt

ISBN no. 978-0-9544193-2-5

Typesetting and design by the author
Printed by Orphans Press Ltd, Leominster

## CONTENTS

## Introduction

After completing my research on another Worcestershire land-owning family, the Vernons of Hanbury, I was asked to give a talk on the Pakingtons, so I started looking into the sources. I soon found that there is a large archive in the Worcestershire Record Office of Pakington family papers, called the Hampton Collection, and, making access easier, it has all been put on microfilm. It is a very varied collection – there are a large number of medieval documents, most of which come from the family's Buckinghamshire properties; there are a certain amount of letters, accounts and other papers from the seventeenth and eighteenth centuries, and, probably the biggest collection of all, there are letters and diaries accumulated by John Somerset Pakington (as he was after 1830) which greatly illuminate his life and which form the basis of this book. In doing my research I quickly realised that this material, covering as it does the whole of his life and both his private and public persona, is most unusual in its scope, and that many of the papers, for example his surviving diaries, have never been systematically accessed before. In his day Pakington was a well-known parliamentary figure, serving as he did in three governments, albeit short lived ones, and I hope this book will bring this rather forgotten figure to life again.

There are, of course, many other publicly available sources for such public figures, not the least of which is Hansard, now available on-line, and I soon realised that to do justice to these many sources I would have to split this account into two parts; this, the first, covers the period till his first ministerial appointment in 1852, near his 53rd birthday, and the second will cover his busy ministerial career until he died, having been raised to the peerage as Lord Hampton, in 1880.

I hope the readers will approve of the many digressions that his career, both in parliament and as a county figure, has taken me into; not only do these throw light on many aspects of Worcestershire history, but they bring back to life many issues that were live in the first half of the nineteenth century, but which today are either forgotten, or only dimly remembered from school history lessons. Many of these are covered in the present volume; there will be more to come in the second.

John Somerset Pakington remains a rather enigmatic man in his views; in his early career he was staunchly Tory, regarding with great distaste any attack or even change in what he regarded as the pillars of the state and of English society: the Protestant Church, the Monarchy, and the Houses of Parliament. But unlike many people he seemed to moderate his views as he got older; perhaps the fact that he had opposed Parliamentary Reform in 1832, only to see it succeed and indeed furthered in 1867 and 1874, made him realise that these issues were never simple, and that most of the many reforms to public life that took place during his time in parliament in fact succeeded even though many had been initially opposed. Indeed on the hustings in the 1847 election, after the great Tory split the year before, he publicly said he could disagree with few of the measures of the Whig prime minister, Lord John Russell.

Religion was, of course, one of the subjects in that period which aroused the greatest controversies; Pakington's attitude was somewhat ambivalent, as although he strongly supported the Protestant church as a pillar of the British establishment, he also publicly stated on a number of occasions that he thought every man had the right to hold his own views, particularly Catholics, and that these should be respected. He even went so far as to support the Maynooth grant against the policy of his own party, and supported a bill to repeal many obsolete pieces of anti-Catholic legislation; but on other occasions he opposed any move that could weaken the Church of England, and, perhaps rather surprisingly, he voted against the admission of Jews to the House of Commons. He would probably have said that the fact that every man is entitled to have his own religious views and to have them respected does not mean that measures have to be taken to advantage those with non-Protestant views.

The other subject on which his views seem to have shifted was education. His time as a magistrate convinced him that more education was a desirable national goal, if only because lack of education seemed to him to be characteristic of the criminal classes. The reason it took so long for a compulsory system of national education to be achieved was the religious question; both the Protestant and Catholic churches thought that education should be based on religious teaching, and others, mainly dissenters, preferred a secular basis to teaching; but this meant, of course, that it was almost impossible to find common ground. Pakington seems to have favoured schools based on the Church of England, but at the same time he realised that a national scheme, which he favoured from an early date, would need to be more widely based, and he was interested in schools, such as the King Edward VI school in Birmingham, which managed successfully to accommodate pupils from a wide variety of religious faiths. In the 1860s he came forward with his own scheme for compulsory national education, but that will be covered in the next volume.

Pakington seems to have kept his religious faith throughout his life, and certainly remained a regular church goer. It is perhaps surprising that the various tragedies which are described in this volume, and the insanity of his eldest son which occurred later in his life, did not seem to dent his faith, even though he frequently recorded his thankfulness for the many blessings the Almighty bestowed upon him, some of which turned sour not long afterwards. But in an age before medical science had really started to have much impact on the common diseases of the day people were more ready to accept their own personal tragedies as part of the grand design of the Almighty, which it was not given to those on earth to understand.

John Somerset Pakington's grandson Humphrey, the 5th Baron Hampton, and Humphrey's son Richard, the 6th Baron, co-operated in writing a book about the family based on the extensive archive, which they had duplicated and privately published in 1974, called 'The Pakingtons of Westwood'. I have made use of this where it contains material no longer available, for example the account of Pakington's travels in America, and I am grateful to Johnny Pakington, the present Baron Hampton, and his cousin Thomas Parry, for allowing me to photograph some family portraits.

Apart from the sources I have already mentioned, I have made extensive use of the Berrow's Worcester Journal (usually referred to as 'Berrows' in the text), which was published throughout the period covered by this volume, and is now also available on-line. I have also made use of The Times archive, and in tracing the history of the Droitwich Poor Law Union I have been able to consult the original minute books, held in the Worcestershire Record Office. I also used the Westminster rate books which have helped determine where members of the family lived at different times. I have taken a number of illustrations from Nash's 'Collections for a History of Worcestershire', which I refer to as 'Nash'. I am grateful to Dr Sue Sutton for following up some references in The National Archives, and to John Weedy for supplying illustrations from his collection of Illustrated London News. Last but not least, I am extremely grateful to David Everett for generously offering to read through the proofs, and not only look for typographical errors, but use his extensive knowledge of local history to correct some errors in the narrative, and sharpen up my sometimes over-expansive style.

In trying to get to grips with Pakington's extended family readers might like to refer to the family tree in the Appendix, pages 366 and 367, which also contains a summary of his parliamentary career.

# Chapter 1
# Young Russell

One can assume that the Pakington name originated in one of the villages of the same name, either in Leicestershire or Warwickshire. These are spelt with a 'c', but the family have usually, and always in more recent times, used the form Pakington. The first reference to a Worcestershire Pakington was in 1374 when John Pakington married Elizabeth, daughter and heiress of Thomas Washbourne of Stanford, Worcs. After this John the genealogy is lost, and we have to turn to the marriage of another John Pakington to Margaret Bulfynch of Astley in about 1475 to come to the start of the later Pakington family.

John and Margaret had four sons: Robert, John, Augustine and Humphrey. It was John who founded the family fortune through his work as a leading lawyer. He became a sergeant-at-law and was granted the privilege of wearing his hat in front of the king (he may have advised Henry on his divorce). Later he was given duties on the Council of the Marches. In 1524 he purchased the manor of Hampton Lovett where he built a manor house, described by Leyland as 'a veri goodlye house of brike'. He later bought the manor of Chaddesley Corbett, which included the estate of Harvington, and after the dissolution he acquired for £22 the nunnery at Westwood, an extra-parochial property, on the site of which the family seat was later built. At his death in 1551 John Pakington owned thirty one manors, but left only daughters, and it was his brother Robert who was the ancestor of the later Pakingtons. Robert was MP for the City of London and an active member of the mercers' company. He made an advantageous marriage when he married Agnes, daughter and coheiress of Sir John Baldwin, who had considerable property in Aylesbury and Buckinghamshire, which was inherited on Sir John's death in 1545 by the Pakingtons, and remained in the family for several generations. But by then Robert had been 'barbarously murdered' in 1537 – the circumstances are not known, although Nash suggests he was killed by Papists, as he held strong protestant views.

The other two brothers need not detain us long. Augustine was a lawyer and merchant, and it is known that he acted as an agent for Bishop Cuthbert Tunstall of

Durham while in Amsterdam, where he helped obtain copies of Tyndale's translation of the bible so they could be burned. The last brother, Humphrey, inherited Harvington from his brother John, and, unlike his siblings, remained a strict adherent to Catholicism. His son and his grandson, both named Humphrey, retained this faith, and Harvington Hall, probably built at the end of the sixteenth century, remained a recusant centre. The last Humphrey Pakington of Harvington died in 1637 without sons, after which it descended through his daughter to the Yate family, then at the end of the seventeenth century it came by marriage to the Throckmortons of Coughton. Today it is still a centre for Catholics.

Robert, murdered in 1537, left a son Sir Thomas who later inherited the Buckinghamshire property from his mother, and, on the death of his uncle Sir John in 1551, the Hampton Lovett and Westwood properties, the Chaddesley Corbett manor having been left to his uncle Humphrey. Not a great deal is known about this Sir Thomas, except that he was in dispute with the burgesses of Aylesbury, and when he died in 1571 his son and heir Sir John (1548-1625) inherited. In 1572 Sir John entertained Queen Elizabeth when she was visiting Worcestershire, and she seems to have taken a fancy to him. She had a 'particular tenderness for handsome fellows' – Sir John was over 6 feet tall, and had great physical prowess. No doubt this is how he acquired the nickname 'lusty Pakington', but his time at court damaged his finances and in the following decade he had to retire to his Worcestershire properties. In 1597 his fortunes improved and he married, and carpenter's contracts from 1612 have survived to show that he was building Westwood House, the distinctive brick mansion that still survives. A further description of the house will be found on page 151.

'Lusty' Pakington died in 1625 in Aylesbury. His son and heir Thomas had died a year earlier, having already been made a baronet, so Sir Thomas's son John inherited in 1625 aged only 5. This Sir John, the 2nd baronet, was made a ward of Thomas, 1st Lord Coventry and keeper of the Great Seal, and in about 1640 married Coventry's fourth daughter, Dorothy. During the ensuing civil wars Sir John Pakington was a royalist,

*Once believed to be a portrait of the first Sir John Pakington (d. 1551), this is now thought more likely to be another portrait of 'Lusty' Pakington.*

and paid dearly for his loyalty. Deprived of his parliamentary seat at the outbreak of war in 1642, he was made a commissioner of array for the King, and fought at Edgehill where he was captured and imprisoned in the tower. He was released on payment of a £5,000 fine, only to be fined a further £7,360 on the surrender of Worcester in 1646. No doubt after that he would have tried to keep a 'low profile', but against his will (as he claimed) he was caught up in the battle of Worcester in 1651, when he was charged with high treason. This trial collapsed, but during the Commonwealth he was in trouble with the authorities on two more occasions. Finally on the restoration he was granted £5,000 by the new king, but his wife, Lady Dorothy, reckoned that his adherence to the royal cause had cost him the enormous sum of over £20,000, and had caused the loss of many of his Buckinghamshire estates.

In 1661 Sir John was made high sheriff and returned as a member for Worcester in the restoration parliament, and for the remainder of his career proved himself to be a high Tory, and waged war against the enemies of the church. His wife, Lady Dorothy, who had also become well-known, was a friend of bishops and other senior churchmen, and during the 1650s had lodged Dr Henry Hammond who was under a sort of house arrest in Westwood. In 1660 Charles II wanted to make Hammond the Bishop of Worcester, but he died shortly after, and is buried in Hampton Lovett church.

The 2nd baronet died on new year's day 1680, and was succeeded by his son, another Sir John, who had been born in 1649. Under the influence of his intellectual mother and the Dean of Worcester, George Hickes, the 3rd baronet became an Anglo-Saxon scholar, but was also famous for having a wager with two of his uncles, Samuel Sandys and Thomas Coventry, that the loser of a horse race should pay £1,000 towards a charity that Coventry wished to found in Droitwich, which would be named after the winner. Coventry's horse won, and the Pakington estates were encumbered with lengthy litigation and an annual payment towards the Coventry charity for a long time afterwards.

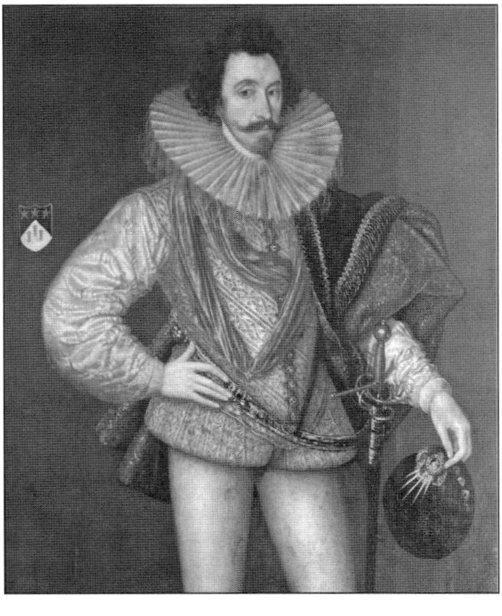

The 3rd baronet died in 1689, and his son and heir, another Sir John, became the 4th baronet at the age of 18. This Sir John continued the family tradition of staunch Toryism, and served as an MP for Worcestershire in a number of parliaments. In 1707 he attacked the union with Scotland on the grounds that it

*Sir John 'Lusty' Pakington (1548-1625).*

might lead to the spread of Presbyterianism, and in 1715 was arrested on suspicion of complicity in the Jacobite rebellion, but managed to escape without charge. Towards the end of his life he served as recorder for Worcester, and a handsome portrait of him at this time still hangs in the Guildhall there. He married Hester, daughter of Sir James Perrott of Haroldstown, Pembrokeshire, and through her inherited property there that remained in the family for 300 years.

After the public figures of the seventeenth century, the eighteenth century Pakingtons were something of a disappointment. The 5th baronet, Sir Herbert Perrott Pakington, got into debt and went to live in Utrecht where he died in 1748 aged only 40, leaving a son John who became the 6th baronet. This Sir John remained a shadowy figure, dying in 1762, leaving his widow Mary an annuity of £500 per annum that she continued to enjoy during her widowhood of 50 years! The 6th baronet had no sons, so the title descended to his brother Herbert, who lived from 1724 to 1795. He married Elizabeth, the brother of Sir Caesar Hawkins. The Hawkins family were distinguished surgeons, with appointments to George II and George III and a seat in Kelston, the village north west of Bath. Sir Herbert, 7th baronet, again seems not to have distinguished himself in any particular way. Fanny Burney visited Westwood in 1777 and left an entry in her journal which described him as 'good natured, civil and uncommonly hospitable, but weak in his wit and conversation', and, as for his wife, she was 'uncultivated as to books, and immoderately fond of her mansion'.

Sir Herbert Pakington's son John was the 8th and last baronet, as he never married. He seems to have led a conventional life as a young man, going to Eton and Oxford, and, elected a fellow of All Souls College in 1782, he was something of a scholar. But later in life he became a recluse, and was reputed to have built the brick wall that still surrounds the park at Westwood. Exactly what it was that caused him to become friendless is not known, but, as we shall see later, he died aged 69 in 1830 an embittered man.

Thus the baronetcy was extinguished, but the 8th baronet had had three siblings, Elizabeth, Herbert Perrott and Dorothy Ann, who was later called Ann Pakington, which name we will continue to use here. Herbert Perrott, an epileptic, took the opportunity of the temporary peace in the French wars in March 1802 to travel abroad. But the

*Lady Dorothy Pakington (1623-79), wife of the royalist Sir John Pakington, 2nd bart.*

resumption of hostilities the following year found him still abroad in Geneva, where he was taken prisoner. A pathetic letter written in Verdun dated October 1803 is preserved, and it seems likely that, as he predicted in his letter, he died there the same year, unmarried and aged about 37.

Ann Pakington, born in 1768 in Somerset, never married, and died in 1846, and will feature frequently in this story. Elizabeth was the only one of the four siblings to marry and have children. Her husband was William Russell, son of the noted Worcester surgeon William Russell MRCS who had been born in Hope Bowdler, Shropshire in 1721, and who served at the Worcester Infirmary from its inception in 1745. He purchased the Powick Court estate, and judging from photographs of it may have rebuilt the house when he purchased it – it was a large three storey five bay rather plain Georgian house set on the road from Worcester to Malvern near the centre of Powick. It was demolished in the 1960s, and replaced by a development of bungalows. In earlier times it was sometimes referred to as Slaughters Court, but in this narrative we will prefer Powick Court.

William Russell junior was one of four children, who were all baptised in All Saints Church, Worcester, so at that time, in the 1750s, the family must have been living in the City, and it was only later that they moved out to Powick Court. The eldest sibling Thomas, after going to Eton and Christ Church, Oxford, gained his MA and MD degree, so chose to follow his father's career, but died young. His brother William chose a more conventional career as a lawyer – he studied at Lincolns Inn and was called to the bar in 1781, before establishing a local practise in Worcester. William first married in about 1780 Mary Cocks, daughter of Joseph Cocks, whose brother Charles had been created 1st Lord Somers of Evesham. This marriage produced a daughter Mary. Mrs Mary Russell died in November 1786, and is commemorated in a monument in Powick church. After praising her virtues as a mother, the inscription continues 'her musical talents were varied and extensive. Taste, sweetness, expression distinguished her song, execution and grace her instrumental harmony; but far more important was her exemplary regard to religious, moral and social

*Sir John Pakington (1671-1727), 4th bart, parliamentarian and high Tory.*

duties; piety and benevolence prevailed in her mind, cheerfulness and simplicity in her manners, in all her conduct the influence of virtue'. Perhaps the memory of her musical talents remained in the Russell household, as long after her death John Somerset Pakington, as he became, was not only a keen concert-goer, but also was a keen amateur singer.

Six years after the death of his first wife on 4th February 1793 William Russell married Elizabeth Pakington in the fine Georgian church of Walcot St Swithins in Bath. It seems that at this time the Pakington family were living in or near Bath, as both Elizabeth and her elder brother John, later the 8th baronet, were baptised in the Bath suburb of Weston, and her younger sister Ann was baptised in Bath Easton. This was not very far from Kelston, the seat of the Hawkins family (see above), so this connection might have been the cause of them living there. Ann later had a house at Hampton Court, Surrey, which remained her main residence, and her brother also spent time there, indeed died at Hampton Court in 1830, so his time at Westwood must have been limited. Being unmarried and with no close relations in the area other than the Russells, with whom he maintained a fairly distant relationship, he probably preferred the company of his sister and the attraction of being near London.

After their marriage Elizabeth and William Russell lived in Powick Court with William's father and daughter Mary (10) from his first marriage. Mary was to remain at home until 1806, when she married Rev. Henry Barry Domvile. Henry Barry had been born in Dublin in 1780, the son of Charles Pocklington who had taken the name Domvile after inheriting from his wife's uncle, Rt Hon. Sir Thomas Domvile. In 1811 he was appointed the Rector of Leigh with Bransford, a parish to the west to Worcester, and in 1830 he became the Rector of Pencombe, a parish somewhat further west over the border in Herefordshire.

Four children were born to William Russell's second wife Elizabeth: William Herbert, Charles Henry, John Somerset and Elizabeth Ann Pakington

*William Russell MRCS (1721-1801) one of the founders of the Worcester Infirmary and grandfather to John Somerset Pakington. He is holding plans for the new Infirmary which replaced the original buildings in Silver Street.*

Russell. Charles Henry Pakington was buried the day after he was born, and Elizabeth married in 1825 at the age of 23 Ferdinand Hanbury Williams of Coldbrook Park just outside Abergavenny in South Wales. The elder boy, William Herbert, was sent to Eton in 1808, and some correspondence between him and his father, mother and brother still exists. This shows that he was ill at Eton, and seems generally to have been of a delicate constitution, and was only there for short periods. He was there again in 1810, when there was a rebellion against the new headmaster, the well-known Dr John Keate. A letter survives from William's father in which he tells William that his mother and brother were very silly to write in person to Dr Keate complaining, 'which I have no doubt was displeasing to him'. Almost unheard of today, in an age when attendance at school was not compulsory 'rebellions' were more common, and his brother was involved in one at his school in Worcester. There were a number of such incidents at Eton, both before and after the Russell boys were there. One popular way of showing disapproval of the Eton headmaster was to give him a 'boo' – a chorus of boos from the boys was effective as it was difficult to pin-point the culprit. Discipline at Eton had been lax under Keate's predecessors, and his attempt to improve things naturally incurred the displeasure of the boys, and later in his first year Keate famously flogged eighty seven boys in one day who refused to line up at school.

John Somerset, the subject of this book, was, in contrast to his brother, of an altogether more robust constitution, and from school wrote of the number of boys he could give a 'licking' to. While William was at Eton, John was at Mr Wheeler's school at Netherton House in Worcester, described in a contemporary engraving as a 'Classical and Oriental Establishment'. In 1810 William was finally withdrawn from Eton, but in the following year his younger brother started his career there. John remained at Eton till late 1814 or early 1815, and meanwhile William, after a short spell at Christ Church, Oxford, was admitted as a pupil to the Middle Temple in London in 1814. Thus the boys' education

*Powick Court, photographed before its demolition and replacement with an estate of bungalows. Photo courtesy of Worcestershire Record Office.*

seems not to have been too badly affected by the death of their father, which occurred in December 1812, after suffering a prolonged period of ill-health. In his will William Russell left his widow an annuity of £700, and annual allowances of £600 to his eldest son, £300 to John Somerset and £150 to his daughter. He refers to his property at Powick, at Bishops Cleeve in Gloucestershire, and in Somerset, and, although not mentioned in the copy of his will, it is known that he appointed Elias Isaac, the banker, of Boughton House, Worcester, as guardian to his children – we will meet the Isaacs on a number of occasions later. But his widow Elizabeth only lived five months after his death, leaving her younger children John aged 14 and Elizabeth aged 11 orphans, and it seems most likely that after their parents had died they were moved to be looked after by their aunt Ann at Hampton Court.

It is not known how far William Herbert Russell's legal career progressed, but at some date around 1817 he married. His bride was Frances Thornhill, who was, in fact, a relative. Her father George Thornhill of Diddington had married Mary Ann Hawkins, the daughter of Sir Caesar Hawkins whose sister Elizabeth had married Sir Herbert Perrott Pakington, the 7th baronet and grandfather of William Herbert, thus making them first cousins once removed. William and Frances took up residence at Southernhay Place near Exeter Cathedral, and the next we know is that William was buried in the cathedral on 15 November 1819. There is a small memorial stone to him in the cathedral nave, which states that he died of a 'rapid decline' on 10th November.

*(Left) Elizabeth Pakington (1762-1813) sister of the 8th and last baronet and second wife of William Russell. (Right) William Russell junior (1751-1812), father of John Somerset Pakington. All these miniatures are from a private collection.*

This left John Somerset as the only son, and heir presumptive to the Pakington estates, although not of course to the baronetcy, which, unless Sir John Pakington, now 59, married and had children, would be extinguished on his death. William Herbert's death may also have been one reason why John Somerset gave up his Oxford studies. He had matriculated to Oriel College, Oxford in February 1818, but gave up in April 1820 soon after his brother's death – he later said that not taking a degree was one of his greatest regrets. But, with both parents dead and only a younger sister at home, it is understandable that John may have felt the need to look after his sister and the family property rather than enjoy life at Oxford. But if he did, he seems to have devoted very little of his time to estate management in Powick, preferring the attractions of London and Cowes in the summer, and country houses and their sport in the winter.

William Herbert had kept a diary, some of which before 1811 survive. The printed book he used as a diary had one month to view, with a single line per day, so most of his entries were necessarily brief. Of greater importance to this present narrative is that fact that after his death his brother gained the same habit, which he kept up until a few weeks before he died. The first one still existing was kept in a publication called 'The Polite Assistant or Commercial Pocket Book and Albion Almanac, Lists of Both Houses of Parliament, Officers of State, Navy and Army, Baronets of

*(Left) William Herbert Russell (1794-1819), William Russell's eldest son, who died childless. (Right) John Somerset Russell (1799-1880), the subject of this book.*

England, and various other articles of useful information. Ruled Pages for occurrences, cash account &c &c For the Year 1820'.

Although diaries now exist for only 21 of the 61 years from 1820 to the year of his death, 1880, it is reasonable to assume that, once established, John continued keeping his diaries for most, if not all, the missing years. Why were they kept? People keep diaries for different reasons – the most ardent diarists probably do it as a way of communicating their thoughts and actions in a way that they could not do verbally so easily to friends or family. Thus most diaries that are kept up for any length of time tend to be fairly full, and written in such a way that an outsider would get some benefit or interest from reading them.

Not so John Somerset Russell, or John as we will call him for the time being. Whereas Pepys averaged at least 500 words per day, and a modern diarist who has had the habit for over 20 years about 250 words per day, Pakington averaged a mere 38 words a day in 1843, as full a year as any. The entries are a mere record of his movements, with whom he dined or otherwise socialised (but the use of surnames only makes it sometimes difficult to identify people), scattered observations about the weather, the quality of the hunting or shooting, and only occasionally his own thoughts or emotions. In earlier diaries in particular there are some notes about payments or receipts, but in no sense are they complete financial account books. The only complete accounts in some years are lists of game shot during the season.

So it is difficult to offer any explanation as to why he kept up his diary so consistently. Although now we are glad he did for providing us with so much extra information about his life, it is doubtful whether he had this in mind at the time, or surely he would have filled them out much more to make them tell a more comprehensible story to an outsider. Perhaps all that can be said in conclusion is that John was a man of great energy, and once he set himself the task of filling in his diary pages he would have thought nothing of completing the task, probably made easier as it is evident that he often wrote up several days at a time.

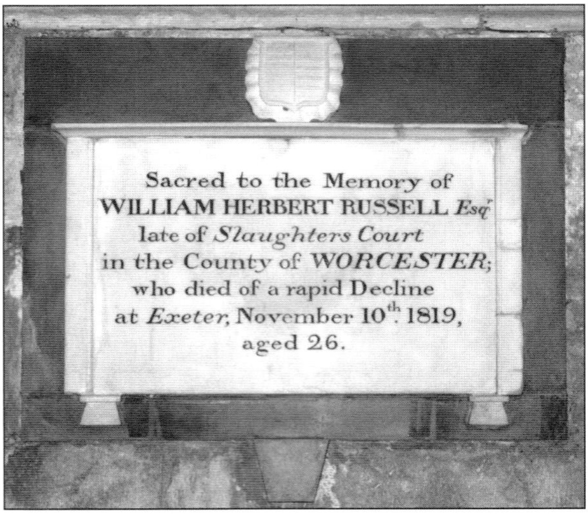


*The memorial to William Herbert Russell in the nave of Exeter cathedral. The shield shows the Russell arms, three bezants, with those of the Thornhills, into whose family William had married.*

The diaries that exist for the years 1820, '21, '22 and '24 have one month to view, leaving one line per day and therefore space for only a brief entry, and even many of these were left blank, but from 1827 the left hand page is confined to seven days, leaving more space. He rarely made use of the right hand page, reserved for accounts. Finally the diary for 1843 (none survive between 1832 and 1843) has seven days covering both facing pages, giving much more space.

In addition to his diaries, John wrote special accounts of some longer journeys he undertook. These were written in a very different style to his daily diaries and in a separate book, with much more detail and many comments about the places he visited, evidently intended to be read by others. Sadly, only one of these still survives. Although we cannot be sure, it seems likely that he wrote an account of a journey he made in August 1820 to the Netherlands (this period is blank in his diary), and a year later he recorded a tour of Scotland in a lengthy account that has survived. In 1833 he sailed to New York and journeyed from there to Canada before returning, and we know a little about this as his account is referred to at some length in 'The Pakingtons of Westwood'. But the original account no longer exists in the family archives. It also seems likely that he left an account of his lengthy three month honeymoon after his first marriage in August 1822, and there were probably other journeys, the accounts of which have been lost.

His first surviving diary, that for 1820, tells us little in the early months, other than that he was at Hampton Court in January dealing with matters relating to the death of his brother, and after attending the 'last ball at Lady Hawes' on 20th he returned to his Oxford college. He evidently kept a horse there as he hunted twice during February, a pastime that he was to enjoy for many years. On 7th February he took his first lesson in French, but we may doubt how much he learned, as he records on three occasions thereafter 'missed French lesson'. He also records missing a flute lesson, but his interest in music seems to have been more serious than that in French, as he enjoyed music all his life, and indeed took part in singing parties and took singing lessons, although it is not recorded whether he played the flute.

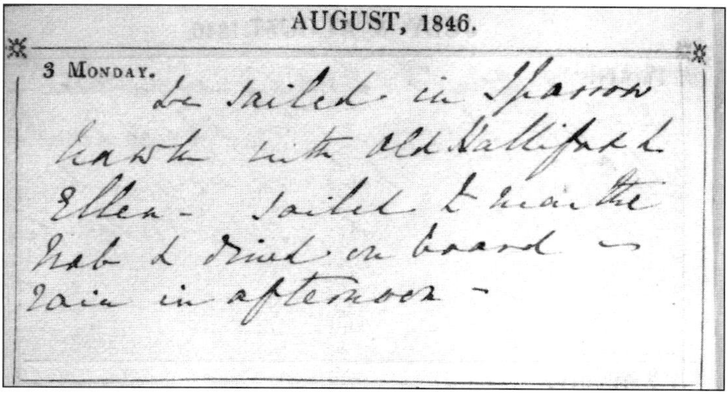
AUGUST, 1846.

3 MONDAY. We sailed in Sparrow hawk with old [illegible] Ellen - sailed to near the Nab & dined on board - rain in afternoon -

*A typical diary entry.*

On 21st March he left Oxford for good, and went to Hampton Court to stay with his aunt, whom he drove to London on 29th – she also seems to have had a house in town. After attending a ball and going to the opera he returned to Hampton Court on 12th April, and on the following day his entry reads 'last time'. What this means must be left to the imagination, but whatever it referred to he must have done again when in Worcester, for the entry for 23rd April reads 'Emit Tsal'. He stayed in Worcester till the end of May, having attended on 23rd May the Eton Montem, an ancient ceremony involving a procession of Eton boys to the village of Salthill. On 29th May he took lodgings in Chapel Place, London, where he remained for two months, and among other activities he attended a Tattersalls' sale at Hyde Park Corner on 16th June when he bought a yearling, indulging his long-time interest in horses.

At the beginning of August he started his four week tour of the Netherlands. Sadly we know nothing more of this, other than the fact that he was accompanied by his long term friend Thomas Hallifax. Hallifax gets numerous entries in the diaries, being John's closest friend over a long period, but we know little about him. He was the grandson of Sir Thomas Hallifax (1722-89), who was the son of a clockmaker who made good in the City of London, and was a founding partner in the bank of Vere, Glyn and Hallifax. This bank later became Glyn, Mills, and eventually was absorbed into the Royal Bank of Scotland. Sir Thomas Hallifax had a son Thomas (1774-1850) who had an estate in Chadacre, Shimpling, Suffolk, where Thomas junior also lived, but he predeceased his father in 1849 aged only 48. Thomas Hallifax jun. never married – in the 1841 census he was living in Berkeley Square with four servants, and described as a banker, although judging by the amount of time he spent on various activities with John, he could not have devoted much time to the family business. Unlike his brother Rev. John Savile Hallifax, Thomas does not seem to have gone to University, neither did he go to Eton, so where John and he met is not known. However, in a diary entry in 1844 when John was again at Chadacre he notes that he 'visited old haunts... and reflected with deep thankfulness on the 26 years of health & happiness which I have passed since I left that place'. Why he had stayed at Chadacre when he was 19 is not known, but it may have been then that he first met Thomas Hallifax.

*The banker Elias Isaac (1778-1841), who became guardian of John Russell on the death of his father in 1812. From a portrait in Boughton Park, now the home of the Worcester Golf Club.*

On his return to London from his continental trip John took new lodgings at 3 Wigmore Street at 120 gns per annum, and a week later engaged a new servant, Charles Muggeridge, at £25 per year, or 14 shillings per week when on board wages. In October he paid a brief visit to Worcester, and on 25th notes that he received £5,200 from Lechmere. This sounds like a land sale to the Lechmeres of Severn End and Rhydd Court – perhaps John was already finding his life-style was not sustained by his income – but he had to share the proceeds with his half-sister Mary's husband Rev. Domvile. A few days later he also notes he had pay £1,000 to Mrs Russell – this would probably have been his brother's widow, and she would have been entitled to a share as well. During November he spent two and a half weeks in Bretton Hall in Yorkshire, presumably enjoying the usual country sports.

John's diary for 1821 is little more informative than that for 1820, and we learn that on 27th January he went to Sweeney Hall in Shropshire for a 'delightful' stay of three weeks, during which time he went to visit 'the ladies of Llangollen' not far away, and hunted as usual, dining with the 'new hunt club of Salop', and the following day attending a ball in Chester given by the officers of the 88th Regiment. Sweeney Hall was the residence of Thomas Netherton Parker, the son of a Worcestershire clergyman, whose son Thomas Browne Parker was a contemporary of Pakington's at Eton and Oriel.

John left Sweeney Hall on his 22nd birthday, 20th February, and spent the next five days at Worcester, visiting his uncle at Westwood. On 26th February he left Worcester by the London mail coach, which would have entailed an uncomfortable 14 hour journey through the night (inside fare: 30 shillings), but one which John took quite regularly. Staying presumably at his Wigmore Street lodgings, he visited Blackheath, a place that occurs regularly for reasons unknown to us, and Dartmouth House. He had been in London less than a week before he returned, and entries in the following weeks show him indulging his favourite pastime of hunting, and dining with his gentry Worcestershire neighbours, choosing somewhere different almost every evening. Destinations included his half-sister Mary and her husband Rev Domvile at Leigh; Mrs Wylde, who would be his aunt Ann Russell who had married Thomas Wylde; Perdiswell Hall just north of Worcester, the home of Sir Henry Wakeman and his son Offley; and Boughton, the home of the Elias Isaac, the founder of the Worcester banking family, with which he was to have dealings over many years. Another was Rhydd Court, on the west bank of the Severn just south of Powick, the home of Sir Anthony Lechmere. The Lechmeres had lived locally since the middle ages, indeed their other seat at Severn End at Hanley Castle, just a little further south, is in contention for being the house in England longest occupied by the same family. Sir Anthony Lechmere was created a baronet by George IV when they met at Croome in 1822 – he thought Lechmere 'a fine specimen of a country gent'. He built a new house, Rhydd Court, in about 1800, which had become his home. He lost his first wife, Mary Berwick, whose name was adopted by several of the later Lechmeres, and married Eleanor Villiers in 1823. He had had a large family with his first wife, including two sons, Edmund, the eldest, born in 1792, and Anthony Berwick, who John calls Berwick, born in 1802, and who was subsequently vicar of the family church at Hanley Castle, and a canon of Worcester cathedral. The families of Lechmere, Berwick and Issac were associated with the Worcester Old Bank, with which John had many dealings.

As regards the hunting, sometimes it was bad, sometimes he had a 'good run', and once a good run was spoiled when his horse Dowager and he were deposited into a brook! About this time he bought a new horse, Mahomet, for 70 gns, although he soon had trouble with it going lame.

On 27th April 1821 John left Worcester for London to take part in the 'season', and the next day attended a public yeomanry dinner. From then until the end of July hardly a day passed without him attending a ball, the opera, a party, or, twice, the King's levée. He regretted not succeeding in obtaining tickets for the coronation of George IV on 19th July, although he was able to see the fireworks in the Park afterwards. On 28th he went with his sister and aunt Ann Pakington to see the coronation at Covent Garden, perhaps a staged version. He also paid several visits to Hampton Court, where his aunt and sister lived, and at least once met his uncle Pakington there. His continuing interest in music is evidenced by his buying a new flute for 9 gns, and attending several music parties. His mysterious visits to Blackheath, often on a Sunday, continued, and more secretive was his putting an 'X' against 32 days scattered throughout his London stay. Later he had the habit of putting an 'X' in the margin of notable days, for example when he married, but this cannot apply to these 'X's, which must mark something that he does not wish posterity to know about.

His stay in London ended abruptly on 2nd August when he left with his friend Thomas Hallifax and a servant for a six week tour of Scotland, his account of which has survived.

*Rhydd Court, a seat of the Lechmeres. Built by Sir Anthony Lechmere, 1st bart, c. 1800, it had its own private chapel. It was later much altered, and in the 1920s badly damaged by fire. Today it is a special school.*

They travelled to York in the Edinburgh mail coach, a journey of some 36 hours, then after resting at York they travelled on to Durham by coach, arriving in time for a late dinner. The next day was Sunday, and they attended the cathedral service, and took a riverside walk. John's verdict: 'a dirty town but fairly situated & the cathedral which is large & handsome as well as the ruins of the old castle are on a high hill hanging over the river, & looking down on the town'. Later they travelled on to Newcastle, and the following morning took a steam boat down the Tyne to North Shields, which John characterises as 'Filth Market'. From there they walked to Tynemouth, but its ruined abbey was something of a disappointment.

Returning to Newcastle, they hired a chaise and went north to Alnwick, going a few miles out of their way to see Warkworth Castle – well worth the diversion, John wrote. The following day, Tuesday, started as usual with viewing the local castle, then in a hired chaise they continued north, passing through Berwick where they dined, and, entering Scotland, they reached Dunbar in the late evening. John's first impression of the Scottish scenery was favourable:

> The Scottish half of our day journey was the finest from being varied with some beautiful glens & one spot in the last stage (Douglass Bridge) is too pretty not to be mentioned – I should mention in justice to the Scottish inns as their reputation is not generally very good that we had not anywhere met with so good accommodation in every aspect since we left London as in the inn kept by Mrs Lang at Dunbar'.

But not everywhere they stayed reached the same standard.

Before leaving Dunbar the next morning they paid a second visit to the castle ruins, then posted on to Edinburgh 'the approach to which is fine, but was very much spoiled to us by thick & rainy weather – it cleared up in the evening & after an early dinner we walked to some of the finest spots in the town, the beauty of which quite answered my high raised expectations'. After this they still had energy left to go to the small, but neat, theatre.

Thursday 9th August was their first day in Edinburgh, and they inspected Holyrood House, but found 'it had little to attract the traveller except for the interesting recollections it inspires'. A visit to the castle was next, and they still found time after dinner to see another play, 'Love in a Cottage'. Next day, after inspecting more of the offi-

*Warkworth Castle, on the coast north of Newcastle.*

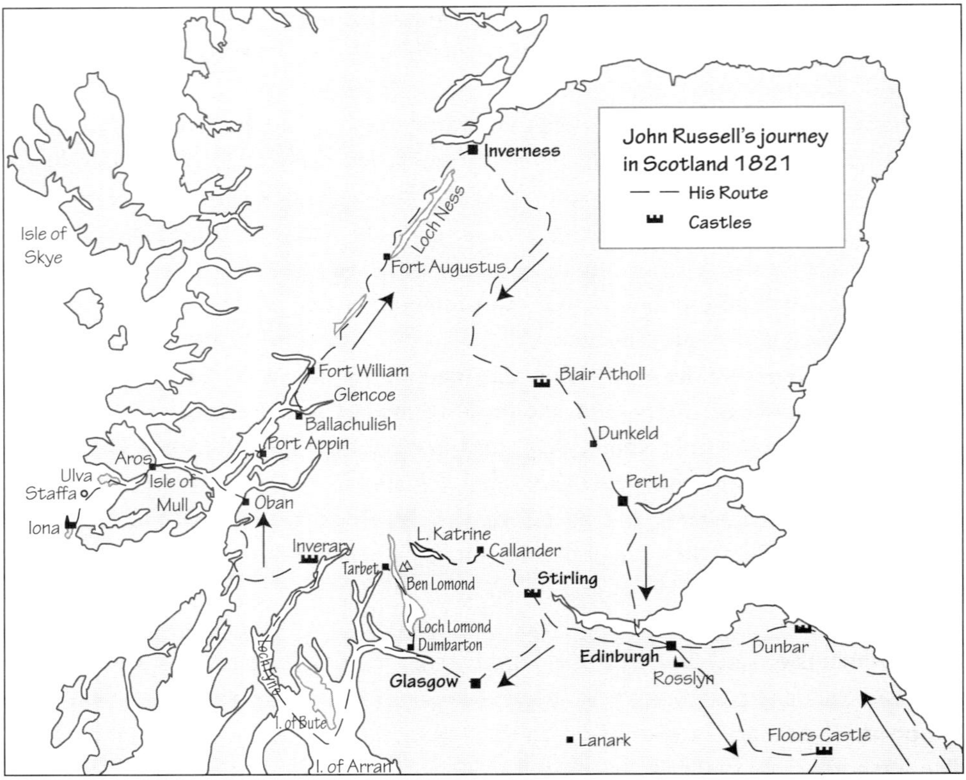


cial buildings in the city, they took a chaise to Roslin where they found the chapel a 'beautiful and perfect ruin'. Then they walked to Hawthornden and back through 'a romantic and richly wooded glen'. On Saturday they walked to the 'echoing rock' on the south side of Arthur's Seat, 'where the voice is returned with more distinc-

*Rosslyn Chapel, Roslin, south of Edinburgh. It is highly decorative, and was founded by William Sinclair, 1st Earl of Caithness, in 1456. What exists today is only part of the original, uncompleted, scheme. From R. W. Billings' 'Baronial & Ecclesiastical Antiquities of Scotland'.*

tiveness than I ever heard', then reached the summit, from where they could see Ben Lomond – presumably they had a guide, but John is very sparing in his mention of underlings.

On Sunday they 'went to St Paul's church in the hope of hearing the celebrated Mr Alison but were disappointed'. This concluded their stay in Edinburgh. On Monday morning they took a steam boat up the Forth to Stirling, but again found the scenery spoilt by thick and rainy weather. But once in Stirling it cleared, and they inspected the castle, which although it had a fine view, was very inferior to that of Edinburgh. After dining they went on to Callander, considered to be the gateway to the Highlands, and found a good inn.

Determined not to waste any time, they had an early walk to Bracklinn Bridge, 'a place that no lover of the picturesque should leave the village without visiting'. The weather was fine, and in a chaise they rode past a series of small lochs to a new inn, whence they walked with a guide through the Trossachs to the head of Loch Katrine. Then 'we got into a boat and visited the island, the cave &c made so famous by Scott's Lady of the Lake – the narrow limits of a memorandum book do not admit of an adequate description of this enchanting scene, & it would be injustice to its beauties to pass it with short encomiums...' Five hours passed on this expedition, after which they had dinner in the little inn before returning to Callander. On the way out they had passed a wedding party going to Callander, and 'one of the party stopped the carriage & offered us whisky having a bottle & glass ready in his hand. Understanding from our driver that they would be hurt if we refused, we complied & it required some persuasion to make the man take money – when we met them again on our return journey they stopped & danced a highland reel to the music of a piper in full highland costume, who accompanied them. It was a pretty scene & their rough hospitality was pleasing in the extreme'.

Their stop in Callander was all too short, for the next day they returned to Stirling, and thence to Glasgow, where they stayed at The Star. The latter part of the journey was again spoiled by bad weather, but this did not stop them seeing yet another ruined castle on the way. The following day they devoted to an excursion to see the Falls of the Clyde, and with a guide they passed the 'well-known establish-

*Callander, with the River Teith and Ben Ledi (2,884 feet) in the background.*

ment of Mr Owen'. But the ideas of the reformer and left-wing non-believer Robert Owen would not have found favour with John, who was much more interested in the beautiful falls. Despite a late return to Glasgow they had energy enough the next day to visit a cotton manufactury and a picture exhibition, before dining at the house of a banker, Mr Dennistown, just outside Glasgow. Here the contacts of John's banker companion Hallifax must have helped, for they also spent some time with another banker, Mr Smith, in Edinburgh.

Later, John was to express an interest in lunatic asylums, and the following day he visited the local one, where he met a university friend of his and his family, the Walkers. On Sunday he again wanted to hear a celebrated preacher, this time a Dr Chalmers, and in St John's church 'my high raised expectations were fully answered & his two sermons (we went to hear him again in the evening) were certainly the two finest I ever heard – his voice & manner are bad but the matter of his discourse so rivets the attention of his hearers that these defects are hardly thought of'.

The next place to be visited was Loch Lomond, so they left Glasgow early on Monday morning by steam boat down the Clyde to Dumbarton, whence they took a coach to the foot of the loch. They were in time to catch the steam boat that plied daily the 18 miles to the head of the loch, where they wanted to see Rob Roy's cave. This turned out to be 'not much worth seeing', but did at least entice them to traverse the whole loch, and see the 'strikingly fine & romantic scenery' in the upper part. They stayed at the Tarbet Inn, a 'neat little inn opposite Ben Lomond', and after dinner still had time to walk the two miles to Loch Long, take a boat trip, and walk back. The following day they had earmarked for their first major hill-climb: Ben Lomond (3,196 feet). They crossed the lake and climbed the four or five miles to the summit, 'almost precipitous' in places, and enjoyed 30 minutes taking in the views, not at their best on that hazy day although 'the sea of mountains to the north & west is truly magnificent', before starting back. The whole trip lasted six hours, and 'we returned well recompensed from our fatiguing excursion'.

The Walkers rejoined them that evening, and they passed the next day boating on Loch Lomond, before returning to Dumbarton that night. The

*Inveraray Castle, the seat of the Dukes of Argyle. Started by Vanburgh, the castle was eventually completed in 1789 for the 5th Duke. From Morris's Country Seats*

next morning they boarded the Glasgow and Inveraray steam boat. After enjoying the scenery rounding the Isle of Bute and seeing some seals they sailed up Loch Fyne to Inveraray, a sail of about 100 miles, arriving at 8.00 in the evening. The following day was passed pleasantly going over the Duke of Argyle's seat of Inveraray Castle and 'walking the beautiful grounds & environs', and in the evening John ascended a hill that overlooked the town and castle 'and was much pleased with the view'. Later the Walkers caught up with them again, and they enjoyed an evening together playing a 'tolerably good piano forte' and singing till a late hour.

The following morning they hired 'a miserable sort of gig for ourselves & a cart for our servant and luggage' to undertake the 32 mile journey to Oban, part of the way with the Walkers. They enjoyed the 'beautiful scenery by which Inveraray is on all sides surrounded, and passed a beautiful waterfall in admiring which we passed some time'. The road went by way of Lochs Awe and Etive, and just as it was getting dark they passed Dunstaffnage Castle, 'one of the finest ruins in Scotland, but it was almost too dark for us to judge of it'.

The next day was Sunday, and not wishing to attend the Gaelic language service in the church, they decided to continue their journey to Mull, and hired a 'very fine boat'. It took them all day to reach Aros, half way up the Sound of Mull, as it became calm. The little inn had only one sitting room 'which was occupied by Capt. & Mrs Hyde Parker who very politely begged us to share it with them – our sleeping room was small but clean & comfortable'.

The object of the trip to Mull was to reach Iona, and to do this they made an early start from Aros, making the short crossing to the western shore of Mull whence they took a boat to the Isle of Ulva. Here they breakfasted, then took another boat to Staffa, where they 'penetrated to the end of the celebrated Cave of Fingal'. From here Iona was a further twelve miles south. This place, 'once the seat of Scottish learning & the burial place of many of the Scottish Kings, it is now a desolate island sprinkled with a few wretched hovels, (amongst them a miserable little inn) containing no remnants of its former polish except the fine ruins of the cathedral & nunnery & some of the tombs of the monarchs'. They saw all this under the guid-

*Iona Abbey. Their guide was an old schoolmaster, 'himself no small curiosity'. From R. W. Billings 'Baronial & Ecclesiastical Antiquities of Scotland'.*

ance of an old school master, 'himself no small curiosity', then set sail back home. But they met strong adverse winds and tides and were forced to stop at Ulva where they were 'reluctantly obliged to put into the wretched little inn again, altho' unprovided with clothes &c'.

They rose very early the following day, glad to be out of their indifferent quarters, but the wind and tide were still against them. After 'four stout rowers' had battled for two or three miles, and feeling increasingly cold, they landed on the side of the Loch and walked to the head where two ponies had been sent to meet them. Back at Aros they breakfasted at 11.00, but were unable to leave due to the easterly gale. The next morning, keen to be on their way, they hired a cart to convey themselves to a place which John calls Auchnanay, 18 miles away on the east of the island. Here they were told a steam boat would call, but it did not come, so they had to stay the night there, Hallifax sleeping on the floor. Next morning, after the boat again failed to appear, they were offered a lift on their boat by Capt. and Mrs Hyde Parker. They all sailed up to Port Appin, 'heartily glad to escape at last from the wretched inns & extortionate charges of Mull'.

Soon after a steam boat appeared, and they all took it up Loch Linnhe passing 'very grand scenery on both sides' to another unidentified place, Soloman Ferry, which must have been near Ballachulish on Loch Leven as they were able to walk there. By now it was 10 o'clock at night and the house was full, but the Parkers managed to get a room. Pakington and Hallifax on the other hand had to 'shake down' in the sitting room, where they slept very well.

After a beautiful early walk on the north side of Loch Leven they hired 'a brace of miserable ponies', and rode east to the 'celebrated' Glencoe. They found this very grand and wild, but not so pleasing as that of the road which leads there. 'On the whole I think Loch Leven & the neighbourhood of the inn of Ballachulish the finest thing we have yet seen in Scotland', John wrote. The next day they again admired the scenery, so much so that they sent their servant on ahead with the baggage and walked the 13 miles to their next stop, Fort William. Here their inn, the Caledonian Hotel, was far superior to any they had stayed in, and 'Fort William is a small neat place hardly large enough to be called a town, & has the remains of a fort, now garrisoned by 16 men'. He regretted that they were too close to Ben Nevis to get the best view of Scotland's highest mountain.

On Sunday 'morning service being in the Gaelic language, we borrowed Bible & prayer books of the Parkers & read the service in our own bedroom'. They took their leave of the Parkers, and hired a gig to take them on to Fort Augustus at the end of Loch Ness. John wrote 'it is a fine romantic drive, in some places extremely wild, & in others softer & more wooded but its pleasures are much diminished to us by the misfortune of a very wet day & our gig horse twice falling down & cutting both his knees shockingly', and the inn there was 'very far inferior to that at Fort William'.

On Monday 'the wind being fair & having little choice of conveyances we sailed in a fishing smack up Loch Ness (24m) & stopped half way to see the celebrated falls of Fyns, which is 200ft perpendicular & considered one of the finest in Europe'. At the head of the Loch they decided to walk the remaining nine miles to Inverness mainly through a forest of fir trees, and in the city they stayed at Bennetts Hotel. There they met two gentlemen they had met at Fort Augustus, and the following day they all toured the 'neat' town, and climbed a nearby hill to get a good view. In the evening they went to a concert featuring Miss Wilson, Mr Welch and Mr Horn – perhaps this was the same Miss Wilson they saw twice in the Edinburgh theatre.

Their timetable not allowing any more time in the Highlands, they made a very early start on the morrow taking the Perth coach as far as Blair Athol. The 80 mile journey took over ten hours. They found 'the country we travelled over is a vast mountainous track, uniformly bleak & barren', but they enjoyed the company of Horn the singer, also in the coach. They found a 'tolerable' inn, and after dinner they walked over the grounds of Blair Athol Castle, the seat of the Duke of Athol. They enjoyed the picturesque waterfalls, but found the house, of mixed date in the Scottish baronial style, 'particularly ugly'.

There was a shortage of horses at Blair, which delayed their start next day, and on the way to Dunkeld they stopped to walk through the beautiful Pass of Killiecrankie. They arrived at Dunkeld at half past three, and they had time to view 'the fine ruin of the old cathedral & afterwards spent a couple of hours in the beautiful grounds of the Duke of Athol here, which is his principal residence – the house is small and not suited to the extreme beauty of the grounds – they contain gravel walks, which measure altogether 53 miles, & one of the finest waterfalls we have seen in the north – the place & the Killicranky pass are certainly two of the most striking spots we have visited' – Dunkeld House is now demolished. Finally that evening they took a chaise to Perth where they stayed at the George Inn.

The next day, Friday 7th September, they returned to Edinburgh, but

*Blair Atholl Castle, the seat of the Dukes of Atholl. Photo David Gowans.*

not before viewing Scone Palace. On the way they noted the island in Loch Leven on which Queen Mary had been imprisoned, but found the lake ugly and otherwise of no interest. Back in Edinburgh they stayed at the Waterloo Hotel, and the next day they saw the gaol and bridewell (institute for young offenders), and dined again with Mr Smith, Hallifax's banking friend. The following day being Sunday, they made another attempt to hear the celebrated Dr Allison at St Paul's English church. Successful this time, John found him 'a good preacher, but did not answer my expectations'.

In Edinburgh they met Sir John and Lady Sinclair, friends of Hallifax, and Sir John gave them a letter of introduction to the Duke of Roxburgh, whose seat was Fleurs (modern Floors) Castle, 40 miles south of the city. Never one to miss the chance of seeing something new, John set off with Hallifax to meet the Duke and Duchess, passing by Melrose Abbey, 'a most beautiful ruin'. They were 'most hospitably received by the old Duke & his charming Duchess' – the Duke, 85, had in 1812 won a case in the House of Lords when his title was disputed. For the next five nights 'we were obliged by the kind hospitality of the Duke & Duchess of Roxburgh to remain at Fleurs in the midst of a cheerful & pleasant party & partaking of all those amusements that make a large house in the country so delightful'. They also paid a visit to nearby Sir Alexander Davies, the local MP, who had 'a very pretty place'.

On Saturday 15th September 'immediately after breakfast we reluctantly bid adieu to the party at the Duke's & proceeded along the Borders to Carlisle, where we arrived between 9 & 10 at night (63m) & once more found ourselves in "Merry England"'. On Sunday they attended service in the 'wretched old cathedral' in Carlisle, and then posted to Kendal, whence, on the Monday, they took the coach to Liverpool. The following day brought them to Sweeney in Shropshire, and on Wednesday 19th September they arrived in Worcester at the end of 'our delightful and happy tour'.

Once back at home John's pattern of life did not change very much. He was involved with the yeomanry cavalry (see chapter 5), and a week in September was devoted to assembling and drilling in Worcester, after which he went to stay at Eastnor Castle. This had been

*Floors Castle, the seat of the Duke of Roxborough. From Morris's Country Seats.*

built by John Somers Cocks, newly created 1st Earl Somers and a first cousin of John's half sister Mary, at the enormous cost of over £85,000 using the young Robert Smirke as architect. The work had only been finished in 1820, so John would have seen the newly built castle in all its splendour. Countess Somers, 60 like her husband, was the daughter and heiress of Rev. Treadway Nash, the well-known Worcestershire historian who had died ten years earlier.

Shortly after this John paid a short visit to London, and went straight to Blackheath. He took in an opera at Covent Garden with Hallifax, and bought a new horse, Marchioness, for 63 gns at Tattersalls, before returning to Worcester after a week's stay. There, he noted, he had arranged his own new lodgings in the city, so it seems he preferred to have his own apartment away from the family home at Powick. This does seem strange in a way, as Powick Court is little more than two miles from the city centre, but it seems probable that his sister Elizabeth had been sent to be brought up by her aunt at Hampton Court after her mother died in 1813, when Elizabeth was not quite 11. This probably explains why in these early diaries she hardly gets a mention. In that case Powick Court might have been shut up, or at most lived in by a caretaker. In his younger days John was known as something of a Dandy, was sometimes addressed in jest as 'Brummell', and was later said to be almost too well dressed, so perhaps he preferred to live in and be visible around the City of Worcester, than to live 30 minutes away.

November was mostly given up to hunting, including two outings with the Duke of Beaufort. On the second he had a capital run of 1 hour 32 minutes and 'killed in the open', tiring his horse Othello. Then on 6th December an important event occurred. He was invited to dine at Boughton with the Isaacs, where he met Mary Slaney for the first time. It is not known what her connection was with Worcester, but there must be a suspicion that someone, possibly his guardians the Isaacs, had planned the meeting with the hope that John would court her. A few days later John called back at Boughton and met her again, then he got himself invited back to dinner and a musical evening when she was again present. The fol-

*Eastnor Castle, near Ledbury, Herefordshire. It has remained with the descendants of Earl Somers till the present day. From Morris's Country Seats.*

lowing day, whether by chance or no is not revealed, he met her walking in the High Street. This was on 13th December, and seems to have been the last time they met that year, as on 23rd he left Worcester by the mail coach and spent Christmas with his aunt, uncle and sister at Hampton Court. Elias's wife Harriet was daughter of Wolyche Whitmore of Dudmaston Hall, Shropshire, so she probably knew the Slaney family, and may have thought that Mary, leading a somewhat lonely existence in Lichfield cathedral close, would make a suitable partner for John. He was only 22 and was probably not thinking too seriously of marriage, but the Isaacs may have thought it would not be a bad thing to find him a wife, so as to moderate his highly active and perhaps extravagant life style.

*Harriet (1787-1867), wife of Elias Isaac. A companion portrait to that of her husband (page 18).*

## Chapter 2
## Married Life

Mary Slaney was the daughter of Moreton Aglionby Slaney, whose family was supposed to have come to Shropshire from the town of Slany near Prague in about 1600. Mary's cousin, Robert Aglionby Slaney of Hatton Grange, Salop, was MP for Shrewsbury at various periods between 1826 and 1862 – John was an MP at the same time, but as Slaney was a noted reformer, they often found themselves in opposite lobbies. Slaney was also a keen naturalist, and wrote 'The Smaller British Birds', published in 1832. Mary's father Moreton had originally lived at Shifnal, but seems to have run into financial difficulties around 1811, and went to live in Prince Edward Isle, Canada, and died at Charlottetown there in 1817. His wife died a year later leaving Mary an orphan. She was then looked after by her aunt Elizabeth (who was her father's sister) and her husband Rev. Dr William Buckeridge DD. He was First Canon Residentiary and Precentor of Lichfield Cathedral as well as having a number of other ecclesiastical appointments, living in The Close. Elizabeth was Dr Buckeridge's second wife, his first, Catherine Hussey, having died in 1787. William and Elizabeth had had two children, both of whom died young, so they must have welcomed the chance to look after their niece.

John made no effort to see Mary during January, when he remained in London. He records singing a duet at Lady Howe's music party on 3rd, but then there are some undecipherable entries that may

*Robert Aglionby Slaney, Mary's cousin, noted reformer and MP for Shrewsbury.*

indicate that he was ill – he 'gave up' functions on three successive days, then records he had '10 leeches' on 11th. During the second half of the month his diary is blank, but he records returning to Worcester on 31st. During February his friends Hallifax and Hunt came to stay, and he took them to see Witley Court and Eastnor Castle amongst other places, and he hunted when he could. On 13th, and on seven successive days (except Sunday) we are treated to 'X's by each entry, but what their significance was we are left to guess. He was with Hallifax and Hunt during this period.

Hunting continued into March, and he devoted a few days to a visit to Cheltenham, where he dined with Mrs Oldnall Russell. William Oldnall Russell was the son of Rev. Samuel Oldnall of Worcester, who had married Mary Russell, the sister of William, John's father, and was therefore his cousin.

Whether John was spending these weeks making up his mind whether to court Miss Slaney, or whether he was already seeing her, is not known, but by late March he had made up his mind. First he went to see his banker, Elias Isaac, no doubt to discuss his finances in the event of his marrying, and possibly also to find out what he could about his intended's fortune. Then two days later, on Saturday 23rd March, he set out for Lichfield. The following day he attended the cathedral twice, and saw Mary, and on Monday he visited the 'young Isaacs' at Needwood, where presumably they were at school. The next day his friend Parker from Sweeney Hall joined him, and on Tuesday they went hunting, Parker riding Marchioness. On Wednesday they attended the Hunt Races near the City, and this entry is followed by 'happy day' underlined. We can only presume that he managed to speak to Mary during the day, and found their relationship starting to blossom. The following day he called on Dr Buckeridge, probably asking permission to court his ward. There was more hunting on Friday and Saturday, and on Sunday he again twice attended the cathedral where Parker played the voluntary, and where he was able to see Mary. On Monday he called on her in the Close, where he received 'white ribbons', and took his leave of the Buckeridge household, returning to Worcester.

*Sir William Oldnall Russell (died 1833), first cousin to John Somerset Russell. Reproduced by permission of the Treasurer and Benchers of the Honourable Society of Lincoln's Inn. Russell had become a lawyer, and three years earlier had achieved some fame by publishing 'A Treatise on Crimes and Misdemeanours', which became a long-lived legal text book. In 1832 he was appointed chief justice of Bengal, but soon fell ill and died the following year on what is now Penang.*

On his first day back John had another interview with Mr Isaac, then spent the rest of the week hunting. He received the sacrament on Sunday in Worcester Cathedral – perhaps he hoped reports of this might get back to Lichfield. The following day he sent a gift of shells to Mary in Lichfield and on Wednesday received her letter of thanks written in formal tones: 'Miss Slaney feels much flattered by Mr Russell's kind recollection of her partiality for shells and is extremely obliged to him for making such a beautiful addition to her collection, which she begs to assure him she values very highly'. A few days later John notes that he saw Mrs Isaac – from a later letter we know that he asked Mrs Isaac to invite their mutual friend to come to stay at Boughton, where he could woo her.

The next day he left for a three week stay in London, probably one he had arranged some time before. He spent time with both Hallifax and Hunt, and also his sister and his aunt at Hampton Court, went to six operas and plays including 'School for Scandal' at Drury Lane and 'Julius Caesar', went twice to Blackheath, went to one ball but had to give one up, and was 'disappointed at House of Commons'. On that day, 30th April, the House was discussing a controversial bill to allow Catholic peers to sit in the House of Lords, whence they had been barred since 1678 – perhaps the interest was such that there was no further room for visitors.

While in London, he must have heard that Mrs Isaac's invitation to Mary Slaney had been turned down, so on 7th May he wrote to her follows:

Dear Miss Slaney,

Severely disappointed by the circumstance of your having declined the recent invitations of our kind and excellent friend Mrs Isaac, and encouraged by your kind acknowledgement of the shells I lately sent you, I hope and trust you will forgive the liberty I take in again writing to you to ask another & far greater favour—

My state of uncertainty and suspense, and my having engaged soon to leave England on a short tour on the continent, induce me now to entreat your permission to come down and continue at Lichfield, the acquaintance I had anxiously hoped to have increased in that house, in which I had the happiness or misfortune, first to meet you—

It would be uncandid & absurd to make this request, and not at the same time know that my feelings towards yourself are those of the warmest affection – the most unqualified admiration and esteem – but believe me my dear Miss Slaney, that neither by this avowal, nor by my request, do I wish to hurry you prematurely into pledging yourself to anything – unwilling to take the step of coming down to Lichfield without the assurance that my doing so would not be displeasing to you, I merely beg of you to allow me to renew my visits to you there – and I request it with the presumptuous hope, that in a further intercourse, I may obtain, from similarity of tastes and feelings, that regard, which I sigh for, as my greatest happiness, altho' I feel fully conscious how little I deserve it—

I beg you to offer my compliments to Dr. and Mrs Buckeridge, and with those feelings of anxiety, which must ever be attended on that affection, I subscribe myself, my dear Miss Slaney, most devotedly & affectionately yours, John Somerset Russell.

By the end of the week John had received a positive answer, so he left on the mail coach for Lichfield on Saturday night 11th May, and saw Mary the next day. With her again on Monday he wasted no time in pressing his suit – his underlined diary entry reads **'in ev'g walk'd with Miss S'y in garden – accepted'**. On Tuesday he 'passed morning with Mary – walked with her in evening'; Wednesday 'ditto ditto', and Thursday 'ditto ditto'. On Friday 'ditto – Mr Slaney came – rainy – evening music with Mary'. As she is not known to have had any brothers, 'Mr Slaney' is most likely to be her uncle Rev. Richard Slaney, Vicar of Penkridge, Staffs. There are more 'dittos' on Saturday, and they also rode to Beaudesert House, the seat of the Marquess of Anglesey on Cannock Chase. Sunday naturally saw him in church twice, and that day's entry concludes with a difficult to read, but underlined note, which seems to be 'got wet with Mary'. Perhaps they were caught in a shower, in an isolated spot. On Tuesday more of her relations, Sir Andrew and Lady Corbet, came to congratulate her and meet their new relation. Sir Andrew was the brother of Mary's late mother Mary Corbet, whose family seat since ancient times had been Acton Reynald Hall in Shropshire. John remained friendly with this family for some time. The Corbets stayed for two days, and after they left Rev. Slaney returned to further his acquaintance.

Once his engagement was settled, John wrote to important people close to him with the news, including his aunt and uncle. His aunt's reply, dated 20th May, has survived, and is interesting to read. She starts 'This letter in answer to yr most welcome intelligence, can only contain a repetition of the congratulations & good wishes which I sent you in my last – but to these I have the pleasure to add that my brother [John's uncle Sir John Pakington] was here on Saturday, & received yr letter & the communication **quite to my satisfaction**. He said he should write to you very soon & I sincerely hope he will write to you as good a letter as you did to him – at any rate that it will be

*Acton Reynald Hall, for a long time the seat of the Corbett family. It is now a ruin.*

a satisfactory one to you'. Miss Pakington says she has told Mrs Russell (wife of William Oldnall Russell, his cousin) and Miss Hawkins. Miss Hawkins was Frances, an unmarried daughter of Sir Caesar Hawkins, Miss Pakington's uncle, thus making them first cousins. The Misses Pakington and Hawkins spent much time together, indeed later shared a house. Miss Pakington continues:

> Indeed my dear John the prospect you have before you gives me real pleasure & I can assure you with truth that these events could contribute more to my comfort than yr being to[o] well settled – whenever I can see Elizabeth [John's sister] make so prudent a choice – I shall again rejoice & think my business in the world is finished.

She then talks of a forthcoming stay with her brother in Cheltenham, and entreats her nephew to write **very soon** 'and tell me particularly of yr Uncle's letter – whether he says anything of seeing the Lady or you – if the latter, and we should be still in Cheltenham, I recommend your riding over there to see him – the first day you are free of cavalry duty'. She ends with a PS 'you may easily believe that I shall **wish** to know when you have ascertained the lady's fortune.'

As to the latter, we may presume that Mary had received no money from the estate of her bankrupted father, but it is known that on the death of her aunt in 1832 she received £4,000 in trust for her life. She may also have benefited under the will of Dr Buckeridge as well, but as far as is known on her marriage in 1822 she was not, financially, a very 'big catch'. The earlier part of the letter confirms our impression that relations between John and his uncle were at best 'distant'; whether he ever wrote to his nephew about his forthcoming marriage is not known.

Sunday 26th marked the end of his two weeks' stay at Lichfield, and on Tuesday he took his fiancée to Worcester, where it had been arranged that she was to stay with the Isaacs.

Mary's stay in Worcester lasted over two weeks, during which time she was introduced to his local relations: his half-sister and her family at Leigh, his aunt Mrs Wylde, and his aunt Miss Pakington, who must have come up to Worcester for the occasion. Apart from a brief spell on yeomanry duty, John spent the whole time with Mary, dining either at Leigh or Boughton. Mary returned to Lichfield on 13th June, and on Sunday 16th John took the mail coach to London. He had various bits of business to attend to before his marriage, and decided to abandon his continental trip. On 26th June he accompanied Hallifax on the steam boat to Calais, but returned immediately to town. During his ten days in London he saw five plays and operas, and arranged to raise £1,000 by selling some government stock.

Once John had seen Hallifax off he returned to Lichfield for two days, then went to Worcester where he had business to attend to at Powick Court. As we have seen, this seems not to have been lived in recently by any of the family, and John would have wanted to prepare it to receive his new bride. This seen to, he returned to Lichfield for a week, then took the mail coach to London, where he gave his sister Elizabeth £50, no doubt to cover her allowance while he was away on his wedding tour. He only had one full day in town and on Sunday night he returned to Lichfield, and gave Mary a present of ear rings. Hallifax was still away, but his sister Ellen came to stay in Lichfield, as did his friend Hunt. On 23rd July he took out a marriage licence, and on 26th he rode to Worcester to make sure everything was ready for his return with his bride. He also called at Westwood for one of his fairly rare visits to his uncle. By now Sir John was 60, and John must have known that he was likely to inherit, but relations between Powick and Westwood seem to have been distant at best.

On Monday 29th July he was back in Lichfield, but again his stay was short as he had to return to London once again to tidy up his affairs there. He raised another £1,000 by selling more government stock, packed, gave up his lodgings, and picked up a new carriage he had ordered. This took two days to reach Lichfield, and at last on 14th August came the big day – 'MARRIED' he notes in his diary, and they immediately set out on their wedding tour. The evening of their marriage they slept at Warwick, the following day in Oxford, and they reached London the next day, when they stayed at Thomas's Hotel in Berkeley Square. Two more days found them in Dover, and on 19th August their continental tour started. It lasted for three months.

Unfortunately, his account of this has not survived (his diary is blank), but a 'laisse passer' exists which shows that the couple travelled with John's servant Charles Muggeridge and a 'femme de chambre' Mary Yates. They visited Paris, Geneva, Genoa, and Milan, and no doubt many other places before landing back at Ramsgate on 20th November. The next day they went on to London and stayed at Dartmouth House for a few days before going on to Hampton Court to see John's sister and aunt, and they also met Hallifax, back from his European tour. On 3rd December they started back for Worcester, sleeping at Oxford on the way. It seems that initially they stayed with his aunt Mrs Wylde, and it was not until 21st December 1822 that

*Lichfield Cathedral, where John Russell married Mary Slaney in 1822. This print dates from 1860, after the restoration work of George Gilbert Scott.*

John proudly notes in his diary '**came to Powick Court**'. Other than a New Year's Eve ball at Lady Denny's, the diary is blank for their first days at the old family home. When the house was put up to let eight years later it was described as 'newly furnished', so John must have done his best to prepare the house for his new bride. For a description of it at that time, see below page 61.

No diary has survived from 1823, his first full year of married life, but there is no reason to think it was much different from that for 1824, which survives. For the first five months of 1824 he remained in Worcestershire, visiting his friends and relations, hunting and shooting. One problem with his diary is that it is very difficult to know whether all the social events he records involved John and his wife, or John alone. 'Mary' occurs only five times during 1824, and the word 'we' only once. As he now had his own settled establishment at Powick Court we can assume that on the numerous occasions when people came to dine that Mary participated fully, but whether this was the case when he dined with the local gentry is not clear. And there is no indication that she had any interest in the several occasions he went out hunting, sometimes at quite distant locations.

On January 6th he went to Westwood to shoot, and on the following day John and his uncle went to Worcester to see the 'great fight'. This boxing match was between the English champion Spring (whose real name was Thomas Winter) and the Irish champion, John Langan. The event had created tremendous interest, and the night before the city was full to overflowing with visitors, and stands had been erected on Pitchcroft, where the fight was to take place. Newspaper accounts differ as to the details, but it seems that at least 30,000 spectators were present (The Morning Post mentions an unlikely 500,000), and people had even climbed the masts of boats in the river to get a view. Spring arrived promptly at midday, but Langham did not come for another hour, and during the wait first one then another stand collapsed, causing much injury, but we can assume that John and his uncle were unharmed. Once stripped, it appeared that Spring was the stronger of the two men, but nevertheless the fight lasted well over two hours, and went to over 40 rounds (again accounts differ) before Langham was floored and counted out. When he recovered he wanted to continue, but neither his seconds nor the umpire, Col Berkeley, would allow it.

John was again at Westwood the next day to shoot, and his social round continued with the Lygons (Earl Beauchamp of Madresfield), the Berkeleys of Spetchley, the Wakemans of Perdiswell, the Bensons of Malvern, and the Winningtons of Stanford all prominent, as well as his relations. One new name crops up – that of John Barneby of Brockhampton, just over the border near Bromyard in Herefordshire. His family had been there since acquiring it through a Habington heiress in the sixteenth century, and Barneby was supposed to be very wealthy. The two Johns were contemporaries at Oxford, and were later Tory MPs together. They spent much time shooting on each other's estates before Barneby's early death in 1846.

That all was not well with Mary was indicated on 2nd March when she consulted Dr Malder, but that is all we hear of any illness that year. There are a number of mentions of rehearsals, a concert at Boughton on 22nd April, and the music week at Worcester on 1st May. John clearly enjoyed singing, and his music making is mentioned on many occasions throughout his life. Perhaps the Isaacs had a predisposition to music, as an earlier Elias Isaac had been appointed organist at Worcester cathedral in 1747. John's first trip away from Worcester was on 7th May, when he drove with Mary in a tilbury (a light open two-wheeler) to Cheltenham for a ten day stay. There they made a number of calls despite his having a bad cold, and attended evening service in Gloucester Cathedral.

Yeomanry cavalry week came up soon after, and Lords Somers and Eastnor came over – Lord Somers of Eastnor Castle was 1st Earl Somers, born in 1760, and Lord Eastnor was his son, John Somers Somers-Cocks, later Viscount Eastnor, born in 1788. On 1st June, not long after the end of cavalry week, John went to London – as he took the over-night mail coach, we may assume that he was not accompanied by his wife. In the two weeks of his stay he managed to go to eight operas and concerts as well as make the obligatory visits to Hampton Court and Blackheath. He also dined with some Slaney relations who had a house in town.

Returning home in the middle of June, nothing more exciting than a return visit of the Slaneys happened during the next month, then on 12th July John and Mary left for a stay in Devon, where they stayed till the end of August. The journey to Ilfracombe took four days, but included a two day stay at Linton. They must have been travelling quite encumbered, and reaching Bridgewater on the first day, a journey of 94 miles (according to his diary) was quite an achievement, although it is possible Mary followed behind at a more reasonable pace, once he had established his lodgings.

The main purpose of the stay was yachting. This is the first time this pastime appears in John's diary, but he must have had some earlier introduction.

*Brockhampton Court, Herefordshire, the seat of the Barneby family. In the 1970s the tenant, an insurance company, removed some Victorian alterations and restored the original Georgian appearance.*

Apart from his wife he was not alone in Ilfracombe – a friend 'Foley' is mentioned several times. We do not know who this Foley was, but if a relation of Baron Foley of Great Witley it was most likely John Hodgetts Hodgetts-Foley, a cousin of the 3rd Lord Foley, who was elected in 1824 as MP for Droitwich, and a contemporary of John's at Oxford. Foley remained an MP, later for the county, till his death in 1861. Like other members of his family he sat in the Whig interest, in opposition to John.

John details his various sailing expeditions in his diary – some were just along the coast, but twice he went to Lundy Island, staying the night. On the first trip John and Foley went on to Tenby on the Pembrokeshire south coast, then made the considerable passage back across to Clovelly, north Devon, before returning to Ilfracombe. On the second trip to Lundy, they went with the main aim of sport, and John records they shot at seals, and shot sea fowl. He also records that he started to sketch – 'made first sketch' on 13th August, and later 'went on water to sketch'. On the next day, his last in Devon, 'went with Miss Armstrong to valley to sketch'. But sketching is not mentioned in later diaries, so we must assume it was a hobby he did not pursue.

He wanted to be back in Worcestershire in time for the start of the shooting season on 1st September, so left Ilfracombe on 26th August, journeying partly by steamboat, arriving home the next day. He duly fitted in several days' shooting early in the month, but another event in which he was involved was looming. This was the Worcester Music Meeting, which we today call the Three Choirs Festival. This was in those days run by stewards who acted as financial guarantors, and John had become one for the 1824 Festival. He had a meeting with his fellow stewards Sir Thomas Phillipps, John H. Hodgetts-Foley, Rev. Edward Rice DD, Rev. John Lynes and Rev. William Vernon of Hanbury on 31st August. After a rehearsal on 14th, the Festival started on 15th September, with a morning performance of Handel's 'Dettingen Te Deum' and 'Zadok the Priest'. The Festival lasted three days (Wednesday to Friday), and there were morning performances in the cathedral, which could last as long as five hours. Evening 'miscellaneous' concerts were held in the College Hall, and there were balls and social events in the Guildhall. On Thursday Handel's 'Messiah' was given in the cathedral, followed by a ball at which, according to Berrows, 400 were present, including John and, we may presume, his wife. Not everything always went to plan. The audience at the evening miscellaneous concert in College Hall suffered from the extreme heat, there being no adequate means of ventilation, and eventually a doctor in the audience took matters into his own hands and smashed a window, bringing applause and cries of "encore" from the audience!

The Festival was clearly a great social event, and had the aim of raising money for charity for the support of clergymen's widows and orphans. In 1824 ticket sales amounted to about £3,000, with an average of about 1,000 seated in the cathedral and somewhat fewer in College Hall. But expenditure, boosted by the engagement of larger musical forces than hitherto, was £3,344, and the stewards had to fund the deficit. Over £800 was collected for charity – The Morning Post commented that 'a certain number of ladies and gentlemen of distinction were stationed in most formidable array at the door [of the cathedral], holding each a plate, to pass which (the ladies at least) and not make a deposit was impossible. We never saw more determined applications. There can be no mendicity society in Worcester'.

One incident is recorded in 'The Pakingtons of Westwood' that happened at this time. Among the party for the Festival staying at Powick Court was D. H. Kelly, an Irish school-friend. Kelly was a man of property, but appears to have married somewhat beneath his station earlier in the year. He was invited to stay at Powick, but not his wife. He accepted, thinking there might be circumstances to explain this surprising arrangement, and took lodgings for his wife in Worcester. It was, however, clear to him on arrival that there was ample room for his wife at Powick Court, and when the Russells made no effort to entertain or even to call on her, the husband became understandably bitter. In the correspondence which followed Kelly wrote 'I sincerely hope you may towards other and more valuable friends pursue a line of conduct more calculated to retain them so, than you have towards D. H. Kelly'.

This does not show the best side of John's character.

The day after the Festival ended there was further excitement in Worcester – John went to see a Mr Graham and his gas filled balloon. Quite a multitude had paid 2s 6d to watch the spectacle and were understandably disappointed when the balloon, with Mrs Graham on board, failed to rise very high due to a lack of gas. However the spectacle was repeated on Monday, with spectators (including John again) allowed to watch gratis, and this time the balloon made a good ascent and was able to travel as far as Aston Somerville in Gloucestershire.

During the remainder of 1824 John and Mary do not seem to have gone very far, the only visits recorded being to Eastnor Castle, Prestwood (the home of John H. Hodgetts-Foley), and, for the first three weeks of November, Staffordshire and Shropshire where they stayed with his wife's cousin Robert Aglionby Slaney at Walford Manor, enjoying the hunting and shooting. One assumes Mary was with him, but she does not get a mention. In December they remained at home, and for Christmas his aunt and sister came. During all this time, of course, there was a great deal of hunting and shooting, and Dr Robert Berkeley of Spetchley Court was often his companion.

No diary exists for 1825 or 1826. The main event of 1825 would have been the marriage of John's sister Elizabeth to Ferdinand Hanbury Williams of Coldbrook Park, just east of Abergavenny in south Wales, in December. The Hanbury Williams had been at Coldbrook since Ferdinand's grandfather's time, and prior to that in Herefordshire, ultimately tracing their descent to the medieval Hanburys of Hanbury, the parish just east of Droitwich. Ferdinand was the same age as John, and had inherited Coldbrook from his uncle John Hanbury Williams in 1815, his father having already died. John visited or met his Welsh relations whenever he could, on one occasion staying with them on the way back from his Devon holiday. Elizabeth and Ferdinand had three children, including one son, another Ferdinand, from whom the later Hanbury Williams's are descended, but Coldbrook Park was sold on the death of Ferdinand in 1887, and nothing now remains of the house.

The following year, 1826, John and Mary's only child was born on 13th July, and christened John Slaney after his mother. It would have been helpful to historians if father and son had not had the same set of initials! Presumably Mary's pregnancy and confinement would have much restricted the summer stay in Devon, which otherwise seems to have been part of his routine. For 1827 we are again favoured with a surviving diary, and in the first few pages we find evidence of an aspect of John's character that was probably just following the fashion of the time – gambling. His diary contains an account of his winnings and losses, and these were mainly for bets with friends on the outcome of billiards, whist or 'ecartes'. Barneby is his most regular opponent, but Hallifax occasionally appears as does John's brother-in-law

*According to tradition, Major Hanbury Leigh of Pontypool Park was left a fortune by Charles Williams of Caerleon, which he used to purchase Coldbrook Park (below) for his son Charles, born in 1709 and renamed Hanbury Williams. The property descended to his nephew Ferdinand, the father-in-law of Elizabeth Russell.*

Hanbury Williams. On a few occasions whist at Westwood is mentioned, so it may be that his uncle was not averse to an occasional flutter. But even by the standards of the time most of the amounts involved were not terribly large, the sums wagered when playing billiards usually being under one pound. Occasionally larger amounts appear, such as the £5 he won off Hallifax on the result of the Derby, the £14 15s he lost one day at whist and, the largest and last one that year, the £25 he won off Tom Coventry after a bet about Billy Crane. We are left to wonder who he was. This last win must have pleased him greatly, as because of that he managed to win a net sum of £4 15s during the year. The fact that he kept a careful note of his winnings and losses indicates that he was in no way a reckless gambler – he just found it added spice to his various activities. As a follower of fashion he would probably not want to be thought unwilling to risk modest sums of money when most of his friends would have done so.

The 1827 diary contains the first mentions of his work as a magistrate – he had been appointed two years before, when nearly 26. On 8th January 1827 he attended quarter sessions and dined with the magistrates, and later in the month attended the gaol committee. In February he visited the gaol for the first time as visiting magistrate. Otherwise most entries were about hunting or shooting, except that on 20th January he noted that he heard of Mrs Harding's death. She would probably have been his late brother's widow – she had married a Mr John Harding after William Herbert's death in 1819. From time to time he shot at Westwood, as on 29th January, when he notes that Mary came over for dinner, but that there was 'no party', indicating perhaps that his uncle did not do much entertaining. He also noted that he attended a Music Society meeting about the forthcoming 1827 festival at the deanery, and agreed to guarantee £50 against any deficiencies (to get a modern equivalent we can add at least two zeros onto the sum). On 9th February he somewhat alarmingly noted that 'Pierpoint operates on baby'. Matthew Pierpoint was a surgeon at the Worcester Infirmary, but as nothing further is heard of any medical problem with the nine month old child, it must have been something minor.

John is thought to have been the last person in Worcestershire to have fought a duel, as a result of a quarrel with John Parker. Parker (1793-1885) was a well-known sporting man and at that time master of the foxhounds. On 27th February they had a blank day hunting at Quarter Ash, and John had a 'quarrel with Mr Parker'. According to 'The Pakingtons of Westwood' Parker had accused Sir John Pakington of shooting foxes on his land, causing the bad hunting. (However, this is not the same story that was shortly to be retailed in Bell's 'Life in London', recounted below.) John felt this impugned family honour, and next day he sent for his friend John Barneby, and consulted him over dinner. The following day they were joined by the Hanbury Williams and Hallifax, and after further family consultation John issued a challenge to Parker in the evening.

The following day, Friday 2nd March, they hunted again, but despite his challenge having become generally known, he did not receive an answer that day. But the next day, in John's own words,

> Barneby received answer in Worcester from Mr Palmer as Parker's second – I went to Worcester but returned on hearing this – made my will & fought duel with Mr P. at Pixham at 5 in afternoon – Parker and Hallifax saw it across river – we shook hands after 1st shot.

More detail is contained in 'The Pakingtons of Westwood':

> To reach the site – a flat stretch on the east bank of the Severn – John's opponent rode over from his house near Spetchley, while John crossed the river by the Pixham Ferry. His good friends Hallifax and Tom Parker stayed behind with the horses, and watched as John and his second were rowed across the water. On the Hams the distance was duly measured out. A little way upstream, on the steep bank which sheltered the Hams, rose the solid shape of Kempsey Church, its beauty giving a false sense of dignity to an act of folly. The order was given, and the two opponents fired in the air. Honour was satisfied, hands were shaken, and next day the two men met as friends in the hunting field... some time after the gathering on Kempsey Hams had dispersed, a party of officials rode up with authority to stop the contest.

It seems very strange to us today that a man with a small child and young wife would risk his life in this way, but duelling was part of the gentlemanly code that John subscribed to, which was followed by people much grander than he – both prime ministers Pitt and Peel were involved in duelling. Soon after this a controversy blew up about 'a paragraph in Bell'. Bell's Life in London was a weekly sporting newspaper, somewhat disrespectful of the establishment, and in the edition of 11th March a letter was published from 'a constant reader' in Worcester, dated 9th March. After introducing the parties to the duel, the letter continued:

> Mr Parker is a staunch foxhunter, of Hibernian descent, and is generally esteemed for his many social qualities; he is also known to be brave as steel; and, standing about six feet, presents a strong contrast to his antagonist, who belongs to a Volunteer Regiment, but is not by any means qualified for a Grenadier Company, nor (between ourselves) is he a very great favourite in the county, of which, by the way, he is a Magistrate. But to the facts: When our pack of hounds was first set up, Mr Parker applied, as is customary, to the neighbouring gentlemen for permission to draw their covers, and, amongst others, to Sir John Pakington, Baronet, of Westwood Park, who readily complied with his wishes, but conditioned, that whenever a fox was found he should not be chased through his Park. A short time since the said covers were drawn, but without effect; and during its progress, the Captain (who is nephew and heir to the Baronet) asked Mr P. "what method he should take if Reynard made for the Park?" To which the latter replied, "Oh! That's all right – I've managed with the keeper, who will spring the dog traps if such a course is taken." Here the matter ended for the time, and they went on drawing. Immediately

> after this conversation, Captain Russell was missing from the field, without the least suspicion of the cause of his absence, when lo! it was afterwards found, that reeking hot with the tale, he had posted to Sir John, and detailed the conversation. The Baronet discharged the keeper instanter, and addressed a letter to Mr Parker, couched in terms of severe invective: and giving Capt. R. as his informant. The affair, as between the principals, went over till Shrove Tuesday; but in the mean time, the Members of the Hunt, having considered the conduct of their Military Member anything but sportsmanlike, or gentlemanly, unanimously voted him to Coventry. On the Shrove Tuesday, while the hounds were out, Captain Russell, not finding himself exactly on velvet, rode up to Mr Parker, and began an explanation; but in such terms, that drew the reply from the Master of the Hounds (accompanied by flourishes of his whip over the head of the Son of Mars), "that were it not for his diminutive size, he would severely double thong him, and cut him in two"!
>
> The dispute, however, was stopped, in order that the day's sport may not be interrupted, but, on Friday morning last, a challenge was delivered to Mr P., leaving the time and place to be named by him. He immediately named the following day, for he could not delay it longer, the Monday being hunting day, and he did not wish his little business with the Captain to interfere with the amusements of the Hunt. On the following day, therefore, the meeting took place – when, according to the hackneyed phraseology of the gentlemen who supplies the duel department in the Morning Post, "the parties behaved with great coolness; and, after exchanging shots (which, of course, were harmless), an amicable adjustment took place, and they left the ground". The Seconds were Officers in the Hereford Militia. On the next hunting day, Mr P. and the Captain shook hands, and all is now in statu quo ante bellum.

From this we understand that Sir John Pakington kept dog traps in the park, possibly to protect game or just because he did not like dogs wandering near the house, and he may also not have wanted the huntsmen's horses crossing the park and damaging the grass. But as Parker wished to ignore this stipulation, to avoid the possibility of the fox hounds being trapped he had arranged with the keeper, unknown to his master, to open them all. This does seem quite possible, but more difficult to believe is that John would have immediately left the hunt to inform his uncle.

John records receiving a copy of Bell's on 16th March, and consulted his uncle, Barneby and Dr Berkeley, and

*Master of the foxhounds John Parker with the Worcestershire hunt.*

wrote to his lawyer cousin Oldnall Russell about it, who later came to stay at Powick Court. But as the correspondent had been anonymous there was probably not a great deal John could do about it, other than put his own side of the story. Accordingly a letter dated 21st March appeared in Bell's from a very un-anonymous John Russell in the edition of 25th March, the main part being 'I write for the purpose of asserting that most of the particulars given in that account are entirely false, and those that have any foundation in fact are stated very incorrectly'.

Whether the account by 'constant reader' is correct, or whether what was written in 'The Pakingtons of Westwood' is correct, or whether yet another version of the story was the truth we shall never know, but a quarrel there certainly was. 'Constant Reader' was clearly no friend of John Russell's, but it is interesting that he, at least, saw John as not such a popular person as John Parker.

Once the season's final hunt took place on 2nd April at Bredon, John was free to go to London, and he took the Retaliator coach on 5th, dining with Hallifax in Wimpole Street. After three visits to Blackheath and one to Hampton Court he 'saw Hallifax and Barneby off in steam boat at Greenwich'. Where they were off to is not known, but one senses a tinge of regret that John was not able to accompany them on their tour. He returned home on 12th by the Aurora coach after which life settled down to the usual routine of social calls, attending quarter sessions, and riding out with Mary, who gets rather more mentions in 1827 than in 1824. Her cousin Sir Andrew Corbet with his young family came to stay, and they all went to Worcester Cathedral for the morning service on Sunday in a carriage. The following day, 30th April, they had a large party for dinner. As well as the Corbets the Wakemans, the Domviles, Mrs Wylde and 'Miss O' dined – quite a large family party. On Tuesday he took the Corbets to see Eastnor Castle, and the party was joined by the Lechmeres and the Temples for dinner. This would be Richard Temple, and his new wife Louisa Rivet-Carnac, but it is doubtful if they brought their one year old son – he would become Sir Richard Temple, the well-known Indian administrator.

On 3rd May he records that the gig had been painted and had a new harness. In the following weeks he often records driving out with Mary to various places in the gig, including Cheltenham where he met his uncle, with whom he dined and slept. On 24th they visited the Hanbury Williams at Coldbrook, and during the visit John and Mary rode to the top of Little Skirrid – although only 700 feet high, it has quite a steep approach. They also received a visit from Mrs Hanbury Leigh, whose husband Capel Hanbury Leigh was Ferdinand's second cousin, and returned the courtesy by visiting the Hanbury Leigh home at Pontypool Park. The Capel Hanburys had been noted iron masters, and John and his brother-in-law rode to see the iron works at Blaenavon. On 30th May the Hanbury Williams' first baby, Mary, was christened.

After ten days' stay John and Mary left for Newport, whence they took a steamer to Clifton, Bristol. The next day was Sunday, and after rising early they attended morning service in Wells Cathedral. After looking over the Bishop's garden they proceeded to Tiverton, where they slept. It must have seemed a long day, as they travelled over 70 miles. Finally on Monday 4th June they arrived in Sidmouth, their home for the next seven weeks. During the first two weeks they only sailed once, to Budleigh Salterton, where they were met with horses and rode back, and on the same day 'baby & I both bathed first time in sea'. His accounts mention payments of 1s 6d for bathing machines. On 18th John went mackerel fishing, catching only two, then two days later he hired a yacht (with, one assumes, a crew) called 'Friends' from Exmouth, and sailed across Lyme Bay to Lyme Regis, where he fouled a post in the harbour, and stayed the night at the Cup Inn. The next day they tried to sail back, but had to give up at Seaton due to contrary winds.

A few days later they were joined by the Hanbury Williams, but John seems to have given up the boat as he only records 'riding out'. On Sunday they all went to Exeter Cathedral where they would have seen William Herbert Russell's memorial, and returned to Sidmouth for tea. Then, after much riding out locally, they all left 'with Capt. Justice for Plymouth in Pim's yacht'. On the first day they reached Babbacombe, and walked over to Torquay where they slept. The next night they reached Dartmouth, where Capt. Justice showed them 'the governor's pictures' – the Naval College was not established then, but there must have been some sort of naval station. They had battled a contrary wind that day, which still blew the following day, so they had to reach their destination, Plymouth, by steam boat in time for the regatta. The Royal Yacht and Britannia were there, which made a fine sight when illuminated in the evening. After just one day in Plymouth, they started their return journey by land to Totnes then down river to Dartmouth. Here the yacht again caught up with them, and after a night's rest they called at Teignmouth to see the artist Thomas Luny's paintings, one of which John ordered at a cost of 2 gns. (Luny, 1759-1837, had been in the Royal Navy during the Napoleonic wars, and later retired to Teignmouth where he was reputed to have painted over 2,000 naval scenes.) Finally they returned to Sidmouth.

Wednesday 25th July marked the end of their stay in Devon, and after staying

*HMS Britannia, a 120 gun first rate, commissioned in 1823, entering Portsmouth harbour.*

overnight in Bath they arrived in Powick the next day. John kept a neat account of all his expenses for their two month stay in Wales and Devon, which totalled £202. The biggest items were housekeeping (£50) and the journey there and back, which totalled about £30. Their lodgings cost £26, and there are several entries for 'billiards', also bathing machines, usually 1s 6d; but bathing the baby was more expensive at 4 shillings.

John only had ten days before leaving for Scotland, and during that time he fitted in quarter sessions, a cricket match, a music party, and entertaining John Barneby, who was on his way back from his trip abroad. His trip to Scotland was to shoot at his uncle's lodge in the Highlands, so we can assume that Mary and little Johnny stayed at home, leaving John free to make haste in the overnight mail from Birmingham to Liverpool. There he met up with Offley Wakeman and his younger brother Edward, and they boarded a steamer to take them to Glasgow, calling at the Isle of Man on the way. The same day they went on to Stirling, and the next to Perth where the Wakemans left for Loch Katrine. John found time to go to the play in Perth, before the next day hiring a gig to reach Braemar, travelling through the Spittal of Glenshee, a journey of fifty miles over difficult terrain – 'a fine drive', he wrote.

Sir John Pakington's shooting lodge was called The Hut, and it must have been close to Braemar as the next morning John hired a pony and was there by breakfast time. Presumably it was a little way down the valley of the Dee, as later in the day Sir John and his nephew rode further down the valley to call on Abergeldie Castle. These social niceties out of the way, John turned his attention to sport. He obviously liked both the shooting and the great open spaces of the Grampians. He considered himself a fine shot, and on the third day out shooting noted that he killed sixteen grouse with eighteen shots. A few days later he went to Burkhall Woods and saw an eagle, a roebuck, black grouse, partridge, snipe and hare, killing sixteen of the poor beasts with nineteen shots. Ptarmigan were to be found higher up, and thrice John shot them, on the second occasion passing the summit of Lochnagar on the way. This mountain, at 3,789 feet is the highest in that part of the Grampians, and for someone not used to mountaineering, was some achievement. The only mention of his uncle was when he arrived, so we must assume that Sir John, now 67, did not undertake any of the arduous expeditions. Altogether John

*'Babbacombe Beach' by Thomas Luny, painted in 1823.*

had ten days' shooting, before leaving at 4.00 in the morning on 30th August. For his return he went on horseback to Glamis. This seems a little indirect and would have entailed a mountainous route of some forty miles, but perhaps he wanted to have a last look at the mountain scenery before going home. He posted from Glamis to Perth and took the coach thence to Glasgow, arriving at midnight, an extremely arduous day's travel.

That night he must have allowed himself little sleep, as the next day he travelled to Greenock and took the Liverpool steamer, where he arrived at 7.00 in the evening, which apparently still allowed him time to go to the theatre and meet some friends. The Birmingham coach left Liverpool at 6.00 the next morning, and, posting from Birmingham, he arrived at Powick the same evening at 11.00 p.m.

Shooting in Scotland seems to have whetted rather than sated John's appetite for the sport, as the very next day he 'shot at home', and two days later killed 23 ½ brace at Brockhampton with Barneby. The Music Festival was coming up, and he discussed arrangements with the Dean a few days before. Hallifax and Mrs Walhouse and her daughters came to stay for the music. The three day Festival followed the same pattern as that three years before, and it began on Tuesday with a performance of Handel's 'Dettingham Te Deum' in the cathedral. According to Berrows, there was a capacity audience of 1,100, 660 of whom sat in the gallery set up against the great east window. 'To the eye of the spectator, the scene was beautiful, the whole space to the extreme east end of the cathedral appearing filled with well dressed persons'. These gallery seats cost 5s; those in the choir 2s 6d. As was usual, there was a sermon, given on this occasion by the eminent high churchman Rev. Walter Farquar Hook, on the somewhat lengthy text from Ephesians 'Be not drunk with wine, in which is excess; but be filled with the Spirit; to yourselves in psalms and hymns and spiritual songs, singing and making melody in your heart to the Lord; Giving thanks always for all things unto God and the Father in the name of our Lord Jesus Christ'. Berrows reported that 'the preacher alluded to, and combated those objections which have been urged against meetings of this description, contending that such Festivals were not inconsistent with the maintenance of devotional feelings and fully sanctioned

*The Spittle of Glenshee with a dusting of snow. The modern A93 is in the background.*

by the practice of the early Christian church'. Appealing for generous donations to the charity, Dr Hook 'drew a most eloquent contrast between the animation and splendour of the scene before him, and the forlorn conditions of those widows and orphans on whose behalf he pleaded'.

Messiah was always performed at the Festivals at that time, in 1827 on Wednesday morning, and that evening 500 went to the ball, tickets costing 7s each. The concert in the College Hall on Wednesday evening was also full to capacity, and for the final day, Thursday, the stewards made hasty arrangements for extra galleries to be constructed in both the Cathedral and College Hall, enabling nearly an extra 600 tickets to be sold in the Cathedral, although as it turned out the extra accommodation in the College Hall was not needed. The 1827 Festival was successful in raising over £1,000 for charity, but the ticket sales of £4,000 left a deficit of £142. The expense was increased by the engagement of 'star' soloists, including three from Europe.

John's diary shows that the following week saw a great deal of socialising again, with his aunt and Miss Harding staying, and the week after was yeomanry week. On Wednesday Lord and Lady Eastnor led a large party of house guests at Powick Court. The following night the house was still full, but with a different set of guests, but the day was spoiled when Mary received 'a bad a/c of Dr Buckeridge'. Friday was the yeomanry 'grand field day', and on Saturday, as the party dispersed, news came of Dr Buckeridge's death. Mary left promptly for Lichfield, and 'baby and I went to Westwood'.

John seems to have had nothing better to do at Westwood than shoot for three days, then on Thursday he returned home by way of Thomas Telford's new bridge at Holt. At last on Friday he made his way to Lichfield. Dr Buckeridge's remains were buried at Tong, Shropshire, and John accompanied the funeral cortege there on Saturday. He remained one more day, Sunday, when he heard Dr Gardiner preach a 'fine funeral sermon' in the cathedral. The following morning he left Lichfield early, as he had arranged to visit his friend Hallifax at his residence at Chadacre Hall, near Bury St Edmunds, Suffolk, for some partridge shooting. He went home first to meet with Barneby, then they travelled together in Barneby's carriage to Cambridge, and met Hallifax the next day at Coldham Hall. Later they went to Chadacre. During their

*Dr Walter Farquar Hook (1798-1875), a high churchman, who later became the celebrated vicar of Leeds.*

ten day stay they attended two balls in Bury and a play, and stayed a night at Ickworth, then the seat of Frederick William Hervey, newly created 1st Marquis of Bristol.

From Suffolk they travelled to London to do some shopping, and after only two nights John travelled home, where Mary had also arrived back from Lichfield. The last two months of the year was given over to hunting, in which John was now committed financially. He noted that on 17th November the membership of the hunt committee was increased to ten, and that he increased his subscription by £10 so he could hunt an extra five days a fortnight. Shooting began to take second place. The social round continued, and his aunt Miss Pakington came to stay for a fortnight. For culture he had to go to Birmingham, and on 27th November took the 'young Isaacs' (this would be Elias's son John Whitmore Isaac then aged 19, and one or more sisters) to the Italian opera, seeing 'Il Barbiere di Siviglia', and the next night the same composer's 'Il Turco'. This still left time to attend a Christian knowledge meeting, and take lessons from Messrs DeBegnis and Lagain to improve his singing.

The day after he returned, John noted laconically in his diary that he 'dined at Temples & heard that Barneby had shot A. Knight', and later that he had died. Thomas Andrew Knight died in a tragic shooting accident that happened at Downton Castle near Ludlow, the seat of the Knight family who descended from Richard Knight, an early iron founder. The report in Berrows does not name the culprit. Shooting accidents were not uncommon in the nineteenth century and seemed to do nothing to dampen enthusiasm for the sport – one of John's relations died in similar tragic circumstances twenty years later, as we shall see.

Hunting continued in December, and John recorded riding out with Parker on a horse-buying expedition – this was the man he had duelled with, so relations had rapidly come back to normal. On 17th December Mary and John rode over to Elmley Castle, where they stayed with the Davies's in their house, Elmley Park. Col Henry Hastings Davies was an MP for Worcester, a veteran of Waterloo and ten years older than John, and in 1824 had married Augusta Ann de Crespigny. John recorded several meetings with them in his diary, but much later in life was to become more intimately connected. The following day John 'hunted, sung and shot' and at night they all went to the Pershore Ball. The next day 'came home for baby & then went to Westwood'. The family stayed there over Christmas, and on five days John shot. It seems his uncle had allowed him the shooting rights over the Westwood estate so relations cannot have been that bad, although earlier in December when he had stayed there for two nights he noted 'bad day' in his diary. Whether this refers to the weather, or his relations with his uncle, is not recorded.

No diary survives from 1828, but that from 1829 does. The entries for the first three months have a familiar look to them, being a report of his social round, and accounts of hunting and shooting. He hunted about every three days, and shot just as often, and some days great was the slaughter he reported. On 23rd January he stayed at Witley Court, the seat of Lord Foley. It had been in this family since the wealthy ironmaster Thomas Foley acquired it in 1655. In 1829 it was the seat of his descendant Thomas, 3rd Lord Foley – he died in 1833, and his son 4th Lord Foley was forced by debt to sell the property to the trustees of Lord Ward in 1837. At Witley John met 'a party of dandies', and the next day 110 pheasants were accounted for in two and three quarter hours. A week later at Blackmore Park, the seat of the Catholic Thomas Hornyold, 85 were killed, John having despatched twenty, and the next day at Madresfield 104 were killed, of which John claims to have accounted for twenty eight. A day later he went to Brockhampton, where Barneby does not seem to have been put off shooting by his accident, but only thirty four birds died – clearly Barneby's resources were not up to those of Earl Beauchamp and Lord Foley. Although most of his visits to the theatre were in London, John recorded going to see the well-known actor William Charles Macready in Sheridan Knowles' play 'Virginius and Matrimony' with some friends. The role of Virginius was one that Macready had made his own, but what brought him to Worcestershire is not known.

At the beginning of April John took the Aurora coach to London with the Hanbury Williams who had been staying with them, and, probably with Hallifax, he saw two Rossini operas 'Ricciardo and Zoraide', and 'The Thieving Magpie', and later in the week Vanbrugh's 'The Provoked Husband'.

Hunting continued during April, including a day at Shrawley Wood when there was a 'violent gale of wind which blew down several trees'. The last day of the season was 1st May, and next day the hunt committee met at Worcester where it was agreed to settle the hunt debt – John later recorded that he was called upon to pay £28 towards this. Possibly due to this unpleasant decision, he stayed in the city to dine with friends at The Star, and did not return home till 1.00 a.m. A few day's later he recorded that he heard of 'Miss Corbet's death' – this would be Judith, aged 27, his wife's cousin. On the same day he heard that his sister Elizabeth was ill and shortly after he had an even more alarming report of her condition, so he hurried down to Coldbrook where he found her already improving. After staying three nights he returned home by taking a

*Park House, Elmley Castle, the seat of Col and Mrs Davies. Demolished in the 1960s, its site, just west of the parish church, is now a housing estate.*

chaise to Hereford, then the coach to Worcester where he was in time to attend a hunt committee meeting. After dining with Berkeley and Acton he came home at night in Berkeley's tandem. A tandem has one horse in front of the other, and was one of the racier ways of travelling.

The following week on 20th May Sir John Pakington paid one of his rare visit to Powick, and stayed three nights. They took a pleasure ride on the Malvern Hills, followed by a visit to the Lygons at Madresfield nearby. On the final day John accompanied his uncle back to Droitwich as far as St Johns, Worcester, where he had to leave him to attend the hunt dinner. From this it would not appear that relations between uncle and nephew were too strained, yet only months later Sir John made his strange will. John was to pay two more visits to Westwood in the next month – perhaps he realised that Sir John was nearing the end of his life.

On 27th May John went to Cheltenham, then the following day on to London by the Berkeley Hunt coach, presumably unaccompanied by Mary. He arranged lodgings in Warwick Street, just east of Regent Street, and judging by the various people he met most of his friends had gone to London as well. The Beauchamps, Thornhills (his late brother's wife's family), Slaney and Davies's are all mentioned. He spent most of two days with Mrs Davies going to a concert in the morning, and 'Don Giovanni' in the evening, and Kensington gardens on another day – he could hardly guess then that she would become his third wife. The Worcestershire gentry were up for the Worcestershire Society dinner, which was held on 29th May. Its purpose was to raise money for apprentices from poor Worcestershire families working in London, but one assumes that this was just an excuse for a good dinner. Tickets cost one guinea, and dinner was at '5 for 6 precisely'. As usual, John was one of the speakers, proposing the toast 'the healths of our absent countrymen, and may those who are not subscribers soon become so'. According to Berrows, John spoke at some length and with his usual ability. On 1st June he went to the House of Commons to hear Sir James Macintosh introduce a motion about Portugal, before going to an exhibition, probably the one held at The Coliseum which included paintings, choice indoor plants, a 'Swiss Cottage', and a 'panorama'. John was obviously impressed by this, as he returned the following day with the inevitable Mrs Davies to see it. The panorama was taken from the top of the dome of St Paul's.

The next day he went with Lady Beauchamp to the Kings Theatre to hear Rossini's 'Semiramide', followed by one act of Barbiere, the entertainment ending, according to The Times, with a divertissement. On 3rd June he returned home by the overnight mail coach, and was soon riding over to Westwood to dine with his uncle. Whether they had anything special to discuss is not revealed, but there may have been another motive in going to Westwood – he had suddenly become keen on fishing. In earlier times a very large lake called the Great Pool had been created, roughly circular and nearly half a mile in diameter. Perhaps it had provided the clay for Westwood's bricks, but now it gave facilities for boating and fishing. On the two days after he returned he recorded fishing at home, probably on the River Teme, but on Monday 8th June he returned to Westwood to stay, and on the following four days simply records 'fished, boated &c'. This had to be interrupted on Saturday as he 'came home to breakfast to superintend the hay', but he returned to Westwood for dinner, and on Monday, Tuesday and Wednesday again 'fished, boated &c'. Now it was time for their summer stay in Devon, and on 25th June they left, but had not gone very far before they were delayed six hours by a wheel catching fire. With mainly wooden components fire was always a danger on coaches, whether through over-enthusiastic application of the brakes, or a tight bearing. On the second day they got as far as Wellington, but the following day they were again delayed by a rear wheel catching fire at Haldon Hill near Exeter Race Course. Nevertheless they still managed to reach Ivy Cottage in Teignmouth, which they had rented for £5 per week.

The first two weeks were marked by bad weather – 1st July was 'thorough wet day & gale of wind in which 3 vessels were wrecked at Sidmouth – saw 2 Indiamen turning down Channel'. They were able to take some rides between showers, and on 9th John noted that he took his first shower bath, so it seems their cottage was well-equipped. July 13th was Johnny's third birthday, and he was taken over to Dawlish where the Temples were staying. Not until 20th does John mention sailing, when they took Mrs Bates' little yacht to Dawlish, where they picked up the Temples and

*Westwood Great Pool, from Nash. Westwood House is in the distance.*

sailed on to Exmouth. The next day he sailed on his own to Exmouth, walking back, then two days later he rode to Torquay to arrange the charter of a yacht called 'Lady Louisa', although she was not delivered to Teignmouth till 2nd August. John made a note of her dimensions in his diary – it had a beam of 7 ft 6 ins, and seems to have been no longer than 30 feet, with a small cabin only 4 ft 6 ins tall, so it would been very much a day boat. In the meantime John and Mary did much riding – a favourite was up Little Haldon Hill just behind Teignmouth, from where one day he could see as far as St Albans Head, over 60 miles away, although John may have been confusing this with Portland Bill, 10 miles nearer, which hides St Albans Head from Torbay.

Bad weather still plagued them after the Lady Louisa arrived, but two days later John and Mary braved very strong winds to sail to the Exmouth regatta. They would have had a hired crew, and John 'sailed for the Cup but was beaten for want of ballast'. The following day the weather was much better and they sailed to Dawlish for the regatta and again raced for the Cup with a couple of friends, against three other yachts. 'I led for the first round but was then beaten by getting under the lee of the land'. In August they had some better weather, and enjoyed riding and sailing along the coast, often with a large party of friends – they even took Johnny out in Lady Louisa once. The Teignmouth regatta took place on the 19th and at last John achieved some success – he won the silver cup – and the day was rounded off with a 'good ball'. At the end of the month the weather turned stormy again, and on 10th September disaster loomed when Lady Louisa dragged her anchor, and was only saved from 'great danger on the bar' when her anchors held again in the narrows.

*Teignmouth – an engraving of c. 1840. Image courtesy of Devon Libraries.*

John had brought his own horses to Devon from Worcestershire, and they were sent home on 7th September, but the family remained till 18th. They took two days to travel to Coldbrook, having taken the steamer from Bristol to Newport. Here they stayed a week with the Hanbury Williams, shooting and socialising with the local gentry, including Edward Coplestone, the Bishop of Llandaff. He was probably known to John as he had been Provost of Oriel College during John's time there, and they all went to hear him preach in Abergavenny church.

Back in Powick on 26th September, John was soon over at Westwood, where he shot on four consecutive days. Briefly back in Powick where Mrs Buckeridge had come to stay, he left Worcester for London on the Sunday evening mail coach, met Hallifax, and spent the rest of the day shopping. The next day they both set out for Hallifax's estate in Suffolk, staying at Coldham Hall and Chadacre where they shot, and attended the Bury ball. After six days John returned to London, then went straight back to Worcestershire where he stayed at Elmley, presumably with the Davies's. There he joined a shooting party for two days before returning home to his family in Powick.

The following week his relations the Slaneys and Domviles were staying. They were joined by other guests, but they all left on Saturday 24th October. This left John free to go and see a yacht he had heard about. She was 'Petrel', lying near Bristol, and he went to view her, staying over-night. The hunting season was well under way, and John records that the committee advanced John Parker, the master, £420. But before any more hunting John wanted to view some more yachts, and over four days in early November he travelled to Southampton, Cowes and then Portsmouth. This trip entailed two overnight journeys on the mail coach, so he had clearly not taken Mary. Shortly after his return he went to shoot at Westwood – 'bad day & bad sport', he recorded. Perhaps this referred to another angry interview with his uncle, who may have heard about his wanting to buy a yacht. But this did not stop John from pursuing his dream, as soon after he wrote offering £700 for 'Druid', a yacht he had seen at Cowes.

Although John went most often to the theatre when in London, he also took the opportunity of hearing artistes when they performed locally. In November he had gone to the Boughton, where the Isaacs were one of the more cultured local families, to hear Garry Linley, probably a singer, and after returning from Southampton he took his wife to hear the Bohemian Brothers, although he does not say where. According to a notice in The Times when they appeared in London 'The Four Brothers will appear in the Costume of their Country singing their most approved Airs…'. A little later John rode with Mary to Worcester to see a panorama of the Battle of Navarino (1827), which he described as 'vile'.

As will already be evident, John enjoyed going to balls, even though on many occasions he was not accompanied by Mary. But she was with him when they joined a party going to the Bromyard Ball, and again the following month when they went to stay at Elmley. The entry for 15th December reads 'shot – thick fog… Pershore Ball at night'. Perhaps it is not surprising that there were so many shooting accidents!

It is probable that Sir John Pakington was at Westwood when John had a 'bad day' there on 11th November, but soon after that Sir John must have gone to Hampton Court. John noted that on 17th December he heard from him, then two days later after 'walking 7 hours in snow' shooting at Westwood when he bagged sixteen pheasants and eleven other animals, he received 'bad account of Sir John from Miss P'. On the following two days the deep snow and very cold weather did not stop him shooting at Westwood, and when he returned home on Christmas Eve he had 'very bad account of Sir John from Mr Dobson'. Boxing Day saw him again at Westwood, and he received another 'bad account', but two days later he received a letter from Sir John himself about shooting, which he notes in his diary followed by two exclamation marks. But John continued to shoot there, and on New Year's Eve another twenty two animals went into his bag.

But after a relatively mundane time in the late 1820s, the early 1830s were to see more important events in John and Mary's lives.

# Chapter 3
# Inheritance and His First Election – 1830 and 1831

On New Year's day, 1830, John received another bad account of his uncle, then on 3rd January another 'much worse, preparatory to the last'. Finally on 8th January John heard of his uncle's death, so he immediately took the mail coach to Oxford and thence to Hampton Court where he 'heard from Miss Pakington of Sir John's unjust will'. The will is dated 17th November and the first witness was a Hampton surgeon, so it may have been made immediately after Sir John had arrived at Hampton Court, having 'given up' on his nephew at the 'bad day' he had three days before. The other two witnesses were hotel waiters, another indication that it was written out in haste, probably by himself, and without legal advice.

It begins with the usual rather brief preliminaries, then continues:

> Having in my own person (who but for the imprudence of some generation going before me should now be in possession of 20,000 per annum in lieu of as many hundreds), & (had my grandfather entailed his estate) of four estates instead of only one, the Welsh one being but a trifling remainder, experienced how necessary entails are to the preservation of property, I wish to make the strictest and most distant one of mine that the law will allow me; and therefore always desire hereby that if any doubtful (I know of none) expressions of my intentions should be construed in unison with this desire, and if anyone should be in any respect disposed to controvert this plain statement of my last will and testament he or she or they should be entirely cut off from any eventual benefit that might otherwise come to themselves or any relative of theirs, which I say would otherwise have accrued to them under the disposition I am hereafter about to point out.

This latter provision was designed to deter his heirs at law from challenging the will, although in the event it proved ineffective.

What Sir John presumably felt was that the sales and mortgages which had much diminished the value of the estate and its income needed reversing, and that if it was run by trustees for a long period, with all the income being ploughed back, then its former worth could be reinstated. So what he did was to leave all the property to trustees, naming Sir William Cooke of Wheatley near Doncaster, and another trustee that he had recently asked Sir William to suggest. The only charge on the income would be an annuity of £1,000 a year to his sister Ann, £700 more than he had been giving her. Otherwise the income would all be kept by the trustees to be re-invested in the estate. He obviously envisaged that Westwood House would be let, and he gave permission to the trustees to raise £4,000 to build stables at Westwood to make it easier to let.

The trustees would hold it for the ultimate beneficiary, who would not be his nephew, nor even his nephew's young son, John Slaney Russell, but a son of John Slaney who would inherit when he reached the age of 25. As John Slaney was not likely to marry for at least another 20 years, it was likely to be around 50 years, 1880, before the property reverted back to Sir John's family. In fact John Slaney never had any children, and Sir John, in the wording of his will, did not allow for the possibility that his nephew might have other sons yet to be born. Had he done so, it would have been 1905 before the property would have reverted to a member of the family. All Sir John allowed for was that John Slaney Pakington would have no children, in which case the property would vest in the grandchildren of his trustee, Sir William Cooke, and children of other persons mentioned, who had no connection with the family, and were yet to be born.

What brought about this strange will, so adverse to the interests of the testator's nephew? In 'The Pakingtons of Westwood' the authors write that Sir John had been fond of John's elder brother William Herbert Russell and had seen in him a worthy successor in due course to the Pakington estates. But not so John, whom he thought likely to be a spendthrift in the manner of some of his predecessors. Humphrey and Richard Pakington may, of course, have known more about these family matters than we can learn from the surviving records. But the present author has seen no evidence to support the idea that Sir John favoured William Herbert, and there is plenty of evidence from his diary that John kept in regular touch with his uncle, even to the extent of visiting him in his Scottish hunting lodge. There is nothing in John's conduct that we know about, other than his rather extravagant way of life, that would make his uncle think that he had in any way besmirched the family honour. He had married a well connected lady (even if her fortune was not great), had already produced a son and heir, and was beginning to take part in public life. Only three years later he would stand for parliament. It is also clear that John was on good terms with his aunt. In a letter to him from 1838 she refers to her 'high opinion I have formed of your principles, and admiration of your character and conduct in every relation of life'. He always went to see her when in London, and she came to see him at Powick on a number of occasions. If Sir John had any rational complaints about his nephew one would have thought this would have biased his sister, but this does not seem to have been the case.

It is more likely, if fault is to be found, that Sir John had become an increasingly bitter man, unmarried and probably with few friends, whose mind increasingly became obsessed by his belief that his ancestors had wasted the family estates, causing him to live in circumstances that were more straightened than they should have been. According to 'The Pakingtons of Westwood' Sir John had become something of a recluse, with the brick wall around the park to reinforce his isolation, and it is certainly true that at his funeral there were no relatives. Berrows recorded the funeral as follows:

> The remains of Sir John Pakington arrived on Wednesday at Westwood Park. During the night they lay in state in the grand saloon, one of the finest tapestried apartments in the kingdom. At twelve o'clock on the following day the body was removed for interment in the family vault at Hampton Lovett Church. The procession was arranged as follows: Tenantry on horseback; Dr Amphlett, Rector of Hampton Lovett, and the Rev. Amphlett in a chaise; two mutes on horseback; a magnificent plume of feathers; the Body in a hearse covered with velvet and plumes and drawn by six beautiful horses; mourning coach and four with T. G. Curtler, Esq, and M. Ricketts, Esq, as mourners; another coach with four domestics; the private carriage of the deceased, drawn by a pair of horses.

Curtler had acted as a legal advisor, and Martin Ricketts was a doctor who owned a lunatic asylum in Droitwich. Perhaps he had been treating Sir John.

In 'The Pakingtons of Westwood' reference is made to a letter written by John's wife Mary to her husband when at Hampton – 'Mrs Wylde thinks as the property is left to your Grandson, we ought to put on very slight mourning'!

John obviously was not expecting a will of this nature, and immediately set his sights on challenging it so that his uncle's property could descend to himself and his aunt. His first move upon hearing the details was to consult his friend Hallifax, and the following day he went to see his lawyer cousin William Oldnall Russell, and John noted that he 'gave me hope'. There would have been at least two grounds on which the will could be challenged – the property had been left to people who were not yet living and were therefore too remote; and although Sir John had named trustees he had not named executors, a fundamental error. Armed with this knowledge John wrote to his friends and relations back in Worcestershire to explain what had happened, and at the same time sent the will up to a Mr Murray – no doubt he was a legal expert suggested by Oldnall Russell. He also noted that he bought the yacht Liberty for £600 – this might have been one of those he saw in November, but he did not record it by name.

Before leaving London he had a further consultation with Oldnall Russell, and also recorded going with Hallifax to 'Domvile the solicitor'. His half sister Mary's eldest son Henry Barry Domvile became a lawyer, but in 1830 he was still a student so it is likely to have been another unidentified Domvile relation.

On 19th January John left Hampton Court early and arrived back at Powick the same day. The next day he consulted two further local lawyers – 'opinions in my favour'. So he then wrote to Sir William Cooke, the first named trustee in Sir John's will, and John's copy of his letter survives. One has the impression that he did not know Sir William. He began by stating that he had been advised that the limitations and provisions of the will were illegal, and that in respect of the reserved rents of the estate Sir John died intestate, as the only reference he makes to the 'fee farm and other rents' have 'never been held to include the reserved annual rents'. In this respect John wrote that he and his sister, as the heirs at law, are for the time being taking possession of these. He stated that he intended to dispute the will generally, and in the meantime he requested permission of Sir William to be able to exercise in the usual way the management of the estate, on the strict understanding that such permission would be given without prejudice. John particularly made the point that there were about 1,000 acres of the estate 'that my late uncle has allowed to lie almost unproductive' that needed dealing with.

Finally John made a plea to Sir William to keep any legal proceedings as short and inexpensive as possible, and suggested that in the hope of avoiding the necessity of having to go to Chancery an action of ejectment might suffice. In writing this John obviously hoped that Sir William would agree that the will would be made void. He suggested that these matters could best to decided by a face to face discussion, and he proposed a meeting either in Worcestershire or London.

The next ten days John spent at home, fitting in a magistrates' committee meeting at the gaol about the new county courts, and a stay at Brockhampton shooting, during which he received 'a cheering letter from O. Russell'. At end of January he left Brockhampton to go directly to London. He must have had a reply from Sir William Cooke, as he met him at his aunt's at Hampton Court, and his friend Curtler (whether Thomas Gale or his solicitor brother John is not recorded) was also present. The three men then went to see someone called Preston. One assumes he was a barrister, and the outcome of the meeting was that Sir William gave over possession of Westwood to John and his aunt. Presumably Sir William was advised that he was not acting outside the terms of his trust in doing this, so at least John was able to deal with the day to day matters of estate management at Westwood, and to dismiss or employ staff as necessary.

Before leaving London John met Sir William once more, and the next day met Oldnall Russell, and bought his aunt a carriage – presumably her increased annuity would allow her lifestyle to improve somewhat. As on a previous occasion John travelled back to Worcestershire stopping at Elmley Castle and the Davies's for a night before arriving back at Powick on 6th February. The first thing he recorded doing was to write to the master of the hunt, John Parker, giving him permission to draw the coverts at Westwood. As John had never recorded doing this before, it sounds as if it had been a bone of contention, and may have been an element in the dispute which led to the duel three years earlier.

John was evidently pleased with what had happened so far, and must have felt that he was already master of the Westwood estate, in practice if not in law. John clearly intended to take up residence at Westwood himself as soon as practical, but repairs and alterations were necessary, and he decided to move into a nearby property on the estate first, so that he would be more easily able to keep an eye on estate matters and work at Westwood House. The property he chose was High Park, a large house on the edge of Westwood Park, approached by a drive off the Droitwich to Ombersley road. He took Mary to see this, and she seems to have been satisfied, as soon afterwards Powick Court was put on the market to rent. It was advertised as follows:

POWICK COURT near WORCESTER
TO BE LET

Furnished, for a term of years, and entered upon immediately:

THE capital Mansion of POWICK COURT, comprises two Entrance Halls, Spacious Dining and Drawing Rooms, Morning Room and Library, six best Bed Rooms with Dressing Rooms attached to three, and a suitable number of Servants Apartments; double Staircase, excellent Cellaring under the House, and all necessary domestic offices, two Coach Houses, Stabling for eight horses, walled Garden clothed with the choicest fruit trees in the greatest perfection; Green House, Flower Gardens, Shrubberies, and Five Acres of superior Pasture Land in front of the Mansion.

The house is newly and handsomely furnished, and the premises calculated in every respect for the accommodation of a family of distinction, situated on the high road from Worcester to the admired and fashionable village of Great Malvern, three miles from the former and five from the latter, and particularly desirable, being in a good neighbourhood for Society and sporting of every description, and nearly in the centre of the Worcestershire Hunt.

About Twenty Acres more of ornamental Pasture Land and several good Fish Ponds may be had with the House if required.

For all Particulars, apply to Mr Hyde, Solicitor, Worcester.

It was let, without much difficulty it seems, to a Mr Biscoe for £75 per annum.

Despite the fact that the will was being disputed, Sir John's creditors wanted to be paid, and John left the clearing up of all these matters to his solicitor, John Curtler. A list of Sir John's debts survives in the archives, and totals £8,181, a very considerable sum at that time. The list begins with several items of unpaid wages for domestic servants, game keepers, day labourers, and shepherds totalling the large amount of £800. The butler alone was owed £228. It is possible this includes a year's wages for his servants that were traditionally paid on death, although there is no provision for this in the will. Nevertheless his servants had obviously worked unpaid for some time before his death. There was also £3,000 that had been borrowed at interest in the last few years. Evidently Sir John had been leading a financially precarious existence, so the bitterness expressed in his will is perhaps understandable. Nevertheless, £460 was expended on his funeral – this seems a large amount for so modest an event, although bringing the body from London would have been expensive. How the creditors were eventually satisfied is not recorded, but Sir John's personal property would have been sold, and eventually everyone seems to have been paid. It seems Sir John had not been immune from the disease he ascribes to his ancestors of living beyond their means. Presumably he thought the trustees appointed in his will would be able to pay off his creditors by careful management of the estates, but this was not to be.

Although Westwood, a prominently set Jacobean house, must have been well-known to Worcestershire people, as Sir John had become a recluse not many would have known the interior, or, for that matter the exterior, very well, as it is set in the middle of the park, and cannot easily be seen close to. It is an unusual house with its four angled wings, and must have been an object of curiosity to anyone interested in such matters. So John wasted no time in showing off what he regarded as his new possession to friends and relations, starting with his wife's uncle Rev. Slaney, then a few days later to the Dean of Worcester. John mentions the Dean several times in his diary, partly in connection with Musical Festival matters in 1827. The Dean at that time had been Dr James Hook, but the following year a new Dean was appointed, Rt Rev. George Murray DD. Murray had been appointed Bishop of Rochester in 1827, and it seems to have been quite usual for this Bishop to hold a supplemental appointment, probably because the income from the rather small diocese was not generous. Earlier Bishops had also been Deans of Westminster. It seems that Murray was active

*High Park, the home of John and Mary Pakington in 1831.*

in both appointments, spending time in Worcester and Kent. John would have met the Murrays soon after the Dean's appointment in 1828, and he first mentions them by name in his diary on 15th February 1830 when, after meeting them in Worcester the previous day, he showed the Dean and his wife, Lady Sarah, round Westwood. By this date the Murrays had had all but one of their eleven children, and the eldest, Harriet, was just 17. The third daughter, Augusta, who was to play a big part in John's later life, was nearly 13.

Other visitors at this time included his relations the Corbets and the Hanbury Williams, and his friends Hallifax and the Foleys, who were all shown Westwood. As something of a celebration on 24th February he arranged for coursing at Westwood for the tenants – no doubt this was the first time this had been allowed for a long time. Then on 1st March what must have been a symbolic event took place – the first meet of the fox hounds at Westwood. 'Great crowd – found in Wassages – good run from Shuters Wood & killed in Randan. Merry lunch at Westwood afterwards…'. Hallifax was still with them, and on 5th March they went rabbit shooting, but John complains, very strangely to our ears, that there were 'no rabbits'! Preparations were by now underway to move to High Park, but first John and Hallifax went to Chipping Norton to hunt with the Duke of Beaufort at Heythrop, where they had a capital run late in the day.

On his return John heard of the death of Rev. Richard Slaney and later attended his funeral at Penkridge church. Back in Droitwich he signed the bond giving his aunt her annuity of £1,000 a year, and two days later met his solicitor Curtler to complete a mortgage on the Westwood estate. At the end of March they were ready to leave Powick to take up residence at High Park, but before doing so John rode with his wife to make a

*Rt Rev. Dr George Murray DD (1784-1860), Bishop of Rochester from 1827 to '60 and Dean of Worcester from 1828 to '45.*

good many local calls, no doubt to explain the new situation to his friends. Tuesday 30th March 1830 was the day when they moved into High Park, and they were immediately greeted by a heavy unseasonal snowfall, six inches deep. But this did not stop John taking his wife to see Westwood after church on Sunday, although one presumes this was not her first visit.

The next day John set out to ride round visiting the tenants of his new estate, but was embarrassed to note in his diary that he fell off his black mare in doing so – he would not have cut his usual smart figure calling on a tenant covered in snow and mud! John Barneby came to stay at High Park, and they took Mary round to see Ombersley Court, the seat of Lord Sandys, and Thomas Telford's new Holt Bridge, both much nearer to High Park than to Powick. John also had a number of other matters to arrange in connection with the estate. He had already had the farm implements and livestock valued, and marked trees for felling (50 oaks, which were valued at £800). After another day's hunting at Westwood he 'looked over Westwood wine cellar', a task which took two days.

No sooner was this complete than John had another important engagement. He had to prepare his new yacht 'Liberty' for the summer, so travelled by Cheltenham and Southampton to Cowes, where he 'passed the day in designing alterations to Liberty', and engaged a master. He was called Denton, and was paid £10 per month when the vessel was in commission, and £1 when not. Later he was also to pay £15 per month for the crew, but whose numbers were not stated. John had the ambition to join the Royal Yacht Club, and registered Liberty with them when in Cowes. On 1st May he noted in his diary with obvious pride 'Elected into the RYC'.

The Royal Yacht Club, or, as it was known after 1833, the Royal Yacht Squadron, was founded in 1815, and was an exclusive assembly of the owners of cruising yachts, with less than 100 ordinary members in 1830 and a number of honorary members drawn from the Royal Navy and European royalty. Members had their own uniform of blue coat with special buttons, white trousers, and a special cap with 'a band of gold lace having a crown and anchor worked on it'. Their yachts were, from about the time of John's membership, allowed to fly the same white ensign as ships of the Royal Navy, which distinguished them, for example, in foreign ports from merchant ships flying the red ensign, so they would not have to pay tonnage dues. A prominent member was the Waterloo veteran the Marquis of Anglesey, and when John met him hunting at Croome in December 1829 he may have lobbied for his joining, as unknown or undesirable applicants could easily be 'black-balled' by the committee. Pakington's membership was to last twelve years, and Liberty was described as a 42 ton cutter in the membership lists. In 1837 a new yacht, 'Ganymede' of 69 tons is listed against his name; but although his membership continued no yacht was registered after 1837, so his entry in parliament probably marked the end of his active yachting career.

John wanted to waste no time in starting the work at Westwood, and on 23rd April noted that he 'passed the day in examining Westwood with Mr Hardwick', and the next day when 'he gave a favourable report on its stability'. This was Philip Hardwick, whose career then was still not very advanced, but whose father and grandfather had been well known architects. Hardwick was then 38 and his best known works, particularly the famous Euston arch and the similar one at Curzon Street in Birmingham, were still some years in the future. One might think that he was a strange choice to advise on an Elizabethan country house, as Hardwick was never noted for this type of work, but perhaps John wanted someone with an established reputation. He would have heard of his recently deceased father, Thomas Hardwick, a well known church architect who had also worked at Hampton Court. The Westwood project seems to have continued for several months, so we will return to it later.

On 3rd May John arrived in London and called on his aunt and Miss Hawkins at Hampton Court. During his brief stay he managed as usual to go twice to the theatre: with his wife's cousin Robert Slaney to see the young Fanny Kemble in Thomas Southerne's 1694 play 'Isabella' at Covent Garden, and with Hallifax to see an entertainment including Bellini's new opera 'Il Pirata' at the King's Theatre. While in London John dined with the Oldnall Russells and, after an early start, went to an exhibition, before leaving at midday for Southampton. The next morning they went across to Cowes to inspect Liberty, and he slept at the Royal Yacht Club.

*A painting of 1895 by Henry Brooks and Alexander Dickinsons showing members of the Royal Yacht Squadron in front of The Castle (their clubhouse). The Kaiser (with white cap) and the Prince of Wales are standing bottom right. Reproduced courtesy of the Royal Yacht Squadron, Cowes.*

After inspecting some of the yachts moored on the River Itchen, John and Hallifax returned to London, and John went with his aunt to the Doctors Commons, the court at which he had hoped to have his uncle's will proved. However, as the will had the defects above mentioned this could not be done. To console himself he went to hear the Italian singer Luigi Lablache in the evening. Back home on 15th May, John remained busy with his social round, and showing his friends Westwood – for example on 20th 'St John, Temples & Isaac came – lionized Westwood…' – lionize is a favourite word of John's, meaning look over or inspect. He also used the lake for boating and fishing at this time. His aunt and Miss Hawkins came to stay at the end of May, and he records driving Mary to Droitwich the day before to do some shopping for them.

Friday 11th June was an important day: 'rent day at Westwood – dined with the tenants & afterwards with party at home…'. The following day he drove to Worcester with Mary to deposit the cash in his bank. Once this important task was out of the way, he felt able to leave Worcestershire for his summer stay in Devon, doubly important this year as he had his new yacht and RYC membership to enjoy. John and his wife made good progress on the first day, stopping to look at and dine at Berkeley Castle. The next day they 'travelled very quick' and arrived at Teignmouth at half past six, and took possession of their house straight away. Liberty was waiting for them, and the next day John spent some time on board preparing it. The Hanbury Williams were also there. The next day he felt ready to go out for his first sail – 'very cold' was his comment. But apparently there were quite a lot of things to be done before she was quite ready, and it was a week after they arrived before he was able to record that he sailed to Torquay with Mary. Stormy weather and church-going delayed further expeditions, but on 29th the weather was fine and they sailed to Salcombe where they dined and slept on board for the first time. The next day they went up river to Kingsbridge and back, probably using Liberty's dinghy, and he bought some 'tea china' to further equip the yacht. The following morning they started at 3.00 a.m.(maybe the tide enforced this uncivilised start) and they reached Teignmouth by noon in heavy seas and hard rain.

Many of his friends and relations were either staying nearby or visited Torbay, and on 1st July we hear that Miss Thornhill, presumably a relation of his late brother's widow, came and accompanied them for a 'beautiful sail with strong breeze to Torquay…'. The next day they sailed in the other direction to Sidmouth and back, but it must have been rougher as 'Miss Thornhill and Williams sick'. The following day they had planned their first long passage to Guernsey, but there was a foul wind, so they had to content themselves with sailing to Brixham, where John dined on board with his sister and her husband, before returning. They were now sailing every day, and on 9th July after a morning sail to Babbicombe, they were joined by Hallifax for their passage across the Channel to Cherbourg. The voyage was accomplished over night, and they spent the day shopping and seeing the docks, sleeping on board after dining at an hotel. The next day Hallifax left them to join another yacht, and the others returned, laying to in the shelter of Cap de la Hague to dine on board.

John Barneby now joined them, and their next trip took them west to Dartmouth, then on to Cawsands Bay just beyond Plymouth, where they had 'foul wind & heavy sea'. The next day they still had 'incessant rain & gale of wind' but they must have found an anchorage or mooring, as the officers of the warship 'Undaunted' sent a boat across to invite them on board, but it was too wet. However the following day, 18th July, the two Johns went to church at Stonehouse in Plymouth, and afterwards visited HMS Caledonia before walking to the obelisk at Mount Edgcumbe. Later they were able to visit 'Undaunted' after all. She was a fifth rate 38 gun ship built in 1807, 155 feet long, about five times the length of Liberty, but not as large as the Caledonia, which was a first rate 120 gun warship. On Monday they sailed on to Falmouth, but they were unable to visit Pendennis Castle due to wind and rain, so they returned to Plymouth the next day for the regatta. The first day was very poor 'no yacht coming for the 1st prize' and they sailed out to see the Eddystone lighthouse before anchoring back in Stonehouse Pool. The second day there was no racing, and John's party visited the naval dockyard in the morning and Mount Edgcumbe after dinner. Friday 23rd July was the second regatta day, and Liberty 'sailed against the Madora for the cup & was beaten by bad luck'. Later he mounted an appeal, which was turned down, and they returned to Teignmouth.

John's aunt was staying nearby and they dined together when they returned from Plymouth, but the next day was the Torquay regatta. John sailed but his wife and sister went there by land, but the regatta committee would not allow Liberty to sail for the cup, so John's attempts to win his races were so far without success. Nevertheless John and Mary went to the regatta ball, and slept on board. A few days later Liberty was painted, which put paid to sailing for a few days and allowed John and Mary to do some riding. On Saturday 31st July they gave a dinner party on board for their friends, a haunch of venison was served, and

*A scene painted c. 1830 showing a frigate, believed to be the Undaunted, off Plymouth with Mount Edgcumbe in the background. © National Maritime Museum, London.*

a band was hired for the occasion. The following week Mary, Miss Thornhill and Hanbury Williams accompanied John on a trip to Dartmouth, where they stayed over-night – John records that they all dined on board, but what the sleeping arrangements were is not recorded!

The climax of the summer sailing season was approaching with regattas at Southampton and Cowes. On 3rd August Mary, John and Hanbury Williams set sail for the Isle of Wight with a fine westerly breeze behind them. After staying overnight in Swanage Bay they sailed on to Portsmouth where they dropped Hanbury Williams. Then they came back to Cowes, where they saw Mr Hallifax with his yacht Julia. This would be Thomas Hallifax's father, also Thomas, a member of the RYC. The Southampton regatta was on Monday 9th August, and Liberty, which 'sailed beautifully', competed against Hebe, Peri, Zephyr and Oberon; 'beat them to windward and came in second', John recorded with some pleasure. Never one to accept second best, he still lodged a complaint with the stewards, but they refused to hear it. The next few days were beset with heavy rain and strong winds, which must have made life on board uncomfortable to say the least, but on Friday 13th they managed to get to Portsmouth to see 'Victory', and attend the Cowes ball in the evening. They were able to watch the Ladies Cup the following day, which saw a great match between Alarm and Miranda. On Sunday they started their journey home, stopping at Swanage overnight before returning to Teignmouth on 16th.

More calling on neighbours continued over the next few days – it is remarkable how many Worcestershire friends and relations were staying locally. John also called to see Miss Johnnes in Torquay a number of times – she would be a relation of Ferdinand Hanbury Williams, whose uncle John had married Elizabeth, daughter of Thomas Johnnes of Hafod House and Croft Castle.

On 23rd August they sailed overnight with friends for Cowes, where they called on Lord Deerhurst (son of the Earl of Coventry of Croome) and Lord Anglesey, and they continued to Portsmouth where they made yet more calls. The following day Liberty raced for the regatta cup, but after the first round disaster struck – she sprang her mast, and had to retire. So they watched the rest of the regatta from the shore, but by the following evening a new mast had been stepped, and they sailed

*Woodbine Cottage, Torquay, the home of Miss Johnnes in 1823. Image courtesy of Devon Libraries.*

back to Teignmouth overnight. They did not land till 7.00 p.m. but still managed to go to the Teignmouth ball. There was only one day's rest before having to sail to Weymouth for yet another regatta and Liberty raced for the cup against Madora and Blue Eyed Maid. 'A fine race', John commented, and Liberty came in second to Madora, beating Blue Eyed Maid by four minutes.

They returned to Teignmouth next day, picking up the Bensons, more Worcestershire friends, at Sidmouth. On the following day they sailed to show them Torquay, before sailing them back to Sidmouth. On Saturday 4th September, John's sail to Torquay was his last of the season, and on Monday they left Teignmouth, arriving home at Powick the next day.

Before recounting the remainder of the year from John's diary, we should return to his efforts to acquire the ownership of his uncle's property. It can be assumed that Sir William Cooke, the trustee named in Sir John's will, shared the unease about the will with everyone else, but Sir William, as an old friend of Sir John, would have wanted to make sure everything was done 'by the book'. He therefore put up what was probably only a nominal defence to John and his aunt's claim to the estate. Evidently it had not been possible to by-pass the Court of Chancery, as on 4th June statements were deposited in the Court by the legal representatives of both sides in the action Russell v. Cooke. The plaintiff's bill rehearsed the will and the fact that the ultimate beneficiaries were not yet born, and 'submit, that under these circumstances, the devises and bequests of the said will are void, save the annuity to Anne Pakington'. The provisions are 'too remote and void' considering that the eldest son of John Russell, the great nephew of the testator to whom the estates are devised for an estate for life 'is not yet in being and there is no other person in being entitled to the benefit of the ulterior limitations in the will and codicil'. The plaintiffs claimed that the coheirs and next of kin of the testator were entitled to the whole and real personal estate and effects subject only to the provisions in the will for securing Miss Pakington's annuity. 'They have entered the estate and have cut down and removed some of the timber growing there and sold the same and have retained in their possession the personal and real estate and receipts and profits as devisees under trust under the will.' The plaintiffs go on to say that, although they recognise the trustees' role in securing the annuity, as they have already made arrangements for this to be paid, they have requested the defendants to surrender the term of the trust to them. But 'the defendants have refused to comply with these requests, and deny that the beneficiaries are too remote and void'.

John had returned from Devon just as the shooting season was starting, and he lost no time in going out shooting, joined by the Hanbury Williams's who had come to stay. The following week was the Music Festival, and John took lodgings in the City. On Tuesday the Festival opening was graced by the presence of the Duchess of Kent and her daughter the Princess Victoria, then only 11 years old, who was described by Berrows as 'interesting'. The royal ladies were received into the cathedral by the Dean, Rt Rev. George Murray, and very much increased the attendance on the opening day. The Dean preached the sermon. The holding of musical concerts, even including religious works, in the cathedral had always been controversial, and continued to remain so as we shall see later, but the Dean preached in favour (he could hardly do otherwise). He also condemned efforts by the government to control and redistribute church property. Reformers were in favour of transferring some of the endowments supporting what some regarded as unnecessarily lavish establishments run by bishops and other church dignitaries to fund badly needed clergymen in the fast growing industrial cities. Later the Dean entertained the royal party in the chapter house, and he and Lady Sarah also gave banquets in the two following days in the chapter house following the morning concerts.

The music festival lasted the usual three days, and opened with a funeral anthem in memory of King George IV, who had died at the end of June. The inevitable Messiah was performed on the second day, there were balls every night, and John remained in the city till the end of the festival on Thursday. After it ended the Corbets, Domviles and Oldnall Russells came to stay, and when they were there John took them round to see Westwood. About the same time we hear of another of John's indulgences – a new 'chariot'. From his accounts we know that this was provided on rental. One presumes this was the same as the new phaeton referred to a few days later and several times thereafter – John must have been proud of it.

During the rest of the year life continued very much as normal: hunting and shooting and having friends at High Park, and staying away. John was now a magistrate at Droitwich petty sessions, and usually attended every other Friday. He was also an important figure in the hunt committee, as he took the chair at the annual dinner on 18th December which went on late enough for him to stay overnight in Worcester. John, Mary and little Johnny appear to have spent Christmas on their own as there is no mention of his aunt or other family coming. 27th December was another rent day, and the tenants were entertained to dinner at High Park.

The year 1831 began with the Epiphany quarter sessions, and a question that had been exercising the court was again raised – the inadequacy of the existing county courts, which were held in the Guildhall. Enlarging the Guildhall had been considered, but this belonged to the city which complicated matters. The country was still suffering from agricultural distress, making many people oppose the idea of spending ratepayers' money building new courts. The discussion was ended when the Earl of Plymouth proposed that the question be adjourned *sine die*, but that a parliamentary bill should be prepared authorising the magistrates to build new courts when things had improved. John attended and was delegated to this committee. On the following day he went to the dispensary ball with Mary, then later in the week went to another ball at Pershore, staying with the Davies's at Elmley Castle.

At last on 25th February the case of Russell v. Cooke, which would settle the matter of Sir John's will, came up for hearing before the master of the rolls. The trial does not seem to have taken long. John's counsel was in the middle of stating his case when the judge stopped him and asked the defendants' counsel, Messrs Turney and Girdlestone, what was their case. They cited various precedents, but the judge ruled that none of these applied to the present case, and gave judgement:

> His Honour doth declare that all the decrees, limitations and trusts in the will and the codicil concerned with the real and personal estate of the testator, purported to be devised and bequested, except for the annuity to Ann Pakington, are too remote and void and that the plaintiffs are entitled as the coheirs in law of the testator to all his real estate and that the plaintiffs and Elizabeth Hanbury Williams are entitled as the next of kin of the testator to all his personal estate subject only to the said annuity.

One of the provisions of the will was that anyone taking possession of the estates should change their name to Pakington. Although the will was no longer valid, such a provision was quite usual, and as John was to inherit the Pakington estates, owned by his ancestors for nearly 300 years, it was natural for him to want to adopt the Pakington name. Accordingly on 15th March it was published in the London Gazette that the King had given licence for him to be called John Somerset Pakington, and to bear the arms of the Pakingtons of Westwood, so we will henceforth use that name.

Now the ownership of the estates were settled, how did it leave John Pakington financially? As sole surviving son of his father William Russell, John had inherited his estates, but these do not seem to have been very extensive – his holdings in Powick in 1840 only amounted to 125 acres, but there were other estates in Worcestershire, Gloucestershire and Somerset. A series of rentals exist from the 1840s and 1850s from the agent who collected his rents from property in Knightwick, Suckley and Bricklehampton in Worcestershire and Bishops Cleeve in Gloucestershire as well as Powick, showing that the net receipts from these amounted to about £900 per year. These look as if they were his paternal estates, out of which an annuity for his late brother's wife would have been paid until she died in 1827. After 1830 a further £75 a year accrued from letting Powick Court.

Although John's marriage settlement has not come down to us, a letter John wrote to Rev. Richard Slaney about it has survived, in which he wrote that the estates in his possession yield 'rather more than £300 a year' net of the jointure he was giving his brother's widow, and there was probably an allowance to be found for his sister Elizabeth until she married in 1825. This was not a very good income to start married life on, even if his wife brought some of her own fortune to the marriage as well.

The estates of the 8th baronet are listed in documents involved in the dispute about the will. Although they do not give acreages, they show the gross annual value of the estate to have been just under £6,000 including Westwood House. The 1840 tithe map of Worcestershire shows Pakington's estates in the county to have amounted to just under 3,000 acres, probably little changed from 1830. However, a carefully written-up series of rentals running from 1832 till Miss Pakington's death in 1846 still exists in the family archives, and these show that during this period the gross annual rents receivable averaged about £4,600, including the Welsh estate which brought in about £320 a year. The difference between this and the £6,000 quoted above is accounted for mainly by the value of Westwood House and Park, for which, of course, no rent was received. Tenants' allowable deductions varied considerably, and included land tax, and, from 1843, income tax, some repairs and improvements, and in bad years a ten per cent deduction of rent was allowed. Deductions averaged £360 a year, leaving a little over £4,000. Miss Pakington's annuity of £1,000 was charged against this first, and other deductions included the £473 still payable to the Coventry Charity, the accountant Thomas Curtler's salary of £150, and a further annuity of £200. The balance was then split between Sir John's joint heirs, John Somerset Pakington and his aunt. This led to Miss Pakington receiving more than her nephew, who would have been left with little more than £1,000 a year to add to the income from his paternal estates. It is clear from the accounts that both John and his aunt borrowed considerable sums of money at different times, and interest, usually at 4%, had to be paid.

One thing is clear from Thomas Curtler's accounts – during this period the estate was being carefully run, and arrears, which were the bane of so many estates, kept under tight control. Only in the first three years of this series do the audits, held at the end of June and December, start with significant arrears, as much as £318 in June 1833, but these debtors were vigorously pursued, and mostly cleared by the next audit. By 1840 Thomas Curtler had got the tenants so well trained that an audit started with no arrears, which must have been a rare event indeed!

So in practice Pakington's income only amounted to that of a moderately well-off gentleman, and it seems to be the case that he always aspired to a higher life-style than his income allowed. We know that some of the difference was made up by raising mortgages – when he took possession of Westwood there were expensive improvements to fund, there was his new yacht and its crew, and there was the considerable amount of travelling that he indulged in throughout his life.

In March 1831 Pakington received the first proposals from Hardwick for the proposed new stables. These were to be placed at the rear (north west) side of the house, with a new washhouse and drying ground behind the stables, so they would not be visible from the house. However, none of these plans were ever put into effect.

The winter continued with the usual round of hunting, shooting and socialising, with the occasional mention of estate management matters. On Monday 14th March Pakington posted up to London, staying in Wimpole Street with Hallifax, while Mary and Johnny went to Lichfield. He managed to see two operas at the

Kings Theatre – Rossini's 'Ricciardo e Zoraide', and 'L'ultimo giorno di Pompei' by the little-known Italian composer Pacini. He fitted in a brief visit to Hampton Court, and returned on Sunday.

Back in Worcester, the committee to determine the best site for the new county courts that Pakington had been appointed to was meeting, but the location proved controversial. A site near the gaol in Castle Street was favoured initially of the grounds of expense, but legal problems arose, and then the present site was preferred. There were further delays during construction as a second parliamentary bill was needed to raise extra finance, and there was even a bricklayers' strike. The new courts in the Shire Hall were finally opened in 1837.

As will be recounted in the next chapter, there was unrest in 1831 about the Reform Bill, and in March Pakington had seen Lord Plymouth about re-establishing a yeomanry cavalry troop (see next chapter). After he had returned from London, Pakington noted that he 'rode round Ombersley parish for recruits in vain', but on 18th and 19th April he held dinners (both 'jolly') in Ombersley and Droitwich and later at the Hadley Bowling Green, which seem to have been more successful.

As we have seen, Pakington had already become involved in county affairs through his appointment as a magistrate, but now, at the age of 32, he was ready to embark on the next stage of his ambitions – a seat in parliament. Its dissolution on 22nd April opened the way for him to become involved in national politics for the first time. Many of Pakington's maternal ancestors had been Tory MPs, but the same cannot be said for his father's family. Nevertheless Pakington showed an early determination to get into parliament, and, like his Pakington ancestors, he was a strong supporter of the Tory party. He first showed these sympathies when, at the nomination of members to represent the county of Worcestershire on 6th May 1831, he proposed Col Henry Lygon, who was standing in the Tory interest, as one of the two members. Political tension was running high at the time, and an excitable crowd was present in the Castle Yard in Worcester to hear the speeches by the three candidates for the two seats. To explain why, it will be necessary to take a brief look at the national political situation as it had developed over the last few years.

After a period of Tory governments, in 1830 parliamentary reform had become a live issue. The abuses of the existing system were well known. It was not so much that the franchise was restricted by a property qualification, but that the distribution of seats had become manifestly unfair. Over two thirds of MPs represented boroughs (usually two MPs for each one), where the property qualification varied from place to place and was often very much in the hands of the borough council or local magnate, called pocket boroughs. Not only that, but many boroughs had declined in size, and in a few notorious examples such as Old Sarum had no population at all (called rotten boroughs), whereas the many new industrial towns, even including such populous places as Birmingham and Manchester, had no MPs at all.

The case for reform was clear – small boroughs should lose their representation, or have it reduced to a single MP, and these seats redistributed to new towns that lacked representation. The property qualification needed to vote should be made uniform throughout the country. It might now be thought that this case was unanswerable, but there was considerable opposition among the upper classes to reform, based mainly on the idea that the existing system worked, so why change it? It had produced a stable government and some general increase in prosperity since the start of the industrial revolution over half a century before. Look at what had happened across the Channel in France – a bloody revolution with most of the aristocracy killed, swings of government between a revolutionary parliament and a dictatorial emperor, twenty years of warfare throughout Europe, defeat and national humiliation, and, even after that, instability was continuing. So it is easy to see that the governing classes were nervous, and many thought that once one started tinkering with the system, who knows where it would end? One should remember that the idea of 'one man one vote', and even less 'one person one vote', was not on most people's horizon, so most would have regarded reform as nothing too dramatic, merely bringing a proven system of government up to date. But of course this produced the counter argument that one should not tinker with something that worked.

Once pressure for reform started to grow, it proved to be irresistible. Even those who were unlikely to gain a vote in any reform and would be content to leave the actual voting to the more propertied members of society felt that all districts should at least have some representation in parliament. When in June 1830 the late and rather unlamented monarch George IV died, the rules still in force at that time meant that parliament had to be dissolved and a new general election held. This took place in August (polling in those days was spread over several weeks), and although as both parties were split and the party system not so developed as it was later it is not possible to be precise about party numbers, the governing Tory party lost ground in the election, as the need for reform had become a live issue.

When parliament re-assembled in November it soon became obvious that the Tory government, under the prime minster the Duke of Wellington in the Lords and Robert Peel in the Commons, would not be able to command a majority. In the debate on the King's speech on 2nd November the Duke of Wellington rather ill-advisedly expressed himself utterly opposed to any measure of reform, and unrest and excitement spread to the streets. On 7th November King William IV had to postpone a visit to the Guildhall due to unruly crowds, and two days later there was further trouble. The climax came a week later when the government presented the new civil list to the Commons, and MPs soon sensed that this was a chance to inflict a defeat. When the votes were counted the Tories had been defeated by 29 votes – Col Lygon did nothing to help his party as he was absent.

Wellington and his ministers immediately resigned, and the King sent for Earl Grey, the Whig leader, to form a new government. Grey himself was in favour of reform, and with his ministers set about preparing a reform bill. It was presented to the House of Commons by Lord John Russell on 1st March 1831.

Many expected the bill would be a fairly moderate measure of reform, but what Lord Russell proposed went much further, and a speech lasting less than an hour changed the course of British history, starting a process that has continued ever since. Most Tories, who might have been prepared to give reluctant support to a lesser measure, realised, as Lord Russell read out the list of sixty boroughs that were to lose all representation and forty seven (including Droitwich and Evesham) which were in future to have only one MP, realised that something much more substantial was being proposed. As Lord Hurd wrote in his biography of Sir Robert Peel 'Tory MPs reacted noisily, at first in shock and then in elation. The government had gone mad; neither parliament nor the people would stomach such a massacre, such an overturning of history'.

We need not describe in detail the passage of the Reform Bill, but the government suffered a number of defeats, and it was realised that a general election, which in the present climate would undoubtedly give the government a greater majority, was necessary. Parliament was dissolved on 22nd April, and in Worcestershire, which returned two MPs and had had only one contested general election in 90 years, there were three candidates.

Since 1780 one of the Worcestershire MPs had been a member of the Lygon family, and in 1831 Henry Beauchamp Lygon (1784-1863) was the Tory candidate. He was the third son of William Lygon of Madresfield Court near Malvern, a member of an old county family that traced their descent back to the

*Henry Beauchamp Lygon (1784-1863), later 4th Earl Beauchamp of Madresfield. From a portrait at Madresfield Court.*

Beauchamps in the early middle ages. In 1780 William Lygon married Catherine Denn, who later received a very large inheritance, and, helped by this at a time when the government were desperate for resources to fight Napoleon, he was created 1st Earl Beauchamp in 1815. The 1st Earl died the following year, and he was succeeded successively by his three elder sons as the 2nd, 3rd and 4th Earls. The eldest, William Beauchamp Lygon, had served as a Worcestershire MP since 1806 and on his elevation to the Lords when he inherited, his younger brother Henry Beauchamp Lygon came forward to replace him at Westminster. Henry had had a distinguished army career, serving with Wellington in Spain. He was elected in 1816 and again in the later elections in 1818, 1820, 1826 and 1830, in each case unopposed.

For most of the nineteenth century thus far the county had returned one Tory and one Whig member, the former a member of the Lygon family, the latter represented by members of the Lyttelton, Foley or Winnington families. But the pressure for reform in 1831 meant that this comfortable arrangement was to be disturbed, as the Whigs decided to put up a second candidate in opposition to Lygon. This led to the first contested election for twenty five years. The Whig candidate chosen to join the standing Whig, Hon. Thomas Henry Foley (a younger son of Lord Foley of Witley Court), was Capt. Hon. Frederick Spencer (1798-1857). Spencer, the second son of Earl Spencer of Althorpe Park, had no local connections, but had strong Whig links as his brother, Viscount Althorpe, was chancellor of the exchequer and a leader of the Whigs in the Commons. Althorpe had a long record as an advocate of reform, and had been one of the architects of the Reform Bill, pushing for it to be as radical as possible. His brother, after an unhappy childhood, had escaped to sea, and by 1831 had risen to the rank of captain in the Royal Navy. Later he was to become a vice-admiral.

Thus the scene was set for the contest. It had been agreed that Pakington would help support Lygon, and Pakington records that Lygon came to see him on 28th

*Capt. Frederick Spencer (1798-1857) MP for Worcestershire then Midhurst. In 1845 he succeeeded his brother to become the 4th Earl Spencer. From the Collection at Althorp.*

April to discuss canvassing. The following day Pakington went to Worcester to attend a meeting at which it was determined that he would be the chairman of Lygon's committee. Despite his long record as an MP, there is no doubt that Lygon was unpopular and seen as an opponent of reform, and both sides indulged in dirty tricks to try and ensure victory. Lygon and Pakington were a number of times accosted in the streets, and the day after the committee meeting 'I & many others went with Lygon to canvass in Cornmarket – assaulted with mud &c by mob & driven into public house'. Berrows reported:

> We are sorry to be under necessity of noticing the gross outrage committed on Col Lygon and his friends in this City on Saturday – while they were engaged in canvassing some of the lowest of the population began throwing mud and stones and behaving otherwise with some violence... they took refuge for a time in the Union Tavern until the constables dispersed the mob. ... Capt Spencer's committee soon issued a notice deprecating this behaviour.

A letter from a priest, Nicholas Sewell, to a colleague describing the events during the election has survived, and was printed in the Transactions of the Worcestershire Archaeological Society in 1994. Sewell, from Maryland, USA, and in favour of reform, described some of the devices used by Lygon and his supporters to try and ward off his opponent. Lygon, he wrote, was supported by the

> Coventrys, Beauchamps, &c and innumerable parsons, above 40 attorneys & plenty of money, and with all their tricks per fas et nefas, will probably lose the election. The Lygonists, before the election began, engaged all the chaises from Dudley & other places to Worcester, all the Inns and beds in the public houses in Worcester, except the Star & Garter (Mr Foley's quarters and committee), & the Bell, Broad Street (Mr Spencer's quarters & committee room) & the Crown in Pump Street, kept by one Lester, a Catholic, who being asked by the [Lygon] party for his beds, refused their petition.

But to counter this 'the loyal inhabitants of Worcester have provided 200 beds in private houses for the reforming voters.' Sewell alleged that nearly all the attorneys in Worcester had been retained with a fee of £10 and £5 per day, and similarly in other towns. Presumably this was to try and challenge the qualification of Whig voters; Sewell alleges that 'they do all they can to prolong the Election by asking Foley's & Spencer's voters many useless questions; they thus detained one company of 12 voters, three hours'.

Sewell reported that Whig landowners had been very active in rallying voters; Robert Berkeley from Spetchley had brought 100 voters, Thomas Charles Hornyold, the Catholic owner of Blackmore Park, had brought 100 from Upton upon Severn and district on a barge, and on another occasion brought voters in a covered cart, 'he riding the fore-horse, waving his hat & huzzaing, as he passed the Star & Garter'.

This campaigning was a prelude to the nominations and polling that began in the Castle Yard in Worcester on 6th May. The sheriff took charge on such occasions, and the procedure was for each candidate to be proposed and seconded, and for the candidates themselves to give a speech. On occasions when there were only two candidates the sheriff then declared the candidates duly elected, and the proceedings were probably quite low key, but in 1831 with three candidates this was not the case and a large crowd had gathered. At the end of proceedings the sheriff would ask for a show of hands, and declare which two candidates he thought had won, then the third candidate would disagree and ask for a poll. A good idea of the excitement of the occasion can be had from the report in the Berrows, which began:

> At an early hour this morning, the City exhibited a scene of activity, preparatory to the nomination for the representation of the County. Between 9 and 10 o'clock the Hon Col Henry Beauchamp Lygon, the Hon. T. H. Foley, and the Hon. Capt. Spencer, RN, passed through this city, accompanied by numerous cavalcades of their respective friends on horseback and in carriages; Col Lygon and Capt. Spencer were preceded by flags and bands of music. As they passed along the streets, the feelings of popular favour or dislike were pretty loudly expressed. Though hisses and groans occasionally saluted the ears of Col Lygon and his friends, the populace exhibited generally good humour. The friends of Col Lygon assembled at Madresfield, where they partook of an elegant breakfast; Mr Foley's friends met at the New Inn, two miles from Worcester, and Capt. Spencer's at The Talbot, in the Tything.

Henry Lygon was the first to be proposed, and Pakington stood forward to do so, but as soon as he started his nomination speech the crowd attempted to shout him down. When at last he managed to make himself heard, he appealed first to the Lygon family's ancient local lineage, and having supplied three MPs:

> I cannot recommend Col Lygon to your notice without referring to the very long period of time during which you have thought it right to place your confidence in him and his family – a period of time, I believe, extending over upwards of forty years; and while I distinctly disclaim as unconstitutional and untenable any attempt to found upon this fact anything like hereditary claim, I appeal to your feelings as honest Englishmen, whether the long standing services and friendships ought to be lightly regarded, and capriciously broken.

Pakington then went on to praise Lygon's record in parliament, having supported the agricultural, commercial and manufacturing interests of the county (although a search through Hansard does not reveal a single speech by Lygon, who was doubtless usually away on military duties), and, probably getting rather short of material, Pakington then referred to action taken by Lygon's brother when he was an MP in support of the Kidderminster carpet industry.

He then turned to the issue of the moment, reform. It was clear to everyone that some sort of reform would happen, and in front of an excitable crowd Pakington could hardly claim that Lygon was opposed to it:

> With regard to Col Lygon, the first point I wish to impress on your minds beyond everything, which I entreat you to carry into your homes, and which I entreat you to noise through the county, is that Col Lygon is not opposed to reform. (Loud laughter.) Gentlemen, I should not have taken so active a part as I have done on his behalf, if he had not most distinctly avowed to the county that he was not averse to moderate concession. (Much hissing.)... I can only say that I should not have supported Col Lygon, and that numerous class throughout the county which is now rallying round his standard would not have given him their support, if he had not sided with the majority of the members of the House of Commons, and if he had not sided with a considerable majority of the respectable classes throughout the country, opposing that rash, most dangerous and most unstatesman-like measure. (Hisses.)

The other charge against Lygon, continued Pakington, was that he was not an independent man, in other words he was what we would call today 'lobby fodder', or possibly even worse, amenable to pecuniary influence. But how could this be, said his proposer, when only two years ago a measure proposed by "the leader of his profession" [the Duke of Wellington and Catholic emancipation] had been opposed by Col Lygon, even though he, Pakington, was in favour of it. "I felt that he was proof against every influence that could be brought to bear against him and I entreat you now not to reject him."

Then Pakington returned to his original theme: "But, Gentlemen, if ancient ties are to be severed – if long and faithful services are to be forgotten – if the stream of popular clamour is to overwhelm every better feeling in its headlong course – then alas! we may fear for the consequences." By 'consequences' Pakington meant the return of Capt. Spencer, and he then turned his oratorical fire power on him.

Spencer, was, Pakington said

> ...the younger son of a Northamptonshire nobleman ("Aye! And a good one too" from the crowd), a country gentlemen whose estates consist of a certain number of planks, called a quarter deck, whose independence rests on the closest possible connection with the treasury bench, and whose interest in the welfare of the county of Worcester turns only on his professions that he will closely adhere to all the wild and visionary schemes of his brother. (Much uproar.) Gentlemen, I shall say nothing against the gallant captain himself – I honour his profession – I love a sailor – and I know many men who have sailed under his flag, and I know that they approve of him in his profession; but he is unfit for a county representative; still more, Gentlemen, is he unfit to represent the county of Worcester, where he is a stranger.

Here Pakington was on firmer ground, as no doubt Spencer had been brought in to fight a seat where it was thought the Whigs stood a chance, and where no local suitable candidate could be found. In fact Spencer's connection with Worcestershire was not to last very long at all. Pakington continued by referring to his two brothers. The elder, Viscount Althorpe, was a well-known radical, and of the younger Pakington said

> there are circumstances of peculiar and painful delicacy which electioneering zeal has brought before the public, or I assure the gallant captain that I would not have wounded his feelings, unjustifiable intruder that I consider him here, by referring to them. I assure you, I assure the gallant candidate, that I make this allusion in no wanton spirit.

What Pakington was referring to was the fact that George Spencer, Capt. Frederick's youngest brother, had recently converted from being an Anglican priest to Roman Catholicism. Pakington himself, although a devoted follower of the Anglican church, always had a desire for tolerating other faiths, and, as we have seen, was in favour of Catholic emancipation in 1829. So his statement on the hustings may have been intended as something of an apology, as it had been reported that placards reading 'NO POPERY' had been seen in the county. But Pakington then rather spoilt this by explaining that he had mentioned it because "Capt. Spencer is unknown to you, and if you find any circumstances connected with his family which are, in your opinion, not favourable to him, it behoves you to beware how you place your confidence in him"! He concluded his proposal by saying he was sure that the electors of the county would be saved from "the discredit of returning a stranger to parliament". The notion that voters owed their loyalty to existing MPs rather than newcomers remained a strong one with Pakington for the whole of his career, and was to recur later more than once, as we shall see.

Capt. Lygon was seconded by John Phillips, formerly of Hanbury Hall, who had been third husband of heiress Emma Vernon before her death in 1818. It is interesting that Thomas Foley, the Whig candidate, was proposed by Thomas Tayler Vernon. He was the heir to the Vernon estates after the death of Phillips, but had been kept from occupying Hanbury Hall till Phillips, having started a young family, eventually moved away from Hanbury in 1829. It seems that Phillips and Vernon were opponents in more ways than one. Col. Lygon himself then gave a short speech, saying he regretted that his vote against the Reform Bill had lost him "the good wishes and support of some of my constituents, but it is satisfactory to me to find that it is this part of my parliamentary conduct alone which has given them displeasure", but he pointed out that on this measure "so many of our wisest statesmen differ". Sensing defeat, he concluded by saying that "in or out of parliament, I beg leave to assure you, that the county of Worcester will always possess my most anxious good wishes".

Thomas Foley was next to be nominated, and gave a short speech about his support for the Reform Bill – "it has been said that the measure is revolutionary; I utterly deny the fact. I think it is most highly constitutional, and that the people of England ought to be fairly represented, and not through the influence of borough-mongers". Finally it was the turn of Capt. Spencer. Firstly he denied that he was a 'treasury candidate', then alluded to placards which he had seen calling him a Catholic, which he did not conceive had been authorised by the committee. At this point Pakington interjected, assuring him that they were not. But Spencer said that Pakington had nevertheless alluded to the subject, and he wished to inform the voters that "I was bred and born a member of the Protestant church of England. I have never deviated from her doctrines, and now, before the county of Worcester, I do declare that I am a Protestant". Before nominations were complete, someone challenged the fact that Capt. Spencer may not have had the necessary property qualification to serve in parliament. But Spencer had been prepared for this, and showed the sheriff a recently executed rent charge in his favour of £600 p.a.

The Sheriff then declared that polling could commence, and the scene can be imagined from the description in Berrows:

> The polling booths are six in number, one for each hundred, with the exception of Halfshire Hundred, to which two are assigned, owing to its numerous population. They are placed in a semi-circle, there being a considerable space between each, a judicious arrangement, which prevents confusion, by dividing the crowd. On the opposite side of the field is a spacious booth for the sheriff, the candidates, and friends &c, and Mr Shutt the barrister (who is retained to adjudicate on disputed votes). To prevent tumult the sheriff has provided a body of constables.

It seems that Col Lygon had also brought some constables, and at the end of the first day's polling they had acted in an aggressive way towards the crowd. When this was criticised the crowd attacked the constables, trying to take away their staves, and considerable fighting took place. Berrows regretted to state 'that several persons were severely, though not dangerously, hurt'.

Through all this excitement enthusiasts for reform must have been disappointed to learn that at the end of the first day's polling Capt. Spencer was trailing badly behind the other candidates, but when he addressed the crowd he said he was expecting this, as his arrangements for bringing voters to the poll were not yet as organised as the other candidates'. But polling lasted a whole week, and Spencer and Foley gradually gained ground, despite Pakington making speeches at the end of each day's polling. At the close of the sixth day Lygon was so far behind that he accepted his committee's advice and retired. The result was Foley 2,034, Spencer 1,765 and Lygon 1,335. Col Lygon was therefore displaced by the two Whig candidates, but he was not long out of parliament. The following year, in the first election after the passing of the

Great Reform Act which had divided Worcestershire into an eastern and a western half, he was returned for the western division, and he remained its representative till he succeeded to the earldom in 1853.

The Whig election triumph in Worcestershire was typical of the national result – the Whigs were returned with a majority of over 100, about as good a result for them as could be achieved considering how many seats were not decided by a free public vote. So the new government set about bringing in a new Reform Bill, but as we shall see its passage was going to be no easy matter.

## Chapter 4
## More Elections – 1831 and 1832

After the general election of May 1831 John Pakington spent a few quiet days at home, launching a new boat on Westwood Great Pool, and on 16th May set off for Southampton where he met Denton, Liberty's hired skipper. They proceeded to Cowes, where Pakington gave orders about the season's yachting, and arranged to rent a cottage later in the summer. Back home he chaired a meeting of Lygon's supporters to discuss their recent defeat. His aunt had come to stay, to be joined a few days later by Mrs Buckeridge and a Miss Buckleston.

At this time, in response to growing national unrest, the Worcestershire Yeomanry Cavalry was reformed. It had originally been formed in 1794 as part of the urgent need to strengthen national defences against a possible French invasion, but as this never took place these units were never called to action, but were kept in place after Waterloo in case they were needed for civil policing duties. By 1827 the county police had been formed, and units that had not seen action for ten years were disbanded, partly in response to the need for national economy, and these included the Worcestershires. The men provided their own horses and were not paid unless on active duty, and the regiment was maintained using much private and voluntary effort. However, the government contributed arms and uniforms and gave members (providing sufficient attendance was proved) exemption from the duty on hair powder and the horse tax. Even so, the cost to the government must have been modest. Less than four years later, with the country, especially the manufacturing districts, in a turmoil, it was decided to reform the county cavalry regiments, and in Worcestershire the Earl of Plymouth agreed to take command, with Lord Lyttelton as Lieutenant Colonel. Pakington must have been quick in coming forward to form a local troop, as he went to see Lord Plymouth on 4th March, and the Droitwich/Westwood troop was one of the initial nine units to be formed. It had Pakington as Captain, Arthur Skey as Lieutenant and John Whitmore Isaac as Cornet (a cornet was the most junior officer rank, who carried the colours). Soon a tenth troop was formed, meaning that the county regiment included about 800 men.

The weapons arrived for the Westwood troop in June, and this was followed by a drill the following day. Although the regiment saw action quelling local disturbances on only a few occasions, local units had to drill regularly, and once a year in September all county units assembled at Worcester for drilling and inspection.

On Monday 13th June Pakington, his wife and four year old Johnny travelled to London in their own phaeton, leaving home at 7.00, and arriving, as he records, at 10.00 p.m. They were staying in an hotel, and Pakington spent much time making calls. On Sunday they took Johnny to the zoological gardens in Regents Park, but whether their main motive was to show Johnny the animals, or to see the royal party who also visited that day (including the Duke of Cambridge with his consort the Princess and Landgravine Augusta of Hesse-Cassell) we can only guess. Royalty was again glimpsed on 22nd June when they 'went to Painted Chamber in the House of Lords to see the King pass to the House – took Johnny'. It was the state opening of parliament, and King William opened his address by referring to reform:

> Having had recourse to that measure for the purpose of ascertaining the sense of my people on the expediency of a Reform in the Representation, I have now to recommend that important question to your earliest and most attentive consideration confident that in any measures which you may prepare for its adjustment, you will carefully adhere to the acknowledged principles of the Constitution, by which the prerogatives of the Crown, the authority of both Houses of Parliament, and the rights and liberties of the people are equally secured.

Sentiments with which few, even Pakington, could disagree.

As well as making calls and dining with his friends, Pakington went to an opera, Rossini's 'Semiramide', and to recitals by Paganini, then at the height of his fame; by Luigi Lablache; and by Pryzi at Lady Shelley's. Whether Mary accompanied him is not stated, but she became ill during their stay, so may not have done. On 16th June

*The Painted Chamber in the old Palace of Westminster in 1799 by William Capon. Created by Henry III, the murals had to be reworked several times. It was destroyed by the fire of 1834. © Palace of Westminster Collection.*

'went to dinner at Blackwall with a large whitebait party – drove down in phaeton'. Whitebait dinners at Gravesend had become a traditional event for the cabinet in June, but this was probably a similar event organised for lesser persons.

Pakington had arranged for Liberty to meet them on the Thames in London, so on 24th June they sailed down to Gravesend with Barneby and other friends. They slept on board, returning the next day, when Pakington dined with Oldnall Russell, noting that Mary was too unwell to go, as she still was the next day when Pakington dined at Lady Beauchamp's. A boating party to Richmond followed, and on 29th June, after watching the Foot Guards on parade, he attended a levée. This was a custom that originated as a formal rising ceremony at the court of Louis XIV in France, but in England it had become a general reception held around midday, attended by a large gathering of people of note, some of whom would be presented to the monarch. It also seems that it was an occasion when addresses were presented to the monarch – on this occasion numerous addresses thanking the King for his late dissolution of parliament and in favour of reform were presented. Those attending were listed in The Times, and comprised over one hundred arranged by rank, headed by three dukes. Capt. Pakington (from his rank in the Worcestershire Yeomanry Cavalry) was one of those 'who had the honour of being presented to his majesty'; he was presented 'on changing his name' by Earl Beauchamp. Another person presented 'by Lt Col Viscount Eastnor' was Capt. Barneby of the Herefordshire militia.

On 1st and 2nd July further trips in Liberty were made down river, and on Sunday Pakington attended service for what may have been the first time in the Chapel Royal. Then the following week the family proceeded in their phaeton to Southampton, then on to Cowes, for their summer sailing holiday. Pakington wanted to see the fleet at Spithead, but as Liberty had not arrived from the Thames he had to hire a cutter. He called on the first of his Worcestershire friends, the Bensons, who were at Ryde. The Liberty arrived that night, and they sailed on her the next day to see the fleet weigh anchor and depart, which was a 'beautiful sight'; however the Bensons became sea sick and had to be put ashore. Their servant Tom had been left at Southampton with the phaeton, and Pakington sailed back there to give him his orders before returning to Cowes. The next day he was back in Southampton to pick up more friends, the Slaneys and Barnebys, and over the weekend they visited Carisbrooke Castle and walked to Norris Castle, James Wyatt's rather fantastical construction looking over the Solent, sometimes used by Queen Victoria before she bought Osborne House.

As in the previous year Pakington now undertook a voyage to Cherbourg – as he wrote that 'Barneby sailed with us', it seems that Mary and Johnny came too. They sailed all night, and after spending the day shopping and sightseeing in Cherbourg, slept on shore, before leaving the next day for Guernsey. But they became becalmed and spent most of the night lying to, before getting there the next morning. After a short stay they sailed for Torquay, but were again becalmed before arriving the next day, when the regatta had already started. Pakington had planned to compete but the stewards would not let him.

Another long trip started on 18th July when they sailed back for Cowes, and 'had a beautiful run there in 10 hours & three quarters'. The next few days were spent making calls in Southampton, Portsmouth and Ryde, where Pakington had an exciting sail 'three reefs and water over the deck'. On 26th July a small squadron of yachts from Cowes, including Liberty, Blue Eyed Maid, Lady of the Lake and Wild Irish Girl, cruised together to the westward, anchoring at Swanage the first night but Pakington sailed on further to Weymouth, where the others caught up the next day. From Weymouth Pakington acted as Commodore, and the next day led the yachts to Sidmouth. He had planned to lead the squadron close to the coast on its passage, but the wind became too light for that, and they did not arrive in Dartmouth till the next morning. From there the whole party went up river and dined at Totnes – presumably they did not use their yachts for this, as the tide and narrow passage would make it very difficult. The squadron was bound for Plymouth, where they arrived next day, but Pakington and his family left the squadron after a day and sailed on to Mounts Bay and Penzance, where they met some friends called Armstrong. After sightseeing for a day they sailed with the Armstrongs to St Michael's Mount, after which they landed their friends and started their two day voyage back to Cowes.

The first three weeks of August were spent in and around the Solent, with a visit to Southampton to see Fanny Kemble again. The climax of the Cowes regatta came on 22nd August. There was a fine race for the Kings Cup, and the fleet arrived at Spithead '& saluted Princess Victoria – splendid sight'.

At the end of August a further trip to Cherbourg was made, this time to compete in the local regatta. There must have been quite a large English contingent there, as Pakington went to two balls including Lord Yarborough's, and a concert. After the ball they set sail at one in the morning and arrived at Cowes nine and a half hours later. Not apparently needing any rest the party went back on board for an early start the next day to Weymouth, where Liberty sailed for another cup. 'Beat my own class', Pakington noted, '& sailed

*Norris Castle on the Isle of Wight. It was built for show, and has, in fact, only four bedrooms being only one room plus a corridor deep.*

very well, but enough time was not given & Gem won – ball in evening'. It sounds as if Liberty was overly handicapped, and again the next day the she was beaten in another race. Liberty raced again four days later against Druid, but disaster struck when her mast was carried away, and she suffered the indignity of being towed home.

Thus ended Pakington's summer sailing holiday at Cowes, as two days after loosing his mast he sailed in Druid, a friend's yacht, to Southampton, then reached Powick the next day, Saturday, presumably with Mary and Johnny. The yeomanry week was coming up, and on Monday Pakington attended a drill at Hewell Grange, then another with Edward Bearcroft's Hanbury troop at Broughton Common. After shooting with Hanbury Williams on Tuesday Pakington attended Hewell again on Wednesday 'to present colours to yeomanry who were received by Col Kean & a grand dinner given to the whole regiment afterwards'. According to Berrows, thousands lined the routes leading to Hewell Grange to see the cavalry, and 'the Noble owner, with his accustomed liberality, gave directions for the Park to be thrown open, and every person and vehicle freely admitted'. The scene is described graphically:

> The scene was now animated and interesting in the highest degree; the ground occupied by the regiment forms an extensive valley, the eminences on each side of which are thickly studied with flourishing trees; at the lower end stands the Hall, remarkable for the simple grandeur of its appearance; adjacent to this, and forming a prominent part of the scene, is a beautiful and expansive sheet of water, on the

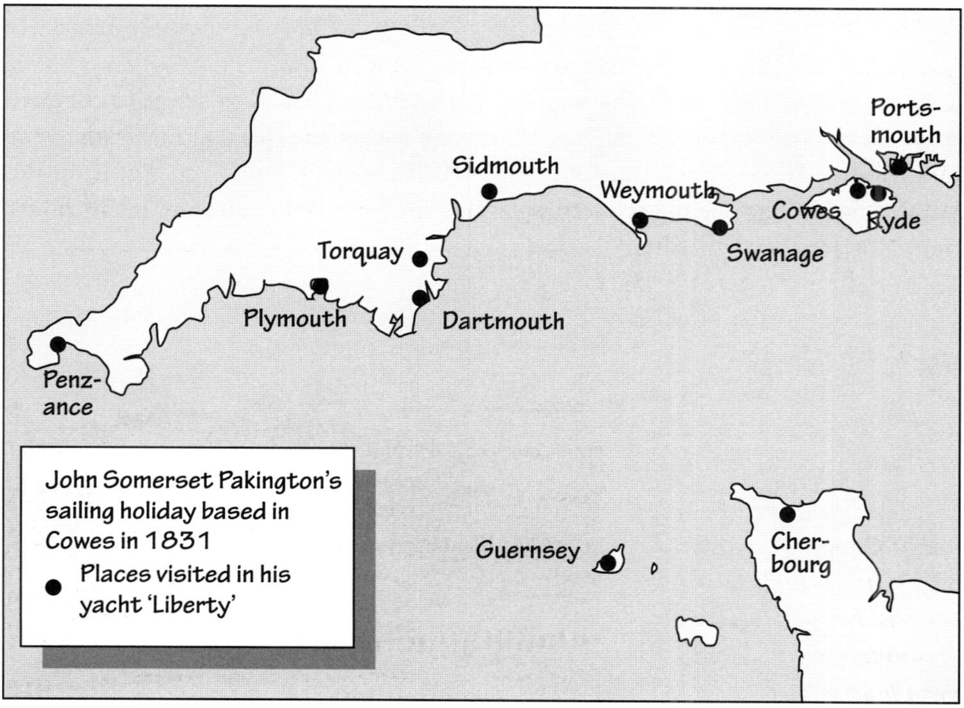

> banks of which are the pleasure grounds, laid out with great taste and elegance, and decorated with an embroidery of the gayest flowers. On the other side of the water the ground gradually rises, till the view is terminated by the woods, here and there slightly tinged with 'the sere and yellow leaf,' giving at once beauty and variety to the landscape. The hills were crowded with spectators; all the surrounding country seemed to have poured forth its population to witness this spectacle.

The Countess of Plymouth presented the colours to the cornets; she made a short speech, saying she had no doubt that when they were called upon they would be always ready to do their duty for the King and country, as Englishmen had always done. A salute was fired, then the regiment, 620 strong, performed various 'evolutions', which the inspecting officer, Col Kean of the 7th Hussars, praised, particularly since the regiment was only four months old. Then the grand dinner took place in a temporary building, in which immense trouble had been taken with the decorations, with flags forming canopies over the tables, and at the upper end a crown, formed of leaves of oak and laurel, supported on each side by a flag. Dinner was at four, and consisted of 'every delicacy of the season; on stands were placed two noble barons of beef'. Afterwards there were the inevitable toasts, with the band playing the national anthem and 'Rule Britannia'. Lord Lyttelton spoke admiringly of the efforts of the Earl of Plymouth in raising the regiment, and continued "in raising this corps for the protection of the crown and the property of the people, the Noble Earl has selected men of character and substance, and I will co-operate most cordially with him for the common benefit of the county". One can imagine that at that Capt. Pakington

*Hewell Grange, from an engraving in Nash. It was replaced by the present building, built on another higher site, at the end of the nineteenth century.*

gave a loud "hear, hear", and joined in the great applause with which the speech was greeted, lasting several minutes. After several more toasts, 'the evening was spent with great conviviality and harmony, and the company separated highly delighted and gratified with the condescension and unexampled liberality of the Noble Earl'.

Miss Hawkins and Pakington's aunt were staying at Westwood at this time, and Pakington met them there. He and Mary also found time to attend the Bewdley Ball on Thursday. On Saturday the yeomanry cavalry marched into Worcester, and the next day they attended the cathedral service. The whole of the next week was devoted to yeomanry matters, culminating in a grand review on Pitchcroft (the large open space, today the site of Worcester racecourse) by General Marriot on Friday 23rd September – 'large party at the mess and at dinner, I was deputed by the officers to address Ld Plymouth & propose his health'.

Pakington's notes for his rather fawning speech have survived, and he began:

> Lord Plymouth, I rise to request your permission to propose our toast, and in so doing, to address myself to your Lordship in the discharge of a duty which I have undertaken with a warmth of pleasure, allayed only by my regret that it has not devolved upon someone of those around me, who are able to do far greater justice to it than I can hope to attain. I am deputed, my Lord, by my brother officers to state that the patriotic energy, the high spirit, the unbounded liberality, with which you have raised, & hitherto commanded us, have excited in our breasts feelings towards your Lordship which I do assure you, are of no ordinary character – feelings, which I own an inability to embody in appropriate language – but the nature of which I may possibly best convey to your Lordship's mind, by the assurance to co-operate with you in your endeavours to preserve the tranquillity of the country, and that we will at all times afford you all the assistance and support, which, as officers, may be in our power – at a time when a spirit of insubordination and disorder was unhappily widely spread abroad through the country, and where consequently, some additional protection became necessary for the security of property your Lordship nobly came forward and by raising this corps of yeomanry, a corps whose services I hope to God will not be required, but which, I believe I am justified in saying is, owing to your Lordship's exertions, already fit to cope with any domestic disturbances which may, unfortunately, afflict the country...

Pakington assured everyone that his political views would remain quite separate:

> My Lord, recent circumstances have made my political opinions in some degree known – I am therefore more desirous to state, that in what I am now saying, there does not mingle one shade of political feeling... and I think that much as there is in your Lordship's conduct which calls for our admiration, there is perhaps no point more remarkable, than the good feeling and good judgement with which you selected the body of officers now around me, from any political class in the county, and it is to me most gratifying, to see men so widely asunder in their opinions upon these points, here assembled together, and united in one bond of friendly union, to promote the common good in our native county.

Pakington wrote that his speech was 'much applauded'.

The Hanbury Williams's remained at High Park till 11th October, and they were soon replaced by the Slaneys, Isaacs and Barneby (John Barneby was not yet married). The Lygons joined them, and life continued with shooting, a visit to the Worcester races, and Droitwich petty sessions. Meanwhile important events were taking place in Westminster. After the election of the Whig government in May a new Reform Bill was passed through the Commons, but met strong resistance in the Lords, where, on 7th October after a debate lasting five days, it was defeated by 41 votes – 21 of the 22 Bishops present opposed it. This led to further unrest in the country – the opposition of the church to reform was particularly resented.

In Worcester rumours had gone around that Guy Fawkes night would become the focus for trouble. Accordingly the mayor and magistrates of Worcester had appealed for volunteer special constables to be sworn, and by Friday evening 400 had been recruited. The home secretary had arranged for a troop of the 7th Hussars, commanded by Capt. Bathurst, to be marched from Kidderminster to Droitwich, and for 100 men of the 91st Foot, under Capt. Lavers, to be marched from Woodstock to Pershore. The special constables had been divided into four divisions and stationed in the city, but during the morning Worcester had been very quiet. In the Nisi Prius court a public meeting under the high sheriff, Osman Ricardo, was held in the morning, with the purpose of passing several resolutions in favour of reform. The speakers included Sir Edward Blount, Capt. Winnington, Col Davies of Elmley Castle and Lord Lyttelton of Hagley Hall, all well-known Whigs, and all reformers. A typical rallying cry was "shall it be said that a band of selfish churchmen and borough mongers could trample on the liberties of England and stop the course of reform? No, the cause must go forward, born on by the wishes of the King, his government and the united voice of a whole people". All the resolutions were passed, including one to send a letter to the King, who was believed to be personally a reformer. In his diary Pakington describes this rather dismissively as a 'radical meeting'; but the word radical usually meant something more extreme, and it is doubtful if the distinguished speakers there, including a man whose widow Pakington would later marry, would think of themselves as radicals.

As Berrows does not mention the pro-reform meeting, the timetable of events that day is not certain, but just before 11.00 a.m. a fire alarm was sounded in the High Street, the engines soon arrived, and the fire was extinguished. But, possibly encouraged by the reform meeting, a crowd had assembled, and trouble soon developed. Windows were broken, and although the mayor held back the party of special constables stationed at the Guildhall hoping the trouble would subside, it only got worse, so the constables attacked the rioters and made some arrests. But the situation was still not under control, so orders were sent express to Droitwich and Pershore to summon the military. Meanwhile the mayor was actively trying to quieten the rioters. The leaders offered to cease trouble-making if two of the men taken prisoner were released, and the mayor agreed. But the mob then gathered outside Worcester gaol and demanded that all the prisoners be let go, which the mayor refused. Then he stood on the steps of the Guildhall and read the Riot Act. A stone hit the mayor, who ordered the Hussars, when they arrived at 1.15 a.m., to clear the streets. They did this by forming a line across the High Street and driving the mob forward. Berrows reported: 'They acted with the greatest temper and forbearance, though much insulted; one or two of the most obstinate of the rioters received sabre cuts, though not very severe ones. ... Two fellows having been very effusive and not moving off, Capt. Bathurst seized one with his right hand and the other with his left, and dragged them on each side of his horse to the Guildhall!'

The 91st Foot arrived about 3.00 a.m., having marched the 9 miles from Pershore in 2 hours, followed at a distance, according to Berrows, by a crowd of vagabonds 'who grossly insulted them'. But by dawn the worst of the trouble had subsided, and the constables and the militia were stationed at key places around the city. Berrows also reported that the Earl of Plymouth came to the city as soon as he heard of the trouble and offered the services of the Yeomanry Cavalry, but by then they were not needed; it also records that Capt. Pakington had consultations with the mayor. Berrows, seeing things from a Tory point of view, was inclined to believe that many of the rioters had come from outside the city and were ne'er-do-wells just intent on making mischief. Some pick-pockets were said to have come from Bristol (where there had been a great deal of trouble) and Birmingham.

Although there were further disturbances over the next few nights, the precautions prevented anything so serious developing. Pakington's diary as usual is very brief: 'radical meeting at Worcester; riot at night'; and the next day, Sunday, 'heard of riots & rode into Worcester to see mayor'. On Monday he records another riot, and on Wednesday he sent Mary to Elmley Castle alone as 'I did not like to leave home'. But the following day 'all remaining quiet I went to Elmley', but he called first at Hartlebury to see the new Bishop, Robert James Carr, before enjoying shooting at the Davies's. How the two men, one very conservative, the other in Pakington's mind a radical, got on is not known!

But although there was no further trouble at Worcester, on Thursday 1st December there was trouble at Stourbridge, and in the evening Pakington received a summons to go there with his troop of yeomanry cavalry. They marched there the next day, and found many other troops assembled, and he was given charge of four of them. Pakington remained at Stourbridge over the weekend. On Saturday night the town 'was in military confusion', and on Monday they escorted a prisoner to Himley. The trouble continued on Tuesday and his troops were out all day – 'troop pelted', Pakington noted. But he received a bad account of Mary, who had been ill, so returned home.

He kept a separate account of his wife's illness, rather in the manner in which he recorded his trip to Scotland, and it appears to have been written in one go, presumably using his diary to jog his memory. The account started on 30th October, which would be when her illness really took hold, and it does seem to have come on quite suddenly, as she had taken full part in the summer's riding and sailing.

Pakington's account is entitled 'Journal of the illness of my dear wife', and started by recording that on Sunday 30th October in the evening she coughed several times, and expressed a fear that a cold was coming on, implying that these symptoms were new. During the next few days the cough increased and she began to feel unwell, and she could not accompany Pakington when he went to dine with Rev. William Vernon, rector of Hanbury, or a few days later with the Skeys at Spring Grove, Bewdley.

In the following week (after the Worcester riots) there was a definite improvement, to the extent she rather reluctantly went on her own to Elmley Castle for a stay, leaving Pakington at home in case of trouble, but he joined her later. The slight improvement continued, and she was able to go with her husband to dinner in Hanbury again, but on 16th she decided not to go to Brockhampton, where Pakington joined a shooting party for four days. They had accepted an invitation to Spring Grove on 22nd, but decided against going. A little later Pakington recorded that, 'in addition to the cough, there was now every night, a considerable degree of low fever, with proportionate increase of weakness during the day…' and at the same time he wrote how, for the first time for a few days, she came down to join him at breakfast, but that this fatigued her so much that she 'did not attempt it again'. Pakington tried to persuade her to see Dr Malden, 'but she felt so assured of being better the next week, that she was very unwilling to do so, & I, little dreaming of the true nature of the case, therefore forbore to press it.' A few days later he noted that she was starting to complain about pain and 'uneasiness in the bones, from lying on them so long on the sofa…'. As he wrote that this is a proof of her loss of flesh as well as strength, we may presume she had started to loose weight. Her appetite had diminished, and she started to retire earlier at night.

On 29th November Mary received a 'bad account of her aunt Mrs Buckeridge', which further depressed her, and she decided that she would, after all, like to see Dr Malden – she felt no better, and had started to suffer from shortness of breath. So on 1st December Dr Malden visited, and pronounced her 'very ill'. He found her left lung affected, and said, most inappropriately to our ears, that 'the ultimate complexion of the case must depend on the effect of the bleeding he had directed for the next morning, & other remedies'. If these were not effective in alleviating her symptoms, 'consumption must ensue'. That evening, Pakington noted that 'she dined and passed the evening with me for the last time, & though weak & ill, without any change in her usual pleasant & cheerful manner…'. But the end of the evening was spoilt by his call to Stourbridge, described earlier. So the following morning she was relieved of 6 ozs of 'highly inflamed blood', which weakened her further, but when Pakington marched to Stourbridge at half past twelve he was 'sanguine that she would soon be pretty well'. From that morning she took to her bed.

Dr Malden was clearly an optimist, as he sent 'repeated good & cheering accounts' to Pakington in Stourbridge, 'which made me hope that all bad symptoms were fast subsiding'. But on Tuesday evening, while still away, his groom brought a letter from Mary and reports from the servants that she was very far from recovering, so he decided to return home at once. 'I arrived at 8.00 p.m. & on going upstairs, I found the poor invalid greatly & sadly changed during my absence', which had only been for four days. She was becoming extremely short of breath, 'the slight exertion of moving to leave her bed had brought on such oppression of breathing as to produce distressing gasping, which continued at intervals during the night'. Her maid was alarmed and Dr Malden called, who pronounced her much worse. The pain in her left side had returned, and Pakington found her so changed in appearance on his return, 'her countenance having all the aspect of the last stage of illness, as to cause me great alarm – she continued however placid & cheerful to an extraordinary degree for one so ill'. Dr Malden, with no more idea of the correct treatment than his contemporaries, 'decided on applying a very strong blister with a view of relieving the lungs by counter imitation'. This made Mary nervous, but she was frightened of a return of the gasping she had suffered from during the night, 'which she told me this evening put her strongly in mind of a similar attack she witnessed in poor Mrs Domvile's last illness… but I had no reason to think that she entertained serious apprehensions about herself…'.

The blister began to rise and break before she went to bed, which made her uncomfortable and led to a sleepless night 'but did not interrupt her sweet calmness of temper…'. Dr Malden came again the next day, and, ever optimistic, 'pronounced her decidedly better, & gave me great hopes, that with care, she might ultimately recover – all acute inflammatory symptoms he considered at an end, without danger of their return, unless from accidental causes, & the only serious danger he now foresaw was the possibility that with returning strength there might not be stamina enough to shake off the consequences of the disease, & chronic symptoms might remain – but upon this point he seemed sanguine – this evening her pulse was down to 80 – and from the appearance of drowsiness the digitalis which had been hitherto needed was to be discontinued, & to give strength the quinine bark to be resorted to'.

On Monday 12th December Pakington wrote 'The improvement in all respects continued, & Dr. Malden said he entertained more hope than he had yet done of perfect recovery, but still there was no return of either appetite or strength, though the breathing was restored to a healthy state, & the cough nearly gone – there was also still entire confinement to bed, & no disposition to leave it.' The improvement lasted all the week, and on Friday she was able to sit on the sofa for tea – 'the exertion was attended with a little cough, but not much fatigue – there was some return of appetite today'.

That marks the end of the account, so we must presume that Mary's improvement was steady after that, and perhaps we should not censure Dr Malden too much as his patient did eventually recover, even though one might say the recovery was despite his best efforts! Bearing in mind that her illness did not last too long, and that the shortness of breath was its main serious symptom, a diagnosis of pleurisy, rather than other lung diseases such as tuberculosis or asthma, seems the most likely.

Pakington passed the rest of December quietly with a little shooting, and he noted he wrote to skipper Denton with an offer of £60 to act for him in 1832. But then, having finished the account of his wife's harrowing illness, he had an accident himself – on the penultimate day of 1831 he wrote 'in riding to Worcester mare fell & badly bruised my leg – brought home in Pierpoint's gig'. The next day he was confined to his bed, and as the first page of his 1832 diary is blank we have to presume that he was unable to go far for some time. He was no better in the second week of the new year as he noted 'confined by effects of fall & low fever'. Only on 14th January was he able to go to Worcester in the carriage with Johnny, and the next day, for the first time since his accident, took a ride on a pony. But his full recovery took some time, and on 19th was still too unwell to go to the dispensary ball.

In February he seems to have fully recovered, and among many engagements he sang at a concert arranged by the Isaacs at Boughton, but the event was rather spoiled when many guests went down with 'bilious attacks' the following day. Just after the defeat of Col Lygon the previous May Pakington had chaired a meeting of Tory supporters, at which thanks had been given to Lygon for his past parliamentary efforts on behalf of the party, and a resolution had been passed to raise a subscription to purchase a piece of plate to present to him. Soon more than 300 men had subscribed the required one guinea, and on 16th February 1832 a grand dinner was held in the Hop Pole Inn in Worcester to present a large silver vase to Col Lygon. Pakington took the chair, and addressing the 228 people present, he opened his speech by saying:

> We offer the silver vase to you, sir, as is inscribed upon the vase itself, in testimony of the high sense we entertain of your long and faithful parliamentary service. (Hear, hear.) For a period of no less than 15 years you have attended in the House of Commons to the varied and complicated interests of this busy county, in a manner alike honourable to you, and satisfactory to your constituents... And now, sir, that advantage has been so eagerly taken of a passing delirium in the public mind to eject you from the seat you filled so well, we cannot reconcile it to our feelings to allow you to retire into private life without possessing some token of our approbation and support. (Cheers.)

Referring to the last election, Pakington continued:

> You stood forward when every grade of political speculator, and every class of religious dissenter, were linked in one unnatural confederacy (cheers) to attack and destroy existing institutions. You, by your spirited conduct, enabled fourteen hundred freeholders of this county to record by their votes their opposition to the rash and dangerous, yet crude and ill-digested schemes of a desperate, incapable, and, I greatly fear, an unprincipled administration. (Cheers.)

Pakington explained that the intention had been to present the vase last October, but due to the general unrest it was thought wise to leave it till now in case the dinner provoked trouble. The meeting seemed to be under the impression that Col Lygon would not stand again for parliament, but, as we have seen this proved incorrect and in fact he enjoyed another twenty years in the Commons before being called to the upper house as Earl Beauchamp.

A few days later Pakington was 33, and he marked the day by visiting Elias Isaac at the Old Bank and 'made arrangements' with him. One suspects this was to procure an overdraft. A few days earlier he had heard of the death of Mrs Buckeridge, Mary's aunt, so on 21st February they went to Lichfield and Rev. George Buckeridge, a cousin of his wife's, accompanied Pakington's party to the internment at Tong, an estate that had belonged to George Durant, a brother-in-law of Mary's great uncle, Rev. Theophilus Buckeridge. Today there are memorials to both Rev. Buckeridge and his wife in the church. Mrs Buckeridge had appointed Pakington an executor in her will, and left £4,000 in trust for Mary, with remainder to Mary's son.

*A view of Torquay from the pier dated 1832, courtesy of Devon Libraries.*

From Lichfield Pakington went directly to London, where he met Hallifax. He called on his aunt, Oldnall Russell, and his architect Hardwick, and after taking in two plays he returned to Powick after a week. Hunting continued, but there had been some problem with the mastership of John Parker, and on 11th March the hunt committee finally dissolved Parker's hunt. On 16th March Mr Hardwick came again to discuss work at Westwood, and Pakington spent a day and a half with him.

The family were due to leave for Torquay at the beginning of April, but first Pakington attended quarter sessions, and as well as the unresolved problem of the proposed new courts there was a discussion on the fees paid to attorneys for attendance and brief at quarter sessions. The attorneys had published a rather bad-tempered pamphlet saying the fees were too low, and threatening non-attendance if not increased. Pakington proposed that the rates be changed as he would not like to drive respectable attorneys from the sessions. Others disagreed – if the court gave way to a threatened strike by attorneys, how could they try artisans who illegally combined for the same reason!? In the end it was agreed to match the fees paid at the assizes. The following day, 3rd April, the family left for Torquay in the phaeton, and his concern for his wife's health is shown by the fact that they took the journey in easy stages stopping at Cheltenham, where he showed Johnny the Pump Rooms, Bath, Taunton, and Exeter, taking five days over a journey that Pakington could do in a single day on his own. They had sent their horses down separately, and they arrived in Torquay soon after, and, no doubt anxious about Mary's health, they took the first week quietly, Pakington noting that his wife rode Gideon for the first time since her illness, and on the second Sunday attended evening service for the first time.

It had been arranged for Liberty to arrive at the end of April, but probably due to continuing bad weather it was 5th May before she arrived. The same day Mary was feeling ill again, and a doctor was called. On Sunday 6th May Pakington notes that he attended church twice (and Mary in the afternoon). Mention of church becomes more common as the diary progresses, and it is only from this point that he usually attended twice on Sundays. Perhaps his religious feelings had been strengthened by his wife's recovery from what appeared at one point to have been a mortal illness. On Monday Dr Scully called, and 'seemed to consider the tendency to active disease of the lungs very great & that she was altogether in a weak state'. But the next day they both went for a short sail, although Pakington and his wife both felt unwell.

As May progressed the weather improved, and they did more sailing as well as the constant round of calling. Perhaps encouraged by the better weather, the Pakingtons arranged to take a party to picnic across the bay, but 'blew & rained hard – party drenched & sick'! The south Devon yeomanry were exercising at Teignmouth so Pakington rode over on Tuesday. He thought the band very good and returned to watch them every day that week. The following week he joined some yachts sailing to Salcombe, where he noted that Mary slept on board for the first time.

Pakington was obviously keeping closely in touch with the political situation, and had recorded the resignation of Lord Grey in early May 1832 when there were further difficulties over the Reform Bill. This led to Britain being without a government for a short period. The difficulty remained with the House of Lords. It was not until the threat of the creation of enough new peers to let it pass that the Lords gave way and passed the Reform Bill on 4th June. There had to be a delay before calling an election under the new franchise as boundaries had to be fixed and voters registered, and the election was fixed for December 1832.

It seems likely that Pakington had decided some time before to stand at the next election. There was even a suggestion that he would have stood in place of Lygon if he had decided not to stand in 1831. Despite the routing of the Tories in 1831 many thought that, once the Reform Bill became law, there would be a reaction and a revival of support for the Tories. So Pakington left Torquay on 22nd June to announce his candidacy, and after spending the first night at Exeter he stayed at Bristol, where he saw the damage the fires started by the rioters the previous November had caused.

The Reform Act had divided the county of Worcestershire into two constituencies, east and west, but had reduced the representation of Droitwich to a single member

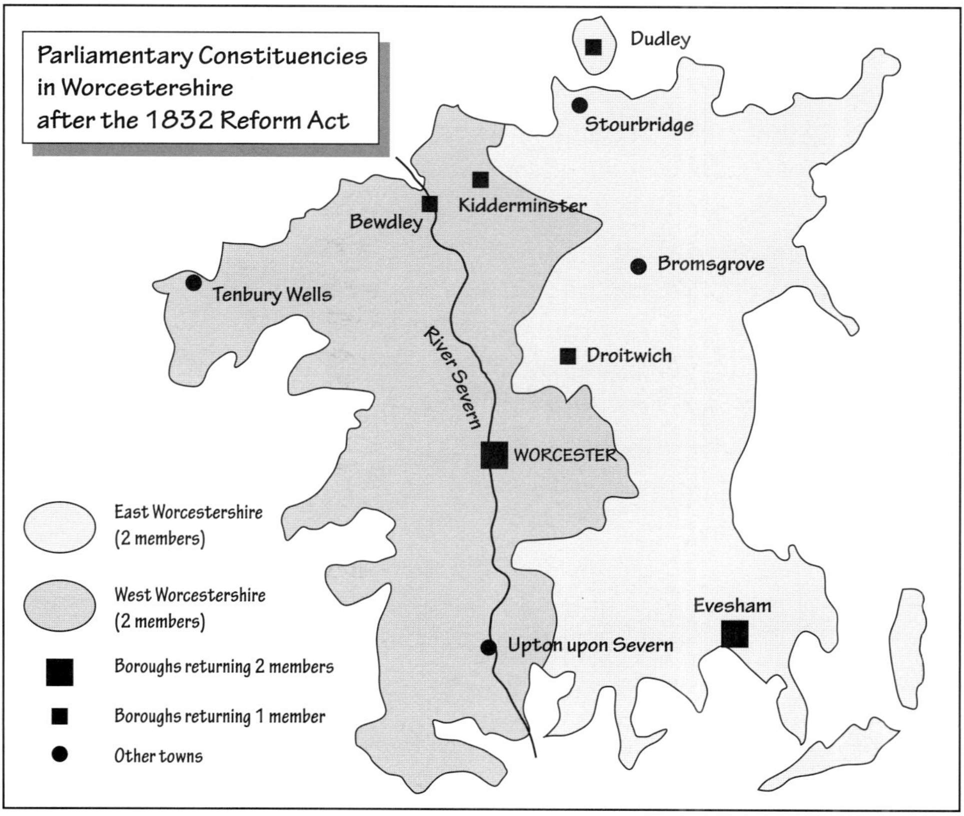

***To the Gentry, Clergy, and Electors, of the***
**EASTERN DIVISION**
***OF THE COUNTY OF WORCESTER***

GENTLEMEN,

IN compliance with the earnest wishes of my Friends, I shall no longer delay the announcement of my intention to become a Candidate for the high honour of representing you in the ensuing Parliament.

I offer myself to your notice as an independent Country Gentlemen, connected with this County by the closest ties both of affection and interest; and if you should place me in the situation to which I venture to aspire, I shall hope that by diligent attention to the discharge of the important duties which will devolve upon me, I may in some measure compensate for my want of ability and experience.

In my general politics I am not disposed to adopt any extreme of party feeling. I entertain fixed but moderate opinions, and I believe that the best interests of the Country would now be essentially promoted by the mitigation on both sides of that party violence which has of late prevailed to so injurious extent.

The leading point in my political creed is an ardent attachment to that Glorious Constitution under which Great Britain has, from the time of the Revolution, enjoyed prosperity and true liberty; —but excellent and unequalled as I consider that Constitution to be, I am not insensible to the fact that no human institution is perfect, and I shall always be ready to support such modifications in our system as may, in my humble judgement, tend to strengthen or improve it.

I shall consider it my duty to answer fairly and frankly whatever enquiries it may be the wish of the Electors to put to me during my canvas, with regard to my political opinions, while I shall deem it a duty not less imperative, should I be honoured with your choice, to enter the House of Commons free and unpledged upon every question.

I have the honour to subscribe myself,

Gentlemen,

Your faithful and most obedient Servant,

JOHN S. PAKINGTON

Westwood Park, June 26th, 1832

as well as enlarge the constituency boundaries. Living near Droitwich in the centre of the county Pakington had a choice of constituencies, and he had probably decided not to stand for his local borough of Droitwich as John Hodgets Hodgets-Foley had been one of its MPs since 1826, and was well established there as a relative of Lord Foley of Witley. West Worcestershire would have two candidates, Col Lygon for the Tories, and Thomas Foley for the Whigs, but it looked as if the eastern division would have two Whig candidates, William Congreve Russell and Thomas Henry Cookes. So it seemed that the eastern division was the best place to try, as there was a good chance of at least one Tory being elected there.

So, wasting no time, Pakington sent a letter to Berrows announcing his intentions, which is reproduced opposite.

One supposes that a contemporary reader would divine that Pakington was putting up as a Tory rather than as a Whig, but the message is clearly designed not to offend the current popular reforming mood, although it certainly could be asked exactly what the candidate was offering the electorate other than a wish to defend the constitution. He probably hoped that the Whigs would only put up one candidate for the constituency, allowing him a free passage, but he soon learned that, at a meeting on 29th June, the Whigs would put up both Russell and Cookes. Both men were new to politics, and Russell, at 54, was an older man. As he was from Birmingham he may have been regarded by some as something of an outsider, which Pakington certainly was not. Before returning to Torquay he wrote about 75 'canvassing letters' – it is not clear what these were as there were over 5,000 electors in the constituency, but perhaps they were for his committee's use as needed. His visit also coincided with quarter sessions, after which he went to Stourbridge and Dudley to meet his local committee, and before leaving Worcestershire on 6th July he recorded that he made 'final arrangements' with his agent Thomas Curtler. Having made all these plans, he must have fancied his chances of winning a seat in the election that was still five months away.

Back in Torquay Pakington was greeted by bad weather, which delayed their trip to Cowes. Once there he attended a RYC meeting and did some sailing before returning to Torquay five days later, when he had the Liberty's bulwarks painted Indian Red. The next day, Sunday 22nd July, Pakington went to church twice and heard 'an excellent sermon on cholera'. The disease was raging in many parts of the country at that time, but it would be interesting to know how it was made the subject for a sermon; perhaps it showed Divine anger for some misdeed of the British people.

A week later Pakington and his family sailed with other yachts to Guernsey and Jersey, but the trip must have been spoiled for Pakington as in Jersey he started to suffer from piles. The next day 'very unwell from piles – obliged to see a medical man – drove about the island & dined large party in evening – piles lanced at night', so even this problem did not stop him from socialising. Returning after a week, Pakington described it as a delightful cruise, but it was another week before he felt well again, causing him to cancel a proposed visit to Worcester to attend an election meeting. As the absence of a newly announced candidate might have seemed odd, he went to the length of sending a medical certificate with his letter to Curtler explaining his absence, which stated that he 'was not in a state of health to undertake a long journey, and that it was necessary for him to avoid for some time anything which was calculated to cause much excitement'. Pakington obviously anticipated that this might cause some people to question whether he would be fit for the actual contest later in the year, and in his letter he actually offered to stand down if the committee felt another candidate would be more suitable, but maintained that his 'sincere zeal in the cause' was undiminished. Berrows did report that it was rumoured that another Tory candidate might come forward, but in the event nothing came of this.

On Sunday he noted a long conversation with Mr Gladstone. As Pakington reserves the title 'Mr' for older people, this would probably be John, later Sir John Gladstone, father of the future prime minister, who was on his grand tour at this time. First a Whig then later a Tory (he was an MP from 1818 till 1827), Sir John Gladstone remained a protectionist and even defended slavery, but despite this he was created a baronet on the same day as Pakington by Peel in 1846. Evidently Gladstone was one of many well-off people spending the summer in Torquay, and in a letter to Pakington written later that winter he remarked that his daughter's health was much improved by cruising with Mary, which he hoped could be resumed next year.

On Monday the Teignmouth regatta was held, but Pakington appears to have been a spectator only, and to celebrate his 10th wedding anniversary the following day he sailed with Mary and Johnny towards Start Point, dined on board, and returned late. A few days later the Pakingtons sailed for Cowes, although his first day there was spoiled by his being 'feverish & unwell'. He recovered to watch the Kings Cup, and returned to Torquay after a week's absence. On Sunday he was impressed to see Admiral Sir Pultney Malcolm's fleet in Torbay, and although the fleet tried to sail the following day, they were driven back by strong winds. Despite these continuing on Tuesday Pakington sailed twice to show friends the fleet, and was invited to board HMS Vernon, a 50 gun frigate.

Now into September, Lady Bolingbroke was holding a music party at which Pakington was going to sing, and after attending a rehearsal he sang a duet with a young lady. Later in the week he and Mary sailed to Fowey and back, seeing Restormel Castle (Pakington never missed the opportunity to see a castle, ruined or otherwise). The following week he sailed in a match against the yachts Paddy and Julia to Sidmouth and Lyme. Despite a favourable reaching wind Liberty was last, and, not for the first time, Pakington put a disputed point to the umpires, but as he does not record the result we may assume it was unfavourable. On 14th and 15th September a new sport appears – wildfowl shooting from the yacht. He noted that he found the skipper, Denton, drunk and decided to discharge him. The season was now drawing to a close, and after riding to Haytor on Dartmoor to see the granite quarries, and some final sailing, Liberty was laid up. Pakington left Torquay on 25th September after a stay of over 4 months. As his journey only took two days, Mary and Johnny probably came separately in the phaeton. Pakington noted that he stayed at Westwood, where it seems that his aunt had been spending some time since Sir John's death. She left on 16th October.

Pakington had to be back as usual for yeomanry duty, and on 29th September marched to Warwick with his troop, where they were to exercise during the following week. He took the opportunity to call on the Gladstones at Leamington Spa – the DNB remarks that Sir John Gladstone 'lived nomadically among the English spas as his wife and daughter took the waters…'.

For most of the rest of the year his diary is taken up with his canvassing and preparations for the election, and possibly because of this Mary and Johnny, who could not have been home very long, returned to Torquay on 25th October. The boundary between the eastern and western divisions of the county lay somewhat east of the river Severn, so the eastern division stretched from Stourbridge and Dudley in the north west and Northfield and Kings Norton in the north east to Broadway and even the detached portion of Shipston upon Stour in the south east, but excluded, of course, the boroughs of Worcester, Droitwich, Evesham, Bewdley, Dudley and Kidderminster, the last two places having been newly enfranchised in 1832.

Pakington had to cover a considerable area, and after starting locally, he worked his way north, with a 'grand public entry into Stourbridge and Dudley – satisfying day' on 19th October. However a few days later a letter appeared in The Times from 'A Looker On', who was clearly no friend of Pakington's, describing his entry into Dudley. (Dudley returned one member under the 1832 Act so was not in Pakington's constituency; but some inhabitants may have had a county vote through owning property there.) 'A little after 2 p.m. he arrived, and had been preceded by a most uncouth sort of band, composed of a drummer and fifer [a shrill tin whistle], several with pots and pans, a large bell, and about 20 with powerful whistles… A person accompanied this party with a handsome flag on which was 'Campbell for Ever'. As Campbell was the local Whig candidate it can be presumed that the ragged band was a spoiler for Pakington's own.

Behind followed about a dozen gentlemen, followed by a brass band and two banners. Pakington followed, 'and about 130 persons on horseback, some few of whom were respectable gentlemen of Dudley and its vicinity, but by far the greater part were yeomanry cavalry in plain clothes…'. The procession wound around Dudley for a period, then when they got back to the town centre a crowd had assembled, and there were two wagons full of people, evidently radical supporters intent on hissing down Pakington. At that point many of the cavalry started charging the wagons and the crowd – 'for about an hour and a half the horsemen constantly in twos or threes or singly charged from their ranks on the people… laying about them with strong riding sticks, and in some instances giving point with the same weapons; and confident I feel, if they had had arms, murder to an immense extent would have been committed.' The 'Looker On' did admit that he saw some stones flying about. No doubt the horsemen would claim that they were attacking the stone throwers and the 'discordant music'. He also admitted that no one was seriously hurt 'although it was only by Divine providence that several were not trampled to death'. Eventually the Riot Act was read, 'and soon after Pakington and his friends left the scene where they had so disgraced themselves'.

This account, exaggerated as it might be, illustrates how tempers could soon fray, and how candidates were quick to protect themselves and scatter the opposition.

Later, on 20th November, he made a similar grand entry into Bromsgrove, which was reported in Berrows. In fact there were two reports, the first stating that he entered the town with a very large party of horsemen of the highest respectability, with his agent Thomas Curtler and Rev. Richard Holmden Amphlett of Hadzor either side of him. After proceeding through the town he addressed the crowd from a window of The Crown Hotel. It is clear from his speech that he had been attacked (which he called 'calumnies and misrepresentations') for being anti-reform and not wishing to forward the interests of the working man. He said that he had even been warned about visiting those places, which included Bromsgrove (and probably Halesowen and Stourbridge too), where feeling was strong against him. In fact he made a point of going there and facing his critics, and he had not so far met with anything other than a decent reception. He was not ashamed to admit he had been against the Reform Bill; but now it was passed he hoped he had been wrong and that it would work to the benefit of the nation. He wished to stress that he was in favour of support for the labouring classes, the bottom of the national pyramid, as he called it, and he was "solicitous to see the condition of the working classes improved" (immense cheering).

The other report, sent by someone rather less favourable, stated that although there was no evidence of any antipathy towards him, only about forty persons listened to his speech (although it was market day), and the loud cheering was only thanks to a carefully orchestrated noise from his attendants.

The day after his visit to Bromsgrove, Pakington noted in his diary: 'Meeting of friends at Droitwich – determined to persevere in election & nearly £3,000 subscribed'. From this it looks likely that Pakington and his friends were having doubts about his chances of success. Pakington's reception was not always as friendly as he would have wished, to put it mildly. Meanwhile costs were rising, and to halt then would have saved a great deal of money. But they 'determined to persevere'.

At the end of October he was able to turn his attention to the south west of the county, and overall recorded in his diary canvassing on thirty three days, and covered nearly every part of the constituency. In 'The Pakingtons of Westwood' the authors imply that his canvassing was rather half-hearted, but this is not the impression one gets from his diary, and he does seem to have put maximum effort to win the contest.

Towards the end of November he made a rapid two day journey to Torquay, where his family had returned and where he remained for the last week of November before arriving back at Westwood on Sunday 2nd December. The fact that this is one of the few Sundays in all his later diaries in which he does not record going to church is to appreciate how much he was trying to cram into a short period, as is the fact that he records only two brief shoots in December. In later times when at home he shot whenever he could, almost daily.

During his canvassing an event occurred that probably did no harm to Pakington's chances. This was a royal progress through Wales and the Midlands by the Duchess of Kent and her daughter the Princess Victoria, the future monarch. After staying in Oakley Park near Ludlow on 3rd and 4th November, they proceeded to Hewell Grange in Worcestershire, where they were to stay with the Earl of Plymouth. On the way they passed through Tenbury Wells, where Berrows reported that 'they were most joyously greeted by upwards of 2,000 persons who assembled to greet them. The bells of the parish church rang a merry peel, and there were several discharges from cannon'. They paused at The Hundred House to take some refreshment, then, accompanied by the Worcester and Upton yeomanry squadrons they crossed the Severn by the new bridge at Holt and arrived in Worcester. The porcelain works of Flight, Barr and Barr arranged for cannon to be discharged as soon as they were seen, and as they crossed the bridge into the city the employees stood on the river bank and waved flags. They stopped at the Hop Pole to change horses, and now the procession, with the royal ladies in the first coach and their attend-

*The Duchess of Kent with her daughter Victoria in 1834. An engraving after a pencil drawing by Sir George Hayter.*

ants (including Sir John Conroy) following, was met by Capt. Pakington and his Westwood squadron of yeomanry cavalry, which escorted it to Droitwich. Here they were presented with a loyal address, and the Hanbury yeomanry took over escort duties as the party proceeded to Bromsgrove. There the Earl of Plymouth had given a dinner to 1,200 Sunday school children (of all denominations, Berrows notes), and afterwards they lined the road from Droitwich, 'and the sight of the children appeared to gratify the royal party much'.

Escort duty from Bromsgrove was taken over by the Tardebigge squadron, and, 'as soon as the Royal party entered the park, the artillery commenced their discharges. At the principal entrance the Duchess and Princess were received by a guard of honour, and the Earl and Countess of Plymouth conducted them into their noble mansion, the band of the cavalry playing "God Save the King"'. In the evening there was a grand dinner, and the royal party left for London the following morning, but not before receiving an address from the inhabitants of Bromsgrove, printed on white satin. After hearing the Duchess's reply the bailiff presented her with 1,000 nails enclosed in a very small quill as a token of loyalty of the Bromsgrove nail manufacturers.

Meanwhile Pakington was hosting another dinner in the George Hotel in Droitwich for members of the Hanbury and Westwood yeomanry squadrons. Over 100 men sat down together with other yeomanry commanders, and after the tables had been cleared Pakington gave the usual loyal toasts 'with his wonted good taste'. He then recounted that a sad event that he had only just heard of cast a shadow over the occa-

*The George, later the Royal Hotel, Droitwich c. 1875, courtesy of Worcestershire Record Office. See also page 145.*

sion. This was the death at the early age of forty four of his friend Edward Henry Bearcroft of Mere Hall in Hanbury. He had collapsed in church the day before, and died at his home later.

After returning from his brief visit to Torquay on 2nd December Pakington's diary for the next two weeks records a constant round of visiting his election committees in various parts of the county and a little last-minute canvassing. His senior supporters arrived at Westwood on Friday 14th December so as to be ready for the big day on the morrow. This was nomination day, and was held on a field adjoining the Worcester road in Droitwich which was chosen as a suitable place to erect the hustings. Again the colour of the occasion can be imagined from the report in Berrows:

> At 10:30 Messrs Cookes and Russell, with a considerable number of horsemen, elegant streamers, etc arrived on the ground, and occupied the whole front of the hustings. Mr. Pakington, who had most splendidly entertained great numbers at Westwood Park, arrived a little before 11. A very numerous body of electors on horseback accompanied him, but as the front of the hustings were preoccupied, they could not approach very near. Some very handsome streamers were exhibited.

Pakington was nominated by James Taylor Esq, who commended his virtues, and said that although his principles were conservative, he would have an independent mind and take decisions based on what he thought would be best for the country, not for his party. (In the days when party politics were less highly organised and whips less powerful, such sentiments were commonly expressed.) Pakington was seconded by John Phillips, who had nominated Col Lygon in 1831. In his speech, Phillips alluded to a subject that he evidently felt strongly about, which was the Beer Laws. Phillips said that he thought beer houses, legal after the Sale of Beer Act of 1830, were dens of all sorts of iniquity, and until they were closed crime and poverty would continue to flourish. As he was speaking about this there were impatient murmurings in the crowd to the effect that there were more important issues at stake, including taxation. Beer shops were a subject that Pakington was take up strongly later.

Before they made their speeches the two other candidates were nominated, firstly Thomas Cookes by Thomas Winnington. His speech was short but it was seconded by Mr Hanford, who had plenty to say against Pakington. After praising Lord Grey and the Reform Act, Hanford said it was hoped that the Tories would all but disappear. "But they have again showed their heads amongst us," he continued, "and we must now give them the coup de grace. ...On what does Mr Pakington rest his claim to be your representative? On his out and out opposition to the Reform Bill?" Hanford said he was willing to believe that Pakington had changed his opinions on this, but to this Pakington interjected "I have undergone no change in my opinions". To rub home the point, Hanford related that in 1831 during the introduction of the Reform Bill, when it was obvious that it would eventually be passed, he suggested to

Pakington (who had presumably intimated his ambition to enter parliament) that if he were to stand as a reformer against Col Lygon, he would have widespread support. But Pakington was steadfastly against the Reform Bill and refused.

Pakington then stood forward and made a speech that Berrows, a staunch Tory supporter, wrote was "much admired for purity of style, clearness of arrangement and chaste elocution". Reading it now, however, it seems over-long and unnecessarily defensive. In his diary, Pakington wrote that he spoke for 1 hour and 45 minutes – the frequent interruptions would have slowed him down. It was obviously an important moment for him, as it was the first occasion he had fully declared his views on various topics in public. He admitted that he had been asked to stand as a pro-reform candidate in 1831, and had even been offered inducements. However, he had refused to sacrifice his principles, which showed that he was a man of independent and steadfast opinions. He then went on to describe the unhappy state of the nation. Ireland was "torn and distracted by a degree of anarchy and discord that never have before affected any civilised or Christian land", the government was running a deficit, and not one interest in England was prosperous. To the charge that he had newly become a reformer, he said that there were many counts to which he was anxious to apply extensive reformation. He wanted "to approach in a temperate and moderate spirit all those great questions which must shortly occupy the attention of the legislature".

He then dealt with a few specific questions. As to the established church, he had been brought up in the tenets of the church, and had from infancy believed in its doctrines; "I believe in my conscience that there never existed a national church so well regulated to promote the temporal and eternal welfare of the people, so truly Christian in its spirit, or so tolerant in its principles". He believed in its connection with the state, but he was not blind to the fact that there were serious imperfections in the allocation of the temporalities of the church. He would approach any measure to improve these on its merits, as he would any measure to introduce commutation of tithes. At present this issue tended to come "between pastor and his flock."

Then he moved to the question of slavery. At that stage although the slave trade had been banned, slavery itself was still legal in Britain's colonies, although there was a move to ban this too. Here Pakington was equivocal. He started by saying that "I yield to no man in detestation of slavery in the abstract, and my wish is that slavery may be discontinued as soon as possible, consistently with the interests of all parties". However, he could not concur with those who thought it could be instantly abolished. Did we not have £100 million of property at stake in the West Indies, as well as a substantial shipping interest there, not to mention exports worth several £million? So we should not adopt any precipitate measures. (Berrows also reported him as having said during the campaign: "I conceive that no humanity may be more false, no injustice greater, than to give liberty to the uncivilised negro; but when the religious instruction and general education, now in progress, shall have had their effect, I believe that the interests of the planter will be promoted rather than retarded by the concession of freedom to those around him.") In fact the abolition of slavery was one of the first acts of the new Whig government in 1833.

Pakington then raised the question of taxation and import duties. He thought that "all raw materials ought to be relieved from taxation for the promotion of our manufacturers, and that in the diminution of taxation, care should be taken to relieve the necessities of the poor rather than the luxuries of the rich". If that sounded like the cry of someone who would also abolish the Corn Laws (the imposition of duty on imported corn to protect British farmers) then he was quick to rectify this: "I boldly say I am an advocate for the support of those [corn] laws which now exist. With regard to free trade in corn, I confess I look on it as out of the question...". Why corn was different to all other imported raw materials, he did not explain. If any change was proposed, "I must be satisfied that any measure that may be introduced will be for the protection of the home grower, and thereby to the benefit of the nation at large, before I, for one, consent to give up anything so good as the present corn laws".

The previous year Pakington had presided at a Tory dinner in support of Col Lygon, and said, in the course of his speech, that Whig supporters were "bankrupt in character and purse". This had caused much offence in the county, and he claimed that it was one reason why the Whigs had decided to put up two candidates for the constituency. Was this opposition personal or political? To us the distinction may seem small, but Pakington objected to the fact that by putting up two candidates the Whigs were effectively trying to disenfranchise local Tory supporters for purely personal reasons – Pakington thought that Tory supporters in the county had the right to be represented in parliament. (This view seems to support proportional representation.) He went on to quote some rather strong statements from Capt. Spencer in 1831 including "...this county, heretofore distinguished only by a servile submission to a Tory faction, roused itself from its degradation, shook off the yoke under which it had groaned for more than half a century...". Surely statements from "public men on public occasions when men's passions are roused, when their feelings are excited, their language will always be proportionally warm. Be it remembered, that any sentences that fell from me, fell from me in public speaking on exciting occasions, and at exciting times." Nearing the end of his speech, Pakington wound himself up to give a stirring peroration:

> Gentlemen, the party who assume the name of liberals, are decrying monopolies, while they are attempting to establish that most intolerable of all monopolies, the monopoly of representatives, and they are shouting with their lips for freedom of election, when they are endeavouring to abrogate to themselves exclusive representation. (Cheers.) If, however, this be a personal opposition, as I should be sorry to think it is, with regard to me it falls utterly harmless; I have long enjoyed the utmost happiness in a private station; if it is not your pleasure to elect me I shall most con-

> tentedly and cheerfully continue in that station; I shall not be the sufferer, but the sufferer will be those thousands of electors who have promised me their support, and who will be virtually disenfranchised if I am defeated. But, gentlemen, whether the opposition to me be personal or political, I predict that it will fail.

John Gladstone, sent a copy of his speech, wrote it expressed 'manly, constitutional and straightforward sentiments'.

But despite all his hard work canvassing and with his committees, the image of Pakington as a reactionary Tory land owner, opposed to reform and with no interest in the lower classes, was impossible for him to escape in the current excitable climate. Polling started on 18th December and Pakington went to speak at Pershore where 'the mob drew my carriage out of town', he noted. Berrows reported that he was 'very warmly received. He addressed the electors from his committee room window, and was loudly cheered. When about to leave the town, the populace would not allow the horses to be put to Mr Pakington's carriage, but drew him themselves to the outskirts'. It seems polling only lasted two days, Tuesday and Wednesday, probably because there were many more polling stations than in pre-reform days. At the close of the second day Pakington knew that he had lost. The two Whigs both polled over 2,500 votes, and Pakington 1,916. But he was not discouraged, and was probably not surprised. He hoped that the expected Tory revival as the decade progressed would give him new opportunities to gain his cherished seat in parliament. But that was still in the future. The Worcestershire result was typical of the nation as a whole, and when the new parliament assembled the Tories, with only 150 seats, were effectively in third place behind the triumphant Whigs with 320 and the Radicals with 190. In the western division of the county the popular Whig Thomas Foley retained his seat, but, with the departure of Capt. Spencer for pastures new, Col Lygon regained his seat for the Tories. But not a single Tory was returned for the Worcestershire boroughs, making the Whig triumph almost complete.

On Friday Pakington 'rode down to meetings to hear opponents duly elected – spoke & much cheered by the people'. On Sunday 22nd December he left for Torquay, taking only two days, arriving just in time for Christmas. He went to church twice on 25th, and again the following Sunday, and on New Year's eve, never one to waste a day, he 'walked with Mary & attended a lecture on thunderstorms & earthquakes; Torquay ball in evening'.

## Chapter 5
## A Visit to America, and Quarter Sessions

Pakington's diaries (assuming he kept them) between 1832 and 1843 have not survived, so our knowledge of his private life at this time is much sparser than for the earlier period. We do know that in 1833 he took his wife and Johnny (whose seventh birthday occurred during the trip) to the USA and Canada, as he left an account that the authors of 'The Pakingtons of Westwood' had access to, but which has since disappeared. While the family were away important events were taking place in the county, but as Pakington was probably unaware of these most of the time he was away, we will first recount the American excursion, based on the account in 'The Pakingtons of Westwood', before returning to politics.

It was only at the end of the 1830s that steam first made a regular appearance on ocean-going ships, the Cunarder 'Britannia' of 1840 being the most famous early steam ship, although she also, of course, carried sail. Prior to that the trans-Atlantic trade was dominated by the sailing ships of the American-based Black Ball line (so called because of its flag with a black ball on a red background). Their New York-built packet ships allowed, despite the vagaries of the north Atlantic winds, a regular twice-monthly service between Liverpool and New York to be established. One of these ships was named Britannia, and it was on this that the Pakington family sailed on 17th April 1833. They would have travelled 'cabin' class. The cheaper 'steerage' class passengers would have had more communal sleeping arrangements. A contemporary description of the Canada, another of the line, launched in 1817, said:

> Her dining cabin offered polished mahogany tables and pillars, sofas, and plush crimson draperies. The men's cabins, brightened by skylights of ground glass in the main deck overhead, had olive-coloured damask silk curtains. In the ladies' cabins the curtains were fine blue silk.

A year later, the Blue Swallowtail Line answered Black Ball with its own ship, the York. To the now-expected mahogany woodwork, the York added a library with a printed catalogue, redwood pillars finished in imitation bronze, and venetian blinds in the cabin doors that allowed ventilation with privacy. Cabin washstands doubled as desks. A Turkish carpet covered the floor and muffled shipboard sounds. The ladies' lounge even featured a small piano flanked by large mirrors.

As was quite usual in those days, a whole menagerie of animals was also kept on board to provide fresh meat, eggs and dairy produce. The journey time westward, against the prevailing winds, averaged 40 days, and could be much longer, and the Britannia called at Dublin on the way out. Pakington had already noted that 'there is nothing objectionable in our fellow passengers', and there was 'much fun among the gentlemen passengers with playing hop, step, and jump, shuffleboard, and suchlike gymnastics'.

On the first Sunday on board there was an impressive service on deck, and Pakington was pleased by 'the decorous attention of most of the steerage passengers'. By the end of that day they were fairly launched upon the Atlantic, and Pakington speaks of their good accommodation, but notes the great creaking of the bulkheads. Two days later they sighted a ship headed for England, and some of the passengers saw a last chance of communicating with home. Letters were hastily written and done up with a 'potato' and, with the two ships as close to each other as possible, the letters were hurled across by an amenable captain, only to 'plop hopelessly into the blue sea'.

They then passed through some very rough weather. Pakington wrote that on one occasion 'delicate sailors among us very ill', although he himself would be used to the ship's movement from his own sailing experience. Regardless of the weather, he was able to enjoy a game of chess, and was happy to write: 'Quite unpractised, but superior to Captain'. On Sunday, May 5th, the sea was tremendously high, and they rolled and pitched more than they had yet done, following a sleepless night. Nonetheless at the evening service the poor chaplain was condemned for giving 'an indescribably bad sermon'.

On the following day they had a favourable wind after nineteen days of calm or adverse winds, and there was 'singing and much fun after dinner in consequence'. On Sunday, May 12th, they were in 'quite a hurricane, so said the mate', and a man fell from the yard, but escaped with minor injuries. Pakington went on deck in

*The Black Ball Line 'Montezuma'. Black Ball Line ships were the first to establish regular fortnightly sailings from Liverpool to New York.*

his 'southwester' with great delight, but during the afternoon service the Britannia shipped much water 'to the dismay of the congregation'. The weather improved, they entered 'the dreaded gulf stream', and next Sunday the services went off satisfactorily amid a peaceful setting of porpoises and birds. Two days later there was a determination 'to hoax the ladies' by telling them that a bank of fog was Nova Scotia. However, it turned out to be the real thing, and the laugh was on the gentlemen. On another day, during a great calm, they 'manned boat with a passenger crew and gave ladies a row round the ship'.

On Sunday May 26th the outward journey was nearly over, and after dinner Pakington was asked to propose the chaplain's health. Two days later the pilot boarded and they dropped anchor. Pakington noted 'a very jolly dinner – was deputed by my brother passengers to propose Captain Sketchley's health'. On the next day they reached New York, after a voyage of six weeks. Although in 'The Pakingtons of Westwood' this was said to be 'unusually long', it is in fact exactly in line with the average quoted earlier.

In New York it took ten attempts before they found satisfactory lodgings. Pakington noted that 'they breakfast at eight, dine at three, drink tea at six, and have supper at nine – all in public. There is none of that rapid eating of which we have heard and read'. No doubt he had read accounts of American life before leaving. The USA was regarded with a great deal of interest at this time, still not 60 years from the Declaration of Independence. The American Constitution was based on very different principles to that in Britain. 'All men are created equal,' declared the Declaration, 'and they are endowed by their creator with certain inalienable rights, and amongst these are life, liberty and the pursuit of happiness'. Although radical reformers in England would have had some sympathy with that, others, such as Pakington, would have thought it a very dubious principle to base government on, and would be very interested to see the consequences first hand.

Many English visitors in the early nineteenth century had written about their experiences, and in what ways the American way of life now differed from that of its British roots. These accounts would have been read with interest by those such as Pakington interested in politics. One such account that he may have read was by Frances Trollope, mother of the novelist, who had visited the USA a few years before and travelled extensively, as well as conducting a business in Cincinnati for a period. Her book, 'Domestic Manners of the Americans', described a male-dominated society, with little evidence of the gentlemanly code of conduct that ruled the lives of people like Pakington, at least in parts of the country away from the large cities. The people, particularly in country areas, displayed a religious fervour and practice much removed from the largely unemotional rites of the church of England. When, on Sunday June 9th, Pakington's family went to church, he commented that 'American preachers seem to believe it best if their hearers are abused and frightened'.

Above all, the idea of equality was deep-rooted throughout society, and Mrs Trollope found it very difficult to engage domestic servants. Those she found behaved very differently from what she was used to. The coexistence of slavery with the principle of equality was something that puzzled many observers of American life including Mrs Trollope, but as the Pakingtons went no further south than Washington they probably did not see slavery first hand.

The following days were spent in sight-seeing, which Pakington considered 'that hardest of all labours', and he took Johnny to see a balloon ascent. They relaxed at the theatre, where Pakington referred to 'a well-dressed and highly respectable audience', except for one man in a box who insisted on sitting with his back to the house. They visited the Navy Yard, a handsome church, a picture gallery, the Athenaeum Reading Room, and a nearby lunatic asylum, confirming Pakington's interest in this type of institution. He also called on Washington Irving, the well known and prolific American writer who had just returned from spending many years in Europe. On an outing one afternoon 'soon found myself in conversation with an intelligent English plaisterer, and later, on hearing a fire alarm, arm in arm with my plebeian friend and pilot I proceeded to the scene of action'.

They then travelled south to Baltimore, where Pakington had to get out and help push the train – 'on a hot day rather hard work'. The Baltimore and Ohio Railway was one of the world's first commercial railways, being contemporaneous with the Liverpool and Manchester, and by 1833 a section west of Baltimore had been constructed, which is probably that which Pakington used. The branch to Washington had not yet been constructed. This would have been Pakington's first, if rather off-putting, railway journey. The London and Birmingham was not to open throughout for another five years, and it was to be almost twenty before Worcester and Droitwich would see trains, although there were Droitwich Road and Worcester Road stations on the Birmingham and Gloucester by 1841.

They went on to Washington, newly laid out, which Pakington calls 'the infant city'. There he heard that he had been nominated for west Worcestershire, and 'that the county of Worcester is in an uproar from one end to the other', but we will return to the election below.

A few days later, on the way to Canada, they visited a church where the preacher claimed that humility was the chiefest of all virtues. Not surprisingly, this went against the grain with Pakington. On July 4th they reached Niagara, and were immensely

*The Baltimore & Ohio Railroad.*

impressed by the falls both by day and by moonlight. Pakington described how the thunderous roar of falling water could be changed to an alarming silence by a shift in the wind. He also wrote contemptuously of 'those hurried thousands who take a peep while dinner is dressed and then pass on'. Visiting Quebec shortly afterwards, they were rowed by officers of the 32nd Regiment down the St Lawrence to see the falls, but 'these will not do' after Niagara.

Moving south again, they spent three days in Boston where they visited a house for the reformation of juvenile offenders, the Athenaeum, a picture gallery, and several factories. They sailed for home from New York on the Caledonia on August 16th, reaching Liverpool on September 10th. Eastbound passages were, of course, much quicker than the reverse, and the passage of twenty five days was a little longer than average at that time.

In summarising his feelings about the United States, Pakington noted that his impression was a favourable one for an infant republic, though he attacks their 'equality nonsense' and states that 'the tendency of democracy once admitted is always downward'. He thought well of the lower middle classes, but claims that 'ideas of republican equality have effects such as a waitress sitting down when her assistance is not wanted, instead of standing at the sideboard'.

Pakington no doubt thought that he could take a break from politics in 1833, as no new election was likely to be held for some time after that of December 1832. However, only four months after the election Thomas Henry Foley's father, Thomas, 3rd Baron Foley of Kidderminster, died. Thomas Henry, being his eldest son, inherited the title and a seat in the House of Lords, leading to a by-election in west Worcestershire. As it happened, Foley's death occurred the day before the family sailed from Liverpool on April 17th. As Lord Foley was only 52 and as Berrows reported his death was 'after a severe illness of a few days', it does not seem likely that Pakington had already planned what to do in the event of Lord Foley's death. But is it possible that he heard of Foley's serious illness shortly before he sailed, and communicated his desire to stand to his friends back home in the event of his death? If not, then local Tories must have put forward his candidature on their own initiative, a brave thing to do as their candidate would not return for at least four months, and so would be

*Niagara: the Canadian Falls.*

invisible to the electorate. On balance it seems most likely that Pakington heard of what was happening before sailing, and managed to communicate his instructions.

Accordingly it was announced in Berrows that, at a meeting at the Hop Pole Inn on 9th May chaired by Thomas Henry Bund, William Dowdeswell of Pull Court proposed and John Williams seconded the motion that John Pakington was a fit and proper person to represent west Worcestershire, that a committee be formed and a subscription entered into. Bund wrote to Berrows, saying that his success was certain, and that he did not identify himself with any party and would follow his own unbiased judgement. The candidate had declared himself publicly against slavery, and that free trade, the bane of our county and city, had received 'his determined reprobation'. None of these statements could be regarded as completely correct, nor indeed was Bund's hope that Pakington would return to this country as quickly as possible – they did not reach New York till the end of May.

His opponent was Capt. Henry Jeffreys Winnington of Stanford Court, who would stand in the Whig interest. The Winningtons were a well known county family which had provided previous members of parliament. Henry's brother Sir Thomas Winnington was the member for Bewdley, and Henry's mother was a daughter of Lord Foley, another Whig family. In view of this, and the fact that he did not actually live in the constituency, it must be wondered why the absent Pakington thought he still had a chance of being elected. The campaign went ahead nevertheless. Nomination day was the following day, Wednesday May 10th, and took place behind The Talbot Inn in Worcester where, according to a report in The Times, as many as 4,500 people had congregated by 9.30 a.m. The occasion seems to have been rather less bad-tempered than at recent elections, possibly because the absence of the Tory candidate had taken away the main focus of the reformers' dislike. Sir Christopher Smith of Eardiston, chairman of the quarter sessions, proposed Capt. Winnington. Trying to put at rest the fears of some that the Reform Act would result in all sorts of people "without honour, character or stake in society" being elected to parliament, he said that both Winnington and Pakington were "honourable as it respected their rank in society and private character". He characterised Winnington as of independent mind and a supporter of the constitution, but in favour of reform that would be generally beneficial. Pakington, on the other hand, an avowed opponent of the present government, would simply be a party hack. "But, should he be chosen, where is he?" (Laughter and cheers) "Where is he to be found? His friends could not pretend to say he could take his seat during this session of parliament... yes, gentlemen, you will not give your sanction to the opinion that the attention of a member of parliament to his duty can be discharged in his absence."

Pakington was proposed by John Williams, standing in for someone else who was unable to be there. Williams had difficulty making himself heard, and in his short speech he said Pakington would give every assistance to the successful working of the

Reform Act, but would the Act "work well if all the House of Commons were on one side? Now, the county sent twelve members to parliament, and only one of them was a Tory; surely they had a right to be represented as well as the others?". Sir Christopher Smith had alluded to Pakington's absence in America, and he acknowledged that it was most unfortunate; "but the passage was now rendered short, and the moment he heard he was elected he would return." (Laughter and "in an air balloon?")

Polling took place on 16th May, and despite the somewhat defensive nature of Pakington's campaign, he came surprisingly close to winning – he polled 1,278 votes against Capt. Winnington's 1,369. Pakington, according to his diary, heard when he was in Washington some time in early July that he had been nominated. When back in New York he read in The Times that he led the first day's poll by 35 votes, so he considered returning to England. But the following day he received a letter informing him that he had lost. One can imagine that his family were somewhat glad that this particular attempt at getting into parliament had not been successful. Pakington wrote a letter to the electors of west Worcestershire from New York dated July 7th, saying how proud he was to have received such a large vote despite having had no political contact with the constituency previously, and that he would personally tender his thanks to the voters when back home in September.

Pakington had been a magistrate since 1825, and attended petty sessions in Droitwich regularly. Magistrates also had another duty, which was to attend the court of quarter sessions, held four times a year in Worcester. In those days before the creation of county councils much of the county administration was conducted at these sessions. A committee of magistrates had to inspect and report on the state of the gaol, and at this time there was much discussion on the need for new facilities, as well as the need for new county courts. The court would set a county rate, and a full report was made of the income and expenditure. The other duty of the magistrates in quarter sessions was to try prisoners who had been held in custody since the last court. These were for crimes more serious than those that could be dealt with in petty sessions, usually held every two weeks, and another major difference was that at quarter sessions the trial was before a jury.

The chairmanship of the meeting on these occasions was an important post. Discussions involving the spending of ratepayers' money could become prolonged, and the chairman was one of the magistrates to try the prisoners. Sir Christopher Smith had occupied this position since 1829, but in early 1834 his wife died. This left him feeling unable to continue in public life, and he resigned at the Easter sessions. At the next sessions the senior magistrate, Rev. George Turberville, took the chair. In a move that had obviously been prepared, he nominated Pakington as chairman, which was unanimously approved. In accepting the post, Pakington said he had not sought the office, "especially when there are upon the bench so many older, more experienced and more able magistrates than myself". Pakington was clearly an ambitious man, and whether he had dropped any hints in the right places is not known, but the fact that he seems to have been the unanimous choice must say something about the regard his fellow magistrates had for his abilities.

The various reports were dealt with first by the court, and this took some or all the first day. There were reports from the visiting magistrates about the state of the gaol, situated on the north side of the lower end of Castle Street opposite the Infirmary, which at this time was being extended and having a sick wing added. It is interesting to see the extent which, even before the reign of Queen Victoria had begun, there was concern that prisoners should be educated and receive religious instruction. At the second sessions of which Pakington was chairman, in October 1834, Dr Beale Cooper gave the visiting magistrate's report. He started by complaining 'that from the numerous and troublesome returns required by the legislature and government, in the past year the labours of the Clerk of the Gaol have been much increased, and recommend in consequence an allowance of £10 a year in addition to his salary…'. The chaplain, Rev. Adlington, stated that 'the attention of the prisoners generally to religious instruction has been satisfactory. The school has been regularly attended, and several of the prisoners have expressed much gratitude for being taught to read'. In this respect, it is to be wondered whether prisoners 175 years later are any better provided for. Modern gaols do, however, cost rather more – in 1835 the court was informed that the cost of maintaining each of the average 176 prisoners in the county gaol was 1s 11½d per week.

Sometimes more trivial matters were discussed, as at Easter 1835 when Major Bund proposed that the advertisements that the court had to place should in future be placed in the Worcestershire Guardian as well as the other papers. Other magistrates supported this proposal, but Mr Hanford objected. He said the proposal was a 'jobbing' transaction (in the old meaning of corrupt), as many magistrates had shares in the Guardian, and he was surprised to find his worthy friend Major Bund lending himself to such a proceeding…. Bund replied vigorously that he repudiated the insinuation of Mr Hanford, and assured him "that I had ever been averse to jobbing of every description". Pakington stepped in to calm what looked like becoming a bad-tempered discussion, and came down on the side of those who wished to advertise more widely, saying, without producing any evidence, that the two older papers (the Worcester Chronicle and Berrows) probably did not circulate so widely in all parts of the county. He proposed that advertisements be placed in future in all Worcester newspapers, which was agreed.

Various pieces of legislation were before parliament at that period which would affect quarter sessions. One bill would allow counsel to address the jury in all cases, rather than only in more serious ones. In 1835 the conservative bench, led by its new chairman, thought that the bill would not be in the interests of justice if brought into effect, and discussed petitioning parliament against it. Pakington said that it would bring trial by jury into contempt, as well as increase expense. He continued:

> Experience shows that the innocent are very rarely, if ever, convicted; while the guilty are sometimes acquitted... If this law is to pass, the session would become a trial of the wit of counsel, and juries would acquit or condemn according as prisoners were lucky or unlucky in the selection of their counsel, and to his success in pleading... I have often noticed the influence of the address of counsel on the jury, in cases of misdemeanour, and that very few juries are competent to detect the intricacies in which they could envelop a subject.

Pakington's objections were in vain and the bill became law. Later Rev. Turberville, in his 'Worcestershire in the Nineteenth Century', stated that 'it is strange how unanimously an arrangement – now admitted on all hands to be a good one – was condemned and found fault with'.

An additional matter had been laid before quarter sessions by the new Poor Law, that of making affiliation orders in the case of illegitimate children whose mothers could not maintain them. The court had power to make a maintenance order against the father, as long as his identity could be proved by both the mother's sworn statement, and evidence that corroborated this 'in some material particular' to the satisfaction of the court. It can be imagined that this was easier said than done, and several applications found magistrates divided as to the truth of the mother's statement. At one court, in seven of the eight cases orders were made for the father to pay amounts averaging 1s 6d per week, but these orders only lasted till the chid was 7. It was stated that the cases cost up to £15 each in attorney's fees, so bringing them was rarely worthwhile. The chairman also remarked that discussing these cases in open court was 'very offensive to public morals, since the evidence adduced too frequently includes details of a nature calculated to disgust any delicate mind'.

The county rate had to be set, and this was generally around one penny, so a gentleman with an income of £1,000 a year would pay £4 3s 4d. In 1834 this rate raised £2,906.

After these matters had been dealt with the session usually divided into two courts to try the prisoners. The numbers to be dealt with seem usually to have been between 50 and 100. First the grand jury, which consisted of more than twenty men, had to examine the cases, and only those in which they deemed there was a case to answer were sent to be tried. (Grand juries were discontinued in 1933 – only the USA still uses this system.) The chairman and deputy chairman of the sessions each conducted the trials, and a petty jury was empanelled to reach the verdicts. Magistrates had a range of punishments for prisoners found guilty: imprisonment for a short period up to eighteen months, with or without a whipping and often including a period of solitary confinement, or transportation for seven or fourteen years, or for life.

Capital punishment was not available, being the prerogative of the assizes, nor were fines as a punishment – most prisoners would have been very poor. It is interesting to look at the first cases Pakington tried in Midsummer 1834, and how the harsh punishment of transportation was imposed for even quite small offences. In fact, as we shall see later, it was becoming more difficult to transport prisoners at this time. Transportation started with confinement in a hulk, which often lasted long enough for the prisoners to be deemed to have served their sentence. In the first case before the chairman the prisoner was found not guilty of stealing some property from his master. The chairman expressed surprise at the jury's verdict, and ordered the prisoner to be detained to face a charge of receiving stolen goods. When he reappeared the following day, the chairman remarked that the offence of servants robbing their masters was so aggravated and so easily committed that the court usually passed a heavy sentence on those convicted of it. However, the circumstances of this case were a little unusual, and the 'merciful' sentence of three months imprisonment was given.

The next case involved three Birmingham teenagers who stole a kettle and a hen and chickens in Northfield. They were known to have a bad character, and were each sentenced to seven years' transportation. The case following involved theft of two sheep by a father and his twelve year old son. The boy, mercifully, was discharged, but his father was found guilty, and sentenced to transportation for life. Two other men given the same sentence had stolen a sheep and a horse. This was followed by a case involving theft of some clothing, and the prisoner, whose second offence it was, was sentenced to fourteen years transportation. In total sixteen men, some as young as seventeen, were sentenced to seven years' transportation for the theft of various fairly minor items including a pair of shoes, and two men to imprisonment for 18 months for passing counterfeit half crowns. Six men and three women were sentenced to imprisonment for twelve months, usually with a period of two or three weeks' solitary confinement, for theft (one sixteen year old lad had stolen seven rabbits from a clergyman), and fourteen men and one woman to six months or less in prison. Teenagers, some as young as thirteen, were often sentenced to short periods of confinement and to be whipped as well.

# Chapter 6
# The New Poor Law

In the same year as Pakington became chairman of the quarter sessions the Poor Law Amendment Act was passed, and we will devote this chapter to the results of this, before reverting to a discussion of his political career. The 1834 Act completely changed the administration of the poor law, which had hitherto been done by the parish overseers giving both outdoor and, where the parish had access to a poor house or workhouse, indoor relief. After the end of the Napoleonic wars the country had suffered a downturn in trade, aggravating poverty, and under pressure to do something the government established a Royal Commission to look into and report on all aspects of the problem, and the new act was based on their report. The arguments for and against the different methods of relieving the poor were many and varied and beyond the scope of this narrative, but one school of thought was that the existing method of giving outdoor relief to able bodied men in the parish actually made poverty worse, and did not encourage people to fend for themselves. Some people felt that outdoor relief should be done away with altogether, offering just the grim prospect of families being split apart and sent to the workhouse. The 1834 Act did not go quite as far as this, but still based the new system around the workhouse. The principle was that the workhouse should give adequate relief for paupers but no more; the strict regime, separation of families, a spartan diet, and almost total loss of liberty meant that the workhouse would be seen as the least attractive alternative and relief only sought there as a last resort.

Parishes were to be grouped in 'unions' so allowing bigger and better organised workhouses to be built, and eventually the thousands of separate parishes in England were grouped into just under 500 unions. Worcestershire had eleven unions, each based in one of the major towns, except that of Martley. The governance of the new system was vested in the three Poor Law Commissioners in London. A number of assistant commissioners were also appointed, and each looked after a district and helped to set up the unions and ensure their proper running. Under the Act there should have been nine assistant commissioners, but more were needed at the outset, although later the numbers were reduced. The Droitwich Union was founded in 1836, and consisted of twenty six parishes (including the four in Droitwich town) including Hanbury and Stock and Bradley in the east, Hartlebury and Lower Mitton in the north, Ombersley in the west, and Claines in the south. Its total population at that time was nearly 16,000. The local unions were run by a board of guardians, each parish having the right to elect a member to the board, and all local JPs were members ex-officio. Potentially, therefore, the boards had a large number of guardians. When the Droitwich board first met on 12th October 1836 there were thirty four in attendance, even though not all parish representatives were present. Nor did all the possible JPs become involved – there must have been an arrangement that only certain justices were to attend meetings, and at Droitwich there was a pool of about seven JPs were who regular attenders. The clergy were much involved, and some boards of guardians had clergymen for chairmen.

Pakington was appointed the first chairman of the Droitwich Board of Guardians, and some insight into his appointment comes from a report in Berrows of a speech he made when being nominated for the 1837 election. He spoke at considerable length on the subject of the Poor Law, and Berrow's report of part of his speech is as follows:

> When the union was first formed at Droitwich, I was waited upon to take the office of chairman, but conceived that some of the clauses were so harsh that I could not carry them into operation, so I did not at first consent to the appointment. So after taking that office, I could fearlessly appeal to the guardians, many of whom are present, whether it had not constantly been my endeavour to administer the law with the greatest regard to the comfort and convenience of those unfortunate persons who sought its protection. (Cries of "yes you have", and loud cheers.) I have a very great objection to the system of imprisonment in the modern workhouse. (Loud cheers) ...I could never assent to make poverty a crime. (Loud cheers.) I would never consent to that rigid imprisonment in the workhouse, which was almost as severe as that inflicted upon those who had broken the laws of the country. (Much applause.)

So despite his generally right-wing stance on many issues, it seems Pakington was never one to make the treatment of the poor as harsh as some would have liked.

Pakington was at the first meeting of the guardians as the representative of Elmley Lovett rather than as a JP, and it was confirmed at the first meeting that he was to be chairman, and that John Howard Galton, the representative from Hadzor, would be his vice-chairman. The guardians were to meet weekly, initially at the George Inn in Droitwich on Wednesday mornings. At their first meeting they were attended by the assistant commissioner for the district, Robert Weale Esq, who attended every few months. They appointed Thomas Lawrence of Droitwich, a solicitor, as clerk at a salary of £90 a year, and agreed to advertise for the medical and relieving officers as required by the Act. The Union was divided into five districts for medical purposes, and three for purposes of outdoor relief. These eight posts were filled as early as 2nd November, and at the same meeting the guardians discussed the food rations to be adopted in the workhouses. Previously it seems that rations or 'dietaries' varied widely between institutions. While many were most ungenerous, others allowed food to be eaten 'without stint'. But the new Poor Law Commissioners, anxious to standardise everything from their base in Somerset House, published a number of standard dietaries, and the Droitwich Guardians decided to adopt dietary no. 3. All these were based mainly on bread. Breakfast was always 6 ozs of bread and 1½ pints of gruel (a type of thin porridge), and supper consisted of 6 ozs of bread and 1½ ozs of cheese. Only dinner varied. A similar ration of bread and cheese was served four times a week, vegetables once, soup once, and meat twice – in Droitwich this was on Thursdays and Sundays. These quantities were for men; women and children had less. Poor as the dietary was, research has shown that it provided sufficient nourishment to keep body and soul together. But there were many cases when the dietary was not properly followed, and in some documented cases the master conspired with the suppliers for the food to be sub-standard to the benefit of both. However, some Unions had conscientious guardians who kept a close watch that the dietary was followed properly. In Droitwich not only was the bread sampled and approved beforehand, but when a baker was found to be supplying underweight loaves he was duly admonished in front of the board.

At their meeting on 2nd November 1836, the guardians received a report on the workhouses already existing in the Union. There were ones at Claines and Ombersley as well as two small ones in Droitwich. There was a discussion on whether any of these could be expanded to form the new union workhouse, but the guardians followed the recommendations of their sub-committee that this would not be money well spent, and they decided that a new workhouse in Droitwich would be a better investment. Accordingly the guardians agreed to look for a site of up to three acres. In the meantime the existing ones at Claines, Ombersley and one at Droitwich would be rented by the guardians from the parish overseers for use until the new one was finished.

A special building committee was appointed to find a site, and to supervise the construct the new workhouse, and no time seems to have been wasted as by January 1837 a new site was ready to be inspected, and soon afterwards its purchase was put in hand. This was on the south side of the present Union Lane, just east of Droitwich station (which was not, of course, then in existence). The young London architect Sampson Kempthorne was appointed to design a workhouse for 200 inmates. Kempthorne designed many workhouses, his father having been friendly with one of the Poor Law Commissioners, and he was no doubt suggested by Weale. Kempthorne had a number of standard plans, which mostly accommodated 300 paupers, so Droitwich must have been considered a 'less pauperised district', as the guardians decided on a smaller version. Although the Droitwich workhouse was demolished many years ago, its plan can be seen on older maps. This matches Kempthorne's standard 200 workhouse plan quite well, and is reproduced here.

A contract was entered into with local builders Messrs Wood, Morris & Preece for £3,050, and a government loan for £3,500 arranged to cover the purchase of the land as well. The design was a standard 'square' one with an entrance block containing a porter's room and guardians' board room. Running back from this was a block with dining room leading to another cross wing with separate sleeping accommodation for the different classes of inmate – there was no question of keeping families together. The master's room was in the centre, with work rooms and other offices lying on each side. Later, an infirmary and chapel were built on the west side. Strangely, the only references to the new building in the guardian's minutes, which still survive, are the occasional authorisation of payments. More detailed matters were left to the building sub-committee, and would in any case have been subject to detailed scrutiny by the Poor Law Commissioners. When complete, many workhouses had the look of a Victorian prison, and indeed in many ways they were similar. Not only was entry and exit closely controlled by the porter, but visitors were only allowed on two weekday mornings a week. Inside the seven different classes of pauper were segregated, only getting together at meal times, and then in silence.

The board of guardians was re-elected every year, the new year starting on Lady Day, so the first board only lasted six months. Not yet an MP, Pakington was able to

*'Workhouse for 200 adapted for the less pauperised districts', one of Sampson Kempthorne's standard designs. The Droitwich workhouse would have been based on this plan.*

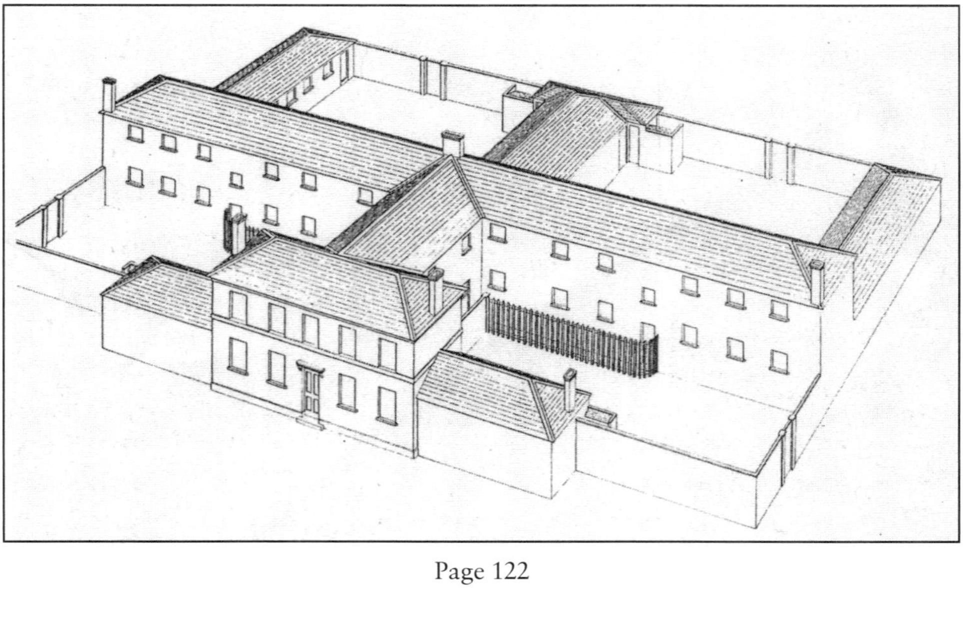

devote much of his time to the new Union, and attended 15 of the first 25 meetings, quite a good record compared with some guardians. At the first meeting of the second board on 5th April 1837 he was re-elected chairman, and Galton his deputy. A vote of thanks was passed for his work so far. Soon afterwards figures produced by the board showed that there were on average 111 inmates in the three workhouses, and that the average daily expenditure on food was five pence (two new pence) per head. Construction of the new workhouse was going ahead, and early in 1838 the Board had to appoint the governor, matron, schoolmistress, nurse and porter (as laid down by the Commissioners) for the new institution. As was a common practise, some of these came from the same family: George Thompson and his wife Ann were to be governor and matron, and their daughter Ann was appointed schoolmistress. Sadly only six months passed before Miss Ann fell ill and had to resign her post. The guardians refused a request from her parents that she be allowed to continue living with them as they could not accept someone outside their control living in the workhouse; consequently her parents resigned their posts as well. One of the relieving officers Stephen Sills and his wife Martha replaced them on a salary of £75 a year, with all found. Another family arrangement was that Samuel Barker and his wife were appointed porter and nurse. Unfortunately this arrangement was also upset early on when Barker was dismissed after returning in an intoxicated state a day after being sent on an errand.

Another appointment was that of the chaplain, no doubt regarded as of some importance by the guardians. Some time later a plain brick chapel was erected next

*Droitwich Workhouse with later additions as shown on an early OS map. Its similarity with Kempthorn's standard plan can be seen.*

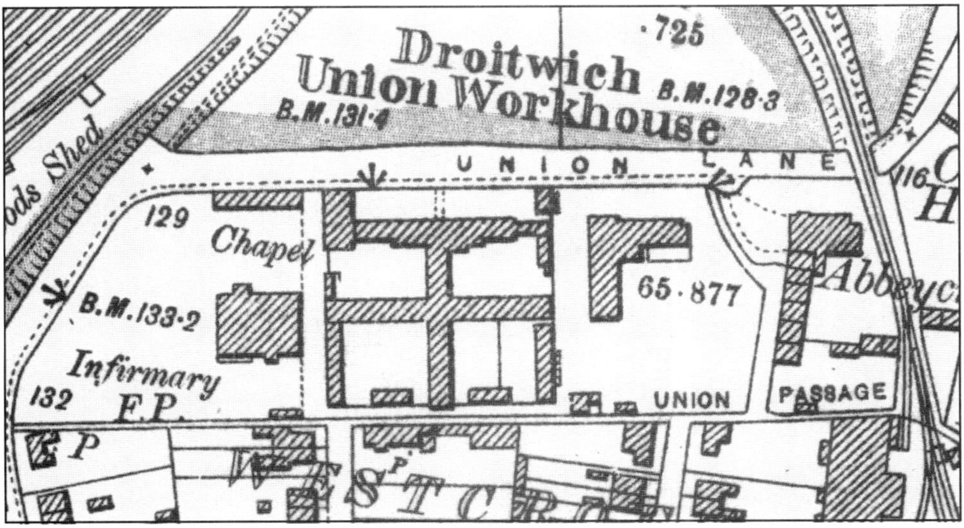

to the workhouse, but at this early period the services would have been held in the dining hall. Later some aged paupers requested they be allowed to attend a local church with the governor, but this was refused. Rev. John Topham, rector of St Andrews, Droitwich, was appointed chaplain at a salary of £40, and he had to hold two services a week. The weekday service was initially left to his discretion, but soon the guardians decided this needed more precise regulation. They stipulated that the service should be held on Thursdays, alternately in the morning and afternoon, this arrangement allowing men on different work patterns to be accommodated at least once a fortnight. Finally a medical officer, William Robson Jaques, was appointed at a salary of £25, and the guardians insisted that he called at the workhouse every day. Among other duties he had to inspect all new arrivals to make sure they were free of disease, and that they had been properly 'cleansed'.

The new building seems to have taken about twelve months to complete, and at the beginning of May 1838 the inmates from the three old workhouses were moved to the new one. The old buildings were returned to their parish overseers. Once the building was finished the builders applied for their final payment, which led, of course, to the guardians inspecting the finished buildings. However, various imperfections were evident, the builders were not paid, and eventually in August the architect was summoned to discuss 'the insufficient state of the building'. The nature of all the defects is not clear from the surviving documents, but poor pointing, particularly of the brickwork of the public faces of the building, was one such. On inspecting the finished building Sampson Kempthorne admitted 'that the works were done in a very unsatisfactory manner and not according to specification'. One might have thought that the architect would have spotted this earlier, but as he was responsible for new workhouses being built all over England he seems to have left everything to the clerk of the works, who proved unsatisfactory.

At the same meeting Messrs Wood and Morris were present, and insisted that they should be paid in full, as they claimed the architect had given them his final certificate. The guardians asked them to produce this, but instead they produced part of a letter from the architect. Kempthorne then admitted that a letter he wrote somewhat injudiciously could have been interpreted by the builders as giving his approval, and they stood their ground and insisted on payment, but the board could not agree to this until the work was satisfactory. Eventually it was provisionally agreed that two 'indifferent' architects should be appointed, one by each side, to arbitrate. However, after the meeting Wood and Morris had second thoughts and withdrew their agreement and instead their attorney sent a final demand for payment.

Meanwhile the Board had appointed a Mr Hunt of Worcester to survey the building, and he produced a list of twenty nine defects that should be put right. Kempthorne seems to have agreed, and wrote to the builders asking for the work to be done. But they would not relent, and in November issued a summons in the name of the Pakington and Galton, the chairman and vice-chairman, for payment of the outstanding amount. Matters dragged on till the following March, neither side being keen to go to court. Eventually the board's clerk, Lawrence, was allowed to negotiate a compromise in which Kempthorne accepted part of the blame and undertook to put right some of the defects at his own expense. A complicating factor was that the builders had contracted with a Mr Sylvester to supply some hot air apparatus that was intended to heat the workshops. It is interesting to note this at a time when most factories would have been unheated. This apparatus had initially not worked satisfactorily but Mr Sylvester declined to put it right and the guardians had to spend further money on new ducts to make it work. As Sylvester was to be paid by the builders, this amount was deducted from their final payment, and Sylvester was not paid in full. The total cost of the workhouse eventually came out at £5,000.

None of the parties to the dispute come out with any credit, particularly the architect, who gave insufficient attention to his commission, and the builders, who must have been aware that they were producing sub-standard work, but who probably thought that standards in workhouses were low anyway.

An important matter that the board had to decide was the nature of the work to be given the able-bodied men. A special committee was appointed to look into this, and they went to Birmingham where they could see different types of flour mills in operation. They saw a new type made by Donaldson & Glasgow that produced a superior type of flour, but this mill was expensive, costing 80 guineas, and needed

*The Droitwich workhouse in 1953, photographed by E. H. Sargeant. Copyright R. H. Sargeant.*

ten men to work abreast, which it was thought was more than would be available. They then visited an existing Birmingham workhouse, where they saw a steel flour mill in operation that only needed three men to work; the flour was not so fine, but would make bread that was just as nourishing. They particularly liked the fact that 'part of the machinery of the dressing machine is connected to a bell, which should the workers stop or loiter immediately on resuming their work rings and gives notice to the miller of their idleness'. The authorities in Birmingham said they were sure that, having had twenty years experience, these mills were the best way of employing able-bodied men. A miller would be needed to supervise things of course, and it was suggested that the governor should allow the workers a more generous diet and 1 penny per bushel of flour ground to be given them when they left.

Assistant commissioner Weale was in attendance at the meeting when this was discussed, and before it concluded he asked the guardians to agree to some new rules on the operation of the workhouse. These included the restriction on visiting hours noted earlier; that the porter should keep a book to note all comers and goers; that a punishment book should be kept (punishment usually consisted of a reduced diet or confinement); and that the rules published by the Poor Law Commissioners should be read out loud after Tuesday morning prayers. Concern for the good health of the inmates was shown by ruling that no-one was to be discharged from the sick wards without a certificate from the medical officer. He should report regularly to the guardians on the state of health of the inmates, and particularly on the appearance of any infectious diseases – in that event the board should take immediate action to stop their spread. This is probably why we find the board borrowing an extra £500 soon after to build 'fever wards' to isolate infectious inmates. The only reference to disease in the board's minutes at this period is that a large number of inmates had 'the itch' (now called scabies). The medical officer sought to have his expense in providing the necessary medicine reimbursed; this was declined.

The treatment of lunatics was a national issue at this time, and one in which the campaigning Lord Ashley (the future Earl of Shaftsbury) was much involved. Those coming from better-off families could be looked after in a private asylum, but pauper lunatics frequently had to endure the most terrible deprivations, and were often confined in workhouses. The Droitwich guardians realised that better was expected; and they were fortunate in that a well-run private asylum already existed in Droitwich, run by Messrs Ricketts and Steward. (This was at the top of what is today called Ricketts Lane.) The guardians agreed to place lunatic paupers in this asylum, for which they would pay 10 shillings a week each, plus 3 gns a year for clothing.

Pakington long held the view that education of poor people was a reform strongly to be desired, and in addition to the schoolmistress the guardians soon thought that it would be necessary to have a schoolmaster as well. One had to be advertised for, but in the meantime an inmate, Richard Rawlins, was found to be suitably quali-

*Rules and regulations displayed at the restored Southwell, Notts, workhouse, owned by The National Trust.*

# RULES AND REGULATIONS

## TO BE OBSERVED BY THE POOR

OF THE

## Southwell Union Workhouse

That in order to preserve the Peace and harmony of the family, all persons in the house shall behave in the most respectful manner to the Master and Matron, and in a quiet orderly and obliging manner towards each other: and that in particular the conduct of the elder part thereof, shall be such as may operate to the good example of the younger branches.

I. That the Master and Matron live in the House, and see that the following Rules be observed.

II. Every Person in health shall rise by six o'Clock the summer half year, and by seven the winter half year, and shall be employed in such labour as their respective age and ability will admit, and commence their work by six o'clock in the Morning, and work till six o'Clock at Night, from Lady-day to Michaelmas; and from seven o'Clock till dark, from Michaelmas to Lady-day, allowing half an hour for breakfast, one hour for dinner, and half an hour for supper; and any one refusing to work, shall for the first offence go without their next meal, and for the second offence be reported to the Overseers, that they may otherwise be punished.

III. That all the poor in the House go to bed by eight o'Clock the summer half year, and by seven o'Clock the winter half year, and that all candles be put out by that time.

IV. That the poor shall have their provisions in a clean and wholesome manner, their breakfast by eight, their dinner at twelve, and their supper at six o'Clock; that no waste be made, nor any provisions carried away; and that Grace shall be said before and after dinner, and none may depart until Grace is said; and their dinner three times a week to be hot meat and vegetables properly cooked.

V. That the House be swept from top to bottom every morning and cleared all over once a week, or so often as the Master and Matron think necessary; and the windows be opened daily.

VI. That none absent themselves from the House without leave, nor stray beyond the time allowed them, on pain of losing their next meal, or of some other punishment; nor may any one be admitted into the House without leave of the Governor.

VII. Any of the poor guilty of stealing, selling their provisions or clothing, or of drunkenness, swearing, quarrelling, fighting, or in any way disturbing the peace of the House, or of being in any way saucy or abusive to the Master or Matron, shall be punished with the utmost severity of the law.

VIII. That all in the House who are able, and can be spared from the duties thereof, shall attend Church or some other Place of Worship twice every Sunday; and those who refuse or neglect to attend, or do not return as soon as Service is over, shall go without their next meal, or be punished in some other way, as the Overseers shall think proper.

IX. No person shall be permitted to bring spirituous liquors into the House, or smoke in any part of the premises, except the hall. Those found transgressing, shall lose their next meal, or be otherwise punished.

X. Any of the poor acting in disobedience of the orders of the Master or Matron, or in contempt of these Orders, shall be taken before a Magistrate, and punished as the law directs.

XI. That these Orders be placed in the hall, dinner-room, or any other place that the Overseers may direct; and that they be read on a Sunday at dinner-time by the Master or Matron, so that the poor may not plead ignorance of the same.

XII. If any of the poor are found defacing or destroying these Rules, they shall be punished by being fed on bread and water only for two days.

THOMAS MARRIOTT. Clerk to the Guardians.

fied. He was asked to be schoolmaster *pro tem,* for which he was allowed the same dietary as the officers. But only two months later George and Elizabeth Goode were appointed schoolmaster and mistress, so presumably poor Rawlins had to resume his inferior dietary!

In 1837 Pakington was elected to parliament, which meant that his attendance at board meetings became irregular, particularly during the first part of the year when parliament was in session. This is illustrated by the fact that, although he continued as chairman, he only attended fourteen of the weekly meetings in the year to Lady Day 1838; even vice-chairman Galton could only manage twenty seven attendances. The most regularly attending JPs were Rev. Thomas Baker (30) and William Ricketts (35), although a few others including Rev. William Amphlett, Sir Offley Wakeman, his brother Rev. Edward Wakeman, and Rev. William Vernon from Hanbury made occasional appearances. This does illustrate a weakness of the system – the erratic appearance of the senior members of the board did not help the continuity of running the union, and on some occasions not a single JP was present, so the Board must have been very dependent on the clerk, Lawrence, to keep things in order. Lawrence himself was far from perfect, and at a meeting in January 1839 the chairman, Pakington, said he had received a personal letter from the Poor Law Commission complaining that letters to the board were often not answered, even after reminders had been sent. Lawrence was admonished, and asked in future to report weekly all correspondence received and sent. He must have felt this was something of an insult, and resigned his position in June. In 'The Scandal of the Andover Workhouse' the author, Ian Anstruther, states that at Andover most of the guardians from the thirty parishes in the Union soon stopped attending meetings, leaving matters to the JPs. At Droitwich attendance during the first eighteen months was usually between fifteen and twenty including only two or three JPs, but numbers later fell. By 1840 only those with a special interest came regularly, and attendance fell to a more manageable eight to ten.

Soon after this Pakington offered to resign the chairmanship owing to his absence at Westminster. The guardians refused to accept his resignation, which must show that they regarded his handling of the dispute about the building as good, and his contacts, which were much wider than those of other guardians as useful. A year later some of the guardians tried to make use of his position as an MP by getting up a petition from the board complaining that there were still more than the nine assistant commissioners provided for in the Act, thus causing unnecessary public expense. However, not all guardians agreed with this, arguing that such a petition was beyond their competence, and although the clerk was ordered to send a petition for Pakington to present to parliament, there is no record of its having been presented. Sometimes Pakington was able to use his position in London to advantage. In February 1841 the Commissioners had followed their usual practise of not allowing outdoor relief to be paid to a female pauper from Droitwich while she was living in

Worcester (so in another union) where she was using her skills in the glove industry. Pakington went in person to see the Commissioners to plead her case, and they promised to reconsider it.

Reference has already been made to various staff problems the Board experienced. In February 1841 a new situation had arisen when a complaint was made about one of the relieving officers, Arthur Granger, behaving improperly towards a female pauper. The Commissioners had strict rules about this: relieving officers must

> treat the sick, the aged and the infirm with marked tenderness and care; that a large portion of claims to relief, which it will probably be his duty to reject, have been created by erroneous impressions fostered by old and vicious modes of relief; and that even the claims originating in fraudulent rapacity will not be allowed to be met with harsh language or angry deportment. He should, and indeed must, so conduct himself as to obtain the respect and confidence even of his claimants; and he should be especially apprised that the Poor Law Commissioners will visit any instances of harsh or unnecessary severity, inattention, or incompetency on his part with immediate dismissal.

It says something of the intention of the new system to be fair to all that complaints by paupers, both inside and outside the workhouse, were duly investigated. On this occasion the guardians held a lengthy enquiry hearing evidence from all concerned, and decided that Granger had indeed been out of order. Some guardians wanted to admonish him, others wanted him dismissed; after a vote the latter course was adopted. A new relieving officer was advertised for, and several applications received. Strangely, Granger was allowed to re-apply, and on the first vote he and another candidate, William Whitney, got the most votes. There was then a run-off vote, which Granger lost. It would certainly have seemed odd to re-appoint him. Another relieving officer, Waterson, ran into financial problems and had to resign, owing the board money as he had not fully accounted for the float he had been given for outdoor relief. It is interesting to note that many of the officers had to give surety on appointment which the board could call on in the event of something like this happening.

Pakington was not present at the meeting that investigated Granger, but after the new board had been elected on 21st April the guardians invited Pakington and Galton to a dinner to be held in their honour at the George Hotel in Droitwich. This might seem odd in view of the few meetings Pakington was able to attend, but he was evidently held in high regard. The Hon. and Rev. William Chetwynd Talbot, vicar of Ombersley, was in the chair and sat between the two guests of honour, referring to them as 'Castor and Pollux' in his speech. He said it was good to have efficient men of business involved in running the union, and referred to opposition to workhouses at meetings and in the press. "But," he concluded, "it is my opinion, if every local Board possessed so valuable a president as our own, these outcries would have been put to silence at once!"

In his reply, Pakington said that he was generally in favour of the changes wrought by the 1834 Act, even though it had been introduced by a Whig government. He said it had become common to speak of the commissioners as tyrants and the workhouses as Bastilles, but he felt that on the whole the Act had worked well. Yes, it was common to decry the whole system, but what would its opponents put in its place? Surely not the previous system:

> I am not guilty of exaggeration when I say that under it the industrious and the idle, the vicious and the well-conducted, were treated with the same indifferent indulgence. The industrious man had no inducement to stimulate him to continue in his industrious habits, or to encourage him in the practice of provident frugality; and the idle man was confirmed in his idleness, because he was enabled to turn to the laws of the country to maintain him in his idleness and vices.

Although the Act had not only been passed to save money, he could not help but allude to the great reduction in the poor rate that had been achieved since 1834 – in 1832 it had raised nationally £7m, and five years later this had been reduced to £4m. Giving further statistics he said that nationally about 100,000 paupers were receiving indoor relief, against about 600,000 receiving outdoor relief. This would have meant an average of about 200 in each union workhouse – Droitwich then had only about half that number. Pakington showed his compassion when he said that it was the aged, the infirm, and those who were otherwise unable to look after themselves who were the proper objects of the law, and he thought they were better off than before. The Droitwich guardians had increased the allowance to such paupers, and the board did not press them to go into the workhouse.

Although it goes beyond the period covered by this chapter, we will briefly discuss the Droitwich Union during the rest of Pakington's chairmanship, as his involvement after he became an MP was limited. Indeed it is rather strange that he kept up his involvement so long – he did not resign until 1865, completing nearly 30 years as chairman. He only averaged about nine attendances a year, and less after the meetings became fortnightly in the 1860s. These were mostly between August and January when parliament was not sitting, although he occasionally managed to fit in one or two during the Easter recess. The irregular attendance of the chairman and other guardians was no doubt a factor in the poor running of many unions, and left much power in the hands of the master. Vice-chairman Galton's attendance was little better than Pakington's, although he remained vice-chairman till he died in 1862. Galton's place was taken by Rev. Thomas Baker, who had usually taken the chair when Pakington was absent. He was elected chairman to succeed Pakington on his resignation in 1865, and his attendance was more regular. It should be noted that on a few occasions after he became a magistrate in 1849 John Slaney Pakington attended board meetings. On one occasion he even took the chair, but his involvement was not long lasting. The business conducted at meetings of the guardians was mostly routine and must have been tedious to many of them. Every item of expenditure had to be recorded and approved. The cost of outdoor relief for the three officers was noted and a new 'float' voted to them. There were usually letters from the Poor Law Commission, many of a circular nature, to be read out. Advertisements for suppliers of the many commodities needed, everything from provisions to the male and female uniforms and to coffins, had to be placed and the chosen suppliers recorded. There was much correspondence with other unions about the correct settlement of and relief for individual paupers. Staff appointments had to be made, and it was this last that caused the guardians the most problems.

Not infrequently one member of staff would make a complaint about another. These had to be investigated, sometimes with the help of an assistant commissioner, and the result was not always conclusive. In 1843 the schoolmistress, Mrs Whitall, was reprimanded by the master, Arthur Sills. Immediately afterwards she complained to the chaplain, Rev. Topham, that Sills had had an inappropriate relationship with the late nurse, Mrs Good. Assistant commissioner Alfred Austin came to investigate, and found no evidence 'of a direct or conclusive nature' to back up the allegation, so Sills was able to continue in post. Mrs Whitall resigned at the same time, but her replacement, not untypically, only lasted 6 months, and yet another had to be found. It is understandable that, unless she had a strong sense of vocation, a young lady schoolmistress would not regard teaching workhouse children as the pinnacle of success. In May 1844 there was another staff problem when the visiting committee of guardians found there was evidence of great negligence on the part of the nurse and matron. The matron, Mrs Sills, had not regularly visited the lying-in wards as she should have done to enquire about the health of those there. In the investigation the master, matron and medical officer all tried to blame the nurse for the unsatisfactory state of affairs, but, as well as the dismissal of the nurse, they were all reprimanded by the guardians. In 1845 there was an investigation into the excessive consumption of food. Assistant commissioner Austin considered that the master and matron, Mr and Mrs Sills, were incompetent and neglectful although not dishonest. They resigned, to be replaced by Henry and Mary Ellins. Soon afterwards the master reported he had found the nurse, Mrs Selina Barton, intoxicated in the workhouse, and she was dismissed, although it took the guardians several weeks to find a replacement, as they advertised twice and received only two applications.

The following year, 1846, the chaplain, Rev. Topham, received complaints that the new master swore, but when he questioned the inmates more closely he could find not one who would confirm this. It has to be assumed that the inmates would have had more regard for their own position vis à vis the master than for the truth when formally questioned. At the same time both the porter and assistant porter complained of the master's conduct towards them, but again Topham came down in favour of the master, finding their complaints frivolous. Soon afterwards the master himself complained of his difficulty of keeping discipline in the workhouse. The guardians decided that this was due to the imperfect classification of the able bodied women, probably meaning that unmarried mothers were not being kept strictly separate from women without children.

Early in 1847 there was another spate of resignations. The nurse, only appointed in November 1846, was said to be incompetent by the medical officer and dismissed. The following week the clerk, Mr Richards, who had been appointed to replace Lawrence, resigned. After advertising, the guardians (including Edward Bearcroft of Mere Hall, Hanbury, making a rare appearance), appointed a solicitor Henry Bearcroft (Edward's younger brother) as clerk, an appointment he maintained for over twenty years. The guardians often found it convenient to keep appointments 'in the family', and in December 1847 Miss Ellins, daughter of the master and matron, was appointed schoolmistress. Unfortunately, only a year later her father was suddenly taken ill and died, and Thomas Chambers was appointed in his place. Miss Ellins continued in post for a while, but in 1850 it was found that she was not suitably qualified to teach the older boys, and resigned.

All workhouses had a porter, who as well as guarding the entrance was expected to be something of a jack of all trades, including being either a tailor or shoe maker. He was often a single man, and allegations of improper behaviour towards the female inmates were not uncommon. Early in 1849 it was alleged that Nash the porter was the father of an inmate's child, but this was not proved. At the same time it was discovered that outsiders were able to gain access to the female paupers' ward at night, with consequences that can be imagined. When the workhouse had first been built, it was on the edge of Droitwich, a little way away from any other housing; but new development was creeping nearer, and eventually it was decided to build a six foot high wall all round the premises to make it more secure. Porters could also succumb to temptation when sent out on errands. In 1855 William Keen, the porter, came back tipsy and abused the master; when summoned before the board he refused to appear, and was dismissed. Reference has already been made to the dismissal of porter Barker after a lengthy absence on a drinking spree.

Only a few months after his appointment, it was found that the master, Thomas Chambers, who had been seen wandering aimlessly around the premises at night, had a history of mental illness, and was dismissed. He was replaced by George Green Gabb. Gabb seemed to have had quite good credentials, having worked under Brunel as inspector of bridges during the construction of the Oxford, Worcester and Wolverhampton railway. His mastership continued without major incident until in March 1853 the schoolmistress, Alice Emuss, was not able to work through illness. Upon investigation it was found she had had a miscarriage. She alleged that George Gabb was the father. Gabb, of course, denied it, and the Poor Law Board were again called in to investigate. However, after giving evidence both Gabb and Emuss resigned and took employment unconnected with the Poor Law. The Commissioners, understandably, did not think there was any point in finalising their investigation, which had produced 'voluminous and conflicting evidence'. However the Droitwich guardians found this unsatisfactory, and Henry Bearcroft wrote to the Poor Law Board that 'the board are much disappointed that an opinion upon the case has not been given by the commissioners, which must operate as but slight encouragement to the board to ask for the opinion of the commissioners in future upon so important a matter'.

So three new appointments had to be made, and Mr and Mrs Robert Layton became the new master and matron, and Miss Mary Ann Smith the schoolmistress. The Laytons stayed three and a half years, before moving to the Hereford workhouse, presumably a better appointment.

Staff problems, of course, were not the only ones the guardians had to deal with. Initially the occupancy had been around 100, but by the winter of 1842 it had risen to near the maximum, which the Poor Law Commissioners had set at 194. A little before this the guardians had recorded the size of the wards. There were three wards for men and three for women and children, where they must have slept at least two to a bed. The accommodation for boys and girls must have been particularly cramped, with thirty girls sleeping in a space 19 feet by 18. To relieve pressure on space the guardians rented a nearby house from one of the medical officers, and another step taken to relieve pressure was to allow more outdoor relief to infirm paupers. Finally in 1844 it was decided to add an extra storey to the building containing the dining hall to give additional sleeping space. One of the problems the guardians had to deal with was that the number of inmates varied widely through the year. In 1845, for example, figures given at the weekly meetings show that there were a little over 200 in January, the coldest time of the year, but that after March the numbers started to decline, and there were little more than 100 inmates at the end of summer, when presumably there was the maximum demand for labour at harvest time. A very cold spell of weather could put an almost unbearable strain on resources.

Although the workhouse was not supposed to be a prison, once inside discipline should have been strictly maintained, and the inmates kept quite separate from the outside world. At a meeting in August 1844 when Pakington was in the chair it was reported that inmates had found a way to communicate with outsiders through the front downstairs windows which gave on to the street. The visiting committee were asked to report what steps could be taken to stop this.

The fact that Pakington remained chairman whilst an MP was used to good effect on a few occasions by the guardians, when they asked him to present petitions to parliament. In 1842, for example, the guardians petitioned that widows should still be entitled to outdoor relief if they went to live in a parish other than that in which their husband had lived. The rule was that the widow was 'settled' in the latter parish, but the petition argued that very often she could find more support in another parish, perhaps where her child lived. The question of relief from poor rates for poor people was a question that had exercised the guardians on several occasions. They were reluctant to exempt occupiers who paid less than £5 a year in rent, but suggested in the same petition that in future the owner of a house rented for less than £5 a year rather than the occupier should be liable. In 1845 another problem was exercising the guardians, that of smoke being emitted from nearby salt workings. A Smoke Prohibition Bill was going through parliament at that time, and in May Pakington presented a petition from the guardians in favour of the bill.

The question of the dietary was discussed from time to time. In 1845 when Pakington was in the chair it was proposed that all inmates over 65 should be allowed tea, bread and butter for breakfast, instead of the usual gruel. But there seems to have been two parties among the guardians and on this occasion the majority of guardians felt this was uncalled for, and it was agreed that this should be allowed only if directed by the medical officer. Ten years later, the question of the children's dietary came up. The Poor Law Board had been told that in Droitwich the dietary was the same for all children from 2 to 9 years old: breakfast 4 ozs of bread plus 1 pint of gruel; dinner included 1½ ozs (sic) of stewed meat twice and 1¼ ozs of bacon twice a week; and supper was 4 ozs of bread and 1 oz cheese every night. The Poor Law Board pointed out, not unreasonably, that children at the upper end of the age range needed more sustenance than those who were infants (it is hard to believe that the master was not in practice already doing this), and directed the guardians to increase the dietary for older children, with the result that all children were given a rather less meagre diet.

In December 1848 Pakington and representatives of other local Boards attended a meeting of the Worcester Guardians to which Jelinger Symons, a poor law schools inspector, had been invited to speak about the need for 'industrial training' of the older boys. The meeting is described in greater detail in a later chapter, but Symons' proposal was that a district

*The famous scene from Oliver Twist. In fact had the children been served the correct dietary, they should not have gone hungry.*

school be established that would in reality be a small farm on which the boys would live and, under a suitable instructor, learn the basics of agriculture. Symons described in some detail a school in Quatt, Shropshire, that was run successfully on these lines. Countering criticism that this would mean giving the workhouse boys a better education than that obtained by children of artisans and labourers, Symons said it was essential to break the cycle of poverty, as otherwise these untrained children became victims of 'hereditary pauperism'.

Pakington reported these ideas to the Droitwich guardians, but as there appeared to be no interest in establishing a Worcestershire District School the subject was dropped. However, the question of industrial training came up again in the summer of 1850. At a Board meeting in May it was reported that the schoolmistress, Miss Ellins, was having difficulty keeping control of the older boys, and it was proposed that in future they be taught by the porter instead. But the Poor Law Board (as the Commission had become in 1847) objected to this proposal, presumably on the grounds that the porter was not qualified, saying that if Miss Ellins was not competent then they should find someone who was. Soon after, possibly prompted by this correspondence, Jelinger Symons paid the workhouse a visit in his capacity as workhouse schools inspector. His report was highly critical saying 'the children are very deficient even in the most elementary and ordinary instruction', and he made similar suggestions to those he had made to the meeting in Worcester, that the older boys should be given industrial training. ('Industrial training' was really a euphemism for being prepared to work as agricultural labourers.) If the board adopted his suggestions, there might actually be a reduction of expenditure, as the government would pay the schoolmaster's salary, and his rations and the rent for the land would be amply repaid by the produce of two or three acres. 'The board would not fail to be pleased with the change produced thereby on the present lazy habits of children which must surely tend to future idling'.

As a result the board set up a committee to examine the proposal, and their report was presented to the guardians on 7th August 1850. They reported 'that upper classes of children can write well but they are not able to understand properly what they read and are so deficient in elementary knowledge as in great measure to justify Mr Symons' remarks, without aiming at a higher standard of instruction than may be generally considered proper for a workhouse school'. They remarked that the present system 'of allowing boys between eleven and sixteen to pass eight hours a day in total idleness is highly objectionable and ought not to be continued'. They recommended the acquisition of about two acres of land and the appointment of a schoolmaster to instruct the older boys.

Pakington was in favour of the idea, and he and the vice-chairman John Howard Galton visited the school at Quatt on 20th August. They seem to have been impressed, as at the board meeting the following week they proposed that the committee's recommendations be put into effect. But many guardians suspected that the whole venture would put an additional burden on the poor rates, and were opposed to it. They probably also thought that pauper children did not deserve all this attention. The meeting was better attended than usual, with many ex-officio (magistrate) guardians present who did not usually attend. Probably Pakington had encouraged them to come as he knew his proposal would be opposed by many of the elected parish guardians.

The proposal, which also included the idea of engaging a schoolmistress who would be able to give the older girls some 'industrial training', was countered by the opposing guardians who proposed an amendment saying, in effect, that the present situation was perfectly adequate and that it would be wrong to give pauper children a better education than to those of independent labourers. In the event the chairman's proposal was carried by 17 votes to 15, although the tone of Berrow's lengthy report on the meeting was somewhat critical of the idea.

So the guardians set about advertising for a schoolmaster 'who should be thoroughly vested in the principles of industrial training', but there were only a few applicants, and none were regarded as having the necessary qualifications. At the same time a committee was appointed to look for a suitable plot of land of two acres or so near the workhouse. Behind the formal minutes one senses that some of the guardians were manoeuvring to try and kill the idea, and this unrest seems to have led to several staff changes. Miss Jane Wicks was appointed the new schoolmistress to replace the ineffective Miss Ellins, but when she was told that no new schoolmaster was to be appointed she resigned after only a few weeks. A new matron, Miss Wooldridge, had also been appointed, but she resigned with Miss Wicks, 'being uncomfortable with her situation'. Finally, in February 1851 it was decided to go ahead with the scheme, except that the porter, William Keen, would be entrusted with the 'industrial training' of the older boys. These boys would be divided into two groups, and each would have three hours of classroom education per day, with three hours on the smallholding, alternating between morning and afternoon. But this proposal meant the porter would be occupied for six hours a day away from his normal post at the entrance, and, perhaps not surprisingly, he objected, saying these duties were incompatible with his other duties, and he could not therefore be responsible for anything that went wrong in his absence.

In the meantime, some of the opposing guardians suspected that the accounts from the Quatt school did not give the whole picture, and it was agreed that a deputation should go to the Bridgnorth Union to examine the books relating to Quatt. They did in fact report that the school incurred an annual loss of about £50. But this controversy rumbled on for some time and reached the pages of Berrows, as the Bridgnorth guardians maintained the Droitwich guardians had got it wrong. However, in April the whole matter seems to have been permanently put on one side when it was resolved not to rent the land the Guardians had been offered, as there was sufficient work to do in the workhouse's own garden to keep the small number of older boys occupied.

Workhouses had always been run on the principle of keeping the seven classes of inmates separate, but obviously pressure on space, not to mention pressure by the inmates, must have meant this principle was not always observed as rigidly as the Poor Law Board intended. In 1856 at a meeting chaired by Pakington and possibly as a result of a suggestion made by the new master, Jesse Aston, it was found that the mothers of illegitimate children were not being kept separate from the other female paupers. A new rule was made that there must be no communication between these classes of women, not even at meal times when food should be brought to the mothers in their ward. The children also had to be kept separate from their mothers, and they were only allowed to meet for one hour a week on Sundays. It is hard for us now to understand the need for this harshness, but illegitimacy was regarded as a great moral sin, and presumably the guardians did not want the morals of the ordinary female paupers contaminated by the loose morals of the unmarried mothers.

It need hardly be said that the sanitary arrangements in the workhouse were very primitive, and early on the guardians had come to an arrangement with the Droitwich Canal Company to discharge sewerage into the canal on payment of sixpence a year. As time went on general standards of public sanitation started to improve as the importance of cleanliness in public health was recognised. In 1864 a Poor Law inspector recommended that the cesspools under the toilets be discontinued, and a new system be used. The recommended method was to have the toilets draining into a channel which would be cleared by frequently flushing water down it to a distant cesspool, but when the guardians asked the architect to make recommendations he found the water supply was insufficient for this method. In any case he felt that the constant damp that would result was not good for health. Instead he recommended the adoption of Rev. Henry Moule's dry earth system, which was based on the discovery that dry earth when placed on top of human waste allowed it quickly to decompose, after which it could used in the garden, or even re-used as dry earth.

The unions, once established, were used for other administrative purposes, including from 1837 the registration of births, marriages and deaths, and the guardians had to find a suitable registrar. Various public health duties were also put on the guardians, including the obligation to remove 'nuisances' (usually connected with effluent from toilets) which were seen as a danger to public health. Cholera was one of the diseases which caused great mortality, and although the exact cause was not known (we now know that infected drinking water is the culprit) it was clear that it spread quickly within certain neighbourhoods. There had been a bad outbreak of cholera in the 1830s, and in 1847 there was a fear that it might attack again, as it was rife in the east, and was spreading towards Europe. At a meeting of the guardians in December

1847, with Pakington in the chair, it was agreed to send a circular to all parish overseers warning of the dangers of open drains and sewers, which should be attended to so as to help stop its spread if the disease should appear in England. There was indeed a bad epidemic in Worcester in the summer of 1849, although it did not affect, as far as is known, the Droitwich workhouse. A national day of thanksgiving was held on November 15th when the epidemic was over.

Milling machines had been purchased in 1838 by the guardians to provide work for the inmates; but after a few years the milling stopped and the miller was discharged. It seems there were not enough able-bodied men to work it. (This indicates that the great majority of inmates were too young, too old, or too sick to look after themselves; most able bodied men were able to find employment.) Shoe making and tailoring was tried for the younger boys, but were unsuccessful. At the suggestion of the vice-chairman, John Howard Galton, mat-making was introduced, with somewhat more success. In 1850, the guardians considered buying a 'Bottens' hard labour crank, but were told by the Poor Law Board that this was not suitable for workhouses. This was because it produced no useful work, and the Board suggested breaking stones as a more useful and appropriate task. The guardians were, however, warned that they should not force a man to break stones for more than four hours against his will.

*'The Stone Breakers' by Gustvae Courbet, 1849.*

# Chapter 7
# An MP at last – 1835 and 1837

The new Whig government elected in December 1832, under Grey in the Lords and Althorpe in the Commons, embarked on a reformist agenda, but soon started to run into trouble. The abolition of slavery caused no major difficulties, but reform of the Irish church ran into problems. The government suffered defeats and defections, most notably from Edward Stanley, heir to the Earldom of Derby, an important figure in the future career of Pakington. Eventually King William IV decided to take matters into his own hands, and, for the last time in Britain, sacked his Whig ministers (Lord Melbourne was now the prime minister), and sent for Wellington. But he declined to take on the premiership, and advised the King to send for his Tory colleague in the lower house, Sir Robert Peel, who happened to be touring Italy with his family. On his rapid return to London on 8th December 1834 he quickly formed a government, and decided to call a general election just two years after the previous one.

Pakington saw this as another chance to enter parliament, and decided to contest the western division of Worcestershire again. On 22nd December, even before the dissolution had been announced, a dinner was held in the Green Dragon Inn at Corse Lawn in the south of the county to promote Lygon and Pakington as the Tory candidates. It was chaired by Sir Anthony Lechmere and reported in Berrows, and Pakington's speech gives some insight into what he and his opponents thought. After a short speech by Lygon, Pakington spoke at length. Comments had obviously been made about his not standing in the division in which he lived, and early in his speech he explained why he was standing for the western rather than the eastern division. This was firstly, he said, to thank those who helped him in his unsuccessful attempt to enter parliament the year before for the same constituency, and secondly, because "I feel that as an English gentleman I have a full and perfect freedom and right to offer myself to any body of electors in the country whom I may desire to represent". While Pakington was quite correct in saying this, he does not seem to have felt the same about Capt. Spencer in 1832, nor on future occasions when an 'outsider' wished to challenge a well-established MP, as he was to become. Then Pakington came to the third reason.

> ...I hold a large property in this [west] division. I lived the greater part of last summer in my paternal residence [Powick], which is in it, and although I am now removed to my other seat, it is so centrally situated in the county that, standing in my park, I shall cast a stone which shall fall in the western division! I say, therefore, that I have a right to seek the representation of either division if I choose, and when I see that your interests and opinions are not fairly represented and you have no other candidate who offers to represent them, I feel bound to come forward to your assistance in this emergency.

His reference to last summer is interesting, as it indicates that he had, for some reason, gone back to live at Powick Court in 1834. What he did not refer to was the unfriendly reception he had received in some of the more industrial parts of the eastern division. Coming to the heart of what he and the Tory party believed in, he continued:

> I say the question is – shall the established church be supported, shall the monarchy be supported, shall our other cherished institutions be supported, or shall they all be left to crumble to pieces under the inroads of a rampant democracy?

Referring to his opponent, the sitting Whig MP Capt. Winnington, he said Winnington had supported measures "which I hold to be totally incompatible with the very existence of the constitution." In the short time Winnington had been an MP, Pakington mentioned three questions on which he had voted in ways totally "destructive of the constitution": Irish church reform, triennial parliaments, and the admission of dissenters to universities. As to the last, their admission to the universities would "be a most fatal blow to the church". After referring to the bad state of agriculture, he said he trusted that a future Tory government would offer more relief to farmers. He felt that the recently issued 'Tamworth manifesto' (an attempt by Peel to set out general principles of government for national consumption) offered the prospect of relief. In that Pakington would eventually be cruelly deceived. Finally, he apologised in advance for having to divert his attention to quarter sessions during the campaign. Berrows reported that his speech was greeted by cheering 'lasting several minutes'.

Shortly afterwards a letter appeared in Berrows from a Whig supporter. He had read the report of this speech, but all he had learned from it was that Mr Pakington had been in America; that he had two seats; that he could throw stones in his park: and that he was chairman of quarter sessions. He learned nothing about specific measures that Pakington might support or oppose.

As newly appointed chairman, Pakington's attendance at quarter sessions in the first few days of January interrupted his campaign. He had stressed at Corse Lawn that politics should not come into these sessions, and they were finished by nomination day, 13th January 1835. An interesting side-light on the campaign and the way land owners still retained the habit of trying to influence results is contained in a letter that Pakington wrote to the Marchioness of Downshire, a relation of Lord Sandys of Ombersley and a land owner there. She had evidently instructed her tenants to vote for the Whig candidate, and, trying to stop the damage that this might do to his chances, Pakington wrote:

> Madam: I hope your ladyship will pardon the liberty I take in trespassing upon you with this letter, on the subject of the instructions which your tenantry in Ombersley have received to vote for Cap. Winnington at the approaching contest for the western division of this county.
>
> I beg to assure your ladyship that no man is more strongly disposed than I am in principle to support rather than attempt to sever the legitimate connection and influence between landlord & tenant, and I would not presume to address you were it not that the case of your Ombersley tenants is in my humble opinion quite a peculiar one.
>
> They are, as your ladyship knows, my dear neighbours – I live on good terms with them – some of them, as in the case of Whitney who has been largely employed by me & is now fitting up my library, & Whitaker who is serjeant in my yeomanry troop, are more closely connected with me and I believe I am correct in stating that they are almost all desirous of supporting me, and will only vote against me in reluctant compliance with your ladyship's injunctions … I would only beg leave to suggest whether under the above circumstances you ladyship would allow such of the tenants as are favourably disposed towards me, to remain neuter by not voting for either candidate.
>
> I beg sincerely to apologise for this intrusion, & have the honour to remain, Madam, with great respect, your ladyship's honourable servant, John Pakington

Thus wrote the man who on many occasions declared that tenants should vote for whomsoever they pleased and not be influenced by their landlord.

A field at the back of The Talbot Inn on The Tything, Worcester, was again the venue for the nomination, and as usual it was a colourful affair. The candidates' supporters assembled at prearranged venues (Westwood for Pakington, Madresfield for Col Lygon, and The Hundred House at Witley, The Crown at Ombersley and the Star & Garter in Worcester for Winnington – presumably it was thought his seat at Stanford was too distant), and substantial breakfasts were provided for them before they left. Winnington, according to Berrows, was first on the ground at 9.30

> accompanied by a vast cavalcade of friends, each wearing a laurel leaf as the distinctive badge of their party. The gallant Captain, on quitting his carriage, entered the sheriff's booth, followed by his brother Sir T E Winnington, Sir Edward Blount

> [the next high sheriff], Robert Berkeley jun. Esq [of Spetchley Park and a future high sheriff], Osman Ricardo [a past sheriff], T C Hornyold Esq [another future sheriff], George Henry Robinson, the member for the City, and others of his more influential supporters, whilst the horsemen took up their position in front of the hustings.'

The nomination was evidently another noisy affair, with the crowd favouring the Whig candidate. First the three proposers spoke of their candidate. Sir Anthony Lechmere proposed the Tory Lygon, Osman Ricardo the Whig Winnington, and Lord Eastnor Pakington. Eastnor was John Somers Somers-Cocks, eldest surviving son of John Somers-Cocks, the 75 year old 1st Earl Somers of Eastnor Castle. Although the founder of the family, John Somers, had been a notable Whig politician between 1680 and 1710, the present generation were of strong Tory persuasion, and the 1st Earl was the author of such books as 'A Defence of the Constitution' and 'A short Treatise on the Dreadful Tendency of Levelling Principles'. Eastnor was at this time MP for Reigate, but was able to spare the time to help his friend gain his first seat. He duly tried to extol the virtues of Pakington, but the crowd clearly preferred Winnington, and he was frequently interrupted.

Then the candidates came forward. Col Lygon made a short speech, much interrupted, then it was Capt. Winnington's turn. But before he really got going, a man called Gutch came forward and asked the sheriff if could pose some questions to Winnington. This was somewhat out of order but eventually was allowed, and Gutch asked how Winnington had voted on a particular clause in the Irish Church Reform Bill (clause 147). As mentioned above, Pakington had referred to this matter at Corse Lawn, saying he believed Winnington had voted for it, and now there was further uproar. It seemed that Winnington refused to answer the question. (This clause, which had become very controversial, allowed the state to appropriate certain revenues of the church. Many who were prepared to accept church reform, drew the line at the government getting its hands on church revenue.) Winnington then went on to defend his record in parliament, ending by saying that 'he promised them another splendid victory over the common enemy of the rights and privileges of the people'.

Pakington's speech was mainly notable for several interruptions, indeed at one point he declined to continue unless the sheriff could restore order. But there was a twist at the end – Winnington came forward and said that the informer who told his opponent that he had voted for clause 147 was wrong – in fact he had opposed it. This put Pakington on the defensive, and he said that if that was the case, why had Winnington not said so after his Corse Lawn speech? This was nothing short of being an electoral trick. But was it also not the case that Winnington voted for the idea of defraying the cost of church repairs out of church property rather than church rates? But Winnington also denied this, and these exchanges seem to have been rather to the detriment of Pakington.

Pakington also made an appearance at the nominations for east Worcestershire. His comment in a speech in 1831 that Worcestershire people were 'bankrupt in character and purse' had been quoted back at him ever since, and at the nominations there was a placard that quoted this statement, ascribing it to Pakington, and to which he objected. Sitting on his horse in front of the hustings, Pakington started to address the meeting but was shouted down by cries of "No Pakington". When he eventually made himself heard, he said he wished to address a question to the two Whig candidates, Messrs Cook and Holland. Was the placard placed by the candidates? Both candidates denied having seen it before that day, to which Pakington said he was satisfied with their gentlemanly answer. He took exception to it as he said it contained an implied falsehood, that the words were intended as personally offensive, which they were not. The date on the placard was also wrong, so as it contained a double falsehood. He hoped he would not see it again.

In the event, Whig reformist feeling was still too strong for two Tories to be elected in west Worcestershire. Col Lygon with 1,945 votes came just ahead of Capt. Winnington with 1,938; Pakington came third with a still respectable 1,773. It is notable that nearly ninety percent of the registered voters went to the poll. Pakington could take some comfort from an analysis of the voting figures. Voters were allowed two votes, and 1,501 voters cast their vote just for Winnington ('plumpers'), whereas 100 more voted for the Lygon/Pakington ticket ('split votes'). This indicated that Tory support was potentially greater than that for the Whigs, but what did for Pakington was that over 300 voters voted for both Lygon and Winnington, indicating a considerable feeling that the present incumbents should not be disturbed.

The new parliament showed a considerable Tory revival, and when all the results were in they found themselves with 290 seats out of 658 – not an absolute majority, but probably enough to keep the government alive for the time being. Peel became the new prime minister, and his 'Tamworth Manifesto' was well received. It promised that the government would promote sensible and well considered reform, but would not 'adopt every popular impression of the day – by promising the instant redress of anything that anybody may call an abuse…'. Peel's first major measure was to reform the Church of England – its problem in those days was not shortage of money, but too much, with many sinecures and over-rich livings, while there was an increasing shortage of churches and clergymen in the new rapidly growing industrial towns. An Ecclesiastical Commission, with power to redistribute the church's income, was established, and was successful in restoring the church's popularity while keeping it as the established church. But when Peel's ministers tackled reform of the Irish church again (where the problem was that a large income was used to benefit the small minority of protestant worshippers) the government suffered a number of defeats, and after serving as prime minister for one hundred days, on 8th April Peel resigned. The King sent for Lord Melbourne, the leader of the Whigs.

Sometime in the previous year, 1834, Conservative Associations for both east and west Worcestershire had been formed, and anniversary dinners for both associations were held in 1835. The meeting of the West Worcestershire Association was held on 23rd September at the Hop Pole in Worcester, under the chairmanship of John Brown Esq of Lea Castle. Col Lygon, the Tory MP for the division, had to send his apologies as he was ill, but he had, however, sent them a buck. The chairman called on Pakington to give the leading speech. He said "I dislike political associations generally and on principal; but there are times unhappily when, as in the dialogue between Brutus and Cassius it was urged 'good reasons must of force give way to better,' and I fear the time has come when good reasons on general grounds against political associations must give way to the better which grow out of the dangers with which they are surrounded". Pakington also regretted that there were some prominent men in the county who supported Conservative principles "but who keep aloof from these associations from objection, on principle, to all political societies". He stressed the need to get rid of the present 'imbecile' Melbourne administration "which has lost the confidence of the King, is opposed by the majority of the English members of the House of Commons (cheers) and which held its existence entirely by the support of the Irish Roman Catholic members – dependent on one man, who avowedly aims at the destruction of the church and the dismemberment of the empire". (Loud cheers.) Pakington was referring, of course, to Daniel O'Connell, MP for Dublin and vigorous campaigner for Catholic and Irish rights.

Two weeks later it was the turn of the East Worcestershire Association, with Pakington in the chair at their meeting at The George in Droitwich. As usual a number of toasts were drunk, the chairman proposing first "Church and King – may the former prove victorious over all its assailants, and be enabled to shed over this country its pure and holy influence; and may the latter long live in the hearts of the people, and protect our glorious institutions in all their purity unimpaired". In his speech, he again expressed the hope that such political associations would in the long term prove unnecessary, "but he must be indeed a sanguine man who does not feel that day to be far distant". He then attacked vexatious queries aimed at Tory voters who had to prove their right to vote in the registration courts – "even my vote has been objected to, though I believe there is no man in east Worcestershire who seriously doubts that I possess a 40 shilling freehold [the county voting qualification]!!". Speaking about the dangers of meddling with the constitution, Pakington said he had recently read a book written some 10 or 12 years before, in which this statement appeared: 'in my mind the greatest of all objections to any broad and general manner of reform is the danger that it will bring with it to all our other institutions.' "These were the words; and by whom, Gentlemen, do you think these words were written? Perhaps you will feel some degree of astonishment when I tell you that the author of these words is none other than Lord John Russell!"

**The 1837 Election**

Despite his failed attempts to win a county seat, Pakington must have looked on his home borough of Droitwich as offering the best potential if a chance could be found for him to contest it on behalf of the Tories. Droitwich was one of those ancient boroughs that had the right to return two members of parliament, and the first record of its doing so was in 1295. But after 1311 the borough apparently chose not to take advantage of this right again till 1554, since when until 1832 it had regularly returned its two members. The electorate was restricted to those owning 'a freehold property in salt', of whom there were probably only about twenty five, and the borough was very much in the hands of the Foley family, which had provided at least one of the two MPs, and sometimes both, for over 100 years before 1832. In this time there had been only one contested election, and that, curiously, involved a Pakington ancestor. As the population of the borough was only about 2,000, the commissioners working from the Great Reform Act not only reduced the representation of Droitwich to a single MP, but considerably enlarged the boundaries to include ten adjoining rural parishes, parts of one more, and several extra-parochial places including Westwood, to make up the requisite population of 5,000. There is an interesting article in Berrows in October 1849 on the history of the constituency, where it was claimed that the Foleys, who were an 'easy, careless sort of people', left the new boundaries to the commissioners, whereas they should have taken more interest so as to avoid this eventual mish-mash of a constituency.

The Foley connection continued after 1832, when John Hodgetts Hodgetts-Foley, one of the two previous MPs, was elected as its single MP, and when the number of electors had only increased to about 290. According to Berrows, Foley, who was a quiet, easy gentlemanly man of no brilliant parts, but of highly honourable reputation, 'performed respectably. He was at his post when he was wanted, and his votes were conscientious and tolerably liberal'.

The 1849 Berrows article tells the story of the 1835 election in some detail. The management of the borough was in the hands of two bailiffs, elected annually at the Court

*The George, later The Royal, Hotel on the corner of Hanbury Street and Queen Street, Droitwich.*

Leet of the Lord of the Manor, Lord Foley, and afterwards it was customary for the bailiffs to hold a dinner to which all the important inhabitants of the borough would be invited. In 1834 something went wrong, and Lord Foley's agent did not invite many people who thought they should have gone; so some general resentment was caused against Foley's agent. Berrows pointed out that there was also some political 'excitement' stemming from the reform controversy, and the result was that a document was circulated in the town 'pledging the signatories that in the event of an election they would give their support to a local gentleman who would consult the interests of the town'. The document carried no name or political agenda, but because of the resentment then current against Foley's agent it was well subscribed, even by many who were not at all Tory. Reading between the lines of the Berrows' report, it seems that Pakington was behind it on behalf of the Tory party.

The dissolution duly occurred in August 1834 and eventually a new parliament was called for 15th February 1835. Berrows continues:

> In due time, there being, as he supposed, no necessity for hurry, Mr Hodgetts-Foley drove over to Droitwich. The first thing he did was to ride out to Westwood Park, to pay his respects to one of his most influential constituents, Capt. Pakington. The Captain was not at home, but Mrs Pakington was. Now Mrs Pakington was, in every way, a charming woman, and Mr Hodgetts-Foley could not resist the pleasure of spending half an hour with her until Capt. Pakington came back. The half hour, amid Mrs Pakington's fascinations, extended itself to an hour, then two, then three, and finally half the day, and into the evening. It was dark ere Mr Hodgetts-Foley found himself on his way back. As he rode into Droitwich he heard an unusual tumult – music, huzzaing, and an uproar. The first thing he heard when he alighted was that Capt. Pakington and Mr John Barneby from Brockhampton House had been canvassing the town all day, and that Mr Barneby was to stand for the borough upon the 'requisition' which had been signed by so many voters! Mr Hodgetts-Foley appeared thunder struck! However he set to work to redeem lost time. He found that he had everything to do. There was no organisation or committee...

*Prestwood Hall, Kingswinford, the seat of John Hodgetts Hodgetts-Foley (1797-1861). He was the grandson of Thomas Foley, 1st Baron Foley of Kidderminster and of Witley Court, and a cousin of the 3rd Baron, who had died in 1833.*

Hodgetts-Foley did not even know the extent of the constituency, and when he looked into it found that the majority were not, as of old, the burgesses and salt makers of Droitwich, but the tenants of Pakington and others in the surrounding villages. Hodgetts-Foley did not know any of them by name, whereas Pakington 'knew every one of them, their wives and children, ducks and chickens, and all about their rents and leases'. Hodgetts-Foley found himself unpopular as well as his agent. He also saw that the Tories were treating the signatories on the document as pledges, and calling on the subscribers to redeem them.

At this point another disaster befell Hodgetts-Foley – his agent left. But, said Berrows, this galvanised Foley and his friends to new action. The departure of his agent was regarded by some as a good thing, and they also found that Barneby was a 'rank old Tory', not popular in the town. So Droitwich itself voted for Hodgetts-Foley, but the surrounding countryside was more Tory inclined, and it was evident that the result was going to be very close. When the result was declared, Barneby won by 128 votes to 125, and the Tories duly celebrated with a dinner at The Barley Mow, Droitwich, on 6th February, at which Pakington spoke. But Hodgetts-Foley did not give up, and petitioned parliament on the basis not only that some of the votes for Barneby were ineligible, but that the voters' register was incorrect in a number of respects. Possibly Hodgetts-Foley simply wanted to cause Barneby inconvenience, as Barneby had already spent a large amount on the election, and was now faced with the expense of defending an election petition.

The petition was heard by a committee of MPs which sat for seven days, concluding on 1st April. Each side was represented by two counsel, and fifty witnesses were brought from Droitwich to the Commons' hearings. Various small alterations were made on behalf of Foley, which brought the result to a tie. Then the committee heard the case for Barneby. The first vote he objected to was that of Viscount Southwell, who was an Irish peer which Barneby claimed made him ineligible to vote. The committee deliberated over this for some time, and eventually decided against the vote, restoring Barneby's majority of one. As there was no point in hearing any more of Barneby's objections the committee declared Barneby duly elected, but ruled that as the petition had not been vexatious each side must pay its own costs, which were estimated at the large sum of £600 each.

After the election Hodgetts-Foley let it be known that he was never again going to stand for Droitwich, a constituency he had represented for five successive parliaments. Soon after, all the Foley property in Worcestershire was sold to Lord Ward, although Hodgetts-Foley continued to live at Prestwood Park.

Some time after the 1835 election it must have been decided that John Barneby would contest east Worcestershire at the next election. In 1835 two Whigs had been elected, Thomas Cookes and Edward Holland, and the Tories obviously fancied their chances of overturning this Whig monopoly. Barneby, who was supposed to be very wealthy, was probably regarded as a good contender for a county seat, which was expensive to contest. In the event, Barneby was elected at the next election as well as another Tory, Horace St Paul, and it was not till 1847 that the Whigs regained representation when Hodgetts-Foley was elected.

On 28th January 1836 Pakington wrote to John Howard Galton of Hadzor that he had heard that Galton would be coming forward to contest Droitwich on behalf of the Whigs at the next election, and that he would like to inform Galton confidentially that he also proposed to contest Droitwich for the Tories, as Barneby was transferring to east Worcestershire. Pakington had heard that Galton was already actually canvassing, even though it was only a year since the last election – the government's position must have seemed precarious, and an early election possible. Not for the first time Pakington wrote that 'I need not say that I fully recognise the right of every independent gentleman to seek the representation of any place he pleases', but although he professes amity to his friend and neighbour, there can be little doubt that he was hoping to deter Galton from standing.

In the event no election was held before King William IV died on 19th June 1837, when, following the practice of the time, parliament was dissolved. Pakington was in France when the King died, and he returned a week later, just in time to start his election campaign, although quarter sessions at the beginning of July intervened again. His letter announcing his campaign appeared in Berrows on 29th June, and on the same day an address appeared from John Howard Galton announcing that he would also be a candidate. This was the first and last time that Galton appeared on the hustings. Unlike Pakington, the Galtons' connection with the district only went back about ten years – they came from the Black Country, where they had made their fortune in the gun manufacturing company of Farmer & Galton. Galton made it clear that he would be standing as a supporter of Lord Melbourne in the Whig interest, and his opponent that he would be on the opposite side.

Nomination day was Tuesday 24th July, and the big news was that Galton, having taken a canvass of the relatively small electorate, had decided to withdraw, leaving Pakington unopposed. Berrows reported:

> The borough, from an early hour in the morning, was the scene of much animation and gaiety, and at about 11 o'clock, Mr Pakington arrived at the court house accompanied by a long train of electors and friends, the cavalcade being preceded by a band, with flags, streamers, etc. The writ having been read, and the mayor sworn to make a faithful return thereto an adjournment took place from the court-house to a specialist hustings erected in a field adjoining to the town. Here, as soon as the mayor had taken his station, and order was restored, the business of the day was further proceeded with. The act against bribery and corruption was read, and at its conclusion the mayor thrice demanded of the electors whom they would have to represent them in Parliament. Cries of "Pakington, Pakington" mingled with vehement cheering, immediately resounded from the assembled throng...

Pakington still had to be nominated and seconded, and his friend W. H. Ricketts performed the former duty. We are in a crisis, he said, and "the period has arrived in which either monarchy or democracy must prevail; in which the constitution must be preserved, or a revolution will ensue." After these dramatic words he praised Mr Galton for his "honourable conduct" in withdrawing, and said he was sure Pakington, when elected, would prove himself a firm supporter of church and state, and to be "a staunch advocate of the local interests of the Borough of Droitwich".

After John Tolley had seconded him, John Pakington gave his address. Unusually, Berrows did not give a full report on account of its length, but nevertheless gave a lengthy summary. He again praised Galton for taking the honourable course, and said that while he was a Conservative, he was no ultra-Tory. He was against Lord Melbourne's government on account of both its ministers, its supporters, and the measures it had tried to adopt. "During the late sessions had it not been attempted to remove the bishops from the House of Lords? – to produce an organic change in the House of Lords itself – to alter the law of primogeniture – and just before the close of the session notice of motion was given to alter the accession to the throne?". At the late Westminster election, several members of the government had actually voted in favour of Mr Leader, "an avowed republican." He would oppose the attempt to appropriate church property for secular purposes, and was against any reform in Ireland that would "raise the Catholics and oppress the Protestants". As to the proposal for the commutation of church rates, he was in favour of toleration of dissenters (who still had to pay church rates) but saw no justice in their claim not to pay church rates. Everyone who bought property knew what payments were attached to it, and if this principle were acceded to, who knew where it might end – even the payment of tithes might be objected to by dissenters!

After referring briefly to foreign policy, he mentioned the unpopular malt tax, but said he would only be in favour of its repeal if sufficient revenue could be found from elsewhere to replace it. Then he mentioned the proposals for a secret ballot. He was all in favour of getting rid of bribery and intimidation at elections, indeed if this was done the Conservatives would probably be the gainers. "There is not only the intimidations of the landlord, but there will also the intimidation of the 'mob'". He therefore publicly declared that "no tenant of mine who thinks it proper to vote against me should on that account leave his farm or suffer in any way"; but a secret ballot was not the answer. "There is also a second objection; I will never consent that the important public function, the exercise of the right of suffrage, should be discharged in secret." (Loud cheers.) "If I am sent to parliament, the electors would want to know, and that very properly, how I record my votes, and so, by parity of reasoning, the non-electors have a right to know how the electors voted", he argued. Ironically, the introduction of the secret ballot in 1874 coincided with the end of Pakington's parliamentary career.

He then mentioned what was to become a favourite topic of his, the need for popular education for the poor. After his experiences at quarter sessions, he had seen so often how "ignorance is the parent of crime", the answer to which had to be a national education scheme. Another of Pakington's special interests was the Poor Law, and he had recently become the chairman of the Droitwich Union, and his comments about workhouses are recorded in the last chapter.

After these more liberal comments on the poor, Pakington finished his speech, and 'preceded by the band, flags, etc, formed a procession round the town amidst the hearty cheers of his partisans. They then returned to the George Hotel, where a large party sat down to a cold collation which had been prepared for the occasion.'

Thus began Pakington's parliamentary career. If The Times is to be believed, it promised well. Summing up the House of Commons on August 14th, a correspondent wrote that the Tories, in addition to their well-known leaders, now had younger men such as Disraeli and Pakington to add to their strength. If Pakington did not have the same glittering success as Disraeli, he fairly quickly started to make a mark.

*Westwood House, from an engraving of 1847, courtesy of the Worcestershire County Record Office. The unusual wings projecting from the four corners are in the same style as the original building, which was built in about 1610, but were clearly added later. They may date from the 1660s after the original manor house at Hampton Lovett had been destroyed in the civil war, and the Restoration had revived the family fortunes.*

**Westwood House**

Not long after becoming an MP, Pakington turned his attention again to Westwood. It is not clear when he and Mary moved into Westwood. After Sir John died in 1830 his sister spent some time there, and it is conceivable that the Pakingtons remained in High Park pending the major repairs that had to be done at Westwood – although their household was there by the time of the 1841 census. At that particular time Mary and Johnny were staying with Pakington's aunt at Hampton Court, and Pakington, who does not appear on the census, must have been away somewhere, but it is interesting to see the size of the establishment at Westwood. There were ten domestic servants living in, five male and five female. The census does not give the particular stations of the servants, but some, including a lady's maid and possibly Pakington's man-servant, would have been missing as the master and mistress were away, so it can be seen that it was a large establishment. In addition there were two game keepers, one at the Lower Lodge and one in the Keepers Lodge, so Pakington did not stint in this direction either.

Although he does not seem to have gone ahead with the new stables proposed by Phillip Hardwick in 1831, he had kept up his connection with the architect, and in

*The lower hall in 1928. Reproduced by courtesy of Country Life.*

the summer of 1837 asked him to propose some major improvements to the house, which Hardwick in a letter described as 'so old and in such bad condition'. Some correspondence survives from Hardwick, and it seems that he was mainly concerned with the first and second floor halls, and the main staircase. In Hardwick's first letter, dated September 5th, he described what he proposed, starting with the hall ceiling, which will consist of ribs and bosses. This was presumably the ground floor hall, in which the present ceiling consists of strapwork which might represent the ribs, but there are no bosses. The Victoria County History states that Hardwick's drawings were in the possession of the then owner, Edward Partington JP, in 1913, but sadly they seem to have been lost since.

Hardwick briefly mentioned the proposed chimney piece which would be of stone with the coat of arms and crest – this is probably still there, although now concealed. He proposed that the walls of the hall above the wainscoting should be stuccoed and jointed in imitation of stone, and the large windows restored. The staircase leading up to the grand hall would have a new ceiling which would be made and painted in an imitation of an oak 'like one of the old roofs', and the walls painted to look like stone. The ceiling at each end of the gallery would be arched, which would allow the architect to insert iron ties to strengthen the walls, which were 'extremely weak' through their great height, and which had one 'great fracture'.

The other big alteration was the addition of extra offices on the north west side of the building. Lack of space for domestic offices was a common problem facing owners of country houses in the nineteenth century, and the additions made here would provide valuable extra space.

By early October Hardwick had obtained estimates for the various parts of the work. These were: repairs to the hall including new windows at the front and the ends, and repairing the porch, with a new vault under the grand hall to strengthen it and new oak wainscoting: £1,480. The remodelled staircase with oak wainscoting (Pakington seems to have rejected Hardwick's earlier suggestion of painted deal) including new iron

*The staircase in 1928, reproduced by courtesy of Country Life*

ties for strengthening £1,754; and the addition of major new space for offices at the rear £2,500, totalling about £5,750. Hardwick was quick to point out that estimates on such a building can be difficult, but suggested that under a good clerk of the works savings might be made.

*The grand first floor hall, reproduced by courtesy of Country Life. The decorative ceiling was probably added in the 1660s at the same time as the four projecting wings. The frieze below the ceiling, painted dark, is from the original building.*

It is evident that work started quite quickly, as the bill from the clerk of the works (James Sharpe) for work starting in late October exists, as does a letter from Hardwick dated 27th December, reporting a discussion he had had with Sharpe. Evidently their main concern was the strength of the whole structure, the building being so tall and in brick with the large internal halls leading to weakness. So Hardwick supported Sharpe's proposal 'to arch the centre part of the house under the staircase'. Work continued in 1838, and it looks as if it had been finished by September, just a year after the start. We do not know what the final cost was, but there is no reason to think it was very different from Hardwick's earlier estimate. But we do know that in January 1838 John Pakington took out a £17,000 mortgage, presumably at least in part to finance these works. There is no evidence of any other major expenditure at this time, so perhaps the balance over and above what was required for the Westwood alterations was used to pay off other mortgages. But Pakington's expenditure was not decreasing. Now he was an MP, and an active one at that, he had additional expenditure having to be in London for most of the parliamentary session, with even more journeys back and forth to Droitwich. And although he was to remain unchallenged as the Droitwich MP for a long time, elections still cost money, with a considerable amount of entertaining and canvassing of his supporters to make sure there was no opening for a Whig to exploit. So Pakington may have used some of this loan to bolster his bank account, but of course such action in the long term can only make matters worse by charging his income with the extra expense of the mortgage interest.

## Chapter 8
## Backbencher 1837-1841

So John Pakington had been successful in getting into parliament, but as always there was a price to pay. Elections were expensive, ruinously so in some cases. Lord Ashley, the future Earl of Shaftsbury, in contesting Dorset in 1830, spent the enormous sum of £15,000, most of it on entertaining, and although he received some help he was left with a debt that was to hang over him for a long time. Although no accounts have come down to us, we can be sure that Pakington's three unsuccessful attempts at a county seat as well as his victory in 1837 cost a great deal of money. In 1832, when he first stood as a Tory, he noted in his diary that on November 21st he had a meeting of his political friends when perhaps there was a doubt about continuing, and that £3,000 had already been subscribed. So clearly some of the costs were met by Tory voters throughout the county, but Pakington himself must have borne much of the expense. Contesting the small borough of Droitwich would have cost a great deal less than contesting a county seat, and a letter from his agents, the brothers Thomas and John Curtler, still exists. John Curtler was a solicitor practising in Droitwich, and probably took the main burden of election work. His brother Thomas Gale Curtler lived in the large Bevere House outside Worcester (once the home of Worcestershire historian Treadway Nash) and was a magistrate and vice chairman of quarter sessions under Pakington's later chairmanship.

Thomas Curtler's letter begins: 'Herewith you receive the election bills and a list of them. I much regret that they amount to so much.' Unfortunately the list no longer exists so we do not know how much they amounted to, and then Curtler goes on to refer to the expenses of registration. Under the 1832 act voters had to be preregistered for the first time (a system that still exists) and there was a small charge for so doing. Much of the work of the candidate and his agent was to ensure that all likely supporting voters were properly registered. Curtler proposed charging the modest sum of £36 to cover out of pocket expenses only for work in registering voters, and in addition £100 as a charge to cover all the rest of the time they had spent in Pakington's support – after all, they were not only his friends, but supporters of the Tory cause. Clearly this was much less than a proper professional charge might have been, and Pakington wrote back saying how grateful he was for this generous gesture. He wished the charge of £100 to cover registration, and for them to make a proper charge for their help at the election. Family tradition is that John Somerset Pakington became something of a spendthrift after he inherited in 1830, and certainly the expenses of three contested county elections plus the one at Droitwich must have been very great. He would have had difficulty meeting these out of his income.

Being an MP also led to expense, both travelling to and living in London. Prior to the railway age, travelling to London would have been slow and uncomfortable, but the opening of the London to Birmingham railway in September 1838 would have made it possible to make the journey in one day. After the opening of the Droitwich Road station on the Birmingham to Gloucester railway in 1841 the journey would have been even easier, but it was not until 1852 that the direct route from Droitwich and Worcester to London was opened. Then there was the considerable expense of maintaining a London home, although in 1837 Pakington was using his aunt's house in Green Street, Mayfair, which she kept as well as one at Hampton Court, as his London base. From a letter from his aunt dated December 1837 we learn that Pakington had asked her to find him a London house so Mary could join him there, and that she was having difficulties in finding one that met his conditions. Probably he had specified a maximum rent, proximity to Westminster and so on, and as far as is known he continued to use Green Street for some years afterwards.

The general election results of 1837 followed the recent trend with the Tories further strengthening their parliamentary representation, but the Whigs still retained an overall majority of 32. This included the uncertain support of the Irish MPs, and there were plenty of issues on which both parties could be divided. In addition, of course, the House of Lords had a built-in Tory majority, so in practice the Whig government, under Viscount Melbourne in the Lords and Lord John Russell in the Commons, was often dependent on Tory support in passing measures, and the period was dubbed as 'government by opposition'. Peel was the undisputed Tory leader in the Commons, and the Duke of Wellington in the Lords.

What was the Palace of Westminster like in 1837? A severe fire had raged through all the southern part of the site on 16th October 1834 and wrought much destruction, but mercifully saved the medieval Westminster Hall. Both the House of Commons chamber in St Stephens Chapel and the House of Lords had been ruined. Some suggested the new palace should not be in Westminster at all but near St James where many MPs lived and had their clubs, but eventually it was decided to rebuild on the existing site, retaining Westminster Hall, and a competition was held in 1835 for a new design. This had to be in the Gothic or Elizabethan styles (it was felt that a classical design would clash with Westminster Abbey), and by the judges' unanimous decision the designs of 40 year old Charles Barry were chosen. Then followed considerable delays, firstly because there was a campaign to overturn the judges' decision, and secondly while parliamentary committees considered the details of the design, and asked Barry to do some considerable modifications. So when Pakington first entered the Palace as an MP a start had not been made on any new work, and both the Lords and Commons were meeting in temporary accommodation. In fact it was not until 1840 that Mrs Barry laid the foundation stone, and the 1850s when the new chambers were complete. When Barry died in 1860 the Palace was by no means complete, and his son Edward continued as architect for a period till 1870, when it was at last largely finished as we see it today.

The new parliament first met on 15th November to choose a speaker. We can assume Pakington was there from the beginning, as his name appears in all the early divisions. The first of these was on 20th November when the house divided after a debate on the Queen's speech. A motion was proposed that the House would undertake further reform of the elective franchise in the present session. Needless to say, Pakington was amongst the 509 members who opposed it.

Among the earliest and most important matters to come before the House of Commons concerned Canada. Canada had originally been mainly settled by the French and was known as New France; but the Treaty of Paris in 1763 ceded most of New France to Britain, and Canada remained thereafter a British colony. In what became known as Upper Canada, the future Ontario, there was continuing British settlement, which was boosted after American independence when 50,000 people migrated there, preferring to remain under British rule. This led in 1791 to the partition of Canada – Lower Canada, roughly the present province of Quebec, was separated from Upper Canada. The former was predominantly French, the latter British. Each province was given an elected legislative assembly, and an appointed legislative council under a governor. Power mostly lay

*The temporary House of Commons chamber in 1835. This was fitted up in the old House of Lords, which moved to the painted chamber.*

with the council, and this led to trouble in Lower Canada, where the assembly demanded more control over spending and eventually refused to act unless its demands were agreed to. This crisis eventually led to armed revolt in 1837, and the government in London proposed to suspend the constitution and impose direct rule until matters could be sorted out. This was the proposal before the House of Commons in January 1838, and it had already been debated for four days when on January 22nd a petition from John Arthur Roebuck was presented to the House. Roebuck, a radical who had lived in Canada but was now an English barrister and, until loosing his seat in 1837, MP for Bath, had been appointed an agent for the legislative assembly of Lower Canada. He prayed the house to be allowed to address it on behalf of the assembly. This was agreed to, and Roebuck then spoke from the bar about the history of the dispute, and claimed that every worsening of the crisis was due to the mishandling of matters by the British government. The assembly had always acted reasonably.

After Roebuck had finished he withdrew and the debate continued. It was as the last speaker of the evening that Pakington rose to make his maiden speech. It had clearly been planned in advance, as his friend Hallifax was in the gallery. Speaking initially about the bill, he took a not very clear line saying that law and order must be upheld, and the interests of the British minority in Lower Canada protected. He also took the Tory party line that the troubles could be blamed on the mal-administration of the Whig government. But then he entered on the subject that was the real reason for his contribution, namely the protestant church in Lower Canada, a subject that he was to come back to on a number of occasions.

What led to Pakington's visit to the America in 1833 is not known. It was probably from general curiosity, but it is known that on his outward passage he met Rev. Robert Cartwright. The Cartwrights were a prominent family from Kingston, Ontario, and although Rev. Cartwright himself was to die young, his son Sir Richard

*John Arthur Roebuck, 1802-79. He had been brought up in Canada, and back in Britain he became a QC and MP, usually opposing the government of the day. His demand for an enquiry into the Crimean War helped destroy Aberdeen's government in 1855.*

Cartwright, and his wife Harriet née Dobbs, became well-known members of Canadian society. The Cartwrights were a loyalist and religious family, and in 1835 Rev. Cartwright wrote to Pakington appealing for a donation towards the expense of a Protestant missionary who had recently been appointed to serve the scattered and remote settlements of the province. Pakington probably visited the Cartwrights while in Canada, and there may have been more correspondence about Protestant affairs there, which led to Pakington's maiden speech in the House of Commons.

His particular complaint was that the government seemed to have decided against, or, as Pakington hoped, was merely hesitating over, the renewal of financial support to the Bishop of Quebec. He had been told by the Society for the Propagation of the Gospel that it was proposed to amalgamate this diocese with that of Montreal after the death of the present Bishop who was in poor health. He wished the government to understand that the "thousands" of British immigrants going to Canada every day, most of whom were Anglicans, expected the protection of the British constitution to extend to their new home. This included the very important matter of religion and religious education.

Thus Pakington made his first plea for the support of the protestant church in Canada during a debate that was really on another subject. Soon afterwards he received a letter from a friend, W. S. Gelly, congratulating him on his maiden speech – 'Go on thus, my friend, fear God and fire low, never speak but when you are sure to hit them, and your senatorial reputation will be established!'. His wife Mary wrote 'I do rejoice, my dearest love, most affectionately and sincerely at the complete success of your debut in the House of Commons, & I also unite with you in your feeling of gratitude for having been able to start yourself so well...'. Berrows commented that 'a speech more truly British has not been delivered on the subject of Canadian grievances... His remarks on the government scheme of conciliation were just and forcible and were repeatedly cheered by the opposition benches: no less admirable were his cutting taunts on the reluctance of ministers to take at the proper time those decisive steps against the disaffected which would have prevented the open rebellion which now assumes so formidable a front'.

Records show that Pakington was a regular attender and voter in the House during this period, and, reading through contemporary debates, one that catches the eye was on 15th February on the ballot. This was a proposal by the well-known radical George Grote to introduce the [secret] 'ballot'. The arguments in favour were seemingly over-whelming. Everyone admitted that corruption and intimidation at elections was getting worse rather than better despite laws against it, and as long as everyone knew how people voted this would seem likely to be difficult to eradicate. Landlords exerting influence over their tenants was the most extensive abuse, but there were other ways in which votes could be influenced or even bought, and it seemed logical that only if votes were cast in secret could this be effectively prevented.

But both Lord John Russell for the Whigs and Sir Robert Peel for the Tories argued strongly against the ballot, and it is interesting to read now the arguments they used. Peel, in particular was quite precise: firstly, he said,

> It is a system totally at variance with all the institutions, usages, and feelings of the people of this country, with all the maxims which have taught them to believe that free discussion, that publicity, that the light of day, that public opinion, are the great checks upon abuse. The people have been habituated to canvassing at elections, to the solicitation of promises, to all the activity and all the artifices, by which, at a contested election, one party seeks to gain a superiority over another. Every voter's inclinations and intentions are known; there is no neutrality, scarcely an instance in which a vote is reserved until the day of election. This may be right, or it may be wrong; but it is the inveterate usage of the country, and all this you hope to counteract by a small piece of cunning machinery, the ballot box.

Secondly, Peel continued, the success of the secret ballot depended on the mechanics of the system working correctly so as to keep votes secret, and he doubted this would be the case. And what would happen to canvassing, during which votes were solicited and promises made? Would it be banned? If not it would induce people to make false promises and turn us into a nation of hypocrites. Yes, he accepted that the system was used in America. Whether it was successful there he did not know, but America was different. They wrote their constitution on a clean slate, and the voter was not used to a poll, whereas the British voter had voted in the present way for hundreds of years, and did not want his habits to be upset by these radical proposals.

To us such arguments seem reactionary in the extreme, but the House of Commons was not ready for another major change in the electoral system only five years after the Great Reform Act, and voted against the motion by more than two to one. Pakington had referred to this subject at his nomination, and, needless to say, joined the majority. Nevertheless nearly 200 MPs voted in favour of the secret ballot, but it was to be almost another forty years until it was introduced.

It was another month before Pakington again addressed the House of Commons. This was on the subject of county coroners, and he sought leave on 20th March to bring in a private members bill. As chairman of quarter sessions, he would have been familiar with the matters dealt with in his bill, although quite why he choose this particular topic is not known. At that time the ancient office of coroner was more important than it is today, and from ancient times they had been elected by all freeholders in the county. These elections, involving more people than the more restricted parliamentary franchise, involved those taking part in great trouble and expense, and Pakington thought it would be for the general good to reform this principle. It would be possible to restrict the electorate in some way, but he felt that doing away with elections altogether was best. In their place he would propose in his bill that magistrates in quarter sessions appoint coroners. The Municipal Reform Act had allowed coroners in towns to be appointed by the town councils, and as there were as yet no county councils, his proposal seemed the next best thing. In addition, his bill would propose various reforms to the office, including increasing their remuneration.

His motion was seconded by Joseph Cripps, who had also tried to bring in bills on the same subject. He wished the hon. member for Droitwich better luck than he had had, although he could not agree that magistrates appointing coroners was a good idea. There was a short debate in which not a single member agreed with Pakington's main proposal, and finally Lord John Russell wound up the debate. While he would have no objection to a bill to achieve some of the reforms that Pakington's bill would propose, this would be better coming from the government, and he certainly could not agree with the proposal that magistrates appoint coroners. For that reason "he would give his negative to the motion". At that, Pakington could see there was no chance of his bill becoming law, and withdrew it.

Just a week after this, Pakington was asked to join his first select committee. In fact the committee had been instituted at the beginning of parliament the previous November, but one of the members, Sir Eardly Wilmot, had had to withdraw. Pakington was appointed in his place – the fact that his friend John Barneby was a member may have helped. Much of the work of the House of Commons is done, of course, by select committees rather than in the House itself, and at any one time there were several committees enquiring into all manner of matters. The usual procedure was for committees to meet around midday and sit during the afternoon, prior to the House sitting, which usually started at 5.00 p.m. Sometimes committees sat for quite short periods before producing a report; other committees sat over several sessions, and produced a number of interim reports. The reports were usually quite short and to the point. The evidence taken at committee sessions and the debates in the committee itself were reported in full and formed part of the report, and this part could be very long. This first committee that Pakington served on was charged with investigating the working of the Highways Act 1835. Parishes were still responsible for the maintenance of highways in their districts, and this act authorised them to combine in the interests of efficiency. But it had not so far been very successful, and the state of the highways was, as ever, a great cause for concern and nuisance.

The committee's report was published in June 1838, and its main recommendation was that the parish unions, created under the Poor Law Amendment Act, should in addition be responsible for maintaining highways in their area, and should be empowered to charge an extra rate for so doing. They also recommended the appointment of paid road surveyors. A bill was introduced, but amended to create separate boards within each union to take charge of highways as boards of guardians were considered to have a wide enough range of responsibilities already. But many MPs thought this would lead to much higher rates, and in the end nothing of any importance was passed.

A subject that caused a great deal of controversy in the 1830s, and indeed for many years after, and about which Pakington felt strongly, was the Sale of Beer Act 1830. Prior to this act, alcoholic drinks could only be sold on premises licensed by the magistrates (as indeed is the case today), but this was a system that it was felt led to an artificial restriction and high prices. Magistrates were said to be in collusion with the big brewers, and the monopoly this produced led to high beer prices. The Sale of Beer Act, introduced by a Tory government as a gesture to increase their popularity with the labouring classes, passed with only 29 votes against it, and was generally welcomed at the time. The act allowed anyone on payment of two guineas for a license (from excise officers, not magistrates) to brew and sell beer on their own premises, the only restriction being that they should close at 10.00 p.m. In addition the act reduced the duty on beer, causing a significant drop in price, which, together with the much greater competition in the sale of beer, caused a 'pot' to be reduced in price from three or four pence previously to about a penny ha'penny. Apart from the obvious benefit to the poorer classes of being able to buy beer more cheaply, beer was regarded as a wholesome drink without the evils attached to gin and other spirits, and it should be remembered that at that time most drinking water was polluted and liable to carry disease.

Immediately on the passing of the Sale of Beer Act, beer houses sprung up everywhere, and within six months 24,000 licenses had been purchased, and later in the decade the number of beer houses approached that of the 56,000 licensed premises. Almost immediately, the Act was blamed for what was perceived to be an increase in working class drunkenness, and the controversy continued on and off till beer houses were brought back under the control of magistrates in 1870. This is not the place to debate the rights and wrongs of the issue – the British have always been perceived as a drunken nation – when it was said that Britain was characterised by beef and beer, one wag asked "why bother about the beef?!". The 1820s had seen a great increase in gin drinking, helped by a large reduction in the duty on spirits in 1825, whereas the consumption of beer had remained static; after the Sale of Beer Act the consumption of beer increased considerably. It certainly seems true that there was an increase in drunkenness in the early 1830s, judging at least by the figures for the arrest of drunks in London, but thereafter arrests declined considerably. It was probably the case that the novelty of the much greater availability of cheap beer did lead to more excessive consumption, but then a new stability was reached.

Another effect of the Sale of Beer Act was to emphasize class distinctions. Beer houses came to be seen as very much a working class institution, and no middle or upper class man (let alone woman) would be seen dead in them. A further effect was that public houses, often referred to as 'gin palaces' had to smarten themselves up and make themselves more attractive in the face of the new competition, and this, it was alleged, further increased the consumption of alcohol. In parliamentary debates the evils of beer houses were said to be that they were dens of iniquity and a breeding ground for crime; outside parliament it was the way they drained the small wages of labourers, leaving little or nothing for his family, and leading to a general increase in poverty, that was thought, with at least some truth, to be their greatest evil.

In the early 1830s the matter was considered again by parliamentary committees, and in 1834 the Act had been strengthened by the increase in the license fee to three guineas and the requirement for the licensee to obtain a certificate of good character signed by six rate-payers. Another important change was the division of beer houses into two sorts: those restricted to the 'take-away' trade, and those allowing consumption inside, although the necessary notice confirming that beer could be 'Drunk on the Premises' led to many ribald jokes.

The matter was raised again in the House of Commons on 10th July 1838 by Lord Egerton, who used strong language to oppose beer houses. His opinion was that the class of houses which allowed consumption on the premises should be banned; "I am now quite satisfied that the introduction of beer shops has been productive of consequences bad in every respect among the working classes, destructive of their habits of foresight and economy, subversive of moral feeling, and ruinous, in many instances, to their families". But the government view was put by the chancellor of the exchequer, Thomas Spring Rice, who did not agree at all with Egerton, and said the Act had been 'wise and prudent'. An alteration of the present law would not, he believed, bring about the improvement in the morals of the population that Egerton believed, and he said any discussion should be based on sound facts and figures, not the hearsay and prejudice that some opponents of the Act used. It was when the Chancellor sat down that Pakington rose to make what must have been his briefest parliamentary speech ever: "I am grateful to the noble Lord [Egerton] for having brought this subject forward. It is almost impossible to over-rate the seriously prejudicial effect which this measure has had upon the morals of the people." This was a subject that

*'Drunk on the Premises' from George Cruickshank's 'Four Hundred Humerous Illustrations'.*

he was return to more than once, and indeed had led a move by the Worcestershire quarter sessions in 1831 to petition parliament for total repeal of the Sale of Beer Act, and this contribution summed up his views.

But opinion was very divided on the subject, and after Pakington two MPs spoke who had similar views: the first, Joseph Hume, objected to

> meddling interferences with the comforts of the poor. I do not understand why the poor man should not be allowed to drink his pot of beer where and when he choses, and where he can get it best and cheapest, whether within the doors of a beer shop or in the street. It is melancholy to see those who are in possession of the highest luxuries so anxious to deprive the poor of every little comfort.

And Henry Warburton asked, tongue in cheek, whether any enquiry should not look into places of entertainment generally, rather than just beer houses: "No doubt their report would be, that at clubs and such places there is much drinking of champagne and other wines, that people spend time there which they had much better spend elsewhere, that there is not a little gambling, &c"! The matter was left that certain documents should be tabled for MP's benefit, but any change in the law would have to wait until the next session.

On 22nd July the question of the church in Canada came up again, when the government asked for a motion of supply (i.e. permission to spend) for £11,790 on the ecclesiastical establishment in Canada. First to speak was Pakington, who complained that the sum was totally insufficient – "the government have encouraged English, Scotch, and Irish subjects to emigrate to the forests of Canada, and they should take care to provide them with that greatest of blessings – Christian instruction". He again objected to the combination of the bishoprics of Quebec and Montreal. But in the short debate that followed, most speakers did not agree. The most often voiced opinion was that encouraging the Church of England as against other sects could lead to similar evils as the establishment of the Anglican church in Ireland. Surely it was better to let the settlers come to their own arrangements about religion, and the way it was financed.

As we have no diary for this period, Pakington's private life can only occasionally be glimpsed. At the end of December 1838 he attended a meeting to discuss the 1839 Worcester Music Festival, chaired by the Bishop. The Festival had long been in financial difficulties, with falling receipts and, according to its critics, too many highly paid star soloists. The stewards had to guarantee £50 towards any loss, and it was now agreed to launch a guarantee fund that could be called upon in the event of the steward's guarantees not being sufficient. The number of stewards was fixed at six, although it was later increased to eight, and Pakington was put in charge of a committee to launch the guarantee fund. By the beginning of February this had reached £640, and Pakington's committee then ceased to function, leaving the management of the Festival to the stewards, of which Pakington was not one in 1839.

Quarter sessions continued as usual, but at the Epiphany sessions starting on 31st December 1838 there was a problem. There was no clerk of the peace, and Lord Foley, who as Lord Lieutenant had the sole power of appointment, was abroad. Having taken legal advice the magistrates decided they had not the power to hold sessions without a clerk. Eventually Lord Foley returned and a clerk was appointed. He was Henry Barry Domvile, who was the son of Pakington's half-sister Mary. Further light is shed on this appointment through a letter that appeared soon after in Berrows, pointing out that the clerk of the peace was a sinecure, for which the rate payers had to find some £500 a year, and in fact the work was done by a deputy. If the deputy was competent, why did we need a highly paid clerk at all?

On January 24th the annual Worcester Glee Club Ball in aid of the dispensary was held, and Pakington was a steward and his wife a patroness. Over 300 persons attended the function in the Guildhall, and £780 was raised for charity. Berrows reported that the event was marred by 'a member of the London swell mob who escaped the vigilance of the police and purchased a ticket and relieved several gentlemen of their purses'! Another Worcester event reported in Berrows was a public meeting to pass various protectionist resolutions. The protectionist Corn Laws were under strong attack by the radicals and the anti-corn law movement, and passions ran high on both sides, something that was to continue without abatement for several years to come. The 'landed interest' greatly feared that parliament would reduce or even abandon the corn laws from the pressure it was under, and meetings such as that held in Worcester on 23rd February 1839 were held throughout the country in an effort to stiffen the government's resistance. A very large crowd gathered for the meeting, and included inevitably what Berrows characterised as 'a few boisterous radicals'. But we can be sure there were more than a few, as their shouts made starting the meeting difficult until, at the suggestion of Pakington, the multitude moved into a larger hall. The usual resolutions in favour of retaining the existing corn laws were passed, and Pakington was the last to speak. In such company he always tried to sound a reasonable man; he had, he said, "read the [abolitionist] statements of Lord Brougham, Mr Villiers and the Manchester Chamber of Commerce and considered them with his fullest attention; but the result is that, connected as I am with the county of Worcestershire, I felt it to be my duty to come down from London to meet you this day, and in a plain, manly, and straightforward way to tell you I am determined to support the principle of the present corn laws." This peroration was greeted by 'great cheering and renewed groans'.

The new session of parliament had begun on 5th February 1839, and a feature of the session was that Pakington presented eighteen petitions. Petitioning parliament (as well as petitioning the monarch) is an ancient right, and until modern times was the only way someone without the vote could have any direct contact with parliament. Various rules were established over time as to the manner of the petition, and it has always been the case that a petition has to be presented to parliament by an MP. Up to the late eighteenth century the number of petitions was fairly moderate, averaging something like one per day when parliament was in session. The petitions were presented by the MP, who either read out the whole petition or at least summarised its points, before the opening of the main business of the House. But in the early nineteenth century the number of petitions started to grow, there being over 17,000 per session in the late 1830s. In 1839 13,657 petitions were presented on 90 different subjects carrying 4.5m signatures. In 1839 the House of Commons only sat on 132 days, so the presentation of petitions risked interfering with the main business of the House, and on a number of occasions MPs considered how best to deal with them. But other than the fact that debate on the issues raised by a petition was strictly banned, no major change was made to the system, which remains essentially the same today.

In 1833 a Committee on Public Petitions was established, which produced regular reports listing all petitions presented, by whom, the number of signatories, and the subject. Although the actual petitions were not kept, specimens were printed in the appendix to the reports. Furthermore the reports kept a running total of the number of signatories to petitions on popular subjects, both for and against, and in this way it was possible to see in which way public opinion was running. It may well have been this latter point that helped make petitioning so popular, as if public opinion was clearly in favour of something, for example the universal penny post that was introduced about this time, its proponents had a big stick to beat the government with.

One of the oddities of the petitioning system is that MPs often presented petitions from people and places with which they had no connection. For example, on March 13th 1839 Pakington presented two petitions on one of his favourite subjects – church extension in Canada. The first one was signed by 26 inhabitants of Astley, a Worcestershire village not far from Droitwich. The second, with 132 signatures, came from the Lincolnshire hamlets of Twyford and Woolsthorpe. It is to be doubted whether the inhabitants of any of those places had much interest in the Episcopalian church in Canada, so one is forced to conclude that Pakington, using whatever methods he could, used the petitioning system to generate as many signatures as possible to support his aim. Before these two petitions, there had already been 2,385 signatures on similar petitions that session. One can imagine how MPs could generate petitions from places near their residence, but, as Pakington had no known connection with distant Lincolnshire, he must have used friends, probably other sympathetic MPs, to produce these petitions. One could argue that all this was something of an abuse of the petitioning system. MPs were using it as a way of furthering their own ends, rather than allowing members of the public to bring a personal or public grievance before the House. But it is also clear that this was not always the case – sometimes corporate bodies or even individuals would petition on matters that were clearly of concern to them, and there are other instances of MPs presenting petitions both for and against a particular topic, although no instance of Pakington doing this has come to light.

So it is clear that the petitioning system was being used by some as a public relations campaign, and the summary of petitions presented in 1839 shows how successful this could be. There were 332 petitions in favour of church extension in Canada and elsewhere carrying a total of 23,826 signatures, and on this subject Pakington was the leading presenter. Repeal of the Corn Laws was a 'hot topic', as it remained into the 1840s, and here the protectionists were on the losing side. Although only 409 petitions were presented for repeal (i.e. for cheaper food), these carried over half a million signatures; there were as many as 3,068 petitions against repeal, but these only carried 318,723 signatures. Small groups of local landowners and farmers would petition against repeal, but there were some large petitions carrying thousands of signatures of workers in the new industrial cities. Pakington only presented one petition (against repeal, naturally) on this subject in 1839, but it was probably demonstrations of public opinion such as this that helped to influence Sir Robert Peel eventually to change his mind on the subject. The year 1839 also saw the largest petitions ever presented, which were those of the Chartists in favour of their aim of universal suffrage. One of these carried over 1.5 million signatures, although it was later claimed that some of these were forgeries. But these Chartist petitions were not able to change the minds of MPs, and it was to be over 50 years before most of their aims were realised.

Another subject that gave rise to great controversy was that of national education. On 12th February 1839 Lord John Russell made a statement to the House about the government's plans for a national scheme. This is a subject that occurs many times in this narrative, and in which Pakington became very interested. As is well known, no universal system of education was introduced into Britain until

*Lord John Russell, as he was known until he was created 1st Earl Russell in 1861. He was a younger son of the 6th Duke of Bedford, and was twice prime minister. He entered the House of Commons in 1813 as a Whig when only 21, and died in 1878.*

Forster's 1870 act, but it was well recognised by all parties that education, particularly of the poorer classes who could not afford to pay, was sadly lacking. The problem that bedevilled all proposals for reform was that of religion. Traditionally, education was the province of the church, and most charitably founded parish schools were attached to the Church of England, indeed right up the present the village school is often to be found adjacent to the parish church. Then in the nineteenth century with increasing freedom of religion Catholics and dissenting Protestants founded their own schools, and yet other schools were founded by societies that believed that education should be non-denominational. Setting up any system of national education against this background was always going to upset one party or another. Countries such as the United States and France had decreed that education should be secular, but such a proposal in Britain was bound to meet opposition from all religious groups, most of which believed that religion should be taught as the foundation of education.

In 1839 it had evidently been rumoured for some time that the government was going to propose a new scheme of education, and as always when rumours abound, all sorts of proposals were said to be under consideration. Accordingly Lord John Russell's statement was designed to outline the government's proposals so as to clear up misunderstandings. Russell outlined the difficulties that attended on the subject, and said that he proposed to appoint a board composed of privy councillors to oversee the development of education and the expenditure of the government grant. This immediately raised all sorts of questions in the House, and the opposition of religious MPs such as the evangelical Lord Ashley (the future Earl of Shaftsbury), who said the scheme "with its privy councillors, its books, its normal schools, and teachers, appears to me to be full of the most alarming mischiefs".

Pakington is not recorded as speaking on that occasion (the debate was brief), but the petitions he presented during the rest of the session all had titles such as 'Petition against any plan of National Education not founded on the Principles of the Established Church', so it is clear which way, at that time at least, his thinking was going. By the end of the 1839 session no less than 3,144 petitions with nearly 400,000 signatures had been presented against the government scheme, with only 104 petitions in favour of it. One has the impression that, unlike the question of corn prices, the ordinary citizen was not so much interested in this subject, and that the opposition to it had been whipped up by those stalwart Anglican churchmen not willing to let education slip from their grasp.

But although he did not take an active part in the parliamentary debate, Pakington did play a prominent part in a Worcester public meeting on 6th April chaired by the Bishop. Its object was the encouragement of extending popular education on the principles of the Church of England, and the first resolution, proposed by Lord Beauchamp and seconded by the Ven. Archdeacon Spooner, was

> that this meeting is strongly impressed with the conviction that the only proper foundation for the education of all classes is religious instruction; that it is highly important that such instruction should be in accordance with the doctrine and discipline of the Church of England and should be afforded as extensively as possible.

Secondly it was proposed that a diocesan board of education should be formed to supervise the widening of religious education, and thirdly that

> it seems desirable that the board should, at the earliest possible period take into consideration, firstly, the propriety and best mode of establishing a [teacher] training school in connection with the diocese; secondly the most effectual way of promoting useful and religious education according to the principles of the Church of England among the middle classes; thirdly to bring all Church of England schools into union with the board; and finally to obtain and circulate accurate information relative to the state of education throughout the diocese.

Pakington proposed this last resolution; the main reason he favoured the extension of popular education was, he said, because uneducated people were much more likely to become criminals. Of the 939 prisoners brought before the magistrates at quarter sessions during an unspecified period only 300 could read and write, and 372 were 'totally ignorant of the common rudiments of education'. Pakington believed that it was through the lack of a moral and religious education that men turned to crime. It followed that education would set them on the straight and narrow, an argument that some may have regarded, even then, as somewhat simplistic. Later, Pakington was to favour a national system of education that catered for all religious sects; but in 1839 he was still strongly in favour of education being based on the principles of the established church, and he criticised the British & Foreign Schools Society as they believed in a more broadly based non-sectarian system of education. He was much more in favour of National Schools, as they based their teaching on the catechism of the Church of England.

Another subject, that has already been mentioned, that Pakington chose for special attention, was to change the Sale of Beer Act of 1830. During 1839 he presented a number of petitions on the subject, starting with one from the Worcestershire quarter sessions, and he also wrote asking the chairmen of other county sessions to do the same. By the end of the session the number of signatures supporting change was only a little larger than the number against it; but again it is noticeable that those against change submitted fewer but larger petitions than those in favour of it, which mainly took the form of petitions signed by a small number of local dignitaries.

As well as presenting petitions, on 5th March 1839 Pakington sought leave to introduce a private member's bill to amend the Sale of Beer Act. Why he should have felt so strongly about this particular subject is not certain, as he had already mentioned the subject in campaigning, and it should be remembered that John Phillips, when seconding him at the 1832 election and who may have been a financial backer of Pakington, had mentioned the importance of reform to the 1830 Act. Another Worcestershire MP, Henry Lygon, introduced a petition in favour of reform to the House, and it was certainly a subject that gave rise to strong passions on both sides.

In introducing his bill to the House, Pakington said that what he proposed was a very moderate reform. He realised that other proposals, for example to prohibit the consumption of beer on the premises, stood little chance of success. He proposed an increase in the minimum rateable value of premises that could be given a licence, and a new residential qualification that would restrict licenses to those who had been in occupation of the premises for twelve months. From the Whig front bench, the chancellor of the exchequer, Thomas Spring Rice, said the government had already made its feelings known in answer to a more radical bill to be introduced in the House of Lords. The government were opposed to any general repeal of the Beer Act, and felt that any change in the rules for licensees should apply both to premises licenced by magistrates and to beer shops, as it would be wrong to discriminate against the latter. He stressed that the interests of up to 50,000 people, who had invested capital in beer shops, had to be taken into account, and he felt any change in the law should be considered most carefully and dispassionately.

The motion to introduce a bill was passed, and Pakington's bill accordingly given a first reading two days later, and on 20th March he rose to propose its second reading. He asked members to recollect that when the Sale of Beer Act had been debated in 1830 opponents had predicted it would have a most prejudicial and dangerous effect on the morals of the people. Not only had the predictions become true, he said, but the Act, "instead of conducing to the comfort of the labouring classes, only pandered to their vices". After the passing of the Act, a committee of the House had been set up to investigate complaints, and a new Act passed to tighten up the rules, but that, Pakington said, had proved a "complete nullity". He realised that it would be said that the interests of existing beer house owners should have their investment protected, but his bill did that, and also "the House will hear, no doubt, of the necessity for free trade in an article so essential to the poorer classes as beer, and of all the monopolies which previously existed. But all this must give way before the paramount consideration of the demoralising tendency of the Sale of Beer Act".

Pakington referred to various statements by medical practitioners and magistrates about the evil effects of beer shops, and "I would call the attention of the House to the case of several persons who have been executed. The two who were executed in Cambridgeshire for the murder of Lord Hardwicke's keeper, in the last moments of their existence, attributed their crimes to the associates they had picked up in beer-shops. The same was said by two men who were executed in Somerset". After this rather macabre evidence, he explained his proposals. It would not be effective to prohibit the consumption of beer on the premises, as this would easily be avoided by crossing the street, jar in hand, and drinking in associated premises. Instead he proposed to increase the rateable value of premises that could be given licenses. His proposal was that only premises rated at £10 p.a. should be eligible for a license, and in towns £15. This, he felt, would ensure the respectability of the parties concerned. His proposal to introduce a residential qualification would stop the practice of brewers erecting special beer houses to sell their produce, although he did not explain why this was a bad thing. Finally, he proposed that the license fee, which had already been raised from two guineas to three, should be increased to five guineas.

In the short debate that followed, all shades of opinion were represented. Some speakers claimed that crime had increased since 1830, others that it had not; but the flavour of what was said was that there was some doubt as to whether any change in the law was needed. MPs again referred to the fact that the working classes were not alone in sometimes consuming to excess. The reformer Joseph Hume said:

> The poor man can enjoy his beer in moderation, and perhaps in that respect sets an example to persons of a higher rank; and I need not refer to club-houses and hells in proof of the immorality and intemperance prevailing in the higher classes. I am warranted in making that statement by what had occurred during the fair in Hyde Park after the Coronation, and the evidence was that there were more persons of the class of the hon. gentleman, in point of rank and property, engaged in riot and drunkenness than of the lower classes!

The only outright supporter of Pakington's proposals was Robert Slaney, who happened to be a cousin of his wife's.

The Bill entered its committee stage on 27th June, but Joseph Hume objected to further progress. He said that the many petitions that Pakington had said the house had received on the subject had been a response to a circular that Pakington himself had sent around the country, pressing the authorities to petition parliament. Hume had collected statistics showing that, in total, since the Sale of Beer Act had came into force 1,008 beer house keepers had been brought be-

*Joseph Hume 1777-1855. He was a Scottish doctor who worked in India, whence he returned with a large fortune in 1808. He entered parliament in 1812 and represented various constituencies, including Montrose from 1841.*

fore the magistrates for offences, against over two and a half times that number of licensed victuallers. He felt that Pakington had not made any case for a change in the law, and that if anything the rules regarding beer house keepers should be relaxed, allowing them to open for the same period as licensed victuallers. But Viscount Dungannon quoted statistics from Liverpool that were at variance with those quoted by Hume, showing that beer house keepers transgressed more often than licensed victuallers, and said

> I believe, if the hon. members were to make inquiries among the clergymen and magistrates from one end of the country to the other – from Northumberland to Cornwall – they would hear that a great portion of the vice and immorality existing among the agricultural classes is to be attributed to the establishment of beer-houses. As a county magistrate, I can state that most of the robberies – not those of a trifling, but many of a much graver character – are concocted in the beer-houses, whose proprietors are, in most cases, men of no capital or property.

The chancellor of the exchequer, Thomas Spring Rice, spoke for the government, and said his main concern was to equalise the laws as regarded beer houses and licensed victuallers. He pointed out that although seventy seven possibly Pakington-inspired petitions had been received calling for a tightening or repeal of the act, these were only signed by 6,420 persons, whereas the nine petitions calling for no change were signed by 20,757, and that no less than 248,000 persons had signed petitions calling for a equalisation of the law between beer houses and licensed victuallers.

He utterly refuted the statements by Viscount Dungannon that all beer shops were 'hot-beds of vice', and wished to draw attention to the large investment that many beer house keepers had made in their premises. It was also not true that beer houses were disreputable places compared with public houses, and he produced figures on rateable value that backed-up this assertion. His only suggestion for change was that licenses should not in future be issued to beer houses rated at less than £5 p.a.

The chancellor then said he wished to deal with the allegation that beer houses had caused an increase in crime. By this time the House must have been struggling to digest the rush of often conflicting statistics before it, but Spring Rice presented Home Office figures that showed that crime had increased more slowly since 1830 than before, indeed in some areas had actually reduced, despite that fact that extra categories of crime were now being included, and the new police forces were recording more crime. In any case, before 1830 many people ascribed crime to the bad influence of public houses and the consumption of gin; now they had found a new target, "but in my opinion crime might rather be imputed to indulgence in ardent spirits than in beer. Certainly it is the opinion of most moralists that crime is more likely to be engendered by habits of spirit drinking than by taking beer", and in support of this view he referred to Hogarth's prints of Beer Street and Gin Lane, which pointed to the evils of spirits as against wholesome beer.

Winding up the debate on whether to go into committee, Pakington refuted all the statistical statements made by the chancellor, saying, in effect, that there were lies, damn lies and statistics – hardly a sensible statement to be made by someone who would later become president of the Statistical Society! He referred to the petitions sent by magistrates from no less than thirty one counties, and finally relied heavily on the macabre evidence of men on the scaffold.

With the House now in committee, the chancellor said that he was against the 12 months' residence qualification, as it would prohibit those houses which were built or adapted specially for the trade, which he felt was not desirable. As regards the proposal to limit licenses to properties rated above £10, this was quite unjust, as there were currently 18,279 public houses rated under this figure. The chancellor proposed a different clause, which would grant licenses to premises above £5 ratable value in districts where the population was under 5,000, £10 where the population was greater, and £15 in the metropolis. But Pakington disagreed. He thought it would exclude very many beer houses in London, whereas in fact he did not believe they were the main source of the problem. So Pakington and the chancellor could not be reconciled, and a division on whether to accept Pakington's £10 figure was lost by 76 votes to 103. A further division on Viscount Sandon's proposal to prohibit the consumption of beer on the premises was defeated. This time the chancellor and Pakington voted together. As the original bill had been defeated it was agreed to leave the matter with the chancellor of the exchequer, and nothing further happened that session.

*Hogarth's prints 'Beer Street' (left) and 'Gin Lane' (right) pointing to the evils of gin as against the health and happiness associated with beer, published in 1751. The debate on the dangers of spirits as against beer was still raging in the 1830s.*

Before returning to beer houses, we should make reference to Pakington's comments on the Prison Bill, a government measure of 1839. This showed, not for the last time, two rather contradictory sides to his character. On 31st May, when the bill was in committee, there was a debate on clause 14. This gave magistrates powers to appoint a chaplain when the number of prisoners of a dissenting religion in a prison reached 50. When Pakington first spoke on the clause, MPs must have thought that he wished to see it enlarged, as he said 50 was an arbitrary number. But then it became clear that he did not wish to see any non-Anglican priests in prisons at all, saying:

> But there is another reason why I am opposed to this clause. When I see the rapid strides which the Roman Catholics are making in this country, I must say that I do not feel at all disposed to make this further concession to them. I am by no means disposed to interfere with that principle of British law by which every man is tolerated, and could hold his theological opinions without let or hindrance; I hold that to be a true principle of our Legislature, but I must nevertheless give my decided opposition to this clause.

But most MPs did not agree, and the clause was adopted after a division. The bill was to receive its third reading on 21st June, and Pakington was the first to rise in the debate. On this occasion he wished to object to the clauses giving magistrates the power to order solitary confinement. He said the government had relied on a report on the penitentiary in Philadelphia, where that system had been in operation, but he believed they had not paid sufficient attention to the report, and wanted to bring their attention to certain figures in it. These showed that mortality had regularly and constantly increased, in fact was twice that in the penitentiary in New Hampshire, where the solitary system was not used. Furthermore, not only was the physical health of prisoners jeopardized, but their mental health also. Among the 318 prisoners in Philadelphia, there had been 14 cases of insanity in quite a short space of time. He felt the government should not take any actions that could be so injurious to the physical and mental health of prisoners. But Lord John Russell replied that all that was being done was to give magistrates certain powers, and after a last ditch attempt to leave out clause 14 was defeated, the bill passed unchanged.

Pakington was appointed to his second select committee in June 1839, probably again at the suggestion of John Barneby, set up to enquire into the lunatic asylum run by John Gilliland in Hereford. It appears that there were several defects in the way the house was run. A license had been obtained for its continuation from the Hereford authorities without following the correct procedure, and the committee suggested a small change in the law to prevent this happening again.

The parliamentary session finished on 27th August, after which MPs retired to their country seats, and took part in more local activities. The big event in Worcester was the Music Festival, which started on 19th September, with a 'Grand Fancy Dress

Ball' held on the final Friday evening. Pakington was recorded as attending the ball, and no doubt was at the concerts as well, but his wife does not seem to have accompanied him. Despite the engagement of a number of celebrity foreign singers, and the reduction in price of the 1 guinea and half guinea tickets to 15 shillings and 7 shillings and 6 pence respectively, the 1839 Festival was a mixed success. Only 600 attended the Wednesday morning concert, and only 124 the Tuesday evening miscellaneous concert, with the result that expenses exceeded the income by over £1,200. This meant that even after the stewards' £400 and the guarantee fund's £746 were used, there was a deficit of £121. Despite encouragement in the columns of Berrows, those attending the ball did not, on the whole, come in fancy dress, although where appropriate some, probably including Pakington as a Captain in the Worcestershire Yeomanry Cavalry, wore military uniforms, which would have brightened things up.

The Festival, as usual, attracted criticism from those who thought it incompatible with a place of religious worship; 'Philoprepes' wrote again to Berrows complaining of the use of dramatic and theatrical singers; of the culmination of the festival in a grand fancy dress ball; and of the fact that the rehearsals that took place on Monday forced performers to travel to Worcester on the Lord's Day. Berrows agreed with these sentiments to the extent that they thought British singers should be employed in place of the foreigners. The Festival, it opined, had been founded as a celebration of local singing talent, and should remain so. This would also make a welcome contribution to reducing the Festival's deficit. One cannot help wondering whether it was partly due to Pakington's influence that these celebrated foreigners appeared at Worcester; when in London he never missed a chance to go to the opera to hear a foreign star, and would no doubt have suggested their appearance before the Worcestershire gentry.

The 1840 parliamentary session opened on 16th January, and on 28th the Tories put down a no confidence motion, which they felt they had a chance of winning. The debate lasted four nights, and Pakington, anxious to make his mark on a more general level in the House, spoke on 29th. He opened his speech:

> As I have long been of the opinion that the dismissal of the present weak and vacillating administration would benefit the country, I cannot consent to give a silent vote on this momentous question. The difficulty I have in grappling with the subject is the superfluity of grounds for charge against them; for there is not one branch of the great affairs of this country that does not afford fair ground for inculpating the government.

He accused them of introducing populist measures to keep the support of the 'ultras' of their party. They had made the [secret] ballot an open question; and the penny post, while certainly popular, would prove to be a drain on national resources. The government had, Pakington said, made appointments that threatened the church and monarchy. He pointed to examples from Canada where two officials, Judge Bolton of Newfoundland and Mr Hagerman, the attorney general of Upper Canada, had been dismissed because they showed too much affection for the links to the mother country and the Protestant church. And men had been advanced in Canada even though they used intemperate language. One, Mr Reddard, was now exiled for treason, and another, Mr Viger, was an agitator and under suspension.

Coming nearer to home, Pakington pointed to what he described as 'the darkest stain upon the conduct of her Majesty's ministers'. Was it not true that they had offered a judicial appointment to Daniel O'Connell, the well known Irish nationalist? (In the following year, 1841, O'Connell became the first Catholic mayor of Dublin.) There had been other appointments of Catholics to government offices. He did not object to this on the grounds of their religion, 'but that they formerly had behaved in a manner which on principle was most objectionable and which made them obnoxious to large bodies of the most loyal and faithful subjects of her Majesty'. Pakington then referred to the recent Birmingham election, when George Muntz, a local industrialist, had been returned as one of its members. Had he not expressed republican opinions at the hustings? Were the government aware of this? Did they sympathise with these radical notions? When Pakington said that Muntz would not have sat on the government side for nothing – he must have his price – he was called to order, and he had to apologise for any suggestion that Muntz had been bribed.

The debate continued for three more nights, and it was not until 4.40 a.m. on the last night, after a three hour speech by Peel, and one nearly as long from Lord John Russell, that the House divided. Nearly 600 MPs voted, and in the event the government survived the 'no confidence' motion by the slim majority of 21.

Pakington was still determined to get something done about beer houses. At the opening of the session he had asked the chancellor of the exchequer (Francis Baring had replaced Thomas Spring Rice) whether he intended to introduce any legislation to amend the Sale of Beer Act this session? In reply, Baring said that he had no present intentions, as he felt the chances of getting all-round agreement on the measure was remote. Pakington then announced that he would seek leave to bring in his own bill again.

This he did, and it was given its second reading on 19th February. He said he need not repeat the arguments he had used in the last session, which showed how important and urgent the legislation was, but now he had a new statistical weapon to fire in the debate. The previous November there had been serious Chartist riots in Newport, Monmouthshire, and Pakington had looked into the prevalence of beer houses in that area. He found that in Dukes Town, which had been the main place of rioting, there were twenty eight beer shops and five public houses, or one in every five houses in the place. This was far more than in another Welsh town, Aberystwyth. Developing his argument, he continued:

> No doubt I might be told that if the people were disposed to rebel, whether there were beer shops or not, these disturbances would have taken place; but no man could deny that they hold out great temptations and opportunities, and I would add that, with two exceptions, all the Chartist meetings and lodges had been held in beer shops. I would ask whether it could be considered essential to the comfort, the welfare, and the rational enjoyment of the working classes, that every fifth house should be a beer shop or a public house?

The new bill was similar to the old one, but Pakington explained that he had modified his proposals for the minimum rateable values for obtaining a license. His bill now proposed £15 for cities and towns, £12 for towns larger than 2,500 persons, and £10 for the rest. He felt that these levels should be sufficient to guarantee their respectability. But having set out his proposals, a new difficulty arose.

This was that after his speech another member, Henry Warburton, pointed out that the standing orders of the House directed that any bill affecting trade or taxation should first be considered by a committee of the whole house, which had not been the case on the present occasion. After some discussion, during which the Speaker appeared to side with Warburton, Pakington withdrew his bill, but not before complaining "of the want of courtesy on the part of the hon. member for Bridport [Warburton], in not having informed me of the want of regularity in the introduction of the bill. He never recollected such a want of courtesy before on the part of one member of the House to another." At this he was reprimanded by the Speaker for his language, at which Pakington said he would 'bow to the chair', but would continue with his campaign the next day.

However, it was not until March 2nd that he was able to have his bill read again for the first time, and on 31st there was a debate on the second reading. The same arguments were rehearsed as had been heard before, but the general feeling was that the bill should go to committee for its details to be examined, and it was read for the second time by a large majority. The bill was considered in committee on 10th June. The proposals for the property qualification were now £15 rateable value in towns of over 10,000 inhabitants, £11 in places with over 2,500 inhabitants, and £8 elsewhere, but these figures were prospective, and existing licensees could continue whatever their rateable value. In addition the licensee had to obtain a certificate of good character from six local ratepayers with houses of the value of at least £12. The bill also proposed to make uniform the hours of opening, which would be not before 5.00 a.m. on weekdays, and not before 1.00 p.m. on Sundays, when they should also be closed between 3.00 p.m. and 5.00 p.m. Various proposals for amending these particulars were proposed, but Pakington had been careful to ensure that sufficient supporters of his bill (including Robert Slaney) were in attendance to ensure that, with one minor exception, these amendments were defeated. After a further attempt by Viscount Sandon to prevent the issuing of new licenses for the consumption of beer on the premises was defeated on 8th July, the bill received its third reading the following day, and passed into law at the end of the session in August.

In the same session, the subject of Canada came up again. The government had introduced the Government of Canada Bill, by which the two Canadian provinces would be united, as they had been before 1791, and by which the government hoped that the recent troubles in Canada could be brought to an end. On 19th May in the debate that the bill go into committee, Pakington spoke first, and at some length. He was strongly against the proposal, and cited a number of objections. These included the very great size of the country and the difficulties of travel at certain seasons, but his real fears were that the interests of the people of Upper Canada, mainly of British origin, and their Protestant church, would be diluted by being only a part of the newly unified Canada. He quoted Pitt and Burke about the rashness of trying to unify two peoples so different in their culture, language, religion and national affiliations. Gladstone was next to speak and said he would support the bill, but he was indebted to his friend, the hon. member for Droitwich, for his "able speech, and for having obtained for the matter additional attention". But the general feeling that day was that unification was desirable, and the bill proceeded. We shall have to leave history to judge whether the unification of Canada has been a success.

Although he spoke on a number of different occasions, Pakington's main activity in the 1841 session was to return to the question of coroners. Despite his unsuccessful attempt in 1838 to effect some reform, mainly in the manner in which the coroners were elected, he felt it worthwhile having another try, and accordingly on 18th February sought leave to introduce a new County Coroners Bill. He explained that coroners were elected by the ancient franchise of all the freeholders. This method was open to abuse, and incurred great expense and inconvenience. There was no register of all the freeholders, which category would include some with freeholds of low value who were not allowed to vote in parliamentary elections, and yet there were others with lease and copyholds worth over forty shillings who could vote in parliamentary elections but who were ineligible to vote for coroners. Furthermore all county freeholders could vote for coroners in just one division of the county, causing elections to be laborious and complicated. His proposal was simple: the franchise should be limited to the same franchise as that for parliamentary elections, and that only voters who lived within the division of the county for which the coroner was to serve could vote. Polling places should be set up in each division, and polling restricted to one day.

This proposal seems eminently sensible, but several speakers objected to the removal of the franchise from some classes of freeholders. One such was Joseph Hume, who said that "in my opinion, by the ancient law of the land, every freeholder, whatever the amount of the value of his freehold might be, has a right to vote for the coroner, on the principle, that the life of the poorest man was of as much importance as that of the richest". But the bill was introduced and given its second reading on March 10th, although several reservations about its provisions were expressed in the debate. However, when the bill went into committee on May 5th, it ran into a series of amendments, and there were no less than nine divisions, some of which introduced changes, although the elective principal remained.

Pakington spoke on two more topics during the session. In March he raised another Canadian question, this time that of Newfoundland. This colony, still separate from the rest of Canada, had always been part of British-settled Canada, but had acquired a large Irish population that was Catholic alongside the settlers of English origin. After some agitation the colony had been granted its own assembly in 1832, but as this had been divided along religious lines it had not been stable, and trouble had occurred at elections, prompting the intervention of the military. Pakington was in contact with a gentleman from the colony, who had given him alarming reports, and he decided to press parliament for a select committee. A poor law bill was going through its committee stage, so the government were reluctant to give time to the matter, but eventually on 30th March Pakington was able to make his statement. The main problem, he thought, was that the assembly was abusing its powers. He had heard that all sorts of unsuitable people had been elected to the assembly, including a fisherman, and someone who was 'merely a domestic servant'. His gentleman friend had even been asked to take the daughter of another member into his service! The assembly were using their powers of patronage to appoint people to posts purely out of political favouritism, and adjusting officials' salaries up or down to try and win votes. The Chief Justice had been abused when he tried to be impartial, and the Speaker had misused his powers to be partial in disputes.

Replying for the government, Lord John Russell said he was aware of these allegations, and the recent regrettable violence at elections. But he was still waiting for reports from the colony and did not want to act precipitately. In any case the hon. member should remember that it would not be practical to apply the same standards that had been developed in the British parliament over more than half a millennium to one that was only a few years old. Additionally, there was incontrovertible evidence that the assembly had been responsible for much good in the colony, making considerable improvements in the infrastructure, and he did not want to be rushed into appointing a committee, which it was vital should be impartial.

Pakington expressed an interest from time to time in imprisonment, or in this case transportation. On 23rd March Viscount Mahon introduced a motion criticising the fact that it had become the regular practise to commute sentences of transportation for seven years to imprisonment in one of the hulks, usually for a shorter period. Mahon wished to emphasise the unsatisfactory nature of using hulks for this purpose. They were unhealthy and overcrowded, whereas transportation offered the convict the chance of a new life in much healthier conditions. According to his figures, transportation was much cheaper, as once the convict was in his new home, the value of his labour was sufficient for his keep. He also believed that criminals dreaded transportation which meant a total separation from their family, quite possibly for ever, much more than a spell in a hulk. (As an aside, it is interesting to note the visiting conditions of the day – in the early stages of the sentence, visits were allowed once every six months for a ten minute period, and both visitor and prisoner were separated by a metal screen, with an officer between them.)

After Lord Russell had defended the government, saying they were just following the recommendations of a committee, Pakington rose and said he fully supported Viscount Mahon. He made the point that judges ought to know what they were sentencing criminals to – a sentence of seven years transportation ought to mean seven years transportation, and not three years in a hulk. Discipline was difficult in hulks, which were overcrowded, and it was well known that, once liberated, criminals would be very likely to revert straight away to their former way of life, something much less likely to happen in Australia.

The government were defeated on the motion by 49 votes to 28, which was something that was happening with increasing frequency. On 18th May 1841, after a long debate on sugar duties ended – they wanted to reduce the duty on foreign sugar, which the Tories opposed on the grounds that it would help slave-owning countries like Brazil and damage the interests of British sugar producers in the West Indies – the government were defeated by 36 votes. Lord Russell hoped they could soldier on, but Peel immediately pounced with a motion of 'no confidence', debated over five days ending on 4th June. Whigs who had dissented in earlier divisions were now dragged into the lobby to support the government. The Tories whips were equally active, and it was said that every single Tory member voted or was paired. The comatose and mortally ill Lord Halyburton, member for Fife, was carried through the lobby. When it was seen that the Tory chief whip, Sir Thomas Freemantle, with his black hair and enormous whiskers was walking to the right hand side of the speaker's chair, indicating he represented the winning side, there was great excitement, and it was announced that the government had been defeated by 312 votes to 311.

*Relief guard arriving at a prison hulk at Deptford 1821.*

Although the prime minister, Melbourne, encouraged by the Queen who disliked Peel, was willing to soldier on, his colleagues insisted that a general election be called, and parliament was dissolved. This unfortunately meant the loss of Pakington's County Coroner's Bill. Berrows carried a leader strongly criticising the outgoing 'shabby' Whig government, talking of their 'unconstitutional' actions. It noted that the Queen's liking for Melbourne was well-known, but voters should not have regard to that. The young Queen would do whatever duty dictated, and support the ministry the country preferred. Berrows was also strongly protectionist, and dismissed the importance of a farthing off the price of sugar and a cheaper loaf in favour of protection to native industry, little knowing that the government about to be elected would abandon protectionism for ever.

Pakington, of course, stood again for Droitwich, and despite only having been in the House of Commons for four years had already made something of a name for himself, and Berrows said that 'his re-election is placed beyond doubt; for no one could, with the least probability of success, oppose a gentleman so much esteemed and in every respect so well qualified to represent that borough'. (It should be noted that less than half the constituencies in 1841 were contested; in the days before the secret ballot it was easier to predict the result of contests particularly in small constituencies; opponents only came forward if they thought they had a good chance of success.)

This is how Berrows reported the Droitwich nomination on July 8th:

> On Thursday last the nomination took place for this borough. At an early hour the inhabitants were bustling about and making preparations – not for a party contest, for we supposed never was a constituency more unanimous than that of Droitwich, as out of about 300 electors, we do not believe that five could be found to vote in opposition to the present honourable member. A body of about 200, consisting of the gentry, tradesmen and agriculturalists, electors of the town and neighbourhood, breakfasted at the George Hotel, and afterwards moved in procession, their numbers being augmented to nearly 400, towards Westwood Park, where they met the honourable candidate, and escorted him back, surrounded by banners, flags, and all the usual paraphernalia of election meetings, to the George Hotel, whence they repaired to the town hall for the formalities and then to the hustings.'

In his nomination, W. H. Ricketts described Pakington as a man of business and of talent, and said he 'had been one of the most constant members in attendance upon all divisions of the house'. Berrows reported Pakington's nomination speech at length. After the usual expressions of gratitude, he reviewed the events of the last four years, coming first to the poor state of the country's finances, introducing his remarks with the rather sexist comment: "I must therefore beg of you to grant me the patience, for I fear I may be unavoidably compelled to address you at some length on subjects which, although important in their results, are dry in their details, and holding out but small attractions to those fair portions of my audience which I am honoured and gratified in seeing around me". He contrasted the 1820s, when the Tories were in power, to the 1830s when the Whigs were; the Tories left the nation's finances in a very good state only to see them brought into deficit by the Whigs.

But the main thrust of his speech was reserved for an attack on the Whig's free trade proposals. The reduction of sugar duties would ruin our interests in the West Indies and favour the slave-owning states; the reduction of timber duties would damage Canada, which only last year had been subjected to the dangerous experiment of unification; and the reduction of corn duties would damage the landowner, his tenant, and therefore the farm worker. Yes, of course it was important to find new markets for our manufactures as the government wanted; but why damage the home market by impoverishing the population in this way? Using many statistics, Pakington attempted to rebut the arguments in favour of duty reduction, and said it certainly would not lead to more stability in the price of corn.

There were a few hecklers in the audience, and Berrows reported that 'here a fellow in the crowd, known by the Regal soubriquet of 'the Duke of York', alias Dick Smith, became exceedingly turbulent in opposition to the views of the speaker, and exhibited two loaves of bread of different sizes, stuck on a pole, from which an inference in favour of the budget scheme was, we suppose, designed to be drawn. The ignorant fellow however was 'quite alone in his glory, and having no supporter, soon slunk into obscurity'. It can be seen from this which side of the argument Berrows was on! After the speech the procession went round the town, and halted at the George Hotel. From a window Pakington addressed the crowd once more, and scattered 'a quantity of silver' amongst them, much to the diversion of the spectators.

Despite the fact that the Whigs had lately announced plans to reduce the duty on corn to meet the demands of the Anti-Corn Law League, the Tories did well in the 1841 election and had sufficient gains to give them an overall majority of between 70 and 80 members. The Whigs had become unpopular partly because it was thought that had acted unconstitutionally as explained above, and the other factor in the election was the popularity of Sir Robert Peel, who, despite being a Tory, was seen as a moderate and responsible leader, not afraid to change his mind when he thought it right, as he had done over Catholic Emancipation in 1829.

According to Berrows, the Pakingtons left for a tour of Germany immediately after the election, planning to return in time for the meeting of the new parliament the following month.

## Chapter 9
## Committee Man 1841-43

The new parliament assembled on 19th August 1841 – Sir Robert Peel was now prime minister, with the Duke of Wellington still leader of the Tories in the Lords. Pakington is recorded as attending regularly, but only spoke once during the remainder of the session.

The next year, 1842, saw the new government get down to business, and the first item on Peel's agenda was the controversial subject of the Corn Laws. The Tory party had traditionally been protectionist, and had opposed Lord Russell's attempt to reform the Corn Laws the year before. Peel himself was a pragmatist, and his previous statements on the subject had never been as forceful as those of some of his colleagues. Peel always believed in doing what he thought was right even if this ran against his own or his party's previous positions. The foremost example was Catholic emancipation in 1829, when Peel had gone against his earlier views to enact what he thought was inevitable. Now in 1842 Peel thought that some change in the corn laws would have to be made. The existing corn law dated from 1828, and imposed a sliding scale of duty on imported corn – high when the price of corn was low but tapering to a nominal amount when the price was high. The intention was that British farmers would be protected when corn was cheap, but after a bad harvest when corn was dear, cheaper foreign corn would be allowed in so as to moderate the increase in the price of food. But the system was open to fraud and the duties were beginning to look very high. Duties on other imported goods were being progressively cut, and the price of corn, which was supposed to have been made more stable by the 1828 law, still fluctuated considerably. Moreover there was mounting pressure from the Anti-Corn Law League and the working population generally for total repeal and cheaper bread.

Peel launched an enquiry, finding out the costs of growing wheat at home and abroad and investigating the fluctuations in the market price, and William Gladstone, then a minister in the Board of Trade (he only later became a Liberal) and something of a free-trader, did much of the work. Finally, Peel decided to propose a new scale of duties, similar in principle to the old system, but much lower, and on 9th February 1842 he outlined his proposals to the House of Commons. He began by pleading for a dispassionate debate on the subject, knowing that emotions could run high, and said he did not believe that the present commercial distress could be blamed on the corn laws as some did, claiming that cheaper bread would mean more cheaply produced manufactures. He said there had been remarkable economic progress in the later 1830s, with the fast growth of mechanical power and manufacturing, leading to a rapid transfer of population from the countryside to the towns, and that some reaction to this was inevitable. Furthermore disruption in the United States and China had reduced demand for British exports. He said the arguments of those who opposed what they called a tax on bread were attractive, and he admitted that the price of bread in some countries, for example, Germany was lower than here. But, Peel said in effect, there was more to life than the price of bread, and he did not accept that the German labourer enjoyed life any more than his counterpart here.

To back up this assertion, Peel quoted figures from an independent source showing that the consumption of meat, sugar and grain, and other staples such as cotton and wool was considerably higher in Britain than in Germany. He was not, of course, claiming that there were not areas in Britain where there was great distress – he quoted Paisley, where the year before there had been great hardship among the weavers when a downturn in trade had thrown many out of work, and in which Peel had taken a great interest. But it was the generality which mattered, and he believed his statistics showed that the British worker was better off than his continental cousin. Up to this point in his speech Peel

*The Duke of Wellington and Sir Robert Peel, Tory leaders in the 1840s. From The Royal Collection ©2010, Her Majesty Queen Elizabeth II.*

had been attacking those who wished for total repeal, and concluded by warning of severe agricultural distress "if the House of Commons should be induced to pledge itself to a total repeal, which we on this side of the House deprecate so much...".

Peel then considered the arguments for a fixed duty per quarter [a quarter was the commonly used measure for grain, being 28 pounds or 12.7 kilos]. But he dismissed these, saying the present system was better, as in a series of steps the duty reduced as the price rose, and was only a nominal one shilling when wheat reached 73 shillings a quarter, thus reducing the impact of high prices on the cost of food. But he pointed out that this rapid reduction introduced distortions and temptations to fraud, as only a small rise in the price of wheat meant imported wheat became very much cheaper. Finally, Peel revealed the new rates of duty that would be in the proposed bill: when wheat was 50 shillings a quarter the duty would be 20 shillings; thereafter there would be a more steady reduction in duty till at 73 shillings the duty would cease altogether.

Looking at this announcement from a modern perspective, it might be thought to be something of a tidying up measure rather than a major reform. At some points in the scale, for example at the bottom and at the highest levels, the duty would be lower, at others little changed; but Peel had made a careful study of all the facts and figures involved, and felt his scheme more rational than the existing one. But it remained complicated – under the new proposals, there would still be twenty one different duty rates depending on the market price.

The only immediate reaction to Peel's speech was from the radical Richard Cobden, who, though very disappointed, said he could not expect "to gather grapes from thorns, or figs from thistles". He denounced the measure as

> an insult to the suffering people – a people whose patience had been extolled by the right honourable baronet who proposed this measure – and a people whose patience deserved very different treatment from the landed aristocracy, and from the cabinet which was the instrument of that aristocracy. This measure proved that the landed aristocracy would, if the people of England permitted them, perpetuate a system of selfish policy, tending not very remotely to the utter destruction of every interest in the country.

*Born in 1804, the reformer Richard Cobden was a leading figure in the Anti-Corn Law League, and was elected MP for Stockport in 1841, then for Rochdale until his death in 1865.*

The Anti-Corn Law League, which was demonstrating outside parliament, was not happy.

The bill came up for its second reading on 9th March, and Pakington was one of those who spoke. Despite having presented a petition from Worcestershire farmers against the bill, he congratulated the government for coming up with such a sensible measure. He felt the method of calculating the average price of corn, which was to be related to that used in the recent Tithe Commutation Act, was sensible and should help do away with fraud, and that all classes of society should benefit. His only regret was that in the debate which had arisen from a heavily defeated motion that the duties on imported corn be removed altogether, the manufacturing interest and the agricultural interest should be so much at odds, and that there should have been so much acrimony. The second reading of the bill was passed by a majority of over 100, many Whigs (although not Lord John Russell) voting with the government.

The affairs of Newfoundland came before the House again, although Pakington's proposed committee had failed to complete its investigation due to the dissolution of parliament. The government's answer to the troubles there was to amalgamate the elected House of Assembly with the appointed Legislative Council. Pakington thought this action the best, and spoke approvingly of it when the bill was in committee, saying there was no longer any need for the committee of enquiry.

Pakington is recorded as having served on four select committees during 1842. The first was set up in March to enquire into 'The state of the different West Indies colonies, particularly the state of the labour market there and the relations between employers and labourers'. Slavery had been abolished in 1834, and the committee examined a variety of witnesses as to the effects of this. Estate owners had generally been against emancipation, and blamed the subsequent depression in the islands' economies on this; but the select committee did not agree and 'believed that the great advantages that have resulted from emancipation have been unchecked and unalloyed by any subsequent evils'. Among the favourable results from emancipation the committee noted an increased desire for religious instruction and general education; a 'growing disposition to take upon themselves the obligations of marriage, and to fulfil the duties of domestic life'; improved morals; and a 'rapid advance in civilization'. The committee admitted that there had been a great reduction in the production of the agricultural staples (principally sugar) particularly in the larger colonies of Jamaica, British Guiana and Trinidad, and that this was mainly due to the scarcity and high price of labour since 1834. The committee found that labourers 'can live in comfort and acquire wealth without, for the most part, labouring on the estates of the planters for more than three of four days a week, and from five to seven hours a day; so that they have no sufficient stimulus to perform an adequate amount of work'. This had caused land prices to fall, and negroes can now obtain land 'on easy terms'.

The committee believed that if their suggestions were acted upon in a spirit of equal justice to both proprietors and labourers, prosperity would be restored; 'and that, under the blessing of Divine Providence, the world may witness the complete success of the great example [of emancipation] which this country has afforded'. But the committee could only make the obvious suggestion of a scheme 'to promote the immigration of a fresh labouring population, to such an extent as to create competition for employment'. Quite how this was to be done without revisiting the shores of West Africa was not explained.

As was always the case, the general election of 1841 had given rise to a number of complaints about the conduct of individual elections, and a special procedure to deal with these had been established in the previous parliament. To investigate each complaint a small select committee was formed, and in April Pakington was made chairman of one to investigate allegations of bribery at the Ipswich election. Omens were not good, as the previous four Ipswich elections had all been successfully challenged. Rigby Wason and George Rennie, both Whigs, had been returned, and the investigation became a matter of public notice, particularly when Wason wished to call the out-going MP, Admiral Thomas Cochrane, as a witness. Cochrane was about to be posted to a Far East naval station, and many thought it unreasonable that the national naval interest might be compromised by someone who many regarded as a corrupt MP.

The committee first met on April 13th with Pakington in the chair, six other committee members, no less than three counsel for the petitioners opposing the election and two of their agents, two counsel for the sitting MPs and their two agents, and a short-hand writer. Counsel had to be paid by the protagonists, so it is perhaps not surprising that Wason had raised the matter of expense in the House the day before, suggesting that the number of counsel representing each side should be limited to one. This was not accepted, but the subject was taken up by The Times, which pointed out that despite the change in the manner of dealing with these matters, committees continued to be very partial, and it pointed to four recent examples where a Tory committee had unseated a Whig member and vice versa. With its Tory chairman, the Ipswich committee had a Tory majority of four to three, but with the evidence coming down heavily against Wason and Rennie, it would be unfair to say its ultimate report was biased. Although The Times was no great admirer of Rigby Wason, it did agree that it could be very expensive to defend one's seat before a select committee, and pointed to the recent Marlow election investigation which had lasted twenty days, and with three counsel for both sides, the legal fees would have come to £1,800. If, as The Times impishly suggested, the result of the enquiry would be decided as soon as the political colour of the chairman was known, why spend all this money to no effect? A simple vote in the House of Commons would be a great deal quicker and cheaper, and achieve the same ends.

After the committee had been sitting for a week, Wason again raised the subject in the House, 'for the purpose of calling the attention of the House to the injustice practised by the majority of the committee, in the different conduct pursued by them towards the witnesses before them, as such witnesses happen to give evidence for or against the political party to which the majority belong'. The Speaker ruled his motion totally out of order, which should have precluded any further discussion, but Pakington, obviously stung by what Wason had said, did make a brief statement 'repelling with the utmost indignation the calumnious and unfounded charge'. The enquiry closed on 24th April, and the chairman was able to give its verdict on the same day. Even the counsel for the sitting members had admitted that there was bribery, but they claimed that it was solely done by the agents, without the knowledge of the candidates. But the committee was unanimous in not accepting this 'ingenious' defence (as The Times put it), and found that there was extensive bribery at the election making it void, and that no new writ should be issued until their report was printed and all the evidence made public.

The third select committee that Pakington served on concerned the Keighley Poor Law Union. Adherence to the new Poor Law had been poorer in the north than in the south, one reason being that the growing new industries in the north were offering plentiful employment at wages that were better than in the more rural areas. For this reason Poor Law guardians in the north resisted building the required new workhouses, and preferred to use methods to relieve poverty that had been found satisfactory in the past. Northerners in general seem to have had a greater resentment at being told how to manage their affairs by the London-based Poor Law Commission than southern unions. In addition northerners felt, not without some justification, that the Commission, by imposing harsh workhouse conditions in agricultural areas of the south, were tending to drive paupers northward where there was more employment. Another problem was that Keighley, on the edge of the Pennines, covered a large area, and the guardians, not being familiar with all parts of their area, had effectively split up the union, with local committees running other parts such as Bradford and Bingley.

These differences were very apparent in a debate on 17th June on the second reading of the Poor Law Bill to renew the commission, when several opponents of the commissioners spoke against it. Pakington was the first speaker to support the status quo. He spoke of the importance of a central body to administer the law nationally, and pointed to several abuses that had been revealed under the old law. Without a central controlling body, how were these abuses to be put right? Of course there were things that had gone wrong under the present system, but they had been brought to light and rectified by the Commissioners. He wound up by saying:

> The primary object of that Act was to restore habits of industry and independence to the English peasantry. I believe that it was well adapted to effect its object, and

> that in many instances it has already succeeded. I believe it to be, in all its principles, a sound and wholesome law, and I will not be deterred by any prejudice or clamour that has been raised, or any unpopularity of which I might be the object, from giving my assent to the bill now before the House.

The Keighley union were one of those in the north that had made and followed their own rules, and early in 1842 an assistant commissioner, Mr Mott, reported on the various transgressions. However, the local MP and chairman of the guardians, William Ferrand, a bluff, tough, plain-speaking Yorkshireman, denied many of the charges of mismanagement in the report, and at the end of June a select committee, including Pakington, was set up to investigate. After only two weeks taking evidence the committee produced their report. It did find irregularities in the operation of the Keighley Board, whilst at the same time found that some of the more extreme allegations of abuses within the workhouse were not supported by evidence.

The last of the committees that Pakington served on was to consider the Parish Constables Bill, which placed parish constables under the control of the rural constabulary. Pakington was against the bill as a whole, as he believed that constables, who were responsible for collecting the parish poor rate, had little to do and were a waste of money, and that rate collection should be a responsibility of the Boards of Guardians.

**The Year 1843**

We must now take a break from Pakington's parliamentary career as the following year, 1843 not only marks the existence of a diary, but some important events in his personal life. As the year opens it is clear that Pakington's wife Mary is ill. He is much taken with quarter sessions for the first few days, and as these finished on Wednesday 4th he received a 'bad account' of Mary from his doctor, Dr Ricketts. He did not get home till half past nine, when he found her 'very weak but looking as usual'. The following day he put off callers and went riding with Johnny, now 16. He noted that Mary was with them as usual in the evening, and even worked on her new slippers! He concluded by noting that she slept in the water bed in the blue room for the first time.

Friday's entry reads 'Last day of poor Mary's life! – weaker & weaker in morning – Ricketts told me she could not survive more than 10 or 12 days & might go at any time – she enjoyed tea with us in saloon & expired at 10 ½ p.m.! God's will be done.' Her death certificate states that she died of consumption, implying she had been ill for some time. As no diaries exist for the few years prior to 1843 we do not know much more, although Mary's illness is referred to in letters from his Aunt – in one dated December 1837 she wrote that she is pleased that 'Mary is no longer an invalid'. We also know from newspaper accounts that for some time before her death she had not been present with her husband at events where it might have been expected. A letter to Mary from a friend exists dated August 1842 from which we learn that the Pakingtons were in Italy and that Mary was very ill, and the writer, whose signature is illegible, expressed alarm at reports she has had of her health and pleads with her to spend the winter in Italy or Madeira, if necessary away from her husband. A milder climate was the only treatment for this dreadful disease, but evidently these appeals were made in vain, for Mary died at Westwood.

The following day brings the first mention of Mrs Milner, who had been staying at Westwood during Mary's illness. She appears regularly in the diary, in London and elsewhere, and Pakington seems to have had quite a close relationship with her. Her identity is not immediately obvious. In fact she was christened Sarah Georgina and was the daughter of Rev. George Buckstone of Bradbourne Hall in Derbyshire. Her sister Catherine married Robert Aglionby Slaney, the Liberal MP for Shrewsbury, who was a cousin of Mary Slaney, which no doubt explains why she was present at Westwood during Mary's last illness. In 1816, when she was 23, she married a clergyman, Rev. George William Thomas Milner, who was rector of Larling in Norfolk, but he died in 1824 without having fathered any children, leaving Sarah a widow for over 50 years. She eventually took a house in Eaton Square, but also spent time in such fashionable places as Brighton and Malvern, and visiting her relations. In 1861 she was recorded staying with her brother German Buckstone, the vicar of Sutton on the Hill in Derbyshire, where the vicarage must been quite crowded for as well as Sarah, Rev. German had his wife and three children, a son-in-law Nathaniel Curzon, German's sister Catherine Slaney, and two more visitors, as well as seven servants.

The day following Mary's death, Mrs Milner and Dr Ricketts wrote letters to friends, and 'Johnny & I in great distress all day'. Callers included Barry Domvile, whom Pakington saw, and Rt Rev. George Murray, Bishop of Rochester, still also the Dean of Worcester, whom he would not see, but he learned that Bishop Murray wanted to invite Pakington to his palace at Bromley, no doubt to get away from the scene of his unhappiness. The funeral was set for Friday 13th, and Pakington became more nervous and agitated as it approached. The day itself was marked by an 'awful gale', and Berrows described how the three mourning coaches were each drawn by four horses with plumes &c. In the first was the vicar, Rev. John Amphlett, Thomas Gale Curtler and Martin Ricketts, in the second Pakington father and son, and in the third the relations Rev. Slaney, Rev. Domvile and his son Barry. These were followed by twenty tenants riding two and two. Although Pakington and Johnny were 'greatly agitated', the arrangements went well, and 'Johnny's conduct throughout was perfect'.

On Sunday 'we went to church in carriage mournful to see whole congregation in black & Amphlett gave us good & judicious sermon which pleased us much – prayers & sermon at home as usual'. Owing to his altered circumstances Pakington much reduced the number of servants at Westwood, parting with his footman, the lady's maid, second groom, kitchen maid and scullery maid. He decided to take Johnny away for a break, and on Thursday 19th January they left in two carriages, Pakington, his son and Mrs Milner in one, and her servants in the other. They travelled to Birmingham where they took the new railway to London, where Pakington went to stay with Hallifax, and Mrs Milner went to her home. The next day, in Hallifax's borrowed brougham, they went to say good bye to Mrs Milner. Then they went to see his aunt in her house in Green Street, Mayfair, who had also been ill – she was now 80.

Johnny had been sent to Eton in 1839, but left the following Easter. Academically he proved quite strong, so there must have been other reasons for withdrawing him so soon. It is not known where he was educated after this until the beginning of 1843 when he was placed with a private tutor in Brighton, after having been at home during the previous summer. So on 21st January Pakington went down to Brighton with Johnny by train. His tutor there was Rev. Anderson, who was probably Rev. James Anderson of 12 Arundel Terrace, as in the 1841 census there were five young men in his household who could have been pupils. After staying briefly in the Albion Hotel, Pakington found suitable lodgings on Monday in 74 Marine Parade, a fashionable house on the sea front.

On Monday 23rd January 1843 Pakington noted something completely unexpected – he was offered the governorship of Van Diemens Land (later called Tasmania) by Lord Mahon, later the 5th Lord Stanhope. Mahon was an MP and had held office as under-secretary for foreign affairs briefly in the 1830s, but other than sitting on the government side of the house, had no known connection either with Australia or Pakington. At that time Van Diemens Land was a separate colony, and served as the principal British penal colony. While the salary would have been very welcome, the prospect of giving up the England he loved, his seat and aspirations in the House of Commons, and contact with his son, all for a little-known country on the far side of the globe that was little more than a glorified prison, did not attract. After considering the matter for 24 hours he wrote refusing the offer.

Pakington stayed in Brighton with Johnny until the end of February, and it was obviously a sad time. Despite some bad weather, father and son spent time riding locally, very much enjoying the South Downs, and as usual some of their friends appeared in Brighton. John Barneby and Thomas Hallifax paid visits, Mrs Milner came down from London, and young Walter Corbet, one of Mary's relations, was there. Pakington took time to visit his aunt at her house in Green Street, London, where she was living with her cousin Frances Hawkins. There, on 22nd February, Miss Hawkins died aged 87.

Presumably Johnny was supposed to be getting tuition from Rev. Anderson, but he was quite ill for a period and missed out on his lessons. His father still seems to have had faith in doctors. When one day Johnny 'was attacked by sickness, which made him very ill all evening', his father sent for Dr Tayler. But when he called he was in a great hurry, and ordered a draught, which never came. The next day Tayler failed to turn up at the promised time, so Pakington told him he would seek other advice, and sent for a Dr Hall, whom Pakington 'liked very much…' and 'gave him immediate medicines'.

On 28th February father and son had a 'painful parting, having been 7 months together'. Johnny moved in with the Andersons, and Pakington went to Bromley to stay with the Bishop of Rochester and his family. There is an 'X' against this day in his diary, which must relate to the Murrays. Augusta Murray was in London when Pakington arrived at Rochester, but she returned next day, and on 2nd March they had a 'delightful ride, I rode much with Miss M & in this ride our intimacy recommenced'.

The Rt Rev. George Murray DD, then 59 and Bishop of Rochester and Dean of Worcester, had married Lady Sarah Maria Drummond, a daughter of the Earl of Kinnoull, and was then 55. They had eleven children (and would have well over fifty grandchildren!). The eldest three were daughters, and the first born son was George, in 1843 still a bachelor and a clergyman. The second son, Francis Henry Murray, was likewise a bachelor and clergyman, and the two youngest, Herbert and Frederick, were 13 and 11 respectively. Of the daughters the eldest, Harriet, had married George Charles Pratt, 2nd Marquis Camden, and had already started a family. The second, Caroline Sophia, had also married, her husband being Sir John Mordaunt of Walton Hall, Warwickshire, and by 1843 they had had four children. The third daughter, Pakington's new amour, was Augusta, born on 18th March 1817, and so coming up to her 26th birthday. The remaining daughters were Mary Louisa, 19, Sarah Maria, nearly 18, and Eleanor Margaret, 14.

As we have seen, the Murrays periodically visited Worcester, and the fact that he wrote 'our intimacy recommenced', and that this was their first meeting for some time, indicates that he had had at least a previous friendship with Augusta. Although his wife had died only two months before, intimacy blossomed quickly between the couple. He went to London to meet her two married sisters, rode with her and her parents to see the Dulwich

*The Bishop's Palace, Bromley. This replaced an earlier building in 1772, and is today part of Bromley Civic Centre. Courtesy of Bromley Local Studies Library.*

Picture Gallery, and they started exchanging gifts – he gave her music, and she gave him 'the book of prayers – her first gift!'.

Pakington stayed in Bromley for a week, before going to London in the Bishop's and Lady Sarah's carriage – 'so ended delightful & I fully believe eventful week at Bromley!'. He was to lodge with his aunt in Green Street for the time being, although he found her in a 'forlorn state of depression and weakness' – the recent death of her cousin must have upset her greatly. On 9th March he attended the House of Commons for the first time this session, and dined twice with Lord Mahon. His friendship with Mrs Milner continued – on 11th he dined 'tête à tête' with her – 'very pleasant'. Presumably she was someone to whom he could unburden himself. Later in the month he saw her almost daily – for example on 25th March – 'dined with Mrs Milner & staid till 11 ½ p.m. Very pleasant'.

The 18th March was Augusta's birthday, and they exchanged gifts, she sending him Abercrombie's 'The Philosophy of Moral Feelings'. The strength of Pakington's rapidly developing feelings can be judged from his entry on 15th 'coming home met Camden's barouch & got tantalizing glimpse of A M'. On Friday 17th March a rather strange incident occurred – 'Rode to Honiton Villas, Kensington, to enquire for Mrs Strange, about Johnny's Love Letter…', and the following day 'Went to Brighton to see Johnny – had happiness to find him, rode etc'. Evidently Johnny had got into some romantic involvement that his father had discovered, and not for the last time. Back in London on Sunday, Pakington took possession of his new seat in the Hanover Chapel, built to provide extra accommodation in the parish of St George's, Hanover Square, but now demolished (below right).

The following week he saw The Marble Co. about a monument for Mary, and before choosing the design went to both St John's Wood church and Hanover Road cemetery. The monument eventually appeared in Hampton Lovett church. Parliament is now mentioned more frequently in his diaries, and on 24th March he wrote 'attended factory education debate & intended to speak but nerves rather failed me'. Much of the debate centred on how far education should be non-denominational, and Pakington would have opposed this. But a few days later he felt strongly enough on another subject to overcome his nerves.

This debate stemmed from the fact that 1842 was marked by great political unrest, mainly due to the agitations of the Anti-Corn Law League, and the Chartists. The government managed to stop any major rioting by promptly sending troops when trouble threatened, and the prime minister was concerned enough to arrange for a cache of arms to installed at his house, Draycott Manor. The magistrates in the affected areas had great difficulty keeping control, and this later led to accusations that they had exceeded their powers. Thomas Duncombe, a well-known radical MP, proposed on 28th March 1843 that a select committee be appointed to enquire into matters raised in various petitions regarding what was alleged to have been the over-reaction and even illegal activities of the magistrates when dealing with the unrest. But, in a long and carefully argued speech, the Attorney General, Sir Frederick Pollock, asked what the purpose of the enquiry would be? If the men had a legal complaint then it should be dealt with in the courts in the normal way. It would be a very major task to go through all the many allegations from different places, bringing witnesses down (some of whom were now in prison), and if it was found that some magistrates had over-reacted, what was then to be done? This was not a suitable matter for an enquiry by members of parliament.

Dudley had been mentioned as one of the places where excessive bail was demanded (£600, which was far too much for a working man), and after the attorney general had sat down Pakington rose to defend Messrs Badger and Cartwright, the two Dudley magistrates whom he knew personally. "I know no gentlemen more fit in every respect to hold the commission of the peace, or more fitted in every respect to do their duty with propriety and advantage than the gentlemen alluded to", he said firmly. It was true, he said, that in the event there was not a great deal of trouble at Dudley, but notice of a public meeting had been given, and at similar meetings in other parts of the country there had been a great deal of trouble, damage to property and other evils. It was therefore entirely understandable that the JPs Badger and Cartwright should wish to take precautions to stop the same thing happening in Dudley. Those who had to stay in prison when they were unable to find the bail, later complained to the Court of Queen's Bench, but their action was dismissed "on the ground that although the magistrates had committed a legal error, yet at the time they had no idea of perpetrating any injustice". He continued:

*The monument to Mary Pakington in Hampton Lovett church.*

> As soon as it became known in the district to which these gentlemen belonged, that the hon. member for Finsbury [Mr Duncombe] intended to come before the House of Commons with a complaint relative to their conduct, a public meeting was called, and I have in my hand a copy of the address voted at that meeting to Messrs Cartwright and Badger. The address acknowledged the deep and lasting sense of obligation felt by the meeting to the magistrates, to the military and yeomanry, and stated that the preservation of the life and property of those signing the document was mainly attributable to their exertions. I need only add that this address is signed by 135 of the most respectable bankers and merchants of the town of Dudley, and at the head of the list I see the name of Lord Ward. I myself have been present at many of the conferences held between the magistrates and the Lord Lieutenant of the county, and have never witnessed more temperance, combined with judicious firmness than I saw manifested upon those occasions... It is a very poor return to men who have, in a great crisis, discharged their duties with zeal and with great activity – it is a poor return to such men for a member of the House of Commons to stand up and attempt to hold them up to public scorn, and to reproach them for conduct for which they are well entitled to public gratitude.

After a long speech by the home secretary, Duncombe rose once more to defend his request. He quoted statutes going back to Edward I stating that a man had a right to bail, and that magistrates had no power to ignore the Habeas Corpus Act, and act in any way they chose just because they did not like a man's politics. In this respect the Judges of the Queen's Bench were wrong. But in the division only 36 MPs voted with Duncombe, and the motion was defeated by a majority of 164.

The only other occasion on which Pakington spoke in the session of 1843 was in May when the House was discussing proposals to make more money available for paying Church of England clergymen. The rapid growth of population in the new industrial towns meant there was a woeful lack of places of worship and clergymen in some areas, and many of the clergy there were very poorly paid. The government did not wish to supply public money at this stage; but the Church itself had great resources which were being investigated and redirected by the Ecclesiastical Commission, which Peel himself had established in 1835. Such inequalities as the income of the Bishop of Durham being £19,000 a year against that of the Bishop of Llandaff at £900 had already been addressed. But sinecures and excesses were only being redirected as they became vacant, meaning progress was inevitably slow; the government was now proposing to use the resources controlled by the Governors of Queen Anne's Bounty to bridge this gap. No public money would be involved.

'Church extension' by which was meant the increase in places of worship and in clergymen to officiate, was a subject dear to Pakington's heart, whether in England or our distant colonies; and he spoke on this occasion to support these new proposals. But he felt they were only a step in the right direction, and agreed with those members who had said the plan would be insufficient to meet the present evils. He agreed that the church's own resources should be fully used first, but if these proved inadequate, he hoped that parliament would not hesitate in providing more resources if asked. It had not proved so difficult to raise money for building new churches; but providing a permanent endowment for the payment of clergy was a much greater problem.

Returning to March 1843, on 29th Pakington rode down to Bromley for a brief visit. The next morning before leaving 'took long & delightful walk before breakfast with Augusta & Mary – after breakfast stayed with A for 1¾ hours'. Then he had to return to London, where he took leave of Mrs Milner, his aunt, and Hallifax, and went to Worcester by railway. This would probably have involved him in going to Birmingham, then taking the Birmingham and Gloucester line to the Worcester Road station at Spetchley, as the Worcester station had not been built at this time. Pakington had to be back for quarter sessions which started on 3rd April, and involved him in two days' heavy work, not being completed until 8.00 p.m. on 4th. On 5th there was a meeting of the Droitwich guardians, after which he met Johnny at Droitwich Road station, coming home from Brighton for Easter.

Having been away since his wife's death, Pakington and Johnny rode around making calls, including the Bishop of Worcester at Hartlebury, and the Peels at Waresley nearby. John Peel DD, brother of the prime minister, was vicar of Stone in Worcestershire and was soon to succeed George Murray as Dean of Worcester.

Pakington had a long-standing interest in improving education, which he felt was the best way of lifting the lower orders out of poverty and crime. Although he believed that education should be based on religious beliefs, he was quite prepared to see due allowance made for the beliefs of dissenters, Roman Catholics and Jews. He had recently written to the head master of King Edwards School in Birmingham, who in his reply had explained how dissenters and others did not have to participate fully in Anglican services. As about one third of the pupils were dissenters, the regime seemed to work well. On 20th April he attended a meeting of the Worcester Diocesan Board of Education in the Guildhall, and did not entirely agree with the complacency of the previous speaker, Lord Lyttelton. Pakington supported the recent government proposals

*Waresley House, Hartlebury, the home (now demolished) of Dr John Peel DD, Dean of Worcester from 1845 to 1874.*

for widening education in the manufacturing districts, where a high proportion of the poorer classes were still illiterate, and said the same was needed in agricultural districts. Affirming his belief that education was the surest way of improving their lot, he said "There are some persons who believe that education will tend to deprive the poor of their industrious habits – I vigorously express my firm dissent from such an opinion".

After Easter, Pakington and Johnny went on a trip to Shropshire, staying first at Walford with the Slaneys (see above page 40) then Sweeney Hall and the Parkers (see above page 19). With Robert Slaney they went to Shrewsbury where he saw the gaol; 'made entry in book concerning the unreasonable severity of their separate system'. Pakington had critical views about solitary confinement. With John Parker they went to view a new church at Oswestry, and the local workhouse. At the end of the month they returned to Westwood and the following day Pakington and his son took the midday train to Euston, and went to Green Street, where they found his aunt 'pretty well'. The following day, Sunday, they went to church in the Hanover Chapel and in the Chapel Royal, and wasted no time in calling on Mrs Milner. Next day Johnny returned to his studies in Brighton, and Pakington called on the Murrays – presumably his comment 'sat some time but not satisfactory' indicates that he missed them. So he cut his losses and dined at the House of Commons, where he heard a 'fine speech' by Sir James Graham outlining the government's latest proposals to give more religious freedom in the operation of the education clauses of the Factories Bill. Compulsory education was to be made a condition of allowing young persons to work in factories, but this idea was eventually dropped.

On 3rd May 'called again on Murrays – most delightful & memorable visit. Stayed lunch & sung afterwards – rec'd permission from Lady Sarah to come at that hour whenever I liked – Aug'a most kind'. But the following day he missed seeing Augusta riding in the park as the Murrays rose late, so he dined with Mrs Milner instead. By now Pakington seemed determined to rapidly advance his relationship, and the following day

> went to Murrays by appointment at 12 – consulted Bishop about Oxford – met Bishop's brother – another happy morning till 3½ intercourse with A M most tender & conclusive. As I found Murrays were going to Bromley tomorrow resolved this evening to write proposal & enclose it to Lady Sarah there – wrote late at night.

The reference to Oxford was no doubt in relation to Johnny – he was due to go to Oxford the following year, and probably wanted advice or help getting him into a college. George Murray had gone to Christ Church, which is the college Johnny was to go to in 1844, so he may well have been able to help, and all five Murray sons had gone to, or were to go, there. The following day he called on the Murrays again, 'saw

A & told her I had written & she must caution Lady S as to opening the letter'. We do not know the contents, but it may well be that Pakington had asked permission to write it on 3rd May, and that it contained an important proposal to Augusta, which is why her mother must not open it.

So all Pakington could do now was to await developments. He had a lengthy lunch with Mrs Milner, rode in the park with the Mordaunts, and dined with Hallifax. 'Nervous and anxious all day'.

But all was to be resolved on Monday, when he 'heard from Augusta & Lady S by post – most charming letters confirming every hope but deferring my visit till Tuesday, as they c'd not see Bishop till this day…'. When he went to the Murray's in Belgrave Square the following day he had 'one of the most memorable & charming days of my life! Went to Belgrave Sq at 12 o'clock received most kindly by Bishop & Lady Sarah – & then Lady S showed me up & left me with Augusta in boudoir – with her except lunch four hours – most heavenly interview'. But that still left time for him to go to the House for the first of a five night debate on a motion to abolish the Corn Laws. On the Friday of that memorable week, Pakington spent all morning discussing the details of a proposed turnpike bill, then he went to Belgrave Square to lunch with Lady Camden (Augusta's eldest sister) and the Mordaunts, who had been told of the engagement, but it had not been made public. Afterwards he 'passed some heavenly hours with Augusta & sang a little', but still went to Westminster to follow the corn law debate in the evening. On Saturday he had some turnpike business at the Home Office, then 'at three rode with Bishop & Lady Sarah & Aug'ta by appoint't took country & pretty ride to Tooting Common &c Aug'ta in new habit & looking well – charming ride – I dined in Belgrave Sq & met Camdens – some sweet moments in boudoir with Aug'ta – very pleasant eve'.

On Monday he 'passed delightful morning with Augusta – gave her enamel & diamond ring as solemn pledge of our attachment'. Two days later Pakington attended another levée, and the month continued with visits to Belgrave Square, attending the House of Commons, a meeting with prime minister to discuss the Canada Corn Bill, the opera, and lunch with Mrs Milner. He

*The house on the north side of Belgrave Square that was the London residence of the Bishop of Rochester and his family until 1846.*

frequently records his pleasure in his encounters with Augusta – on Sunday 21st May 'interview with Aug'ta this day as heavenly as anything on earth can be!' and the next day 'delicious evening with Aug'ta in boudoir'.

On 24th May there was a meeting of the Severn Commissioners, and, as a leading member, he followed his usual practice of attending everything he could. So he travelled to Worcester by train on 23rd, and attended the meeting the next day, returning on 25th. The Commissioners had been appointed under an Act of 1842 to improve the navigation of the river, and to allow boats of a maximum of 6 feet draught to come up river as far as Stourport. Proposals to allow sea going vessels to come as far as Worcester had first been made in the 1780s, but these, and later proposals, were always met by staunch opposition from Gloucester interests, who feared that it would allow trade to by-pass that city to the advantage of places further up-stream. As always, there was less rational opposition. It would make the flooding worse, the slow-flowing water would be unhealthy, and so on, and this led to parliamentary battles in the 1830s when a bill was first brought forward. The expense of the battles consumed most of the capital originally subscribed to the proposed company, and eventually an act of 1842 put the work in the hands of thirty commissioners representing all local interests, of which Pakington was a leading member. The money was to be raised by public subscription, and the Staffordshire & Worcestershire Canal Company, chaired by Lord Hatherton, whose canal fed into the Severn at Stourport, acted as a major guarantor. Once the bill was passed, work got under way quite quickly, and the four weirs, at Lincomb just downstream from Stourport, at Holt, at Bevere, and at Diglis just south of Worcester, took little more than a year to complete. To pacify local interests weirs further downstream were not part of the original plan, where the depth was to be maintained by dredging.

Although the idea of connecting the Bristol Channel with the Worcester & Birmingham and the Staffordshire & Worcestershire Canals with all their links to the industrial midlands seemed very attractive, once the project was finished it never realised its potential as the railway network was superseding it. Goods could be transported from Birmingham to Gloucester docks, for example, by a direct train service in less than a day, whereas it would take several days with transhipment at Worcester, using the canals and river.

Back in London, Pakington returned to the routine of calls at Belgrave Square and attending the House of Commons. On 27th May 'rec'd from her beautiful ring with her hair in it as pledge of 'Mutual Love'', and after practicing in the morning took part in a musical evening with the family. On 30th they attended the consecration of a new church, and 'most happy morning – first time of attending church with Aug'ta since engagement – great happiness in kneeling & praying side by side throughout the solemn & impressive service of consecration'. The following day he took Augusta and her mother to meet his aunt – they 'sat some time – this gave me great pleasure'.

But a couple of days later Pakington felt ill, 'more ill than I had done for many years'. Perhaps the emotional upheaval and non-stop activity of recent days was catching up with him. Nevertheless he sat by Augusta singing at night – 'very ill but pretty good voice!'. The next day, Sunday, he stayed in all day, and wrote to Augusta in the morning, receiving a charming letter back from her in the afternoon.

On Monday he had further rehearsals for a musical evening at the Murrays in the morning, then at 5.00 p.m. left for Brighton to meet Johnny, and they dined at the Albion Hotel, 'I much exhausted'. On Monday he felt himself recovering, and his mood was helped when Johnny saw the ring Augusta had given him on his desk, '& this led to me telling him all in evening! – he received intelligence delightfully'. The next day after Johnny had repeated his pleasure at his father's prospects, Pakington had to travel back to London to sing in the Murrays' music party. He was still very weak, but 'to my surprise I sing well'. On Saturday they all went up to Bromley for the weekend: 'most heavenly to be with her at Bromley again…'. Not for the first time, Sunday saw them take a walk before breakfast, and after going to church twice they spent a private and delightful evening together, 'close of it not to be forgotten – on the whole a day of such unchequered happiness as this world does not often afford, & as ought to inspire the most grateful reflecting'.

Although the engagement was still supposed to be secret, an ever-wider circle of relations were told, and Augusta's clergyman brother Francis came to see Pakington on Tuesday, and was most cordial 'to my great & agreeable surprise'. One supposes that as it was still not six months since his wife's death, such an early engagement would be frowned on by some, which is why it was not being published abroad. Pakington wanted his son to meet his new step-mother as soon as possible, so on Thursday 15th June he travelled up from Brighton for the day, and there was a 'delightful' meeting between them. 'Johnny's manner everything I could wish, & his subsequent letter delightful'.

The following Monday the Murrays had yet another music party at which Pakington sang; 'happy moments when concert over'. On Wednesday there is a rare touch of humour when Pakington writes 'went down to Belgrave Sq in such a state that I was marched off at once to Bedlam! i.e. went there by appointment with Bishop & Lord Camden – interesting but painful sight – saw & conversed with McNaughton', whom he thought insane. Earlier that year Daniel McNaughton had shot and killed the Prime Minister's private secretary believing him to be Peel, but eventually he was deemed to be insane, whence the McNaughton rules about criminal insanity.

On Saturday Pakington had to return to Worcestershire as quarter sessions were to be held the following week. On the first day Thomas Lea of Astley Hall proposed the discontinuation of the rural police, which he thought not worth their cost. But Pakington disagreed; 'I spoke with much effect – & was unusually cheered by the bench – motion negatived by triumphant majority'. Pakington often noted that the quarter sessions tired him, but that day he noted that he was 'less tired than usual by exertions of first day'. Wednesday was another long day, in which he 'tried one tiresome case of assault by Sir Thomas Phillipps – fined him £10'. Sir Thomas was a prominent but irascible county figure, famous for his book collection, who lived on Middle Hill, Broadway, and when George Cooper, collector of Her Majesty's taxes, arrived to collect arrears of £1 6s 2d, Phillipps refused to pay, because, he later explained, he only owed £2 based on his poor law assessment, and Cooper had made his own higher assessment of £3 6s 2d. Phillipps attempted to eject Cooper, and eventually there was a scuffle during which it was alleged that Cooper was hit over the head with a 'garden paddle'. Cooper tried to distrain on some horses, but the stables were locked. Eventually Phillipps paid up. Phillips' co-defendants, who it was alleged had helped in the assault on Cooper, were found not guilty, but Phillips himself was found guilty. A no doubt exasperated chairman fined him £10 for common assault.

Although some of the Murray family had seen Westwood when Pakington first took possession of it, the children probably had not, so he had some prints made and sent them to Lady Mordaunt and Lady Camden, his future sisters-in-law.

The following Saturday Pakington joined the Murrays in a trip across the river to Southfleet, and on Sunday, full of feeling, Pakington makes one of his longest diary entries, which is worth reproducing verbatim:

> Sunday 2nd July – A day never to be forgotten – most happy & most impressive & cannot in either respect be surpassed or excelled till our wedding day – Augusta & I rec'd the Holy Communion side by side together for the first time since our engagement & it was administered by George & Francis – the first time she had ever heard them officiate – for her this was a much affecting combination – she felt it much & I feared she would have been quite upset after returning to the pew. We went to afternoon service – Francis preached in morning, George in eve – both good. Dined early & enjoyed shady walk – after tea we returned to drawing room by ourselves – read together Shuttleworth Sermon on Felix - & before going to bed enjoyed moments of intense feeling – we hoped & I trust not presumptuously that our prayers were heard & that the blessing of God had that day been upon us.

Monday was 'another most charming day', and they went to see the nearby Cobham Hall, the seat of the Earl of Darnley. Although Pakington enjoyed the park scenery, he found the house 'disappointing'. The visit lasted through Monday into Tuesday, and included a tête à tête in Augusta's boudoir, a shady walk, and some singing. On his return on Tuesday evening he wrote 'so ended 4 days of no common bliss & which ought to inspire no common thankfulness'. On Wednesday he was brought down to earth with the rather mundane business of the turnpike committee and Coroners Bill in the House of Commons.

The next few days he shared between Belgrave Square and the House of Commons, and another long entry on Sunday ends:

> I have here space to remark & I cannot make such an entry on a more appropriate day than that specially set apart for religious observance how deeply grateful I ought & I trust I do feel for the inestimable blessing that every interview with her whom I have selected for my future wife indicates my admiration & respect for her charming mind & character & thus strengthens an affection which rests upon such foundations – may God make me as thankful as I ought to be.

Thankfulness for his blessings was a constant theme of Pakington's life, and reveals what was perhaps the most religious aspect of his character.

July 13th was Johnny's 17th birthday, and his father went to Brighton, observing that 'I thank God that he is as perfect as I can desire in both the mind & body'. Returning to town next day, Pakington received three notes from Augusta, and spent much of the next few days at Belgrave Square. But London society was beginning to break up now at the end of the season – the Camdens left town, and on 18th July the Murrays also left for Bromley. There was an exhibition of cartoons in Westminster Hall which were competing to be included in the decoration of the new Houses of Parliament. Pakington went twice, including a visit to 'lionize' them with Augusta and Lady Kinnoull (Augusta's mother's sister-in-law). 'Much pleased' he wrote. Pakington's last Sunday with Augusta showed his sentimental side, as they passed their 'last happy evening in the boudoir', reading Shuttleworth's 'Sermon on Prayer', leaving her at 11 after 'a delicious interview'.

Shorty after this Pakington had the first of several sittings for Thorburn, and later Augusta also sat for him. This was the Scottish born miniaturist Robert Thorburn (1818-85), and a miniature still exists in a private collection. It is a pity that the accompanying miniature portrait of Augusta seems to have been lost.

Pakington's interest in prisons has already been noted, and on 20th July he went to Pentonville 'to see model prison

*This miniature of John Pakington is in a private collection, but the sitter appears younger than 44, which he would have been when he sat for Thorburn.*

in action' with his fellow Tory MP and friend Hon. Robert Clive of Oakley Park, who represented south Shropshire. Clive had married Lady Harriet Windsor, daughter of 5th Earl of Plymouth, thus giving a Worcestershire connection. (After Clive's death in 1854 his widow Harriet was created Baroness Windsor in her own right, and her grandson Robert Windsor-Clive became 1st Earl of Plymouth of Hewell Grange of the 3rd creation in 1905.)

In the 1840s the idea of fixed term imprisonment as a punishment was still quite new, as hitherto the main forms of punishment were imposition of a fine, transportation, incarceration in a hulk, or execution. The reduced use of the death penalty in the late eighteenth century had led to a great increase in transportation, but now there was pressure from the colonies and elsewhere to reduce this form of punishment. For the first time the government was forced to consider how best to imprison criminals for fixed terms. Use of hulks was never considered other than an unsatisfactory expedient. Gaols were mainly designed to hold prisoners awaiting trial, and were of limited capacity, some were very ancient and often, like Worcester gaol, somewhat insecure. The first purpose-built prison to hold long term prisoners was Millbank in London, opened in 1813, and was followed by Pentonville which had been opened in 1843. Pentonville consisted of five radiating wings so that warders could have a view down each corridor from a central station. It was designed to hold 520 prisoners on the 'separate' system, which we would today call solitary confinement. Each cell was 13 feet by 7 with a high window (later, of course, such cells would often house two men). Although prisoners exercised and went to chapel together, communication was forbidden, and when together they wore masks. This system was first tried in America, and was based on the theory that allowing criminals to associate freely with other criminals would simply breed even worse criminals. The disadvantage was that it also led to a significant occurrence of mental illness and suicide, and was expensive.

Pakington had not been to the opera recently, but now the Murrays were in Bromley he had more time, and accompanied Lady Harriet

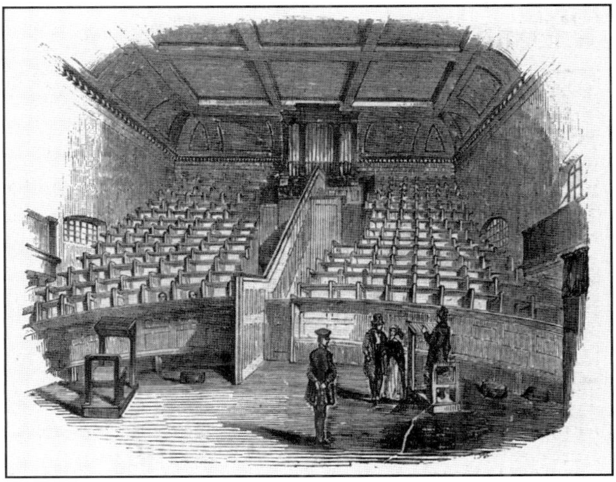

*Pentonville Prison, opened in 1843. This view of the chapel, which was attended daily, shows how the prisoners sat in separate cubicles that prevented them seeing each other. From the Illustrated London News.*

Clive and two of her daughters Henrietta (23) and Mary (14) to Exeter Hall to see Spohr's 'The Fall of Babylon'. The following day Pakington rode to Bromley for the weekend. On Sunday in the morning service he used the new prayer book given him by Augusta for the first time, and, prevented from going to evening service by the weather, 'passed whole evening most happily reading &c with Augusta'. He stayed till Tuesday morning after 'three blissful days', starting for London before 8.00. After a Thorburn sitting he spent the rest of the day busy at home in Green Street, finding the House of Commons counted out when he went at night to attend a debate on national education. No doubt the lateness of the season meant increasing numbers of MPs had left town. The next day he found the House in session, and he voted on a clause in the Coroners Bill concerning whether coroners should be paid one shilling or one shilling and sixpence per mile for travelling. Afterwards he found time to dine with Hallifax, then go to the Theatre Royal, Haymarket at 10.00 p.m. where he saw 'Double bedded room', at which he had a good laugh. On the same bill was Macbeth, but we assume he arrived after that had finished.

During the week he decided to sell some of his journals and papers to Newmans, the antiquarian booksellers at 235 High Holborn. Perhaps he was a hoarder of these things, and had to clear space out for other books. Later in life he had a large collection of antiquarian books including prayer books and bibles. The last weekend of July found Pakington again at Bromley, where he stayed for the following week. On Tuesday Johnny came from Brighton to join them, and everyone seems to have had a happy time – on Thursday 'Augusta & I took delicious walk over the old ground hallowed by happy recollections in evening, played chess again with Bishop & then sung old favourites'.

Sadly, the next day the 'happy party' broke up and the Murrays departed to Stowe where the Duke of Buckingham was entertaining the King of Hanover. Pakington went with Johnny to Cowes, where they met 'old Hallifax', his friend's father. He was also a member of the Royal Yacht Squadron, and on his son's yacht Camilla they sailed to Southampton on Sunday to collect Thomas Hallifax. They enjoyed two days' sailing and walking before having to return to London on Tuesday to meet Augusta for another sitting at Thorburn's. Later Pakington took Johnny to the opera to see Rossini's 'Semiramide', and the following night to 'Cure for Love' at the Haymarket, which sounds something of a rather lighter nature.

After Thorburn requested another sitting, Pakington had to delay his return to Worcestershire, and paid a final visit to Bromley, where he was able to enjoy a moonlit walk in the garden before retiring. On 11th August, after a final pre-breakfast walk with Augusta, Pakington and Johnny rode to London, where they caught the train back home, walking the final three miles from Droitwich Road to Westwood. There he found his aunt with another Hawkins cousin and a Mrs Lowther. That did not affect his enjoyment the next day of sailing their new boat 'Lady of the Lake' on the Great Pool, and doing some duck shooting. On Monday, after calling to see Barry Domvile, the sick son of his half sister Mary Domvile, he went to Worcester and found it 'in commotion'. Queen Adelaide, the Queen Dowager, had taken Witley Court, where she had arrived the previous Tuesday to great fanfare – The Times noted that Miss Pakington's carriage was seen at Holt when Queen Adelaide passed through. She visited Worcester on Monday, and almost every building in the city was decorated in her honour. A tremendous downpour later gave flash floods and washed away roads, catching Pakington on the way home. But the following day he was able to go to Witley to add his name to the list of callers, and there was another thunder storm in the evening. Another member of the Hawkins family came to stay during the week – Caesar Hawkins, the grandson of Sir Caesar Hawkins whose sister married Herbert Pakington, 7th bart, another in the long line of surgeons this family produced.

While in Droitwich, Pakington had a yeomanry cavalry drill (only eleven men came), went recruiting in Ombersley, and went to see Barry Domvile, again, but was only able to see his father as he was so ill. He had lunch with the Galtons at Hadzor Hall, where the splendid gardens were well-known locally. After less than two weeks he returned to London where he was met by Bishop Murray, who took him down to Bromley and his dear Augusta. He was able to stay with the Murrays for five days, and wrote 'passed this day & every succeeding day while here in the exclusive enjoyment of Augusta's society, & in unspeakable happiness'. On Tuesday Lady Sarah took her youngest children with, Pakington wrote, a party of 40 cousins, to see Windsor, leaving him alone with Augusta for the day. The next day, before leaving, Pakington had his

*A theatre bill advertising the performance of 'Semiramide' seen by Pakington and his son in 1843. As was usual at that time, the evening included 'extras' – a 'pas de deux' in the interval, and a 'New Ballet Divertissement' as a conclusion. The leading operatic singers are all Italian. Reproduced courtsey of the Shakespeare Centre Library and Archive.*

first kiss from Lady Sarah, then left with Augusta's younger brother Robert to keep Johnny company travelling to Droitwich to attend the funeral of Barry Domvile, who had died just after Pakington last left Droitwich.

Pakington, Johnny and Robert were at Westwood for two and a half weeks, the boys spending much time sailing, and Pakington shooting, attending the Droitwich board of guardians, having another drill, and entertaining the Hanbury Williams whom he let into his secret. Letters were exchanged with Augusta every day. On 18th September Johnny and Robert left to return to London, but Pakington wanted to go to the Birmingham Music Festival, which lasted three days, ending with Messiah on 21st. The next day he wasted no time in returning to Augusta, who was staying with her family at Bayham, the estate belonging to Lord Camden near Lamberhurst in Kent. On their reunion he wrote 'a sitting room to ourselves seems to have bound us up in each other with a depth of feeling beyond anything we have yet experienced, & to have made us feel as if the happy ceremony had already joined us in sacred union'. There were medieval abbey ruins on the estate, which Pakington went to see of course, but his main interest at this time was on the relationship with Augusta, and a few days later records 'éclaircissement between us, continued in second long walk after lunch & which made us both feel happier and better satisfied'. The latter part of their stay was spent at Wildernesse, another Camden property, and after a stay of ten days Pakington left early after Augusta had made breakfast for him, and got to Westwood the same day, where he found his aunt well.

On his first day back he had a meeting of the Droitwich Guardians, and records that he was 'full of the happy days I have just passed & quite unhinged by parting'. The next day was the first of yeomanry week, and on the first morning a very 'melancholy accident' happened to 'poor Wakeman' (Sir Offley Wakeman, 2nd bart) – in the wet conditions his horse slipped, falling on him and crushing his leg, causing a long-lasting injury. There was a second

*Queen Adelaide during her widowhood. Born Princess Adelaide of Saxe-Meiningen in 1792, she married Prince William in 1818 when it was clear that he was heir to his elder brother George IV. But the couple had no surviving children, and when William IV died in 1837 his niece the Princess Victoria became Queen. During her widowhood the Queen dowager spent three years from 1843 in Witley Court. She died in 1849.*

accident the same day when an artillery man suffered serious injury to both hands – an artillery piece exploded before he had properly withdrawn the ram-rod. On Sunday a third tragedy took place – Pakington was due to go to the cathedral with Robert Henry Clive, the Colonel Commander of the Yeomanry Cavalry, but news of the death of Henry, brother of Joseph Martin, the cavalry's major, came through and Clive had to break it to Martin. Henry Martin, of Hook Common near Upton upon Severn, had been suffering from 'an affliction'. He was due to go to London for an operation, but at the last minute changed his mind, and died when a gun he was carrying discharged as he was leaving his house. At the inquest the jury found it was an accident, but Pakington refers to it in his diary as a suicide.

Yeomanry week culminated on Wednesday 11th October, when there was a review on Pitchcroft attended by Queen Adelaide. The weather had been wet and it was spoilt, Pakington wrote, by 'mud and splash'.

The Michaelmas quarter sessions opened under Pakington's chairmanship on 16th October, and an early matter to be dealt with was one that evidently troubled the chairman. Some time previously one of the magistrates, George Ellins, had published a letter in the Worcester Chronicle that accused a fellow magistrate, W. H. Ricketts, of 'corruption and jobbing' in the course of carrying out his duties as a magistrate and member of the police committee. A meeting of the magistrates had been held and at the January sessions a committee was appointed to investigate. At the April sessions, after some opposition, their report was read out confirming that a gross libel had been committed on Ricketts. Ellins had appealed to Lord Lyttelton, the Lord Lieutenant, claiming that the proceedings of the magistrates in this matter were beyond their powers and illegal. Lyttelton then conducted his own investigation, in front of counsel both for Ellins and for the magistrates' committee. He concluded the magistrates had no power to do what they had done, and the Lord Chancellor agreed that the magistrates' action was without authority and highly

*George William Lyttelton, 4th Baron Lyttelton of Hagley Hall, 1817-76. He married Mary Glynne in a double wedding when her sister Catherine married William Gladstone. He had a brief period of office under Peel in 1846, but was mainly interested in church and local affairs. He was a manic depressive and died by his own hand.*

irregular. Lyttelton concluded that 'I cannot doubt that the magistrates will consider it their duty carefully to avoid any similar proceedings for the future, and to confine themselves to the exercise of their judicial duties…'.

Naturally the magistrates assembled that day did not like to be lectured on what they could and could not do, even if by such a distinguished person as Lord Lyttelton. A short discussion had taken place at the midsummer sessions in which the chairman had taken the view that it needed delicate handling. As the letter had only recently been received, its consideration should be postponed till the next, Michaelmas, sessions. Not everyone agreed, but the chairman was supported on a division by 32 votes to 11. So Pakington now explained that he had consulted widely, and he saw no point at all in having a long discussion on the matter. He proposed simply to pass on to the next business, being the best way to retain the dignity of the court, while showing due respect for the Lord Lieutenant. Not everyone agreed that simply ignoring Lyttelton's letter was the best way, but in the end that was what was done. (This was not quite the end of this matter. In the spring sessions the following year, Lord Lyttelton, not agreeing with the fact that his letter had not been entered into the court's records, and feeling therefore that the magistrates might conduct another erroneous enquiry in future, appeared personally and restated his opinion, but said he had no further proposal to make. As he got up to leave he was asked to propose a motion, but declined, and the chairman, Pakington, said any further discussion would be out of order.)

The day after sessions finished there must have been a little panic at Westwood, as 'heard from Lord Howe that Queen & Duchess of Gloucester would come to Westwood tomorrow'. This was the Queen Dowager now living at Witley Court – Lord Howe was one of her entourage. The next day, however, the household at Westwood was informed that the Queen had a cold and would not come. However 'Duchess of Gloucester [a daughter of George III] with all court came at 12 ½ lionised house & lunched – all went off well'. After they had gone Pakington still had time to travel to Walton, the home of the Mordaunts, where the Bishop and Lady Sarah had come to stay, bringing Augusta. Pakington had a most happy four days at Walton, the only cloud being a Mr Miller who came to dinner on the last night, 'but we did not let him mar the pleasure of an evening'.

Pakington's engagement had not yet been made public, but rumours were no doubt circulating, and the next morning he received a 'kind and satisfactory' letter from Mrs Milner 'enquiring as to engagement'. He replied the following day. But a few days later 'we were much distressed by letter form Mrs Milner in morning which though most kind as from herself contained things which hurt me much'. We can only imagine that although she sent her personal best wishes for their happiness, she felt that many people would say, or had already said, that their engagement was too soon after Mary's death.

Later in the day they had another engagement – the Murrays and Pakington had been asked to meet the Duchess of Gloucester at Hewell, and to dine. He records that he avoided Augusta at dinner – perhaps because his engagement was still unannounced – and instead conversed with the Duchess. Two days later the Murrays progressed to the Old Deanery at Worcester (Bishop Murray was still Dean there), and naturally Pakington joined them. He spent most of the day with Augusta, except for a visit with Bishop Murray to the Bishop of Worcester's palace nearby. The Old Deanery at Worcester was in the Guesten Hall, the fourteenth century open hall used by the Prior of Worcester for the reception of guests, and after the Reformation its interior, which had been entirely open, was divided up and had a variety of uses. At this time it was evidently deemed unsatisfactory as the Deanery, which was soon to be transferred to the Bishop's Palace, the bishop not needing this accommodation. After the Dean moved out the Guesten Hall was partially demolished and its magnificent medieval timber roof used on a new church then being built in the city. Later still it was taken to the Avoncroft Museum of Buildings, but the ruins of the Guesten Hall still stand today in the College Green. The Murrays returned to Worcester in November to take possession of the Palace, which we will now call the Deanery.

On Monday 30th October Pakington was invited by Queen Adelaide to Witley Court, where he had a pleasant musical evening, singing 'The Treasures of the Deep' in a trio with the Duchess of Kent and Lord Barrington. The next day, making calls from Kidderminster to Hartlebury, his mare 'fell & gave me terrific fall – I thank God that in his great mercy I escaped with so little injury'. On 1st November he returned to London by train with the Murrays. They went on to Bromley, but Pakington went to his aunt's new house in Westbourne Street where he was staying. Two days later she had an accident. A wheel came off the vehicle she was travelling in, and she was 'capsized in the mud – much frightened but little hurt'. The same day he went on to Bromley, where he found Johnny up from Brighton, and noted the next day that Augusta does not want him to be seen in church until the Bromley Ball, held two days later. Instead they read divine service together, and

*Walton Hall c. 1810, which was replaced by the present building, now an hotel, in 1858. From 'Capt. Saunders Warwickshire Drawings', courtesy of Shakespeare Centre Library and Archive.*

in the evening the Bishop confirmed Johnny, 'all were much affected by this impressive & interesting ceremony'. Pakington was also pleased to note that Augusta received a beautiful congratulatory letter from Mrs Milner, and writing her answer engaged Augusta for most of Monday. Hearing that an engagement he had at Westwood had been postponed, Pakington resolved to stay as long as possible, and it was not till Monday 13th that he left Bromley 'after a most happy visit of 9 days, but A & I have now become so completely united in feeling & affection that every separation is very painful'. He called on his aunt in London, but still managed to be at Westwood by 9.00 p.m.

Next day he called on 'poor Fanny' (Frances, the widow of Henry Domvile), and later George Murray came to Westwood for the night, and he and Pakington spent some time talking 'about Miss Childe's letters and Augusta', presumably someone else who did not approve of his early engagement.

It was the time of the year for shooting parties in country houses, and in November Pakington spent time at Stanford, the home of the Winningtons, and Ingestre, the seat of the Chetwynd-Talbots, Earls of Hensol – a member of the family was vicar of Ombersley. Back from Ingestre on Saturday 25th November, he spent time with Augusta and the Murrays who were installing themselves in the new Deanery. On this and other occasions when they were in Worcester he would return to Westwood for the evening, which he often passed on his own. Perhaps he was reluctant for it to be known that he was spending so much time with the Murrays. The following Monday he was 'busy all morning in painful search amongst dear Mary's things for presents as momentos for Slaneys', then after spending the next day with Augusta, he went in the evening for a shooting party at Brockhampton with Barneby. While there he heard that Johnny was poorly in Brighton, which spoiled his visit, but once back at Westwood he heard he had recovered. The Murrays were still in Worcester, and dined with Pakington at Madresfield on 1st December. He managed to spend all the following day at the Deanery, and practiced duets with Augusta.

Concerned about Johnny, on Monday 4th December Pakington set off by train to see him. He spent the first night in London with Hallifax, where he met Mr Hallifax senior and his bank-

*The Bishop's Palace, Worcester, which was used as the Deanery from 1843. From Valentine Green's History of Worcester 1796.*

ing partner George Glyn. In Brighton the following day he found Johnny 'better but weak', and got back to London in time to dine at the Carlton Club with Lord Ashley. Returning to Worcester, he slept (unusually) at the Deanery after attending their music party, and remained there for two days. Over the weekend he had to entertain his late wife's cousin Robert Slaney, who left on Monday 11th. That night Pakington had been invited to sleep at the Deanery, but heard that the Murrays had been invited to dine with the Queen Dowager at Witley. He was determined to keep his engagement there nonetheless, but when he got to Worcester he found that they were to sleep at Witley as well. He still decided to stay, so played chess there with a Mrs Harrison until he went to bed. The Murrays arrived back at midday, which left Pakington two hours with Augusta till he had to go and meet Johnny, coming home from Brighton, whom he thankfully found in much improved health.

On December 14th Johnny dined and slept at the Deanery, while Pakington joined the Murrays at a musical evening at the Isaacs' at Boughton. The next day Pakington went to enquire about Fanny Domvile. She had been pregnant when her husband died in August, and on 11th December had given birth to her fourth child, christened Barry Francis Domvile. The same day Pakington bought Barry's yeomanry uniforms for £46 – perhaps this was to help his widow. Pakington and Johnny stayed again that night at the Deanery. Edmund Lechmere was also there, and when Lady Sarah informed Mrs Lechmere of the engagement, 'she evinced great pleasure & kindness'. The engagement had still not been made public.

Monday 18th December marked the start of the Assizes, but after attending the grand jury Pakington spent most of that and the following day sitting with Augusta, who was ill, and left Johnny to sit in court observing proceedings. On Wednesday Francis Murray came over to shoot, and gave a 'very poor account of Augusta', which made Pakington uncomfortable all day. Although the sport was fair, neither Francis nor Edward Wakeman, his other guest, were good shots. Augusta was better the next day, and Pakington attended an East Worcestershire Conservative Association meeting, where only Ricketts joined him. The next day, after a meeting of the Severn Commissioners, he stayed at the Deanery where archdeacon Godsall was a guest – Augusta was still convalescing, and after dinner when Pakington went to sit with her, Godsall could not think what had become of him!

After attending morning service at Hampton with Johnny, they spent the rest of the Christmas day in the Deanery, going to evening service in the cathedral, and later had 'delightful moments with Augusta in little room'. On Boxing Day they all went to Eastnor Castle. They went out shooting the following day and had fine views and a beautiful day, but 'moderate sport'. Afterwards 'Lady Sarah delighted me by admitting me to her room to sit with Augusta'. In the evening they made music, and Lord Mexborough, one of the guests, sang comic songs. They all enjoyed the shooting and singing so much that they extended the party till Saturday 30th. Johnny and his father spent that evening again at the Deanery where he had 'had most happy and affecting interview with dearest Augusta & Lady Sarah, talking of the close of this eventful year – so ended one of the most agreeable visits and most happy Xmas weeks I have passed... Lady Sarah's kiss to Augusta & myself as we sat on sofa not to be forgotten'. Pakington's summary of the year is as follows:

> I cannot close the records of this chequered & eventful year which has witnessed the termination of a happy union of 20 years & the commencement of another connection no less dear & tender without endeavouring to express my deep & grateful sense of the great & unmerited mercies & blessings which the goodness of God has vouchsafed to me – I humbly hope that affliction has been so far blessed to me as to have strengthened & improved my character by making me more than ever sensible of my own unworthiness & my entire dependence upon the mercy of the Almighty, and more than ever conscious of the happiness as well as the duty of endeavouring to lead a Christian life – when I reflect upon the bright prospects which cheered the close of the year, & the tender attachment which has given a charm to its last months I earnestly pray that if it pleases God to realize my hopes, I may bear with humility such great enjoyment & that through my future life I may be enabled to fulfil every duty to the dear boy with whom I am now blessed & to my dear future wife, both of whom I so tenderly love.

And he introduces 1844 by writing

> In the course of this to me important year I am engaged again to undertake the sacred & happy duties of married life. I thank God for having led me to a choice, which is confirmed by every feeling of my heart and judgement – may it please Him to bless an attachment which I believe is as mutually deep as was ever felt, and to realise those happy prospects which we are now permitted to indulge!

## Chapter 10
## His second marriage 1844-46

Pakington spent the first three days of January 1844 presiding over quarter sessions, and any free time was devoted to Augusta, who was still with her family in Worcester. On the 4th the Murrays went to Kinlet, the home of the Childe family, but Pakington declined to go as it was the anniversary of the week of 'poor dear Mary's death'. Johnny was still at home, and he and his father rode twice to Lincombe to see the new weir that had been built just south of Stourport. After the second visit they travelled on to Walford to stay with the Slaneys. On their first evening he attended a 'nice dance', but his thoughts were elsewhere and he did not enjoy it. From Walford they moved on to Acton Reynald to stay with the Corbets where they enjoyed the usual hunting and shooting, and returned to Worcester on 18th January.

Early in January Pakington had expressed a little surprise to find his son with the Murrays in the Deanery. The day after his return when Pakington went to Worcester early, he remarked 'cautioned Johnny about Eleanor'. It appears that he was forming a relationship with Eleanor Murray, and Pakington was obviously not keen for his son to get involved with his future sister-on-law, not least because Johnny was 17 and Eleanor 15.

A problem that was to dog Pakington throughout his life was money. The following day he shot with Thomas Curtler, whom he had invited over after examining his bank statements the night before, which left him 'out of spirits'. He discussed the situation with Curtler, and the following day he told Augusta 'about vexation about money affairs & increasing debt', but it is not evident from his diary that there was any noticeable change in his behaviour after that.

Now the works on the Severn were progressing well, Pakington presided over a grand celebratory dinner that was held in the Guildhall on 25th January. The main object of the event was to present a silver service to John Wheeley Lea, of Lea & Perrins Sauce fame, who, from the time he was Mayor of Worcester in 1835, had tirelessly worked to see the project come to fruition. As usual on these occasions there was toast after toast, giving the opportunity for speech making. First was the loyal toast, then one to the Queen Dowager, followed by one to Prince Albert and the rest of the royal family. Toasts to the army and navy followed, and in his reply on behalf on the navy Capt. Gabriel paid tribute to Pakington, who was one of those who "did good by stealth and blushed to find it fame". After a toast to the Lord Lieutenant of the County, these preliminary toasts were followed by Pakington's tribute and toast to Lea, and Lea's reply, toasting those who had subscribed to the silver service.

Pakington then proposed a toast to the success of the Severn Commission, followed by one to the Bishop and Clergy. The Mayor then stood up and proposed the health of the 'worthy chairman', and this was followed by toasts to the MPs for the county, then the MPs for Worcester City. Pakington then spoke about Lord Ward, who had been an enthusiastic supporter of the project, and proposed his health, followed by toasts to the Mayor and Corporation, and John Dent, the glover who was president of the chamber of commerce. Reverting to the Severn improvements, Pakington next proposed the health of Lord Hatherton and the committee of the Staffordshire Canal Company, followed by toasts to two more consistent friends of the project, Col. Davies MP and Capt. Winnington MP, remarking that although they were both Whigs, this had never interfered with their private friendship. Then after a toast to a former Mayor, Mr Evans, Lord Hatherton rose to propose what he called the most important toast of the evening, one to William Cubitt, the project's chief engineer. Cubitt, one of the leading civil engineers of his day, spoke of the importance of his assistants, and said the success of the Lincombe weir in not leading to flooding or any of the other dangers that some had predicted, should be repeated at the lower weirs that would be finished later in the year. Berrows reported that he finished by saying something of the navigation below Worcester, but unfortunately did not report the details. It would be interesting to know whether he was as optimistic about this section as he was about the rest – as we shall see, the lower section would need much more work before it could take the same boats as the upper section.

John Lea then proposed a toast to Leader Williams, the resident engineer, which was followed by toasts to the clerk to the commission, John Waters, and the contractors, Grissell & Peto. Capt. Winnington toasted the subscribers to the fund to obtain the Act, and in reply it was said they were already getting a return insofar as coal was now one shilling per ton cheaper. Then, after a toast to Mr Hornyold and the vice-presidents, a toast was proposed to the salmon fisheries association – the salmon catch had much reduced in recent years, and one problem was that the close season was not the same on all stretches of the river. Pakington had said he would introduce a bill into parliament to regularise this. Finally the chairman proposed a toast to 'the traders of the Severn and tributary canals, as also to the trade of Worcester'. This made a total of twenty four toasts, but Pakington was still able to end a busy day by singing at a 'large & excellent concert at the Deanery – I thank God for giving me health, strength & ability so to get through & enjoy the day'.

Although he seems to have softened his views a little later, at this time Pakington was an ardent protectionist. Like many of his kind, he was alarmed at the increasing impact of the Anti-Corn Law League. In some areas 'anti-League' movements had sprung up, and in Worcester on 27th January a meeting was held to set up an anti-League movement in the county. The meeting was poorly attended, and Phipps Onslow took the chair. Francis Woodward proposed the first motion that the 'Worcestershire Agricultural Protection Society is to protect British Agriculture not only against the threatened innovations of the Anti-Corn Law League, but to oppose all measures that may be brought forward having a tendency to deprive the agriculturalist of the protection to which he is justly entitled'. The second motion 'to raise a subscription to oppose the Anti-Corn Law League, who are distributing vast numbers of printed tracts containing the grossest falsehoods and misstatements' was seconded by Pakington. In his speech, he said that he did not wish to make any detailed comments about the recent proposals to change the rates of duty on imported corn, but just wanted to establish the principle that the 'agricultural interest is entitled to protection, that the protection must be given by the government, and that some powerful organisation must be formed to counter the dangerous conspiracy of the League'. No doubt that statement drew vigorous applause.

Another new development of this time was that Bishop Murray offered to have Johnny in his household to be educated, presumably by the tutors already there to educate the young Murrays, rather than remain in Brighton. His father was pleased to accept. While the Murrays were still in Worcestershire Pakington was keen to show them Augusta's future home, so on 29th January they all 'came over to see Westwood & lunch. Lionized them everywhere & I showed Lady Sarah my proposed arrangements for dear Augusta's happiness'. The following day there was the hunt ball, and a large party assembled at the Deanery to attend. On 1st February Pakington left for London, leaving Johnny at the Deanery to 'commence his residence with the dear family who had so kindly offered to receive him for a time'.

Parliament opened on the same day, and Pakington attended the debate on the Queen's speech. Next morning he called on Mrs Milner, where he stayed for four hours and had an 'interesting & affecting conversation as to past & future'. On Saturday he travelled to the estate of his friend Hallifax at Chadacre in Suffolk, and while there walked to the nearby village of Hawkedon where he 'visited old haunts... and reflected with deep thankfulness on the 26 years of health & happiness which I have passed since I left that place' (see page 18). The main purpose of his visit seems to have been to attend the Bury fancy dress ball, which was 'very good', and the following day returned to London, where he met the Murrays and Johnny at Euston Square and passed a 'delicious' half hour with them before they had to go on to Bromley. Pakington dined with Mrs Milner, where he felt tired, and 'conversation took wrong turn & we were disappointed'. But the following day he 'lunched & sat 3 hours with Mrs Milner – compensated for last night – most interesting conversation on my attachment to Augusta'.

Pakington spent the following two weekends with the Murrays, the second at Wildernesse, and, not for the first time, he records that 'deep feelings of gratitude filled my mind this day when I reflected as I did much, on my happy connection with such a family'. He could not be with Augusta on his 45th birthday on 20th February but he had 'a most tender & affecting note' from her, and he had 'a long interview with Mrs Milner', and after attending the House sat with his aunt. The following day Pakington was able to move the second reading of his County Coroners Bill, but it was agreed to postpone debate on the detail till a later stage to allow more time for the nine-day debate on the State of Ireland that was in progress. This debate finished at 4.00 a.m. on Saturday morning, but Pakington still left early for Bromley, and spent the weekend with Augusta.

Quarter sessions, which had been adjourned from January, were due to take place the following week, so Pakington travelled to Worcester. A remark by Thomas Curtler offended Pakington but fortunately the day of duels had passed, and the offence was forgotten after an exchange of letters. Pakington spent the rest of the week discussing the covers with his game keeper and marking trees with Curtler. On Saturday he returned to London and stayed with his aunt, who had moved to Westbourne Street in Mayfair in 1840, and on Sunday he continued to Bromley. Heavy rain on Monday made him postpone his departure, and he spent time talking over his financial prospects with his future parents-in-law, and it was also agreed that Johnny would remain in their household.

In March Pakington chaired a select committee looking into the petition alleging that John Collett's election to the borough of Athlone had been tainted by bribery. After three meetings counsel for the petitioners withdrew when it became obvious that the evidence was not going to support the claims, and John Collett retained his seat.

With his marriage not very far off, Pakington was making the necessary preparations for his new bride, and decided to buy a new carriage. Turners were one of the best known carriage makers in London, and after visiting them he decided on a barouche. By this time the Murrays had moved back to their house in Belgrave Square. Augusta was able to have a long interview with Mrs Milner, 'and they were delighted with each other', and the next day Pakington found her 'much affected by interview with Augusta'. Later that day, Friday 15th March, he attended the House for the first day's debate on Lord Ashley's Ten Hour Bill to reduce the hours of work for children in factories. Then on the second concluding day he tried to speak but 'could not get in'. He voted with Lord Ashley, while Peel and many other Tories, voted against – on this occasion Lord Ashley carried the day by a narrow majority. This day, 18th March, was Augusta's 27th birthday, and Pakington went to visit her in Bromley, but he could not stay long as he had to attend a Commons committee, as well as voting in the evening.

Designs for the new barouche were coming on and Pakington and Augusta, now back in Belgrave Square, went to see drawings at Turners on Tuesday. On Friday there was another debate on the Ten Hours Bill, and again Pakington tried twice to speak but could not. As before, he voted with Ashley, opposing allowing children to work 12 hours per day, when he was on the winning side, but voting in favour of 10 hours, which was defeated, leaving nothing decided. Despite his forthcoming marriage, Pakington was heavily involved in Commons business, and the following week was appointed chairman of a new committee to investigate alternative proposals for railways to Newbury, which occupied much of his time all that week. He still had time to dine with Mrs Milner, where he had an 'interesting but rather melancholy evening'.

Parliament adjourned for Easter the next week. Pakington took leave of Augusta and went to Westwood – taking the 1.00 p.m. train to Birmingham, he was usually at Westwood by 9.00 in the evening. At home he had many estate matters to deal with, and on Easter Sunday, 7th April, he started writing 'announcement' letters, presumably with news of his engagement and marriage date, a little over a year since Augusta had accepted him. Quarter sessions took place immediately after Easter, and as soon as these were finished he was back in London, and slept at his aunt's in Westbourne Street. After one night there on Friday he rode on down to Bromley, where he met Johnny and Augusta. There had been some disagreement about the jointure in his marriage settlement, but this was settled by a 'satisfactory conversation' with the Bishop, and of course he had a 'happy meeting and delightful evening' with Augusta. On Saturday they read each other's 'congratulatory letters', and Pakington stayed till Wednesday when he, Johnny and Augusta rode up to London. Augusta showed him the new house her family were taking in Eaton Place. They moved into their new home the following Monday, and on that evening Pakington left them to settle in and had a 'very pleasant tête à tête with Mrs Milner'. The following day he joined the family for a celebratory lunch, but the occasion was spoiled by the fact that Augusta's grandmother, Lady George Murray, was seriously ill.

Now that parliament was back in session, Pakington had various duties there, including the competing lines to Newbury, controverted election, and medical relief committees. The first committee was the first to be set up under a new system to investigate alternative railway proposals. Pakington chaired the com-

*A barouche. It had four seats, two facing two, and a seat for the driver.*

mittee of five, all chosen so they had no local interests and could view the matter dispassionately. They had to choose between two lines from London to Newbury, one promoted by the London & South Western Railway Company which ran via Basingstoke, and the other by the Great Western Railway which formed a branch from their main line at Reading. The committee was asked to look at wider issues, and after some fairly intensive few days' hearings the they reported promptly to the House, and recommended the LSW line through Basingstoke. Their reasons were that, although looking purely at the line between Newbury and London the GWR proposal was the best, they considered that the LSW route offered better communications between London and Winchester, Southampton and the coast. He also noted that the roads between Reading and Newbury were better than the other route's and in addition there was already a canal, although, as was pointed out in the House, this could be said to show that traffic between Reading and Newbury was heavier than from Basingstoke.

When the report was laid before parliament, Charles Russell proposed that consideration be postponed. He pointed to the various advantages in terms of distance and levels that the GWR route would provide, but as Russell was also chairman of the Great Western Railway he clearly had a vested interest. The following speakers all pointed to the fact that the decision of the committee was unanimous and not subject to local bias, and that the House, having set up this new system, ought to abide by it, a view supported by the prime minister. The House divided and by a large majority received the report. Pakington noted in his diary that he was 'vindicated', although it would perhaps be fairer to say that it was the integrity of the committee that was vindicated rather than their decision. In fact in this instance history did not treat Pakington very kindly. The GWR were soon able to build their line, which today forms part of the main line from London to Exeter, and no line from Basingstoke to Newbury was ever built.

*A modern photo of 55 Eaton Place, to which the Murrays moved in 1844.*

The Medical Relief Committee was set up to investigate ways in which paupers received medical attention, and in particular the allegations made by Thomas King, an ex-resident of Nacton workhouse in the Woodbridge Union, Suffolk. He had petitioned the House of Commons, complaining that sick and elderly paupers had been left to die in their beds uncared for, and that several deaths, which should have been reported to the coroner, were not. Thomas King was, unusually, quite literate as he had been a schoolmaster, and had first complained to the Poor Law Commissioners, who had appointed an assistant commissioner, Sir John Walsham, to investigate. His report entirely blamed the nurse for lack of attention to her duty, and the master and matron escaped with only mild admonition, even though they admitted they had been ignorant of many of the matters alleged by King. King felt the report was a whitewash, and a local stir was created. Eventually the select committee was appointed to look into medical relief generally. King was nothing if not forthright in his allegations, and later in the year, after he had imputed some more wrong-doings to some of the guardians, they felt enough was enough, and sued him for libel. This prompted adverse comment in The Times, and when the matter came to court the judge felt that binding over King to keep the peace was sufficient punishment.

The Controverted Elections Committee was set up to look into how disputed elections were dealt with under new legislation of the previous parliament. Their report was brief – they recommended no change, except reducing the number of members on such committees from seven to three.

The only other time Pakington is recorded as speaking in 1844 was in March, when he sought leave to bring in a Quarter Sessions Bill. Drawing on his experiences as chairman, he complained about the fact that Recorders, who were an essential part of the proceedings, had unlimited powers to postpone sessions under the Municipal Reform Act. He felt this acted against the interests of justice, and he quoted two recent incidents at the Worcestershire quarter sessions when at the last minute the recorder announced a postponement of six weeks in one case and four weeks in another. The jury had already assembled, and everyone found this very inconvenient. It also meant prisoners awaiting trial had to spend more time in prison, even though they might prove to be innocent. He sought leave to introduce a bill to regulate this in some way; but on 18th April, at the request of Sir James Graham, the home secretary, Pakington agreed to withdraw the bill. He took comfort from the fact that, as Graham had pointed out, at least public attention had been drawn to the issue.

In the latter half of May, Pakington divided his time between Eaton Place and Lord Camden's, the House of Commons, and Westbourne Street, where he was lodging. Although it seems that Augusta had a miniature painted the year before, she was now sitting for a portrait by William Mulready – this may have been the son of the well known painter of Irish scenes, who specialised in portraits. The painting was not liked, but the artist was able to effect some improvements. Pakington also mentioned sitting for Richard Dighton for a sessions portrait – if completed, this seems to have been lost. The portrait that hung for many years in the Worcestershire

County Hall was painted six years later. At the end of May Pakington paid a brief visit to Westwood, the main purpose of which seems to have been to set out some new stables. As soon as he was back in London he met his future father-in-law and a solicitor to finalise the marriage settlement. The final deed has not come down to us, but a draft has, in which Marquis Camden, Richard Temple of The Nash, and Rev. George Murray (Augusta's brother) were appointed trustees. Pakington would receive £1,000 from the Bishop after the marriage, and the sum of £7,000 was given to the trustees for the benefit of any children, the interest from which would be given to Pakington. He would secure an annuity of £1,000 for his widow should he die first. Although not large, these amounts would have been welcome to Pakington, as his income was derived mostly from agricultural rents, and agriculture at that time was not prosperous – the previous year Berrows had reported that Pakington and many other landlords had allowed their tenants a ten percent reduction in their rents.

The Hanbury Williams were in town, and were introduced to the Murrays for the first time. The following day was the last Sunday Pakington and his fiancée spent together before they married. It was a 'cold day in point of weather but most warm happy & delightful feeling – rec'd sacrament with dear Augusta previous to our now approaching marriage – the next time we kneel together at the altar of God it will be for the sacred purpose of being united for ever'.

On 29th May the trousseau and wedding presents were laid out for inspection in Eaton Place. Johnny and the younger Murrays came up from Bromley to see the new carriage, and they all went to see the Panorama of Hong Kong. This was displayed in Burford's Panorama House in Leicester Square, built specially to display these 360° representations of places of interest. It showed the newly established colony of Victoria on Hong Kong Island.

Last minute preparations for the wedding included having his teeth cleaned, getting a special marriage license from Doctors Commons, and going to Thorburn for some alterations to the miniature portrait. The Murrays all went to Bromley on Saturday 1st June while Johnny went to his father's, and they went to the opera on Saturday night. On Sunday father and son went round to the Camdens and Mourdants to take their leave, then dined with Miss Pakington before going to evening service at Paddington church. Pakington's final goodbyes were saved for Mrs Milner, with whom he lunched on Monday, before going to the House to arrange pairs during his honeymoon. He received several expressions of goodwill from fellow MPs.

Tuesday 4th June was the great day, and Pakington and Johnny went down to Bromley in their new carriage 'with Clive', probably his friend Robert Clive, who may have acted as 'best man'. At 2.15 p.m. he and Augusta were married in the Palace by the Bishop of Rochester. There does not seem to have been a wedding breakfast, as at 4.00 p.m. they started on their honeymoon. Pakington and Augusta had very much enjoyed their stay at Lord Camden's estate at Bayham the previous year, and had arranged to spend their honeymoon there. The Bayham Hall that Pakington and his bride stayed in is now known as the dower house, and is picturesquely situated adjacent to the ruins of Bayham Abbey.

Their first day of married life was spent quietly 'in great happiness but in much excitement & strong feeling', and they only went out for a short walk round their 'old & happy haunts'. Pakington noted that Augusta received an 'affecting & beautiful letter from Mrs Milner'. During their stay at Bayham they rode and walked about locally enjoying the summer weather and local beauty spots. On one day he noted 'one of those bright days which come now & then to show how happy mortals are permitted to be – in warmth of mutual affection'. Feeling, perhaps, that now he was married to a Bishop's daughter he should keep up his religious observance even more punctiliously than before, on the first Monday morning he 'commenced morning prayers with servants'. Another innovation was to dine earlier, leaving plenty of time afterwards for an excursion. So in the second week they dined at 3.00 p.m., and came home to tea at 9.00 p.m. – 'we much liked our change of hours'. However, their dinner time was soon put back till 4.00 p.m. Their excursions included one to Tunbridge Wells where they saw the Hawkinses and exchanged gifts of Tunbridge ware, and another to Dover where they enjoyed a day by the sea. After a fortnight Johnny joined them, and after three and a half weeks of 'happiness & enjoyment as great as ever was vouchsafed to human beings' their stay was over, and they returned to London. It is not quite clear where they stayed at the commencement of their married life, but it seems most likely they had rooms with the Murrays in Eaton Place.

After a few days Pakington had to return to Worcester for quarter sessions, and on Thursday morning he inspected the new stables at Westwood before returning to London by train. Back in town the newly weds spent time making calls, and for the first time dined in Eaton Place with his two sisters-in-law, making 'a happy party of three couples'. They called several times on Pakington's aunt, who was 'weak', but whom he delighted 'by offering to dine with her at her little party next day'. At the party venison was served, probably from Westwood,

*The old Bayham Hall, now known as the Dower House. The new Bayham Hall was built in 1870 nearby. Part of the abbey ruins can be seen in the foreground.*

as his aunt's letters often end with a request for more game. Augusta was introduced to Miss Pakington's friends, who were 'much pleased' with her. Now their uncle, Pakington took the younger Murray girls with the Camdens to Her Majesty's Theatre on Thursday evening where they had a box. The opera was 'Anna Bolena' by Donizetti, but as was the custom in those days other items were added to the bill afterwards. These included a fantasia on the horn, the Saragossa dance, the second act of William Tell – 'the best act', The Times critic opined, and concluded by writing 'what time the entertainment ended, we cannot conceive. Our acquaintance with the matter ceased at twelve o'clock, and there was still 'La Vivandiere' to come…'.

The following Saturday Pakington again took the girls out with Johnny to a military review in Hyde Park. It must have been a magnificent occasions, as several leading army battalions had assembled, and at 11.00 the Duke of Wellington (commander in chief), Field Marshal the Duke of Cambridge, and a large number of military top brass took the field. Wellington meticulously reviewed the troops, after which they all marched past, then fired by company while the cavalry went through their 'evolutions'. Afterwards he took Johnny to see the pictures and sculptures in Westminster Hall, and in the evening there was a big family dinner party. Johnny returned to Bromley soon after, and although Pakington does not say so, it seems likely that he accompanied the Bishop and his wife and four children on a foreign tour starting on 15th July.

As already noted, Bishop Murray went to Christ Church, Oxford, and probably helped Johnny Pakington gain entry there. In fact all five of the bishop's sons went to Christ Church, and Johnny Pakington and Robert Murray went up together as they matriculated on the same day, 16th October 1844. Johnny does not seem to have spent much time in Oxford that autumn, as a month later he was with the Murrays in Worcester, and only in the following year did he get involved in university affairs. He obtained his BA and MA degrees, and was also an active member of the Oxford Union Society in 1845 and 1846. Founded in 1823, the Union, like its counterpart at Cambridge, held debates conducted in something of an imitation of those in parliament, indeed many members of both Unions have gone on to become prominent politicians. Johnny was admitted to membership in April 1845, remained so till Lent 1847, and was a committee member in Michaelmas 1845 and Lent 1847. Records of the debates survive, and he was noted as a speaker on a number of occasions. The first such debate was in April and May 1845 when the motion was 'That Sir Robert Peel's government has forfeited the confidence of the country'. Although his father was later to vote against Peel's bill to repeal the Corn Laws, at this stage he could be counted a supporter of the government, and his son spoke in favour of Peel and against the motion. The debate evidently aroused great feeling, as despite the fact that only about 100 took part, it was adjourned no less than three times, lasting four weeks. In the event, Peel's supporters outnumbered his opponents by 63 to 39.

Later in the spring Johnny is recorded as speaking against capital punishment, and against the delegation of the judicial functions of the House of Lords to a small professional section. Then in November 1845 he spoke against the motion 'that Lord Ashley's uniform advocacy of a law to keep down the hours of labour, while supporting those laws whose object is to keep up the price of food, together with his recent letter to his constituents, entirely vitiates his claim to be considered a statesman'. Lord Ashley, later 7th Earl of Shaftsbury and famous for pushing bills though parliament regulating the hours of work of children in factories, was a complicated character, in many ways a traditional Conservative and committed Christian, and opposed the repeal of the Corn Laws. This contrasted with his zeal in campaigning on behalf of child factory workers, as well as for the more enlightened treatment of lunatics. Johnny wrote to his father, who had given him some background on Ashley, after the debate enclosing a verbatim copy of his speech. In it he neither agreed nor disagreed with the motion, but instead mainly attacked the proposer, saying that the motion meant very little. All MPs could be called statesmen, and his various campaigns were no more than a right thinking Englishman might espouse. Unusually, Johnny walked out after his speech, and did not vote.

Although the level of debate in the Union was probably quite high, and no doubt the debates, such as the one on Ashley, gave undergraduates the opportunity for showing off their wit and culture, the general tone was still conservative. It was still only fifteen years since Peel, when the University MP, had been vilified for proposing Catholic emancipation, and another motion in 1846 'that Landlords are justified in influencing the votes of their tenants' was carried by 22 votes to 17. Unlike his father, Johnny succeeded in gaining his BA degree, as well as spending some time studying in the Inner Temple, but it was not until 1865 that he took his MA which then, as now, was a formality for Oxbridge graduates.

Pakington and his wife left Johnny with the Murrays in July 1844. Shortly afterwards Augusta fell ill after eating some 'stale spinach', and they travelled to Westwood on 17th, and took possession of the 'new furnished apartments'. The next day she expressed herself 'delighted with the tenantry', and they were both 'much affected & excited at coming home'. A week later they left for Pencombe where Rev. Henry Barry Domvile was the rector, and where they met Fanny, the widow of Henry Barry jun., and her four children. They had an outing to lionize Hampton Court (not to be confused with Hampton Court in Surrey) and met the Arkwrights, whose seat it was, and who had remodelled the house, which Pakington was 'much pleased' with. From Pencombe they travelled to Coldbrook to spend five days with the Hanbury Williams, coming back home on Saturday 3rd August in a 'storm of violent wind & rain which lasted all day'. The next week Pakington had to attend a meeting of the Severn Commissioners, and afterwards they all travelled to the new weir at Lincombe whence they travelled back to Bevere by boat, stopping to dine at Holt Fleet.

A week later Pakington noted that a ride to Hanbury will be 'Augusta's last ride at present, as she had the happiness of finding from this time that she is in the family way'. By now Johnny had joined them, the Murrays were staying in Worcester, and Miss Pakington came for a period as well. An intensive round of calling and being called on continued till, when staying at Hagley with Lord Lyttelton, Augusta feared she was having a miscarriage. Nothing amiss happened, but she stayed there resting over the weekend while her husband went home. Monday marked the first day of the shooting season, and Pakington father and son spent all morning shooting before returning to Hagley, where Pakington found his wife 'better & pretty safe for present'. He spent the night there, and the next day described the pretty scene at Hagley with a cricket match taking place. He took a walk on the Clent Hills, and noted with amusement that, not recognised, he was refused re-admission to the park when he returned.

Thursday 12th September was the start of the yeomanry week, and Augusta and Miss Pakington went to Worcester to see the regiment march in. As her husband was staying in Worcester, Augusta stayed with her family at the Deanery. On Sunday, as well as attending the cathedral twice, Pakington walked down to Diglis to inspect progress on the new lock and weir. On Monday he did something that he does not seem to have done before – he travelled to London and back in the same day. Leaving home at 5.30 a.m. with Johnny, he and a deputation of Severn Commissioners took the 8.30 a.m. train from Birmingham to London, where they were to attend the Board

*Bevere lock and weir, on the Severn north of Worcester. It used a bend of the river, and the lock was made in the bend. It was one of four built to improve navigation between Stourport and Worcester.*

of Trade on unspecified business. Johnny continued on to Bromley, but Pakington returned to Birmingham on the 5.30 p.m. train, and he noted that he had 'travelled 250 miles & did business & shopping in town!'.

At the end of the week Bishop Murray joined them, and Pakington was busy preparing for the quarter sessions the following week. On Sunday he had a bad throat and 'was in fright about sessions – ladies doctored me no end!'. But the sessions seemed to pass without incident, and on the same day Miss Pakington and her friend Miss Young left Westwood after their long stay. Sessions lasted three days, and the third day, Wednesday, was particularly 'heavy', lasting from 9.00 a.m. till 8.15 p.m. One trial lasted four hours and created much interest on account of the respectability of the accused. 'Augusta & Caroline had great luck to come & hear it – much complimented on summing up', he noted.

The trial was of two farmers, Ephraim Swan and John Patrick, who farmed land near Kyre Park, the seat of William Lacon Childe, and in which there was a herd of deer. The deer keeper noticed that a distinctive buck had gone missing, and there were signs of a dead animal having been dragged out of the park near Swan's farm. The main evidence was from George Passey, a youth of '15 or 16 years old', who had climbed a tree and claims to have seen the prisoners removing the dead buck from

*A cricket match taking place with Hagley Hall forming the back-drop. This is a modern photograph, but the scene in the 1840s would have been similar.*

the park. There was obviously the question of how far the evidence of a youth could be relied on, but Pakington's main concern in his summing up was how far the jury should have regard to the respectable status of the accused. This is Berrows' report:

> In conclusion, he [Pakington] alluded to the station of life occupied by the prisoners, and to the consideration as to how far their position in that respect should weigh with the jury in deciding upon their verdict. He was sure the jury would not allow their feelings to be warped by this consideration to the detriment of justice, and he then told them what he considered was the correct view to be taken of such circumstances attending a trial of the nature before them. It was, he thought, their duty to give the prisoners the benefit of the superior station which they occupied in society in precisely the same manner, but not further, as they would allow evidence of previous good character to weigh in the balance. When the evidence of guilt was of a doubtful nature, then a superior station of life would, in the same manner as a good name, have its influence in strengthening these doubts. But supposing a prisoner ranked in a superior station of life to the usual class of offenders, and his guilt was established, then his superior station rather added to the enormity of the offence. Therefore the station of life or previous good character should be allowed to weigh only in cases of doubt, and they should decide upon the guilt or innocence of a prisoner solely upon the evidence adduced before them.

The notion that respectable persons should be given the benefit of the doubt, and a suggestion that Passey may have been coerced into giving his evidence, led the jury to find the prisoners not guilty, at which there was a short round of applause in court. Reading the evidence now, however, it does seem strong against the accused.

Immediately sessions ended John and Augusta left for a stay at Eastnor where they met the Mordaunts, but after only two nights they were back at home by themselves, and 'most happy to be so'. Pakington was soon on the move again, calling on the Rev. Pearson at Witley where he met Prince Ernest of Philipsthal, who was doubtless visiting Queen Adelaide. The next day, after presiding at an Odd Fellows dinner in Droitwich, he went to Witley to dine with the dowager Queen, where he also met the Duchess of Gloucester. Augusta, pregnant and with a heavy cold, stayed at home. Pakington travelled to London the next day with Lord Hatherton and other men involved with the Severn navigation and met with Lord Dalhousie, vice-president of the Board of Trade. What their mission was is not recorded. Berrows said they went to discuss the railway, presumably expressing their concerns about the spread of the railway network and the effects it would have on the new Severn navigation. After this meeting Pakington took the Bromley coach to spend a night with the Murrays, and returned the next day. At the Bishop's suggestion, he used the Greenwich railway, the earliest steam railway to be built into London.

At the end of October they were due to stay at the Mordaunt's seat at Walton near Wellesbourne for ten days. Augusta, getting better but still poorly, followed a day later. Three of the days there were spent shooting, and with obvious satisfaction Pakington records that he accounted for 164 of the 600 birds shot. They spent a day in Stratford and 'lionized' the church, but Pakington does not seem to have joined other guests who went to hear Charles Kemble, the well known but aging Shakespearean actor. The following week Pakington 'went in phaeton to christening of poor Fanny's posthumous boy – Dow. Lady Winnington Godmother – poor Wood & myself Godfathers – melancholy ceremony – Augusta unwell & could not go'. The Murrays were coming to Worcester, and Johnny took the opportunity to join his father, and they spent a day shooting together. The younger Murrays with other guests formed a house party at Westwood on Saturday 16th November, and on the Monday the 'ladies came to pass long morning while gentlemen shot'.

A stay at the Childe's seat at Kinlet followed, and back home Augusta was starting to show some interest in doing local charity work, and she went to discuss 'the poor' with the rector of Hampton, Rev. Joseph Amphlett. Pakington never went long without referring to money problems of his own, and at the end of November he had a long talk with Thomas Curtler, his friend and agent, about 'private affairs'. At the beginning of December the weather turned very cold, and during a short visit to Madresfield Pakington had a severe 'stomach attack', leaving him unwell for several days. When he recovered he went to London leaving Augusta with her family in Worcester, and called on his aunt. There he 'found dinner party assembled at Miss P's – Burslem & lots of ladies'. He had only one full day in town and did some shopping, not forgetting to have lunch with Mrs Milner, then travelled directly back to Croome Park, the seat of the Coventry family, where he met Augusta. She was not well, so after enjoying a day's shooting in the evening he 'sung alone on account of Augusta's cold'.

Back home he mentions the 'railway plans'. The route of the Oxford, Worcester & Wolverhampton railway, then being planned, after leaving Droitwich was to pass through some of the Westwood estate and within yards of Hampton Lovett church – it is perhaps surprising that a route a little further away could not have been found. The weather remained very cold, and Johnny and young Robert Murray skated. As on most Sundays, Pakington records that prayers were said at Westwood.

On 9th and 23rd December Pakington attended public meetings held in Worcester to discuss plans for the next Music Meeting, which would be held in Worcester. The Bishop of Worcester took the chair, and Bishop Murray, in his capacity as Dean of Worcester, was by his side. The chairman opened the meeting by referring to objections that had been raised against holding the Music Meeting in the cathedral, but said he attached no weight to these. He felt the advantages of the Music Meeting much outweighed any disadvantage. He said "I can never enter a cathedral to hear sacred music without my feelings of devotion being extremely enhanced thereby and without, as it were, feeling my soul to be elevated from earth to heaven". And it must not be forgotten that at Worcester nearly £1,100 had been raised for the clergy's widows and orphans. The Dean concurred, and confirmed that he himself and the chapter were willing to grant the use of the cathedral for the festival.

Each year stewards were appointed, and each guaranteed a maximum of £50 towards the expenses. However, after a discussion on the likely expenses the following year this was reduced to £40. Pakington spoke at some length, referring to an anonymous letter that had appeared the previous week in Berrows, attacking the present arrangements. The writer thought the Festival should restrict itself much more closely to religious observance, and proposed various changes. Firstly, the grand ball, which was advertised and held in conjunction with the Festival, was a 'giant grievance', and, if it was to be held at all (Hereford had dropped it, he claimed) it should be totally separated, with different stewards and advertising. No self-respecting clergyman would be seen at such an event. Secondly, he objected to the use of big-name London singers, as this tended to draw attention away from the religious nature of the performances. He also pointed out that Handel's oratorios, much performed at the festivals, had not really been written for performance in church, but rather for the more dramatic setting of a theatre. He felt that only Messiah was suitable for the Festival, and that only if more integrated into a religious service. And there was much more in the same vein.

Close as he regarded himself to the Church of England, it can be imagined that Pakington had little sympathy with some of these sentiments, although it is to be noted that in the later advertisements for the 1845 festival, the ball was advertised in a separate box, with a shorter list of 'lay' stewards, who were the main festival stewards without the six clerics. What had led to the decay of the festivals, Pakington said, was not this, but the increasing facilities for hearing top quality performances caused by the great increase in musical appreciation amongst the populace. He pointed to such as the Birmingham Festival, where one could hear oratorios in the magnificent town hall, and Exeter Hall in London, where large forces sang for an admittance of only five shillings. The Worcester Music Festivals would have to become more competitive, and reduce costs. Three of the last four festivals had lasted four days, and there had been some poor attendances. He thought that three days should be the maximum. He also thought that some of the expensive soloists could be replaced by choral singing. At the close of the meeting those present were invited to subscribe to the 'guarantee fund', and, never backward in coming forward, Pakington promised £20, the same as the Bishop and Earl Beauchamp, but more than the Dean and some others.

Christmas was approaching, and on 23rd a tenants' dinner was held, which 'went off well'. On Christmas Eve Augusta followed up her earlier resolve to help the local poor, and went visiting with Mrs Amphlett, the rector's wife. On Christmas Day they were invited to the Deanery for dinner, and Johnny and his father walked. After this six mile exercise they must have been ready for dinner, but in fact dinner was ready for them as he mistook the time and kept the party waiting. On Boxing Day Pakington and the Bishop amused themselves by playing chess. Both men were quite good, and the result was 'very even'. Back at Westwood on Sunday 29th, Pakington records 'so foggy that we never left the house – but day of great domestic happiness & engagement – much as we have been blessed this year we have known few happier days than this last Sunday of the memorable 1844'. On New Year's Eve he again gave thanks for the 'remarkable blessings & mercies' he had received, and 'for the hopes for the future which I am permitted to indulge', hopes that sadly were not all to be fully realised.

We have no diary for 1845, but we know a sad event occurred in April, when Augusta gave birth to a daughter, Edith. Her life only lasted a short time, and she was buried in Hampton Lovett church on April 6th. From Hansard we learn that Pakington only addressed the House of Commons once in 1845, which was on his favourite subject of providing religious instruction. In this case it was in Australia, and during a debate on the Waste Lands (Australia) Bill he urged the government to increase the grant of £30,000 they had already made towards religious instruction in New South Wales. The Bill authorised the Governor of the colony to lease waste lands, which would provide a new source of income.

We also know that he served on at least five parliamentary select committees. Perhaps the most interesting was set up to report on the merits of atmospheric railways against those of conventional locomotive-hauled ones. Atmospheric railways worked on the principle of having a tube of 15 inches (more on gradients) between the rails, that had a slot along the top into which a blade with a piston attached was carried by the locomotive carriage of the train. The tube was evacuated using pumping stations at regular intervals along the line, and the train was literally sucked along by allowing air to be introduced behind the train. At that time there was only one working atmospheric railway in existence, that between Dun Laoghaire and Dalkey in Ireland, a

*A section of atmospheric railway track reconstructed at the Didcot Railway Centre. It was the difficulty of maintining a good seal on the central slot that proved its weakness.*

length of less than two miles, which had opened in 1844. The principle had given rise to much interest from railway engineers, as it was thought to have the potential for greater speeds, and to be able to cope with steeper gradients than conventional engines. The London and Croydon Railway was to be built on the atmospheric principle, and Brunel had also proposed that the more important South Devon Railway, with its steep grades, would do the same.

The committee on which Pakington served took evidence, much of it conflicting, from various railway engineers, and its report showed that it had been attracted by some of the system's claimed advantages. In particular, it was regarded as potentially safer than conventional railways. The report showed that many of the fairly frequent railway accidents of the period would have been avoided using the atmospheric system. This was because it was proposed that these railways should be single track, and by its very nature two trains could not run on this track in opposing directions, but the committee gave scant regard to the substantial limitation on capacity this would create. Neither did they enquire into the major technical problems that would arise at junctions and crossings, or, as proposed on the South Devon, when the diameter of the tube changed.

The committee's report failed to come down strongly in favour of one system or the other, saying that only experience would determine the matter. In fact, the South Devon Railway was built the following year as an atmospheric railway, although only the section from Exeter to Newton Abbott ever became operational in this way. The main problem, which the committee had not foreseen, was that it proved difficult to maintain the vacuum in the tube, as the leather seals used for this purpose quickly deteriorated (especially along the coastal section). After only a year both the South Devon and London and Croydon railways abandoned this technology, and reverted to conventional steam power.

Pakington was on other select committees in 1845. One was to classify railway bills so they could go to the appropriate select committee, and another investigated dealing in railway shares by Mr Hignett, solicitor to the Board of Ordnance in Woolwich, whose premises were affected by two competing railway schemes (he and two members of the board were found to have acted corruptly). There was a committee to look into the rules concerned the treatment of private bills in parliament, and another, which Pakington chaired, investigated allegations of wrong-doing in the recent election at Dartmouth.

Perhaps the most important committee on which he sat was to look into proposals for building new courts of justice to replace the ancient ones at the Palace of Westminster. In earlier times, the Common Law Courts and Court of Equity had been inside Westminster Hall. Later they were accommodated in a building built against the west side of the Hall, but this was restricted in size and height. It was generally agreed that it would be desirable to build new courts of justice on a site between The Strand and Chancery Lane near the Inns of Court, which then had some very poor property on it, and was large enough to accommodate the courts then at Westminster, other legal offices then occupying different sites in the City, and provide more barristers' chambers which could be let at attractive rents.

Sir Charles Barry was the principal witness before the committee. He was the architect of the new Palace of Westminster, then still under construction, and had proposed the scheme to build the new courts elsewhere to improve the appearance of the new Palace. He was examined on an alternative idea of building further courts around and enclosing Palace Yard, but Barry was adamant that this would be an inadequate solution, and it would further detract from his new Palace.

Barry's evidence and that of other witnesses made it clear that the present arrangements were very unsatisfactory, and that the proposed plan would be a great advance. It was even suggested that much of the cost could be defrayed by building new cham-

*The plan included in the select committee report on the scheme to provide new courts of justice. It shows the proposed new buildings surrounding New Palace Yard which would have provided extra accomomdation for the Royal Courts of Justice. Old Westminster Hall is coloured dark near the centre, and the additional court buildings built by Sir John Soane in the 1820s immediately below it. The proposed new buildings enclose New Palace Yard to the left of Westminster Hall, with a grand entrance in the corner. Perhaps fortunately the scheme was never carried out, and Westminster Hall and the Yard remain open to the street. The newly completed Palace of Westminster lies between Westminster Hall and the Thames and is shown in outline.*

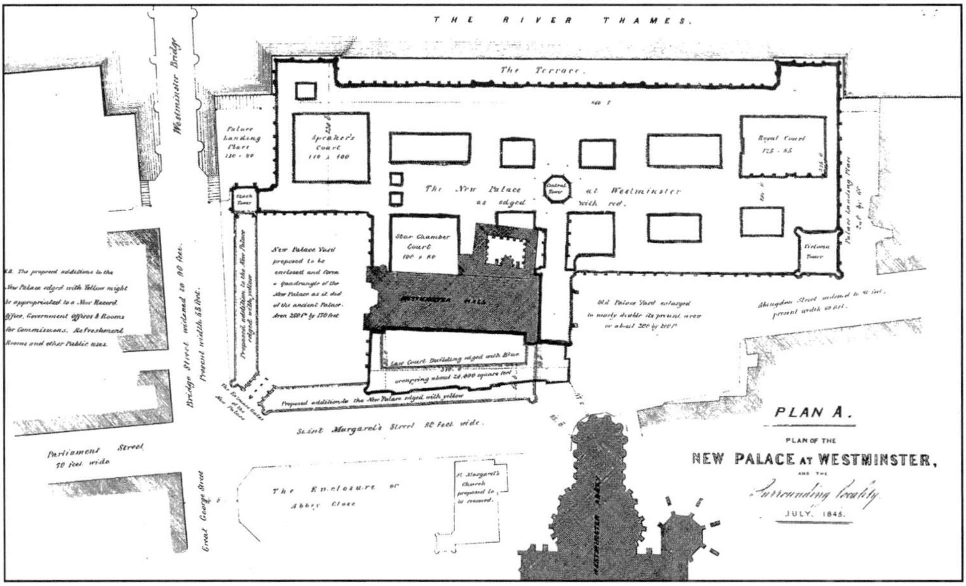

bers for letting on both sides of the proposed new Courts of Justice. But it was to be twenty five years until the new building in The Strand was started. Barry by then was dead, but George Street's Royal Courts of Justice occupy the same site as Barry proposed, and remain for Londoners to admire today.

The great issue in parliament in 1845 was the Maynooth grant. The Maynooth seminary is in county Kildare, where Catholic priests were and still are trained. It had been founded by William Pitt in 1795 as part of the preparations for the union of the British and Irish parliaments and received a grant of £9,000 a year. It was alleged that Maynooth was sending priests out to the Irish countryside bent on fomenting trouble. Peel felt that this problem could be cured by some measures of reform and being more generous to Maynooth, and proposed that the grant be increased to £25,000 a year. This became a very controversial issue, and was debated at great length in parliament. Right-wing Tories (including Benjamin Disraeli) bitterly opposed it, and any further conciliation with the Catholics.

The debate on the second reading lasted no less than six nights, and finally at 3.30 a.m. on the morning of 18th April the government had a majority of 147, with most Whigs supporting Peel. Pakington had previously made comments about not encouraging the spread of Roman Catholicism, but, surprisingly, voted with Peel for the increased grant. Despite his staunch Anglicanism he supported the toleration, but not the encouragement, of other sects. Pakington may have sensed that the prime minister was coming to the end of his period in office, and his loyalty may have been influenced by his powers of patronage.

## Chapter 11
## The Andover Union Scandal 1845-46

Although the events comprising the Andover workhouse scandal overlap those of the preceding and following chapters, it is best to describe them as a continuous narrative. Pakington himself only played a minor part in the events, but, as it has been largely forgotten since, it is worth telling the story again. Pakington himself was interested enough to devote much time in the first half of 1846 to attending the select committee hearings, and was active in the compilation of the committee's report.

As we have seen, Pakington acted as chairman of the Droitwich Union from its inception in 1836, so was familiar with the workings of the Poor Law Amendment Act. So far as he made his views known, he seems to have felt that it worked well. There is no evidence that the Droitwich Union was not well run, although within twelve months of its first meeting Pakington became an MP and therefore was an irregular attender of meetings of the Guardians. He generally took a keen interest in things he became involved in, and the Droitwich workhouse seems to have been run in the spirit of the 1834 Act, even though many, of course, were bitterly opposed to the whole concept. One notable opponent was John Walter, proprietor of The Times newspaper, which campaigned tirelessly against the 1834 Bill, and after it became law it exposed every sign of wrong-doing in workhouses, and also campaigned against the Poor Law Commissioners, who were regarded as embodying the evils of the system.

Apart from its general harshness, one problem with the 1834 Act was that, without careful supervision, it tended to lead to abuses. It was very much dependent on the good-will and public spirit of the Poor Law Guardians, and the ability and fair mindedness of the workhouse masters, who were often given a great deal of power by their Boards. Failures in all these areas were present in what became the Andover Union scandal.

It had become the practice in many workhouses to set the inmates to work crushing and grinding bones, sometimes by hand, sometimes using suitable mills. The product was used as a fertiliser. This may not, at first glance, seem such a bad thing, as the labour led to a useful product and disposed of the considerable waste produced at slaughter houses. But the bones were sometimes in a state of considerable decomposition, giving off an evil smell that was regarded by some as disgusting and not fit even for a workhouse. Worse, as we shall see, it gave hungry inmates the temptation to use the bones as a source of food. Anti-workhouse campaigners used bone crushing as symbolic of the worse aspects of the workhouse. In July 1844 they succeeded in getting an order for Boards of Guardians to report to parliament whether they employed the inmates in crushing bones, whether the value of sales outweighed the cost of the work, and whether they tendered when selling the fertiliser (at Andover, there was a suggestion that the guardians acquired the fertiliser for their personal profit).

Many Boards of Guardians, although now subject to the various acts of parliament and the over-riding authority of the Poor Law Commissioners, came from a long tradition of independence in the administration of the Poor Law, and did not like being told what to do by outsiders, and simply ignored instructions from above. In many cases they were within their strict legal rights in so doing. A contemporary example of this concerned the Boston Guardians, where it was revealed that they made men seeking relief work within the workhouse labour on a treadmill, which produced no useful result. The more men on the wheel, the heavier the weights were set to counteract the work. The government and the commissioners were united in condemning the practise, but the guardians simply ignored the instructions sent them, and a complicated legal process had to be gone through before it was stopped.

*The three Poor Law Commissioners at the time of the 1846 Andover scandal. Sir George Cornewall Lewis (left) had scceeded his father as a commissioner in 1839. In 1847 he became a Liberal MP, and held various government offices. (Centre) Sir Edmund Walker Head was a commissioner from 1841 to 1847. (Right) Sir George Nicholls was one of the original 1834 commissioners, and later wrote some histories of the poor laws. Lewis and Head from Hulton Archive, Getty Images.*

In 1845 rumours began to circulate, spread by men who had left the workhouse, about conditions at Andover. Not only were men employed in the unpleasant task of crushing bones, but that they were so hungry that when a shipment arrived they set on to it like hungry wolves to find fresh ('green') ones that may still have had flesh adhering to them. Some had even found the marrow very welcome, and ate that as well. The chairman of the Andover board was Rev. Christopher Dodson, who had held this position since the first meeting in 1837. He was very firm in his views about the necessary unpleasantness of the workhouse, and was persistent in turning down any request for amelioration. Most of the guardians shared his views (if, indeed, they took any interest in it) but one of the few who had more humanitarian views was a local gentleman, Hugh Mundy. He had heard the rumours, and decided to investigate. He took a long statement from an old lag, Samuel Green, who been transported for seven years for stealing a kettle, and returned to enter the workhouse. Green's statement confirmed the worst aspects of the rumours.

Mundy tried to get his colleagues to agree to stop the practise of crushing bones, but failed, so wrote to his MP, Ralph Etwall. Etwall was a friend of a reforming and radical member John Wakley, who was a doctor and surgeon, and the founder of 'The Lancet'. So on 1st August 1845 Wakley asked the home secretary, Sir James Graham, whether these stories were true. Graham expressed disgust:

> I cannot believe in the existence of such an abuse as is embodied in the statement just made. The House must have heard that statement with horror... If the facts alleged are true I am quite satisfied that they would have been represented to me, and had they been so represented, I would have insisted on the fullest investigation of them... I shall institute an enquiry this very night.

A few days later Graham was asked again whether he had heard anything from the Poor Law Commissioners, which he had not; but he said they had told him that they had never heard of such a thing. But that was not quite correct as the day before, the commissioners had sent the local assistant commissioner, Henry Parker, to inves-

*Edwin Chadwick was secretary to the Poor Law Commissioners from 1834 till they were abolished in 1847. Disappointed not to have been one himself, his relations with the three commissioners was not good, and he became the focus of much of the hatred poured upon the commission. The evidence he gave to the parliamentary select committee on the Andover scandal was damaging to the commissioners and helped lead to their replacement by a board in 1847. Chadwick is best known for his work over many years improving the sanitary state of towns. Hulton Archive, Getty Images.*

tigate. According to The Times, Parker's investigation was short and conducted mainly in the presence of Colin McDougal, the master.

Of all the characters involved in the Andover scandal, McDougal should come off worst, although much of the later controversy concerned not him but assistant commissioner Parker and the Poor Law Commissioners. McDougal was a Scot and 44 when appointed the workhouse master in 1837. He had been in the army – the commissioners recommended the appointment of military personnel as being likely to have the right kind of background. McDougal had been a sergeant, had fought at Waterloo, and had been injured when his horse fell on him, causing painful problems with his legs and chest. The other characters in the saga, particularly Parker, and Board chairman Dodson, could be accused of being heartless and unfeeling, but this was because of an honest belief that the workhouse system would only succeed if the workhouse was made as unattractive as possible. There is no evidence that they were either dishonest or gratuitously cruel, but McDougal was both of these things. The bone crushing scandal stemmed from the fact that the inmates were desperately hungry –they were not supposed to be generously fed, but the dietary should have been adequate. The hunger at Andover arose because McDougal had got into the habit of creaming off some of the rations for his own use or profit. Evidence was particularly brought forward that extra rations ordered by the medical officer, for example for expectant mothers, were charged for but not supplied. In addition, some workhouse property had been seen in the home of his son-in-law.

Apart from being dishonest, he had other personal traits that were hardly likely to inspire the inmates to higher levels of morality. He made a habit of spending Saturday nights drinking, and returned to the workhouse drunk; he was sometimes even drunk when reading morning prayers or grace. And he saw nothing wrong in making advances to females inmates; more than one pauper admitted sleeping with him under either threats or promises of more rations. Mrs McDougal does not come out of he saga well either. On one occasion when an inmate, Hannah Joyce, for the second time found her infant dead in her arms in bed, Mrs McDougal believed she was guilty of murder (even though an inquest found the child had died of bronchitis), treated her abominably, and encouraged the other inmates to shout abuse at her when she finally left.

When assistant commissioner Parker reported back to the Poor Law Commissioners they ordered him to undertake a more detailed local enquiry, and this opened in Andover on Saturday August 16th 1845. However, the master complained he had not been given enough time to go through the account books in which it was alleged there were irregularities, and he had also been ill. Parker, therefore, adjourned the enquiry till Monday week. The Times correspondent felt this was unnecessary, but was pleased when Parker announced that the enquiry would be open to the public. Accordingly a large crowd, including Etwall the MP, and counsel for the various parties involved, gathered when the enquiry finally opened in the workhouse hall on 25th August.

It did not take long for Parker to show his bias in favour of the existing establishment. One reason for the matter coming to light was the complaint of the medical officer, Thomas Westlake, that the extra rations he had ordered for various sick or nursing inmates were given either only partially or not at all. But Parker pointed out that the book used by Westlake to order these rations was not the correct one as ordered by the Poor Law Commissioners. Westlake replied that he was following the system laid down by McDougal, and that he had never been told what the correct procedure was. Parker said he should have known, and implied that this was a good enough reason for the master not to give the extra rations.

The charges against McDougal that had to be considered by the enquiry were as follows: that he failed to give the correct dietary not only to the sick but to the regular inmates and that some food that should have gone to the inmates was instead fed to his pigs and horses; that he used workhouse property including blankets, soap and food for the benefit of his daughter and son-in-law, Mr and Mrs Holly, who lived nearby; that the Hollys' clothes were sent to the workhouse laundry for washing; that McDougal took liberties with the female inmates, touching them and addressing them improperly; and that he was frequently inebriated. Numerous witnesses were called to support these charges (all reported verbatim in The Times), and there was to be further enquiry into the bone crushing allegations, before McDougal would have been called to give evidence in his defence. But at the end of day thirteen the enquiry abruptly ended when Mr Westlake, who was regarded as the accuser of McDougal, received a letter from the Poor Law Commissioners stating that they were concerned about the length of time the enquiry was taking, and that they had now decided to end it and allow Westlake to prefer criminal charges against McDougal on any one of the matters already investigated.

But the enquiry was only adjourned, and when it resumed on Saturday 20th September events took a rather dramatic course when McDougal's counsel, Mr Missing, announced that he had advised his client to take no further part in the enquiry and would announce his resignation from his post to the Board of Guardians' meeting later that day. Missing said this was because insufficient time had been allowed for his client to prepare evidence to rebut the charges of improper sexual conduct. But it has to be assumed that the evidence against McDougal was so strong that he was advised that nothing was to be gained from continuing except further humiliation. Assistant commissioner Parker then joined the guardians in the board room, it being a board day, but when he was told that they wished to retain McDougal for a further month until a new master started Parker said this was unacceptable. The meeting ended with the chairman and vice-chairman bad-temperedly walking out saying they would resign.

Had Parker allowed the board to select a new and more suitable master, things at the Andover workhouse might have settled down and the Andover scandal not become such a well-known epitome of the evils of the 1834 act. However, on hearing of the departure of McDougal, Parker immediately thought of helping someone whom he knew to be out of work, a man named George Price, whom he put forward as a replacement. It was not long before rumours began to circulate that Price was not all that a caring master should be. The Times, on 3rd October, published a report that said he bore a remarkable resemblance to a gentleman of the same name who had resigned from the Oxford workhouse earlier in the year after an enquiry had found him guilty of cruelty towards the inmates. It was indeed the same person, and when this became known there was uproar in the town, where it was said that they wanted him 'at no price'! When the Poor Law Commissioners got to hear about it, they delved into their records and found the report from the Oxford investigation, but they had not looked at it as by then Price had resigned. They criticised their assistant commissioner, who made the rather unlikely defence that he did not know about the Oxford business. The Andover board were told at their meeting on 11th October that Price was unsuitable and that they would have to look for someone else. Eventually they appointed Mr and Mrs Blyth as the new master and matron, who, perhaps thankfully, have since passed into obscurity.

*The Andover Workhouse, from the Illustrated London News 1846. The front block still survives, converted into flats.*

By now the Poor Law Commissioners were becoming disenchanted with Parker. He had, they thought, needlessly prolonged the enquiry, he had shown bias during it by leaning towards defending McDougal and opposing Westlake, and now he had shown appalling judgement by appointing someone equally unsuitable. Accordingly one of the commissioners, Sir George Nicholls, wrote to Parker requesting him to resign (this was usually done to offer someone the alternative to a humiliating public dismissal), which accordingly he did on 16th October. As can be imagined, relations between the Andover Guardians and their medical officer Westlake were not good, and at the board meeting on 25th October they dismissed Westlake through 'lack of confidence'. But again the Poor Law Commissioners were not happy, and (as they had the power to do) refused to accept his dismissal and ordered him to continue in post. It is to be wondered, in any case, whether their meeting on 25th was legal – the chairman (Rev. Dodson) and vice chairman had resigned at the end of the enquiry, and Rev. G. W. Smythe appointed the new chairman. But then Rev. Dodson, having got over his fit of anger, decided he would rather continue, and took the chair on 25th without Smythe having relinquished his post.

We must now turn our spotlight on the House of Commons, as the Andover MP, Ralph Etwall, was determined that more light should be shed on the scandal, with the ultimate hope that it might damage the Poor Law Commissioners, and that some change there might be effected. In the House on 4th February 1846 the subject was raised by Capt. George Pechell, who had previously campaigned against the evils of bone-crushing. He asked the home secretary, Sir James Graham, to ensure that the practice would at last be stopped. Graham said that it had been found that about 150 Unions used bone crushing as employment, and the Commissioners had issued an order that they cease on January 1st. Some Unions had pleaded for an extension of time, but Sir James was pleased to say that the nine extensions granted would all come to an end on 1st April. Ralph Etwall then spoke and said he proposed to bring forward a motion on the subject of Andover. He said the enquiry held by assistant commissioner Parker was not regarded as satisfactory by the public. He wished to point out that as there was no mill in the workhouse and the bones had to be crushed by manual pounding, which was particularly revolting. A week later Capt. Pechell questioned the home secretary again as to why the return of all the workhouses that employed bone crushing and the names of all their chairmen and vice-chairmen ordered last year was not yet available. He observed that:

> During the recess, while the right hon. baronet [Sir J. Graham] and other hon. members of this House were recreating themselves on the moors or on the banks of the Rhine, I took the opportunity of visiting a Poor Law workhouse – or, as it was called in the country, a Poor Law 'bastille'. Now, it so happened that a mill for the grinding or crushing of bones for the purposes of manure was erected in that very 'bastille', and it was shown to me as one of the features of the place. When

> I saw the place, I thought it was a depôt for bone of a very different description. When the right hon. baronet stated last session that this intolerable nuisance should wholly cease, I relied upon that declaration; and I certainly did not expect that in November or December last I would witness a continuance of this most objectionable system.

Then on 5th March Etwall was able to bring forward his motion that a select committee be appointed to investigate the administration and management of the Andover Union and workhouse. He spoke at some length about the evils that had been revealed there, and in some detail explained the defalcations of McDougal in obtaining all sorts of personal benefits at the expense of the paupers. He reiterated his objections to bone crushing, and even alleged that some of the bones delivered to the Andover workhouse came from an old cemetery that was being dug up in the course of building a new church in the town. Sir James Graham rose to speak for the government, and began by regretting that so much parliamentary time was being taken up by what he called "a workhouse squabble in the south of England". He went over all the complaints that had been made about Andover, and one by one showed that they had now been addressed. There was a new master, better auditing, no more bone crushing, a better dietary, and so on. So he felt there was no need for another enquiry, and proposed instead that the report of Parker's enquiry be laid before the House, which he hoped would close the matter.

Mr Wakley then spoke, and said that no-one thought the matter had been satisfactorily dealt with. The commissioners had appointed a man, Parker, to conduct the enquiry who had every reason not to reach an unsatisfactory verdict as he himself was supposed to have been keeping watch on the union. The enquiry was terminated prematurely, so some matters and

*Sir James Graham, 1792-1861. He was first elected as a Whig in 1818, and held office under Lord Grey. In 1834 he left the Whigs over the Irish church question, and in 1838 was elected as a Tory MP, but he always remained on the moderate wing of the party. From 1841 to 1846 he served as home secretary under Peel. He represented six different constituencies during his parliamentary career.*

some witnesses were not heard. Parker had then been dismissed even though he had been an assistant commissioner for ten years. Even the guardians themselves were now petitioning parliament for an enquiry. The debate continued for some time, and all the speakers were in favour of an enquiry. Much of the debate turned on the treatment of assistant commissioner Parker. Since resigning he had been active in claiming himself to have been ill-used, and had published a pamphlet in self-defence. Several MPs had read this and claimed he had made out a good case. If he had been dismissed for 'insubordination', then the public had a right to know what this meant and on what occasion it had occurred. All he had done was to obey the instructions of the Commissioners in the way the enquiry was held and terminated. He believed he had been made a scapegoat for all the evils that had been revealed by the enquiry and which had embarrassed the Commissioners.

A Worcestershire MP, Peter Borthwick, who represented Evesham, made one of the more colourful speeches; describing the horrors visited on the Andover paupers he said:

> If the details which the hon. member for Andover had presented to the House to-night had been told of some distant or savage land into which civilization had never entered, and where Christianity was unknown, they might have regarded the statement as surcharged, that the picture was over-coloured, and that it was hardly in human imagination to invent details so horrible. They would have assumed that some foundation must exist for such a representation, and the spirit of English benevolence would have been roused to meet the evil. Public meetings would have been held, subscriptions would have been loyally entered into, missionaries would have been sent forth to reclaim, if not within the pale of Christianity, at least within the pale of humanity, persons who were suffering such wretched privations. Would they then pause in the same good work, because the sufferers were their own fellow countrymen, and the remedy was in their own hands, and could be applied without trouble? The sufferers were Englishmen; the tyranny under which they suffered was a law enacted by this House.

At the end of the debate the home secretary had to admit defeat, and said he would therefore grant the enquiry. However, he did not agree that it should also encompass an investigation into the dismissal of Parker, as he strongly believed that the Poor Law Commission could not function unless it had unfettered powers of appointment and dismissal. It would be wrong if every time an officer was dismissed this should be subject of a House of Commons enquiry – we may presume that Sir James Graham would not have been a friend of modern unfair dismissal legislation! So Sir James withdrew his motion opposing the enquiry, but opposed an amendment directing that the enquiry should also look into the circumstances surrounding Parker's dismissal. There was then a division, and despite the Tory government having at that time a majority in the Commons, the amendment was carried by 92 vote to 69.

The select committee was duly appointed, with seven Tories, including Pakington, and eight Liberals. Although this might seem to be a fair division, two of the Tories, Benjamin Disraeli and Sir William Jolliffe had voted for the extension of the enquiry to cover Parker's dismissal so might be considered anti-Commission, as did all the Liberals on the committee who had voted. Only Lord Courtney, John Pakington, and John Manners-Sutton, the under secretary of state for the Home Office, had actually opposed the extension of the enquiry on 5th March. So the committee turned out to be very much anti-Commission, and much of the time of their hearings was spent in internal disputes that reflected these divisions.

The committee first met on 20th March, and perhaps rather strangely chose Courtenay as chairman. He was categorised as a 'youth' and 'very young man' in The Times – actually he was nearly 39, so that was hardly fair. The committee then adjourned till after Easter, and begun their work in earnest on 24th April. In all the committee sat forty eight times until their last meeting on 17th August, which just gave them time to produce their report before the parliamentary session ended at the end of the month. Some of the committee meetings lasted as long as eight hours, so they must have sat for well over 200 hours. The chairman seems in the end to have done a reasonably good job (according to The Times, at least), but most of the interrogation of witnesses was carried out by the three anti-Poor Law campaigners, Pechell, Wakley and William Christie, who attended every session. Pakington attended all the first sixteen meetings, but business in Worcestershire kept him away from hearings on 24th and 26th June. In July he divided his time between London and Dover, where Augusta was staying for three weeks, and he missed more meetings because of that. In August they went to Cowes, missing another meeting, although he returned for meetings on four consecutive days from 5th to 8th August. Then, determined to do some sailing, he returned to Cowes and missed some more meetings.

There was some drama at the last meeting – at the very end Manners-Sutton, the junior minister, objected to a question put by William Christie. The room was cleared, and Manners-Sutton accused Christie of putting a question just for the benefit of The Times correspondent, which accusation Christie said he treated with contempt. Manners-Sutton then seems to have lost his temper and left the committee room, but as he did so he challenged Christie to a duel. The challenge was taken seriously by the other committee members and Henry Parker, who had attended the committee hearings throughout, was dispatched to the police court to ask for a warrant forbidding Manners-Sutton to commit a breach of the peace. An officer was dispatched to give the warrant to Manners-Sutton, who duly attended the next morning, when everything was smoothed over, Manners-Sutton having regained his composure.

Although Pakington had not attended the final committee hearings, he had been present when the final form of the report was discussed on 18th August, when there was a vote on one of the more damning paragraphs about the Poor Law Commissioners, which read:

> That on a review of the conduct of the Commissioners towards Mr Parker... the committee are of opinion that their conduct has been irregular and arbitrary, not in accordance with the statute under which they exercise their functions, and such as to shake pubic confidence in their administration of the law.

Only four members of the committee opposed this condemnation of the Commissioners: Sir John Walsh, Manners-Sutton, Pakington and James Stuart-Wortley, and the Tories Benjamin Disraeli and Sir William Jolliffe joined the Liberals in approving it. Although it can be imagined that the committee were more or less unanimous in condemning the inhuman regime at Andover, these four, it seems, were not prepared to go so far as to try and overturn the Commission, believing that, with proper management and control, the existing Poor Law regime could be made to work.

Bearing in mind the voluminous evidence they took, the final report of the committee is relatively brief. Firstly, it dealt with the way outdoor relief was offered in the Union. The committee felt too much discretion was left to the relieving officers, that the board itself should interview applicants where possible, that it was wrong to withhold relief from elderly or partially disabled paupers unless they came into the workhouse (although the committee accepted this was the policy of the Commissioners), and that it was wrong to insist on paupers offered temporary relief performing labour in the workhouse first. With regard to the workhouse itself, the committee found Mr and Mrs McDougal 'utterly unfit' to be master and matron. They particularly referred to the cruelty inflicted on Hannah Joyce, and that had the visiting committee of the Board of Guardians done their job properly many of the abuses would not have taken place. On the question of the dietary, the committee noted that initially at Andover dietary no. 3 was followed, but when this was subsequently improved by the Commission no improvement was made at Andover. Indeed the inmates frequently got less than they should due to the dishonesty of the master.

The committee found that nearly all the Union books were being improperly kept, and that merely a glance at these by the assistant commissioner would have shown that to be the case. But then the committee went on to partly excuse Parker, saying they received evidence of his hard work, and pointed out that even when there were twelve assistant commissioners the Poor Law Commissioners stated that there were not enough to supervise their unions as they should. When their number was further reduced to nine, the committee felt it was clear that they could not be expected to do their job properly. However, they also said that Parker placed much too much reliance on the Andover Board. One cannot help feel that different factions on the committee pulled in different directions on this point, and that had Parker been somewhat sharper and less trusting he should have been able to see some of the failings.

The committee began their comments on Mr Parker's enquiry and later dismissal by making the obvious comment that it was wrong to ask assistant commissioners to investigate complaints within their own district. They then criticised the Commissioners for abruptly trying to end the enquiry before all the evidence had been heard. Their final paragraph in this sections reads as follows:

> That, whatever feelings the Commissioners may have entertained with regard to Mr Parker's mode of conducting the Andover enquiry, or his defective superintendence of the Andover Union, the time and the manner of Mr Parker's removal from his office appear to them, after full consideration of the whole case, to have been such as to give him just cause of complaint, and to have been inconsistent with a discreet exercise of that power of dismissing their subordinate officers which the law has entrusted to the Commissioners.

In phrasing it thus, one could argue that the committee glossed over Parker's obvious bias in conducting the enquiry, and his laxity in not inspecting the Andover Union more carefully, and the committee had therefore displayed some bias towards Parker and against the Commissioners. This accorded with its make-up, and Pakington and his fellow Tories did not feel entirely happy with it. Finally the committee criticised the manner in which Parker was invited to resign – the Commissioners acted in haste and did not give Parker the right to put his own point of view first.

As a postscript to the committee's report, it was clear to the new Liberal government that the Poor Law Commissioners did not hold the confidence of either the country or House of Commons, and the following year, 1847, the Commission, which was to expire anyway that year, was replaced by a Board which included the lord president of the council, the lord privy seal, the home secretary and the chancellor of the exchequer. This gave parliament a much more direct control over its activities. Not, of course, that that stopped all criticism of the workhouse system, but at least it made it more difficult to accuse those in charge of behaving arbitrarily and without control.

## Chapter 12
## The Year 1846 and the Corn Law Debate

New year 1846 found John Pakington with his wife and son at Westwood. As usual quarter sessions occupied the first week of the new year, and Pakington notes in his diary that he addressed the grand jury on the subject of county finance. It was noted that there was a balance of over £3,000 in hand at the end of November, and this would enable the rates to be as low, Pakington said, as he could ever remember, ¼d rate for the county, and ½d for the police. He spoke proudly of the fact that the county expenditure, apart from the police rate, had gone down from £21,614 in 1840 to £15,474. He said, however, that the county was facing considerable expenditure on the new county lunatic asylum, but as Pakington's involvement in its establishment stretched over the next five years, we will discuss the new asylum in the next chapter.

After the Epiphany quarter sessions Pakington had received 'so bad an account of Miss P that we put off dinner party & went to London – found poor Miss P rallied a little', and while in town he saw his architect Hardwick, and they returned together to Westwood, where they discussed plans for alterations. Probably in the same connection, Pakington saw Isaac at the Worcester Bank the next day and 'settled business', which probably meant some form of extra loan or overdraft. The following day, 15th January, the name of Boyle occurs in the diary for the first time – this would be George Frederick Boyle, the younger half-brother and heir to the childless 5th Earl of Glasgow, and who had been a contemporary and friend of Johnny's at Christ Church, Oxford. Johnny was to marry his sister Diana in 1849. Next day Boyle joined a shooting party, and Pakington enjoyed 'capital sport', and ninety head were killed, of which Pakington accounted for forty. He notes that they wanted 'better guns', and he refers to Boyle and Wakeman as 'moughs'. This word does not appear in the Oxford English Dictionary, but we may assume it was not intended as a compliment!

Meanwhile, further bad news about his aunt's health had reached him. So he and Augusta returned to London, and passed the evening with Miss Pakington in Westbourne Street, where they found she was 'torpid, and did not fully know us'.

They spent most of the next two days with her, and during spells of consciousness she 'blessed us both'. On Tuesday 20th January they received a note that she had died early that morning. The rest of the week was spent writing letters, going through her papers, and settling with her landlady, coachman and servants. They were able to return to Westwood on Friday, then on Tuesday, after Miss Pakington's remains lay in the hall at Westwood overnight, the funeral was held in Hampton Lovett church. Although she would not have been well-known locally, she did represent the last of old Pakington line, and her passing was marked, Pakington notes, on the following Sunday when all the tenants wore mourning and hat bands. Her will, which had been the subject of a delicate correspondence between her and her nephew, left all her property to Pakington other than a few bequests, thus at last making him sole owner of the Westwood estate, and substantially increasing his income.

On 5th February the household left Droitwich for the season in London, and the next day combined another visit to Westbourne Street to sort out his late aunt's affairs with going to the House of Commons. In fact the session had already begun, and on 26th January the prime minister had addressed the house with regard to all the railway legislation that was to come before them during the year. This was the height of the railway boom, as the following figures show. In 1843, forty eight railways bills had come before the House; in 1844, one hundred and eighteen; and in the present session no less than 815 bills had already been brought before the Board of Trade (which was a necessary preliminary). In 1845, the House had run out of time to consider all of them – the Board of Trade did not pass them to the House until April. So in 1846 it was proposed that a select committee considered how best they should be dealt with. A debate took place in which several interesting points were raised: bearing in mind the enormous amount of capital required to construct all these schemes, should

*The monument to Dorothy Ann Pakington, John Pakington's aunt, in Hampton Lovett church. The monument also commemorates her father, Sir Herbert Perrott Pakington, her mother, Elizabeth Pakington née Hawkins, and her brother, Sir John Pakington, the 8th baronet, who had died in 1830, and to whom apparently there was no earlier memorial.*

parliament try and put a limit on the amount of the nation's capital that would be absorbed? Should the committee be peripatetic and take evidence outside London? How far generally should the government interfere with free trade – was a 'light touch' or a 'heavy touch' required? At the end of the debate the committee was approved under the chairmanship of Lord Granville Somerset (chancellor of the Duchy of Lancaster) and fourteen other members including Pakington.

The committee soon got down to business, and once in London Pakington attended its meetings. On 12th February the chairman moved that an additional committee be appointed, to be called the Classification Committee. It would consider all the proposed bills and group them so that competing projects were considered together by the appropriate select committee. Five members would be on this committee, again including Pakington. It had many sittings, most of which he attended, and which overlapped with sittings of the Andover Committee, as described in the previous chapter. He was also nominated to serve on the Amalgamation Committee on 24th March, which was to consider the whole question of the amalgamation of railway companies. Finally, he mentions another committee in his diary, the Rackets Vote committee. So 1846 must have been Pakington's busiest year in the House of Commons so far, and he later recorded that he attended over four committee meetings per week during the session.

Two days after he arrived in London in February, Pakington and his wife went to Danbury, Essex, where his father-in-law had, the previous year, purchased Danbury Place for use as an episcopal palace. The original Elizabethan house had lately been rebuilt by the owner. On Monday, leaving Augusta in Danbury, he returned to London for committee business and to attend the first day of the great Corn Law debate. He remained in London all week, returning to Danbury for the weekend, and returned to London on Monday, as the Corn Law debate was continuing.

The Corn Laws were the great issue of 1846, and were to have serious long term consequences for Peel, the Tory party and Pakington himself. The event that trig-

*In 1845, the Diocese of London was considered too large and it was decided to detach from it the counties of Essex and Hertfordshire and add them to Rochester. The Bishop of Rochester had to move nearer the centre of his enlarged sphere, and bought Danbury Place. From Morris's Country Seats.*

gered these happenings was the failure of the Irish potato harvest in late 1845. The English harvest was bad, but supplies of corn would be boosted by foreign imports, which would have a low duty if the market price rose. But there was much worse news from Ireland. As wheat did not prosper in the wet Irish climate, the population had become almost entirely dependent on the potato, which had proved itself well suited to conditions there. But as with all monocultures this presented a much increased risk of some pest or disease affecting the crop, and so it proved. As the harvest was brought in, reports started circulating that the tubers, afflicted by a fungus, quickly rotted, and despite efforts to find some way of using them, proved inedible.

This is not the place to give a detailed account of the Irish potato famine, or the various steps the government in London took to relieve the hardship. In the long term, the main effect was to start the depopulation of the Irish countryside, which continued for a considerable time, and meant that Ireland is almost unique among developed nations in having a lower population now than 200 years ago. At one point the population had halved. As we have noted before, Peel's rhetoric in favour of protectionism had not been as strong as that of some of his colleagues, and it may be that the arguments he put forward in its defence in 1842 when introducing the new Corn Law may have sounded as unconvincing to himself as they do to us now. So he informed his rather startled cabinet in November 1845 that total repeal was the only way forward. The Duke of Wellington, the aging Tory leader in the Lords, thought Peel had lost his nerve: "Rotten potatoes have done it all. They have put Peel in a damned fright". But Wellington's priority was that Peel should continue to govern as prime minister, so he promised his continuing support.

Peel failed to get the whole-hearted backing of his cabinet, and felt he could not proceed without it. He therefore resigned in December 1845, and the Queen sent for Lord John Russell to form a government. But Russell was not decisive, and ran into problems when some potential ministers refused to serve if Palmerston was in the cabinet, so eventually had to tell the Queen that he had failed. She therefore sent for Peel once more. His position was now different. Before, he had been elected by popular vote; now he was prime minister at the request of the Queen. He could therefore appeal to the loyalty of his colleagues to the Queen, and was thus able to form a government. Some, however, such as Edward Stanley, later as Earl of Derby the prime minister, would still not serve.

Peel's proposal for complete abolition was first debated in the House in January 1846. The debate on sending the repeal bill to committee started on 9th February, and lasted twelve nights. Peel's impassioned speech on 16th February, which lasted more than two hours, covered many topics. It was typically full of facts and figures, and showed throughout his humanity, rationalism, and belief in his own correctness. He began by referring to the split in the Tory party caused by his conversion to the principles of free trade. He spoke about the events of the previous November, when he had tendered his resignation to the Queen, and had told her that he would support in broad terms various measures, including the repeal of the corn laws and an increase in military estimates, that he believed that his probable successor, Lord John Russell, would propose. So he was in no way responsible for Russell's failure to form a Whig government. It would have been easy for him in the short term to court party loyalty by supporting the protectionists and keep the duty on corn at the present high level. But Peel firmly believed that that course would have been wrong for the country and difficult to sustain against such a strong tide of public opinion, and thus wrong for the party in the long term. Peel was a man of honour. When people accused him of being the mere hired advocate of free-traders, they should consider that, when appointed to office, ministers have to take an oath in the presence of the sovereign including the words 'that in all matters to be treated and debated in council, I will, faithfully, openly and truly, declare my mind and opinion according to my heart and conscience'. How, therefore, could he go against his deeply held views in the matter before the House that night?

He then spoke about the four million people in Ireland who were on the verge of suffering a catastrophe. In case any member felt that reports of the potato blight were exaggerated, Peel read out reports that he had received recently from responsible people there, saying that in some districts nearly all last year's potato harvest was unusable. Even in areas where some of the harvest was saved, scarcely enough potatoes survived to provide this year's seed potatoes, so the situation later in the year would be even worse than it was now. How could anyone still press for duties, not only on wheat but on all foodstuffs, to remain high when all these millions of people faced starvation? In past crises of this kind an order in council had been issued for the temporary suspension of duties. However, as parliament was now sitting, the matter had to be brought before the legislature, and of one thing he was sure – if only a temporary suspension was agreed to now, it would never be possible to reinstate the old corn laws. The only sensible course of action now was to agree to a permanent repeal.

Peel then attacked some of those who had spoken in favour of protection. He gave several examples of trades where ruin had been forecast when the last round of duty reductions had been enacted in 1842, but the trade had prospered despite an increase in imports, and he supplied many figures to back up his claim. Reduced prices, he pointed out, led to an increase in demand for those products, which benefited all producers, at home and overseas. One of the examples he gave referred to wallpaper, on which he proposed the duty should be reduced. "It is claimed," he said, "that foreign wallpaper has better patterns than ours; but there is nothing in the physical constitution of Englishmen to prevent them from drawing as good patterns as Frenchmen, if you will stimulate them to exertion by competition." Such a claim has a very modern ring about it. The same applied to corn; protected by tariff walls farmers could get away with inefficient methods and still make a profit. But, he claimed, using the latest advances in agricultural science yields could be increased by as much as sixty percent. This could only come about by the application of capital which would be stimulated by increased competition. As a gesture towards this he announced that there would be government financial aid for land drainage schemes – this was one of the means by which big improvements in yields could be brought about.

Winding himself up to a powerful peroration, Peel again attacked those who were attempting to wreck the government bill by proposing to postpone discussion six months (this was a favourite parliamentary device to kill a measure). Did they not remember, he asked, that in the recent Queen's speech she had said that parliament would discuss and decide on our future commercial policy? How could that be debated if it was put on the shelf for six months? Members had a duty to do what they had agreed to on that occasion. "Advance or Recede" was his battle cry. "May God grant that by your decision of this night you may have laid in store for yourselves the consolation of reflecting that such calamities [as that in Ireland] are, in truth, the dispensations of Providence – that they have not been caused, they have not been aggravated by laws of man restricting, in the hour of scarcity, the supply of food". These were his final words spoken before the House adjourned at 2.00 a.m.

Pakington's diary comment that this was a 'splendid speech' is interesting. Of course, he may just have been referring to Peel's considerable powers of oratory and his command of the subject replete with facts and figures. Nevertheless, if Pakington was such an opponent of free trade as he had claimed at earlier Worcestershire meetings, would he still have noted this in his diary? One has to suspect that really Pakington agreed with much that Peel had argued, and it was only his traditional country Tory position that did not allow him to vote with Peel. Such may in fact have applied to many Tory MPs. And it is to be noted that Pakington did not feel strongly enough to speak in the debate.

In the final division on 27th February the bill was sent to committee by a majority of 97, all but eleven Whigs voting with the government. But the vote showed how split the Tories were – over two thirds of the party voted against, and if one discounts government ministers who were obliged to vote 'aye', probably only about 70 back-bench Tories out of about 370 were in favour of repeal. Certainly Pakington was not one of them, and he joined his protectionist colleagues in the lobby. There was a similar result after the debate on the second reading on 27th March, and again Pakington opposed it.

Apart from his Commons' committees and evening attendances in the House he found time for the usual round of social activities, attending a levée in St James Palace with his father-in-law on 18th February, and a few days later he was taken by 'young Hardwick' to see the new hall that Philip Hardwick senior had been responsible for at Lincoln's Inn. This would be Philip Charles Hardwick (1822-92), the son of Philip

Hardwick, who by now had health problems that restricted his mobility. Hardwick junior, although not in the front rank of architects, established a successful country house practise, but it is not always easy to discover whether work belonged to father or son at this period.

The following week he skipped one of his committee appearances and went to Oxford to see Johnny, dining in Christ Church hall and 'wining with Johnny', before returning to town the next morning. Then on 26th his sister-in-law Eleanor, not yet 18, was presented to the Queen at a 'drawing room'. Pakington was in attendance, but Augusta was not well enough to come. A 'drawing room' was similar to a levée when people were presented to the Queen and Prince Albert, but most of those present at the latter were officials, and therefore men, whereas at a 'drawing room' society ladies were presented. They were grand occasions. The Queen and Prince Albert were attended by twenty one Lords and Ladies-in-waiting of differing status; the Duchess of Kent and the Duke and Duchess of Cambridge with their attendants were there; the gentlemen at arms were on duty in the throne room and at various doorways; and the Yeomen of the Guard wore their splendid coronation uniform. Firstly various diplomatic presentations were made in the throne room, and the diplomatic circle in attendance comprised thirty eight diplomats, some with their wives and families, and there was a 'general circle' of about fifty palace officials and attendants. Then followed the presentations of the ladies of which there were eighty-six. Some were there on the occasion of their marriage or some other important event; the rest were presumably debutantes; each was presented by a lady relation; Eleanor was presented by her mother. Then just to round things off there were over two hundred gentlemen present, mostly members of the establishment including most of the cabinet.

A month later Pakington and Augusta attended another drawing room, and on that occasion it was Augusta who was presented by her mother.

Another of Pakington's sisters-in-law had been staying at Danbury. She was Lady Caroline Mordaunt, who had six children aged between one and nine. The previous September she had been tragically widowed when her husband, Sir John Mordaunt, one of the MPs for Warwickshire, had died after a shooting accident near his seat at Walton Hall. He had been out shooting with a friend in his park and had climbed over a fence. When his friend followed him over the fence he had not properly secured his shotgun, and accidentally discharged it into the back of Sir John's legs. For a time it was thought he would recover, but after suffering for several days he died. Pakington wrote 'poor Caroline – my heart aches for her sufferings' with feeling, having six small children to look after. Augusta was ill all the week on her sister's account. Soon afterwards a committee was formed to arrange for a monument to be erected, but if this was concluded, its location is now uncertain. Tragedy was to strike this family again in the 1860s, when Sir John's eldest son, Sir Charles, married

Harriet Moncrieffe. His new wife proved something of a free spirit, and the Prince of Wales was amongst her admirers. When their first child was born and Harriet admitted it was illegitimate, a lengthy and expensive divorce case ensued, complicated by the fact that Harriet was for a time declared to be insane.

At the beginning of March Pakington and young Hardwick went to Westwood to review progress on some alterations. Pakington was alarmed and annoyed to find cracks in the hall, so he had to stop the decoration, but Hardwick convinced him that they were coming from the flue and were not serious. He was also concerned by Augusta's possible gynaecological problems after the scare about a miscarriage the previous year. As she was still having some 'symptoms' Pakington consulted the obstetric physician Sir Charles Locock, well-known for attending Queen Victoria's confinements using chloroform. But Sir Charles could find nothing seriously wrong, but did have some leeches applied.

On 11th March Pakington spoke twice in the House – in support of his Salmon Fisheries Bill, and on Catholic relief. He had introduced a bill to protect salmon the previous year – it provided for a close season and a minimum net size and was connected with the new works on the River Severn. It had been modified in committee and not passed, and in the current year he reintroduced it. The Catholic Relief Bill was an attempt to sweep away some remaining restrictions on Roman Catholics. Catholic emancipation had come a long way since it started with the Acts of 1788 and 1791, and the important Emancipation Act of 1829. But many older acts, some going back to Queen Elizabeth's time, remained on the statute book, some enforced but many not, and the 1846 bill would have swept away many of them. Some were just indignities, such as the requirement for teachers to be licensed by Anglican bishops even if they were teaching in a Catholic school. There was even some doubt as to whether the Statute of Praemunire, which made illegal any appeal to a foreign power over the heads of the English courts, could still be made to apply to Catholics. (This statute, which dated back to the fourteenth century and was mainly aimed at restricting the power of the Pope in England, was only formally repealed in 1967, which was probably just as well as otherwise those taking Britain into the Common Market, which allowed for foreign courts to overrule British ones, might have been guilty under it.)

Most of those who spoke in the debate on the bill supported it to a degree, but there was still unhappiness on the part of many who saw it as re-introducing Papal power in England, which was against the constitution. Pakington, although a committed Anglican, strongly supported religious toleration, and in his short speech said he would have voted in favour of Catholic Emancipation in 1829, and he did vote for the Maynooth grant. The established church of this country ought to rest on the affections and religious faith of the people, he said, rather than the force of law. But he felt some aspects of the bill went too far in favour of Roman Catholics, so although he would vote for the second reading, he would press for some changes in committee. The bill was approved by a large majority, and the day's sitting finished early enough for Pakington to take Augusta and her sister Eleanor to a concert of ancient music in the evening.

Two days later the House was busy discussing the detail of the tariff reductions proposed by Peel, but Pakington noted in his diary 'did not return to House, not wishing to vote on tariff questions'. There is obviously another hint in this that he was more favourably disposed to Peel's free trade than he liked to admit, and as the voting was now consistently against protection he did not see any point in being on the losing side, which he did not really agree with anyway.

The following day is the first time the name Andover appears in the diary – his work on the select committee was described in the last chapter. On that same day Johnny came down from Oxford, and stayed with his father in London. A week later Augusta began to think she was pregnant again, 'so she must be cautious' her husband wrote. The next day, Saturday, Johnny and his father went to the Lyceum to see the celebrated American dwarf, General Tom Thumb, in a play specially written for him. Pakington was very impressed; he was 'a wonderful sight! The extreme smallness of this little creature combined with activity & intellect is a new variety of the wonderful workings of God'. Another theatre visit followed the next Tuesday to see Donizetti's opera 'Linda de Chimouni'; this was followed by a 'pretty ballet'.

Pakington had to return to Worcestershire for the Easter sessions, and took the late mail train arriving in Droitwich at 2.30 a.m., staying at The George. Earlier in the day he had heard that Augusta was definitely expecting – 'I am most thankful for her having the blessing of such a prospect, before the first anniversary of her former loss returns'. The next day, as the household had removed to London, he stayed in quarters at the court in Worcester, where he presided on Monday and Tuesday, when business was light. Hardwick came to review progress at Westwood – Pakington was pleased – and after attending the

*Charles Sherwood Stratton (left) with his wife, a giant, and another dwarf. He hardly grew at all after he was 6 months old in 1838, and was 3ft 4 ins tall when he died in 1883. He enjoyed a successful career with Barnum's circus, appearing twice in London before Queen Victoria.*

Institute of Mechanics and Severn Commissioners meetings, he returned to London, changing trains in Birmingham, where he had time to order a hot-house. Leaving Birmingham at 5.45 p.m. he reached his London residence by 10.30 p.m.

The following day was Good Friday, and as Johnny had gone to Danbury Pakington and his wife had the Murray's house at Eaton Place to themselves over Easter. On Monday he went to see Hardwick to discuss the progress of work at Westwood, and on the following day he had another theatre evening with Johnny. They saw three comedies at the Haymarket – 'all good in their respective ways & much amused'. For the weekend after Easter, as parliament was not sitting they had booked rooms to stay at Richmond. Pakington would have had fond memories of this district from the time when his aunt lived at Hampton Court, and he calls this their 'little honey-moon'. On Friday morning they went riding on donkeys, and were 'much struck by beauty of place'. Wet weather after lunch kept them indoors, and they played chess with each other for the first time. The following day they explored Richmond Park as far as Petersham, and on Sunday went to morning service at Hampton Court Chapel.

Back in London, Pakington was much engaged looking at horses, before buying a bay horse at Shakell's for £65 – one measure of inflation would equate this with the price of a good quality saloon car today. The following day he fell for and bought a bay cob bantam at Collins'. On the next day, Friday, Johnny returned to Oxford, and Pakington attended the first meeting of the Andover committee, and for the next two months most of his time was spent attending committees and sitting in the chamber. Much time was taken up in the Commons the following week by William Smith O'Brien. Pakington notes the two debates in his diary, although an indication that he did not always write his diary every day is given by the fact that he got the days wrong. O'Brien was, despite being a protestant and a member of a land-owning family, a well-known Irish nationalist. He had recently refused to attend meetings of one of the committees established to consider railway schemes. As only five members served on each committee, by a resolution of the house passed in

*William Smith O'Brien (1803-64). He was second son of Sir Edward O'Brien, 4th bart, of Dromoland Castle, and received a conventional upper class education. Before his banishment he was leader of the Young Ireland movement. Transported to Tasmania he tried to escape and had an adventurous life.*

February attendance was made compulsory. O'Brien had written to the chairman of the Selection Committee (which chose members to sit on select committees), Thomas Bucknal-Escourt, to explain that because of his principal belief that Ireland ought to govern itself he would only sit on committees that considered matters to do with Ireland. He felt that only Irish members should involve themselves with Irish affairs, so why should he intermeddle with English or Scottish affairs?

His refusal to obey an order of the House made him potentially guilty of contempt, for which he would be imprisoned by the serjeant at arms. On Tuesday 28th April there was a long debate. Bucknall-Escourt recited at length the sequence of events that had led to the present situation, and was followed by Daniel O'Connell, who used various legal arguments to try to prove that O'Brien could not be guilty of contempt, even citing a statute of Henry VIII. Two other Irish members, Edmund Roche and John O'Connell, supported O'Brien and said the House would be unwise to push the matter too far in view of the delicate state of relations between Ireland and England. Some English members, including Peel himself, expressed some sympathy with O'Brien but felt that rules were rules and had to be obeyed. Other speakers were less sympathetic. But at the end of the debate some element of moderation was introduced by adjourning it until Thursday to give O'Brien a chance to change his mind. But that was not to be. On Thursday his friends appealed that he be given the right to express his views more freely on the matter, but this was against the rules of the House, and at the end of the debate the serjeant at arms was instructed to take him into custody. On 22nd May Daniel O'Connell made another attempt, using a legalistic argument, to prove that O'Brien's imprisonment had been illegal. Although he found little sympathy among his fellow MPs, at the next sitting the government proposed that he be released as the authority of the House had been upheld and O'Brien sufficiently punished, although O'Brien himself apparently wished to remain in prison. At least it can be said in favour of O'Brien that he was consistent in his views, to the extent that two years later he became involved in a misconceived rebellion in Ireland, for which he was sentenced to death. Unwilling for him to be made a martyr, he was instead transported to Van Diemen's land, which, although he eventually returned, marked the end of his political career.

On 28th April Pakington noted that he went to a meeting of the Society for the Propagation of the Gospel in Hanover Square rooms – an 'important and influential meeting', according to The Times. The society dated back to 1701, and was formed to spread the benefits of the gospel to places which had hitherto been ignorant. Although the Society's income had grown enormously since its formation, its potential work had increased even more as the British Empire had expanded into Africa and other un-Christian parts of the globe. As was usual at such meetings various resolutions were passed. The first, proposed by the Bishop of Winchester, stated that emigrants to these distant countries needed much more attention to their spiritual needs than was presently provided – this, of course, was a subject that Pakington had shown interest in. George Byng MP seconded the resolution, and as he sat down he gave a cheque for £100 to the cause, amidst loud applause. The second resolution, proposed by the Bishop of St David's, proposed that 'The connection into which this Christian country has been brought, through its commercial and political relations with vast numbers of the heathen, imposes upon it the duty of imparting to them the blessings of the Gospel'. The Bishop of Jamaica, Aubrey Spencer, who had recently been translated from the diocese of Newfoundland, proposed the third resolution which supported the work of the Society generally. The fourth, which proposed opening local British branches to raise funds, was proposed by Lord Sandon. This was seconded by William Manning, then archdeacon of Winchester. It may have been to hear him that Pakington attended, as he noted in his diary that he was 'a very fine speaker'. Manning had acquired the reputation of being an eloquent and earnest preacher, and Pakington had on previous occasions gone to hear notable preachers when opportunity arose. Manning was very high church, and had followed Newman as Oxford University preacher, and in 1851, like Newman, converted to Rome. His career as a Catholic priest culminated when he was appointed Archbishop of London and later a Cardinal.

The following week Pakington went with his father-in-law to look at a house in Eaton Square. The Murrays had moved from Belgrave Square to nearby Eaton Place in 1844, and the rather grander Eaton Square lies just a little further south. It seems that Pakington and Augusta had been living with her parents, and now for the first time he was planning to have his own London home.

Although in earlier years Pakington does not always record whether or where he went to church, in 1846 he recorded on most Sundays going to church, usually twice. Although he had his favourite places, he also enjoyed going somewhere different, often with Bishop Murray. On 7th May they went to St Paul's, where they heard the Bishop of St David's 'preach for 1 hour 20 minutes'. The following Sunday he went with Augusta to the recently opened St Michael's, Chester Square, where he was 'not quite satisfied' by Mr Harrison, the preacher. Unusually he missed the afternoon service due to 'conversation with Augusta'.

On 15th May there was the final lengthy debate on the third reading on the bill to repeal the Corn Laws. Pakington was there and noted 'powerful speech by Disraeli'. The future prime minister started by trying to demolish the arguments in favour of free trade, indeed he claimed the Liberal leaders had abandoned many of their arguments already. Disraeli, rather in the manner of Peel, used statistics and quoted reports he had received from foreign countries to prove the protectionist case. Somehow, however, his arguments were more disparate than Peel's, and presented in a way that owed more to a desire to sway the house by oratory than by a logical, rational case.

Using his undoubted power of oratory, Disraeli described the bounteous fields of counties such as Lincolnshire, that had become so productive under protectionism, and how they might revert to their former unproductive state if the measure passed. Then he became more personal, and not only attacked Peel but also the hundred and twelve members of his own party who had followed their leader and changed from being protectionists to being free traders. In one of his more colourful allusions, he compared this to the mass conversion of the Saxons by Charlemagne. "When I saw the hundred and twelve fall into rank and file, I was irresistibly reminded of that memorable incident on the banks of the Rhine".

He said Peel had been accused of treachery, of seeking power only to use it to follow different policies from those on which he had been elected. But, he continued,

> I entirely acquit the right hon. gentleman of any such intention. I do it for this reason: that when I examine the career of this minister, which has now filled a great space in the parliamentary history of this country, I find that for between thirty and forty years… the right hon. gentleman has traded on the ideas and intelligence of others. His life has been one great appropriation clause. He is a burglar of others' intellect.

In his biography of Peel, Lord Hurd claims that Disraeli, when an ambitious young MP in 1841, had written to the new prime minister Peel seeking an appointment, only to have his request ignored. In his reply to Disraeli, winding up the debate, Peel referred to this when he said:

*Born a Jew, Disraeli converted to Christianity, and entered parliament as a Tory at the same time as John Pakington in 1837. Thought by some to be an opportunist, he was passed over by Peel in his 1841 government, and, hurt, frequently opposed Peel thereafter. This portrait was painted by Sir Francis Grant when Disraeli became chancellor of the exchequer in 1852. Twice prime minister, he also wrote several novels.*

> Sir, I foresaw that the course which I have taken from a sense of public duty would expose me to serious sacrifices. I foresaw as its inevitable result, that I must forfeit friendships which I most highly valued – that I must interrupt political relations in which I felt a sincere pride; but the smallest of all the penalties which I anticipated were the continued venomous attacks of the Member for Shrewsbury [Disraeli]. Sir, I will only say of that hon. gentleman, that if he, after reviewing the whole of my public life – a life extending over thirty years previously to my accession to office in 1841 – if he then entertained the opinion of me which he now professes; if he thought I was guilty of these petty larcenies from Mr Horner and others, it is a little surprising that in the spring of 1841, after his long experience of my public career, he should have been prepared to give me his confidence. It is still more surprising that he should have been ready – as I think he was – to unite his fortunes with mine in office, thus implying the strongest proof which any public man can give of confidence in the honour and integrity of a minister of the crown.

Lord Hurd claims that if Peel had had Disraeli's 1841 letter in his hand that night to prove his point, it might have caused a big set-back to his rival's career. Whether this would have been the case we shall never know, but certainly Disraeli used the power of his oratory to the utmost, and if a few inconvenient facts were ignored as he piled accusation upon accusation, then so be it. The result of the vote, when again the combined forces of the Liberals and the Peelite Tories won the day, was a forgone conclusion. Disraeli used the big occasion not in any hope that his side would win, but to further his own ambitions of achieving office within his party.

How far Pakington agreed with Disraeli's arguments we will have to conjecture, but his use of the adjective 'powerful' could certainly not be quarrelled with. It is perhaps significant that he used that word rather than 'convincing'. Certainly the House was well attended by those wishing to hear the great men of the day speak, and the division took place at quarter past four in the morning, and the repeal bill was passed with a majority of ninety-eight. Pakington voted again against repeal, and one bitter protectionist MP, Elliot Yorke, delayed MPs' bedtime even further by proposing the bill should have a new name: 'The Foreign Lands Improvement Bill'! Pakington retired at quarter to five, and was therefore up late the following day, and spent the afternoon quietly riding in the park with the Bishop, the Camdens and Augusta's unmarried sisters. Augusta herself had been unwell; but that day he was pleased to note 'Augusta better & alarm passed off'.

On Sunday evening Pakington went by the late mail train to Birmingham, where he slept, and the following morning was able to reach Westwood by 10.00. Presumably he went to inspect progress on the renovations, as he returned to town that night, getting home at 11.15 p.m.

On 25th May Pakington recorded that he had 'good fortune to hear Lord Stanley's great speech on Corn Laws' in the Lords. Stanley said that all principal countries had laws to protect their domestic agriculture, and quoted from past statesmen who had all supported some form of protection. He continued:

> I dispute that which has been held to be an indisputable axiom; and I contend that the inference, the *prima facie* inference, is that all statesmen of former times in this country and all other countries at the present day, have not been wholly destitute of political wisdom and political sagacity. I cannot believe that not a single beam of enlightenment dispelled the universal darkness, till that which flashed simultaneously and with such marvellous power of conversion upon the statesmen of the present age, in the month of November last.

Stanley then paid a personal tribute to the Duke of Wellington, now his opponent and, in great contrast to Disraeli ten days before, to Peel himself. Peel must have known the damage to himself that would occur through his change of mind, but, continued Stanley, "I cannot but think that he conscientiously believed the emergency of the case required this course to be pursued". But Peel was too influenced by the "brawling torrent of agitation" and should have recognised the "deep current of public opinion", which Stanley believed was still in favour of protection. He had therefore achieved a "fatal triumph" and compromised the independence of parliament.

Stanley then launched on a long passage quoting statistics on prices, tonnages imported, and employment numbers, all to bolster his protectionist arguments. Unfortunately, it is evident that these figures could be used to strengthen either side of the debate, as Peel and Disraeli had already demonstrated. Finally Stanley returned to his argument about the dangers of rushing into action, particularly in response to popular clamour. He said the House of Lords had a long and vital tradition of forming its own judgement on matters such as this; and if the House succeeded in leading the country back to a wiser course, then

> it will be proud of having withstood alike the seductions of power, and the threats of popular clamour; proud of having succeeded in saving your country from this great delusion, this hazardous and fearful experiment. Your best reward, my Lords, will be the approval of your own consciences; but doubt not but that you will have a further reward in the approbation of a grateful and admiring nation, to which you will have given just cause to exclaim, 'Thank God, we have a House of Lords!'.

Later speakers that night, while congratulating Stanley on his speech, complained of its length – it lasted over three hours, long even by the standards of the time.

The following day Augusta's condition again gave rise to concern, and her husband thought there was a more serious chance of a miscarriage. Nevertheless her condition did not cause him to lessen his activities. The Andover committee meetings were taking place every few days, and on 27th May he attended a meeting of the Incorporated Society for Promoting the Education of the Poor in the Principles of the Established Church (to give what Pakington calls 'The Education Society' its full name) at the Central School at Westminster. The Archbishop of Canterbury and eight other bishops were on the platform, and in the audience were many clergy and other distinguished persons. After a prayer, the girl pupils were examined by the Bishop of Lichfield on the scriptures. Their answers (according to The Times) showed that they had not learned the scriptures by rote, but intelligently and in a right and religious spirit. Then the boys went through a similar ordeal when they were examined on history, geography and scripture, and again 'acquitted themselves very creditably'. Then all the pupils went through their 'musical exercises'.

Then followed a series of resolutions. First the annual report, describing the work of the Society, which mainly involved training new male and female teachers, was read and adopted. Then, after a resolution praising the work of the society, Pakington proposed a resolution 'That this meeting regards with much satisfaction the progress made by diocesan and district boards throughout the kingdom in the establishment of training schools'. He said "I witnessed with great pleasure the exhibition of the scholars, more especially their proficiency in music and singing, and I hope that one of the objects of the society will be to extend throughout the country an improved system of musical teaching by means of their training masters, so that an improvement will take place in our congregational psalmody". The Times reported that the meeting lasted five hours.

Two days later on 29th May tragedy struck. After returning from a Worcestershire Society dinner, he found Augusta had been 'taken ill & after seven hours suffering she miscarried at 4 a.m.'. However, she seems to have recovered well, and the following week Pakington was able to leave her and go to see Johnny at Oxford. After boating and dining in hall, he attended a 'fine debate' in the Union in the evening – this was the period when Johnny was active in the Oxford Union, as recorded earlier. At this time the London season was in full swing. On 4th June his friend Hallifax had his ball, and on the same day Johnny passed through town on his way to boating at Eton. But Pakington's priorities lay in parliament, and he missed a party and a concert to which he had been invited as he wished to attend a debate on the Poor Removal Bill. He spoke briefly in favour of the proposal, which did not succeed, that settlements would become Union-wide, rather than confined to a parish. Hitherto, a pauper's parish of birth ('settlement') was responsible for his relief, even if administered by the Union workhouse.

On that Saturday he went back to Westwood for a brief visit. He saw both Curtlers (John and Thomas), and presumably inspected progress at Westwood. There had been a heat-wave that week, and it was too hot to walk to Hampton Lovett church – 'hottest morning I ever felt in England' he noted, but it did rain in the evening. On Monday he travelled back. On both journeys he travelled by Great Western express – as there was no direct line to Worcester yet, this would have been from Paddington to

Gloucester (opened in 1844), then by the Birmingham and Gloucester to Droitwich Road. This route was not any faster than the one from Euston via Birmingham – he left London at 8.30 a.m. and arrived home at 3.15 p.m., a journey of over 6 hours.

The Corn Law Repeal Bill was still going through the Lords, and was opposed, as we have seen, by many Tory peers, led by Lord Stanley. But the Duke of Wellington, still the leader of the Tories in the Lords, after initial hesitation in which he confessed he hardly understood the matter, worked hard to bring the Tory peers into line. After Lord John Russell ensured the support of the Whig peers by suggesting that if the bill failed it might do permanent damage to the House of Lords, the bill passed on 25th June without a division.

By this time Peel's enemies had sensed another chance of defeating him. The Protection of Life (Irish) Bill (usually called the Coercion Bill) was going through parliament, and the Whigs had decided to oppose it. The debate on the second reading, which introduced measures, including a curfew in the most troublesome areas, to clamp down on violent crime in Ireland, started on 8th June. On the third night, Monday 15th June, Pakington was there, and listened to another of Disraeli's strong attacks upon Peel, which he noted without comment in his diary. Pakington often expressed his concern over the dreadful state of affairs in Ireland, and must have regretted that it was producing as much violence, albeit verbal, in the Commons as across the Irish Sea. Disraeli again accused Peel of inconsistency, this time on the Catholic question, and made lengthy references to speeches Peel made in the 1820s in the run-up to Catholic Emancipation in 1829, to prove his point. Pakington was a practical man, and may have wondered how Disraeli could have spoken at such length without any reference to the subject of the debate at all. In his diary, he noted 'Peel's triumphant vindication against attack', referring to the prime minister's short but firm denial of Disraeli's claims made immediately after Disraeli sat down. This does rather indicate with whom Pakington's sympathies lay.

The debate on the Coercion Bill ran over six nights, but there was other business to be discussed which meant the sixth and final night of the debate was not held until June 25th. One matter that interposed itself was a debate on the railway gauge question, which Pakington attended. The Great Western Railway and its extensions had been built on the seven foot broad gauge, and all other early railways on the standard gauge. Pakington would have seen the inconvenience of the change of gauge when he travelled by the Great Western express earlier in the month, as the GW line to Gloucester was broad gauge, and there it met the Birmingham and Gloucester railway, built on the standard gauge. It was quickly recognised that having two different gauges in what was fast becoming a national network was a great inconvenience, and it soon became obvious that the standard gauge would predominate. So all proposals for new lines unconnected with the Great Western were now for standard gauge lines, and it was thought desirable for parliament to formalise its policy on the matter. So on 16th June the government proposed the adoption of a set of resolutions setting out future policy. These amounted to a decision not to allow any more broad gauge lines to be built north of the GW line to Bristol, excepting some short branch lines.

Sir George Clerk, vice-president of the Board of Trade, proposed the resolutions, and explained that they had considered whether it would be practical to abandon the broad gauge altogether. But this would cost around one million pounds, and it would not be right either to ask the Great Western, or the public, to find this money. In addition it would mean the abandonment of a system that was generally accepted as being superior to the standard gauge. It allowed for more powerful engines and faster speeds, and greater accommodation of passengers and goods. So there was no alternative to living with the present inconveniences, and in the debate this was generally accepted, but there was considerable discussion on some of the detail, which Pakington would have listened to with interest.

Meanwhile the debate on the Coercion Bill was rumbling on, and reached its final night the following Thursday 25th June. Earlier in the century, there had been several other similar bills all restricting the normal freedoms in Ireland to try and deal with civil unrest, and they had usually been passed by an overwhelming majority. But now, with many more reforming and radical MPs in the House, opposition to it was strong. Many speakers pointed out that the bill did not tackle the root cause of Irish discontent, and until this was put right the troubles would continue. Joseph Hume, the radical Scottish doctor who represented at different times English, Scottish and Irish constituencies, produced an impressive set of figures that showed not only that crime was worst where poverty was worst, but also how bad poverty was. In the four poorest counties, Kerry, Mayo, Clare and Cork, as many as sixty one percent of families lived in 'mud cabins having only one room'. The average age at death was only 23 (in a typical English rural parish at this time it would have been at least 40). The homicide rate in those counties was over double that in less poverty-stricken parts of Ireland.

*A photograph of dual gauge track at the Didcot Railway Centre, showing the complicated points work necessary. The broad gauge remained in use on the Great Western railway until finally abolished in 1892.*

During the debate there was a little drama, when messengers from the House of Lords revealed that the Corn Law Repeal Bill had finally passed. This is supposed to have made MPs feel that there was nothing now to be lost by defeating the government. So the Coercion Bill was defeated by 292 to 219 votes, and the following day Peel resigned, opening the way to a Liberal government under Lord John Russell. Pakington had gone to Worcestershire the day before the final vote, so was paired as someone supporting the bill.

Despite his busy life, Pakington still found time to go to the theatre. On 17th he saw the 'Ethiopian Serenaders' at a party given by a Mrs Miles. They were a popular group of five Americans dressed in ordinary evening costume, having, according to The Times, 'their hands and face painted black wearing a black wig of a woolly texture playing the banjo, accordion, tambourine and a type of castanets. ...The spokesman of the party used 'clown in the ring' humour disguised in 'nigger' dialect'. They sang American negro 'minstrelsy', which The Times correspondent found suffered from 'the extreme sameness of style'. The best song was the railroad overture, imitating the sounds of a railroad train. The following night Pakington went to the opera to see Bellini's 'I Puritani', after which was performed the last scene from the composer's 'La Sonnambula'. Some time the following day, 19th June, he received a note asking him to call on the prime minister, and when there on 20th had a 'gratifying interview in which he announced fulfilment of promise of baronetcy as Queen's pleasure was taken & said he thought me right on my vote on corn'.

The mention of the word 'promise' sounds as if Peel had already promised to see if could obtain a baronetcy for him. Pakington had already achieved many of his ambitions by entering parliament and occupying a number of important positions in Worcestershire, as well as having a fine wife and a young male heir. He would not have thought too highly of his uncle, the 8th and last baronet of the first creation, but he would have been keenly aware of his earlier forbears, and their distinctive and historic creation of Westwood House and park. What could be more natural than wishing to become another in the long line of Sir John Pakingtons? There is one slight mystery about the timing of his meeting with Peel. Pakington's baronetcy, as well as a few others, was announced on 27th June as being on the occasion of the resignation of the prime minister, but his meeting with Peel was, according to his diary at least, several days before the government's defeat on 25th June. So it seems that Peel must have anticipated his defeat and have been preparing an honours list from the beginning of the debate – the only other explanation is that Sir John (as we shall now call him) got the date of the meeting wrong in his diary, but this seems unlikely.

Sir John's brief visit to Worcester was in connection with the Worcester Infirmary. This institution, which had been founded just over 100 years previously, had a connection with his grandfather, William Russell, who was a long-serving surgeon at the Infirmary, but otherwise Sir John himself does not seem to have been involved in it. Despite his other heavy commitments, Sir John had been appointed to a subcommittee of the Infirmary set up to examine the rules, although in fact he does not seem to have attended any of its meetings. This had arisen out of an incident the previous year, when a committee was looking into some complaints about treatment in the Infirmary. The doctors wanted to attend, as they believed they had the right to do under the original rules, which stated that all subscribers of two guineas, and all medical staff, were governors. When the chairman told them not to attend, the doctors, annoyed, came nevertheless and demanded entry. An animated discussion followed, as a result of which a committee was formed to look into the matter, consisting of Thomas Curtler, Lord Lyttelton, Sir John Pakington, Dr Spooner and a few others.

The result of all this was the meeting on the day following the defeat of the government, at which Curtler was to propose some changes in the rules to allow committees with limited membership to be set up. The question had obviously aroused much interest in the City, and over two hundred attended according to Berrows. Dr Jonas Malden commenced proceedings by reading a memorandum signed by himself, Charles Hastings, and four other doctors. This purported to show that the medical staff had always played a central part in the management of the Infirmary, and 'have always been considered members of all committees or boards'.

Thomas Curtler then rose to speak in favour of the changes which the committee proposed. He said it was quite wrong to claim, as the doctors had done, that it was proposed to take away from them the right to participate in the management of the Infirmary, but that there were obviously occasions when small committees were needed to investigate matters such as possible abuses. He quoted some figures which he claimed showed that the expense of running the Infirmary had steadily increased in recent years, whereas the number of in-patients had declined a little. This needed investigating. He also had found an entry in the ledger which showed that a pupil had been admitted on the payment of a £99 premium. But the rules of the Infirmary were that £200 should be paid; again this should be investigated. He did not mean to cast aspersions about anyone present, but, human nature being what it was, things did sometimes go wrong, and practical ways must exit to investigate them.

Sir John then rose to speak:

> ... the present rules make every governor an ex-officio member of every committee. Now I was not aware, until the committee appointed in December last, of the existence of that rule, and I must say, without using any harsher term, that a rule more opposed to public business, more indefensible, or more absurd in itself, ever rested on the books of any institution. My surprise at hearing it was so great, that it could only be exceeded by the fact that gentlemen could get up in this room and oppose its alteration.

He thought the case made out by the medical gentlemen was weak, and it was ridiculous to suppose that the change would substitute 'secret' for open committees.

> Perhaps no-one is more conversant with the working of Parliamentary Select Committees than I am, having been connected with them in different investigations for the last five months, and I do not think the public are aware how large a proportion of parliamentary business devolves on Select Committees. But are they 'secret' committees? Nothing was so much at variance with their constitution or intention. They dare not transact their business secretly. They act under great responsibility. I care not whether they are committees of the House of Commons or this Institution. Their reports have to be made public, and the evidence they report upon must be made public also, and it is only by Select Committees that any business can be carried on in a proper way. It is ridiculous to suppose that 658 members of the House of Commons could be at liberty to attend on any Committee. If I had been convinced by the medical gentlemen's memorandum and were to return to Westminster and tell my fellow members that Select Committees are 'secret' and should now be open to all MPs, I can imagine my worthy friend Dr Hastings, after reading the report in the morning paper, saying 'Good God, have you seen this speech of Pakington's, we have made a convert of him with a vengeance; here he is telling the 658 members of the House of Commons they all ought to attend on Select Committees. Surely he is not fit to be member for Droitwich, but should be locked up in my asylum there'. Dr Hastings is manager of a good asylum there, you know. (Laughter.) How is the business of the county or the gaol to be managed, and who would be so absurd to move at a quarter sessions that the whole magistracy of the county should attend?

Of course, Sir John said, the medical men should be represented on committees, and he would propose that on every committee there should be one surgeon and one physician from the Infirmary, chosen by themselves.

The eminent Dr Charles Hastings then rose, and said that at present the body of governors appointed twelve of their number to meet weekly to manage the institution's affairs, but every governor had a right to attend these meetings, which was a 'great fundamental principle of the institution'. If Mr Curtler's propositions were adopted, these weekly meetings would turn into 'secret' committees, and medical men would be turned away – "go about your business, you have no right here…". What medical men, Hastings asked, would have his character whispered away in a 'secret committee'? He concluded by asking why, as the present system was working so well, Mr Curtler wanted to change it. He would challenge anyone to find an institution better managed – "the medical management of the Worcester Infirmary is as good as any in the Kingdom".

The meeting continued in the same somewhat bad-tempered vein for nearly four hours, and it can be gathered that the medical men present did not get on very well with the formidable Thomas Curtler, and they resented any idea of weakening their involvement in the management of the Infirmary. When at last the chairman was able to end the discussion and call for a show of hands, Curtler's proposals were rejected by a large majority, the doctors having obviously made a greater impression on the meeting than Sir John's and Curtler's strong language.

Despite not getting back to Westwood till 4.30 p.m., Sir John and Johnny, who had come up with him, were able to get back to London that evening, Friday 26th June. In fact Pakington might have stayed in Worcester for another few days, as on Monday the midsummer quarter sessions were held, which he missed, and he evidently preferred the various other engagements he had, including a visit on Saturday to the Home Office and College of Heralds in connection with the baronetcy. On Saturday afternoon he travelled with Augusta and the two youngest Murray boys, Herbert and Freddy, to Dover. On Monday he returned to London, and heard Peel announce his resignation in the Commons, and the following day 'gazetted as a baronet this day & the old title of my maternal ancestors thus satisfactorily revived'. On Tuesday and Wednesday he attended meetings of the Andover committee, then returned to Dover.

The newly created baronet spent his first day back in Dover sitting on the beach with Lady Pakington and going to the end of the pier. The next day he chartered a yacht and took Augusta for her first sail, which they enjoyed very much. But he was unable to distance himself from Westminster, returning again on Monday for more select committee meetings, including an examination of Poor Law Commissioner George Nicholls. He still found time for another evening with the Ethiopian Serenaders and a call on Mrs Milner. He returned again to Dover on Wednesday and had another sail, and the Bishop and his daughter Eleanor came down to join them on Saturday. On Monday he returned yet again to attend the Andover committee, and returned to Dover the next day, allowing them to go on an excursion to Sandgate, Deal and Walmer Castle. He was back in the Commons

*Sir Charles Hastings, 1787-1866. The son of a Shropshire clergyman and trained in Edinburgh, he was a surgeon at the Worcester Infirmary. In 1832 he founded the Provincial and Medical Surgical Association, which later became the BMA. He was also worked hard for improved housing and sanitation in Worcester.*

on Thursday when he spoke on the Poor Removal Bill, and attended an Andover committee meeting on Friday. On the former, he showed his more humanitarian side. He spoke about the hardship and suffering caused by the removal of paupers from their place of residence to their parish of settlement, particularly in the case of widows where it was quite wrong to remove them from places where they were well known and cared for, to somewhere where they had no friends or support.

He was able to spend a final weekend at Dover, visiting the Castle, before going for a few days to the Camden property at Wilderness, and returning to London for yet more meetings of the Andover committee. He paid a lightning visit to Westwood over the next weekend, and after conducting some local business on Monday morning returned in the afternoon in time to meet the Bishop and Lady Sarah and attend a grand concert party given by the Duke of Wellington in Apsley House attended by the Duchess of Gloucester, the Duke and Duchess of Cambridge and other royal personages. The Bishop and Lady Sarah then went to Danbury, leaving their youngest daughter Eleanor with Sir John and Lady Augusta. There were meetings of the Andover committee, and on Thursday he took Augusta to see Paul Delaroche's celebrated portrait of Napoleon at Colnaghi's in Pall Mall. This must have appealed to the English as it showed the emperor at Versailles in 1814 having suffered his first defeat at the hands of the allies. Although not painted from life, The Times reported that 'the likeness appears perfect', and depicts him in 'utter physical and moral depression… the victorious hero of a hundred battles is reduced to the feebleness of a child'. In the evening Sir John took Augusta and Eleanor to hear the Ethiopians Serenaders – this was the third time he had seen them this year.

On Saturday 1st August they all went down to Southampton where they were met by Hallifax, who took them on a 'beautiful sail' to Cowes. There they met Hallifax's father, and took possession of a cottage. They were able to sail to and attend the Southampton regatta for two days before Sir John had to return to London again for meetings of the Andover committee. The following week he at last had the whole week to enjoy some sailing with Hallifax and Lord Ilchester, missing some Andover meet-

*'Napoleon at Versailles', by Paul Delaroche, currently exhibited at Osborne House. From The Royal Collection © H. M. Queen Elizabeth II.*

ings, but he still felt he had to return the following Tuesday 18th August to attend the last two meetings of the committee. In his diary he recorded '87 committee attendances this session!'. On Thursday evening he was able to enjoy another long weekend sailing before returning to London on Tuesday. A London butler was needed, and he engaged a Mr Davies at £50 per annum. They spent the weekend at Danbury, and after returning to town on Tuesday finally left London for the season, taking their barouche and horses with them to Birmingham. Augusta was unwell, having been 'abominably shaken' till they got to Wolverton where they were able to change carriages.

From Birmingham they posted to Hewell, where there was to be a meeting of the Worcestershire Archery Society, which seems to have been a very popular occupation of county society at that time. Owing to the alterations at Westwood they temporarily moved to West Ford House just north of Droitwich. On 7th September Johnny, who had been journeying on the continent, returned – 'I had the blessing of seeing him safe & well after his travels'.

The following week was yeomanry week, and on Thursday 10th September the Westwood troop marched to Worcester led by Sir John and Johnny, who had joined for the first time as a cornet. Berrows gives a good description of the week's action, which was attended by fine weather. The initial assembly was at Pitchcroft, and after a short drill they were addressed by the Colonel, the Hon. Robert Henry Clive, on matters of discipline. The involvement of Clive, the younger son of Edward Clive, 1st Earl Powis, and grandson of Clive of India, with the Worcestershire Yeomanry Cavalry came through his wife Harriet, who was daughter of Other Hickman Windsor, 5th Earl of Plymouth of Hewell Grange, and whose brother Other Archer Windsor, the 6th Earl, had been Colonel till his early death in 1833 (see page 203).

On Friday the Yeomanry assembled again at Pitchcroft for exercises, and the following day they marched down to Kempsey, where there was a large open space next to the Severn called Kempsey Ham. There they exercised again before marching back to the City preceded by an 'admirable band' in the afternoon. That evening a body of carabineers practised shooting at a special target set up at Pitchcroft. On Sunday the troop attended divine service in the cathedral – one imagines this was an occasion for dressing up. On Monday there was

*West Ford House as it is today. It is the home of the Droitwich Golf Club, situated on Ford Lane just north of the town.*

again drill at Kempsey, and in the evening there was a shooting competition for the carabineers. On Tuesday there was drill on Pitchcroft and a competition for the best horse in each troop. Berrows records that after the awards Lord Ward (the Lt Col), Sir John Pakington, Major Martin and other officers rode up to the winner from the Worcester troop, Sgt Major Wagstaff, 'and expressed themselves in high terms of this very superior animal... the best in the regiment. We hear that Lord Ward expressed a wish to purchase it...'. Unfortunately it was later found that this horse was not properly harnessed. It did not have a crupper, and was therefore disqualified, prompting a letter in Berrows from a disgruntled Sgt Major Wagstaff.

On Wednesday morning was the final review at Kempsey before Col Hankey of the Dragoon Guards, when the eleven troops assembled, each under its own captain. Berrows lists a total of twenty two manoeuvres they then went through, watched by an 'immense' crowd of spectators, leaving hardly a conveyance in the City. The steamer Sabrina helped by making regular trips as well. At the conclusion of the manoeuvres, the regiment formed close columns of squadrons, the officers at the head, and Col Hankey then addressed them. He congratulated Col Clive upon the general appearance of the regiment, saying what a source of pride it must be to him to have under his command such a fine body of men. "I have been present at many reviews of yeomanry cavalry," he concluded, "but I have never witnessed a better field day in my life; the precision, steadiness, and soldier-like manner in which the day's duty has been gone through has my highest praise, and reflects great credit on both officers and men."

The following morning before the regiment disbanded, Col Clive made some concluding remarks. After congratulating the men on the way discipline had been maintained during the week, both on the field and in their quarters, he introduced a critical note when he said he was disappointed by

*The Derbyshire Yeomanry Cavalry. Although uniforms varied from county to county, this scene, with mounted volunteers watched by their captain, must have been similar to that witnessed in Worcester during yeomanry cavalry week.*

the poor turn-out at some of the local drills during the summer, and even during the week just past some men had only turned out for the last day or two 'to the great injury to the rest of the regiment'.

The social side of the week was important, and Sir John notes that Augusta attended officers' tea parties every evening at which she sang. On Sunday there was a meeting of the officers to arrange for a portrait of Col Clive to be obtained by private subscription. Later they decided it should be painted by the well known British portraitist Henry Pickersgill. Some of the officers entertained their troops to dinner during the week, although it was not recorded that Pakington did so this year. On the final night a grand dinner was held to entertain Col Hankey, attended by over one hundred. It was Johnny's first experience of yeomanry week – he 'performed well, and liked the week very much'.

With most members of the county gentry in their homes, the rest of September saw great socialising, and one of the highlights was a grand archery fête and ball held by Lord Ward at Witley Court. Purchased by Lord Ward's trustees from the Foleys some years before, Witley Court had been occupied by the dowager Queen Adelaide until earlier that year, but now Lord Ward, still a bachelor, had taken possession, having just returned from a long continental tour. The Pakingtons were there

*'Grand Meeting of the Devon & Cornwall Archery Societies', 1832, reproduced by courtesy of Devon Libraries. This gives a good idea of the scene at the meetings of the Worcestershire Society at various country houses.*

with Johnny, together with most of county society. The park was thrown open to all-comers for the occasion, and the spectators watched the archery, which lasted all afternoon. It took place, Berrows poetically reported, in a spot 'beautifully adapted for the purpose, consisting of gentle undulations of smooth turf, with groups of trees scattered here and there… the herds of deer with which this park is stocked, occasionally disclosed themselves from the neighbouring coverts, and taking a distant glance at the Robin Hoods and Maid Marions scampered away again to conceal their dappled sides in the surrounding thickets'. The yeomanry band played in the park all afternoon to provide additional entertainment.

Dinner in the large picture gallery 'was a truly sumptuous banquet – the array of gold and silver plate was magnificent in the extreme'. After more archery the prizes were awarded. One of the attractions of archery was that both ladies and gentlemen could take part, and the first lady's prize was won by Miss Clive, probably Henrietta Sarah, the eldest child of Col Clive, and the second by Miss Pepys, probably Emily, elder daughter of the Bishop of Worcester. Capt. Clowes won the gentleman's prize, with John Howard Galton of Hadzor Hall second. After the prize-giving, tea was served, then at 9.00 the ball started in the library with music by Weippert's Quadrille Band, 'and was kept up with ardour till an early hour'. Berrows summed up the event:

*Witley Court from the south in the early nineteenth century, courtesy of the Worcestershire Record Office. The house was started in 1655 by ironmaster Thomas Foley, grandfather of Thomas, 1st Lord Foley of Kidderminster, and was progressively enlarged by later owners. This illustration shows the portico added by John Nash c. 1800. In the 1850s the architect Samuel Daukes remodelled the house for the new owner Lord Ward on grand Italianate lines.*

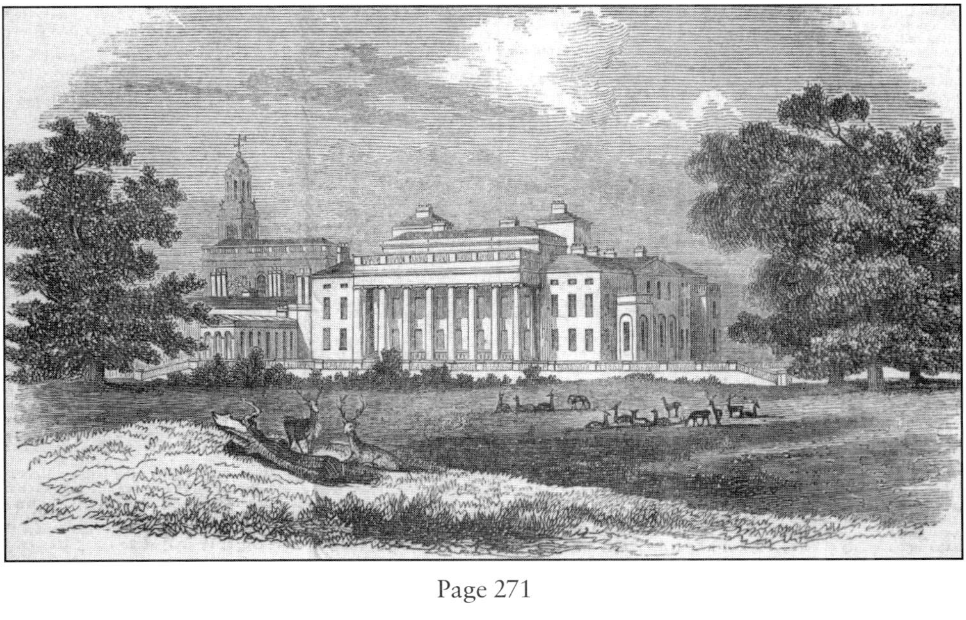

'the whole arrangements were commensurate with his Lordship's wealth, station and liberality, and were carried out in a style of princely magnificence. The whole proved to be one of the most brilliant fêtes which our county has ever witnessed'.

The following week another big event was held, this time given by the Very Rev. John Peel, the new Dean of Worcester, at Waresley, to mark the coming of age of his son, Robert Augustus Peel. Robert had been a contemporary of Johnny's at Christ Church, Oxford, but although Johnny had ridden over to Waresley earlier in the day to meet his Christ Church friends, the Pakingtons were not invited to the ball, Sir John noted ruefully in his diary. Robert Augustus had a younger brother Herbert Richard who would also go up to Christ Church, but whose life ended sadly when he committed suicide in 1885 after suffering badly from gout.

During October Sir John was busy with local affairs attending many meetings, including one of the Worcester Agricultural Society, when at the dinner he proposed one of the toasts. The final toast that evening was to John Slaney Pakington, to which Johnny briefly replied that that was his first attendance at a meeting of that sort, but would certainly not be his last. This was also the shooting season, and although Sir John records going out on a number of occasions, there were few of the big society shoots of the past, his usual companion being Johnny. On 9th October Sir John, Johnny and Galton attended the Staffordshire yeomanry review at Lichfield, where they all donned their uniforms again. A few days later they split up, Johnny going to Danbury before going up to Oxford, and Sir John and Lady Augusta went to Weston Park for a few day's stay with Lord Bradford, a visit somewhat spoiled by rain.

Quarter sessions began on 18th October, and Lady Augusta went to Walton to see her sister Caroline. Sessions lasted three days, after which Sir John rode to Malvern where Mrs Milner was now living, and on Friday he travelled to Coldbrook to spend the weekend with his sister's family. Both Sir John and Lady Augusta returned to Westwood on Monday, and on Wednesday Philip Hardwick junior came to see about the roof and gables there. At the end of October they enjoyed a weekend at the Foley Arms in Malvern, where he noted an early morning walk up the hill and seeing Mrs Milner in the evenings. The day after they came back home on Monday 2nd November, he went by rail to Rugby to see Capel Hanbury Williams – this would have been his nephew Ferdinand Capel, then aged 13 and at Rugby School. The next day they took the train again, this time to Oxford where they met Johnny and Lady Augusta's brother Robert. On previous occasions Sir John had dined in college hall when in Oxford, probably using his status as a prominent politician as an entry, but today was Gaudy Day which precluded it.

The next day they all went on to London, where his father entered Johnny as a pupil at the Inner Temple. Unlike his father, Johnny was to get his BA and MA degrees from Oxford, but it was probably never intended that he should take his legal studies very far. It was quite usual for young men to be educated at either one of the Inns of Court or at Oxbridge, or both. The main point of the legal studies was that anyone with a landed estate or other family wealth would need a working knowledge of real estate law, trusts and settlements, and other legal matters. Sir John was conscious of his own deficiencies in not having taken his education as far as he might, and wanted to be sure his son did not make the same mistake. Johnny returned to Oxford that evening, and his father and step-mother went to one of M. Julian's promenade concerts, at which it was advertised that four military bands had been engaged in addition to M. Julian's own concert orchestra.

As far as is known, since first being elected an MP in 1837 Sir John had not had his own establishment in London. Initially he stayed with his aunt in Green Street, and after his marriage to Augusta, in her father's house in Belgrave Square. Development of Belgravia, part of the Grosvenor estate, was proceeding apace at this time, and the Bishop had moved into a new house in Eaton Place earlier in the year, and now Sir John and his wife had determined to take a lease on one of the new houses in nearby Eaton Square. Early in November they went to see their new house with the Bishop and his wife, and chose some wallpapers for it, then on Saturday afternoon they returned to Westwood by train, but not before calling on 'poor Barneby'. Sir John's old friend was terminally ill, dying at the end of the month from what may have been some form of cancer of the spine.

Back home, on Monday he signed the conveyance of land for the Droitwich to Kidderminster part of the Oxford, Worcester and Wolverhampton railway, for which he received a very welcome £12,742. At an OWW meeting in 1849 a committee highlighted the high price that had been paid for some of the land, and as well as the Duke of Marlborough and Lord Ward, the '£10,000 paid to Sir John Pakington for injury done to his house' was mentioned. As the nearest approach of the railway is over one mile from Westwood House and leaves the Park untouched, it is difficult to see what this injury was, and possibly the committee's report was inaccurate. Evidently the amount paid to Sir John had seemed very high and he had driven a hard bargain, perhaps helped by his influential position as an MP. On the same day Sir John attended a Lunatic Asylum committee meeting – this project will be described in the next chapter. There followed a stay at Hartlebury Castle where they were entertained by Bishop Pepys and his wife – while there, they all went off to view the progress of Lincombe weir on the Severn.

The following week they went visiting again, first to Winterdyne, the house overlooking the Severn just south of Bewdley lived in by carpet manufacturer Thomas Pardoe. Earlier in the century it had been the home of John Phillips and his wife Emma, the Vernon heiress, who were unable to occupy Hanbury Hall while her first husband, the 1st Marquis of Exeter, was alive. After their night at Winterdyne Sir John left early to attend a meeting of the Droitwich Guardians, and later returned to Winterdyne and to take his wife home. The following day they went to stay with the Dean of St Asaph in Cradley near Malvern, but Augusta developed what her husband called a nettle rash in the evening, which confined her to her room all next day. Nevertheless, he went to Malvern to lunch with Mrs Milner. But, concerned for his wife, he managed to fit in a visit to Dr James Gully, well known for his water-cures at Malvern, and the next day they called on him again by appointment.

On 28th November they left Westford House and returned at last 'to our great joy' to Westwood. Augusta's nettle rash cleared up and the next week, despite very frosty weather, Sir John was able to enjoy shooting including a day at Ombersley with Lord Sandys. The following Tuesday he attended the funeral of John Barneby – 'felt much on making so melancholy a visit to Brockhampton', he wrote. Barneby's death created a vacancy in the representation for East Worcestershire, and both Capt. George Rushout and John Hodgetts Hodgetts-Foley offered themselves as candidates for the Tories and Whigs respectively. But on 11th December the East Worcestershire Conservative Association met under the chairmanship of Sir John to discuss the situation. The meeting was initially covered in great secrecy, but eventually it emerged that it was felt that a contested election should be avoided at that point, as in any case a general election would have to be held soon, and it was therefore agreed that a deputation should see Hodgetts-Foley and, if he agreed to withdraw his candidacy now, to offer no opposition to him at the next election if he put his name forward again in place of the retiring Tory member, James Arthur Taylor, thus splitting the representation of the county. Hodgetts-Foley agreed to this and withdrew. This stratagem would reduce the Tory representation in the county and was opposed by many, including Berrows. This controversy continued into the New Year, and will be discussed in chapter 14.

*Dr James Manby Gully, from a caricature in Vanity Fair. His 'hydrotherapy' or water cure became very popular at Malvern, and was a very spartan regime, with much bathing in different kinds of baths, long walks, simple food and no alcohol. Unlike most Spas, Malvern water was distinguished by its purity. Among his famous patients were Charles Darwin and Alfred, Lord Tennyson. Late in life, his affair with a married woman led him to be a suspect in the Charles Bravo poisoning case.*

The frosty weather continued, and Sir John, who seems to have regularly monitored the temperature, records it as 10°F at 7.00 a.m., and still only 14°F at 11.00 on 14th. But this did not prevent him going to London the following day, firstly to check on progress at Eaton Square, and then to see Hardwick junior about Westwood. Back on 17th, he was very annoyed to find that someone had been tampering with the weir that held back the Great Pool at Westwood 'without orders', and consequently it was damaged and losing water.

The following day he had to attend another funeral, that of Col Henry Davies of Elmley Park. We have seen that Pakington had been a frequent visitor at Elmley, and knew the family well. The Colonel had fought with Wellington in the Peninsular War and at Waterloo, after which he had retired on half pay and turned his attention to politics. From 1818 he had represented the City of Worcester in the Whig interest at Westminster, and he seems to have been a genuine reformer, as Berrows commentated that he had been known as 'a Whig, and something more…'. He had declared himself in favour of the secret ballot and of church reform in Ireland – in a speech in 1834 he had said:

> For what greater absurdity could there be than where there are whole districts comprising 13 or 14,000 souls with scarcely a Protestant in them, with a rich endowment attached, and the clerical personage who has had the good fortune to obtain the living spending the money he derives therefrom on the Continent or some other watering place in this country. I would abolish all livings in which there were not a sufficient number of Protestants to form a congregation.

He seems to have been well respected and honest, and his political views apparently did not compromise his relationship with Sir John.

The frost continued through Christmas but it did not stop Sir John and his son shooting, including a large party on Christmas Eve, and on Boxing day they travelled to Malvern to lunch with Mrs Milner, and to call on Dr Gully. The frost had caused the Great Pool to freeze over, and Johnny gave his father a pair of skaits (as he calls them) and some lessons – '1st attempt since boyhood', his father noted.

On the final day of the year a meeting of the Severn Commissioners was chaired by Sir John, and in his diary he noted simply that the meeting was to declare the navigation open. But in fact there were several critical voices raised at the meeting. Sir John made an initial speech in which he hoped that the accomplishment of that great work, the improvement of the navigation of the river, would prove eminently beneficial to the commerce of the Vale of Severn. He admitted that other forms of transport [railways] had come into operation since the works were first thought of, but he still had no doubt but that the great work would be found highly useful. Under the Act, once the chief engineer for the project had reported the works complete, the navigation had to be declared open and the collection of tolls at the various locks had to start.

But after the optimistic start several speakers cast doubt whether vessels drawing six feet would be able to transverse the whole length from Stourport to Gloucester throughout the year. Several people pointed out that William Cubitt, the chief engineer, who was not present, had relied on reports from other engineers to complete his report, as he had not visited the works himself since September. Others asked whether the width of the dredging was sufficient for two boats to pass each other, and those from Tewkesbury pointed out that navigation on the Avon had been adversely affected by the works. Some would have preferred to adjourn the meeting (at which it was suggested that their motives were mainly to delay imposition of the tolls!), but Sir John said that, under the Act, they had no alternative now but to open the works and impose tolls.

The doubts expressed at the meeting about the navigation below Diglis were to be proved well founded.

Sir John concluded the year 1846 by giving dinner to his tenants.

# Chapter 13
# The Powick Lunatic Asylum

At the Epiphany quarter sessions in 1846, Sir John had reported the favourable position of the county's finances, but pointed out that it faced considerable expenditure on a new county lunatic asylum, required under the Lunatic Asylums and Pauper Lunatic Act of 1845, although he himself thought that the insistence by the legislature that counties make provision for these unfortunates in this way was not before time. As Sir John was very much involved with the establishment of Worcestershire's new asylum between 1846 and 1851 we will devote this chapter to describing its establishment.

Up to this time there was no formal provision for caring for pauper lunatics. Those from better-off families could be put into a private asylum, of which there was one in Droitwich run by William Ricketts, but those without means would probably end up in a workhouse. Some boards of guardians, including (as we have seen) those in Droitwich contracted with private asylums to look after lunatics in their area. But not all could be accommodated there, and the terrible condition of those for whom no proper care could be taken was highlighted by Lord Ashley, who investigated the provision for lunatics in London, and proposed better care. The 1845 act provided that counties must either build their own asylum to house pauper lunatics, or join with neighbouring counties in so doing. At the Michaelmas quarter sessions in 1846 an asylum committee was appointed under Sir John's chairmanship with eleven other members (the Victorians seem to have loved large committees). At their first meeting they agreed to send a circular to all Worcestershire unions to enquire how many pauper lunatics there were in their districts, but at the next meeting in December it was reported that the response had not been very satisfactory. It was also considered whether it would be sensible to join any of the adjoining counties. But Staffordshire, Gloucestershire and Shropshire had already made their own arrangements, leaving Warwickshire and Herefordshire. The former county was said to have too many lunatics (over 400 – the large population of Birmingham was then included), leaving just Herefordshire. Some members cast doubt on the wisdom and savings to be achieved by combining with another county, and as Herefordshire had failed to respond, this idea was dropped.

It was first proposed that the asylum should be built to hold 175 lunatics, but Osman Ricardo suggested building a larger one to hold 200, which would be big enough to include the City of Worcester, which was agreed. Sir John resisted a suggestion to increase capacity to 230. It was thought that one third of lunatics could remain in workhouses as 'certainly harmless', thus reducing the need for special accommodation.

The purpose of the new asylum was not only to 'alleviate the sufferings of unfortunate individuals who may require our protection and care; but also the means of effecting their cure in a very large proportion and thereby restoring them to their families and friends'. As it was to be a joint asylum with the City of Worcester, the committee had to look for a site within five miles of Shire Hall, accessible by good roads, in an open and airy situation on gravel and rocky subsoil and with a good water supply. The new Commissioners for Lunacy insisted that the buildings be made fireproof and that there must be one acre of grounds for every ten patients with uninterrupted country views, and that galleries and wards should be arranged so that the medical officer might pass through all of them without retracing his steps.

Early in 1847 advertisements were placed for a suitable estate of between twenty five and forty acres, and after a number of replies had been received it was eventually agreed to buy from a Mr Stallard an estate at Powick called 'White Chimneys', for which the committee offered £2,800, which he accepted. However, the Coventry trustees refused to sell a small area adjacent that the committee wished to add to it, so Sir John opportunistically stepped in and offered a small area of his own land near Powick Court, for which he was paid £541. This made the total area just under 30 acres. It was also agreed at this time that the joint county/city committee would consist of eleven county magistrates and four from the city, and that the costs of the project would be split so that the county paid eight ninths, and the city the rest.

Sir John was therefore able to report good progress at the midsummer sessions in 1847, and soon afterwards it was agreed to advertise for architects to submit plans. To encourage this they offered prizes of £50, £30 and £20 for the three best submissions. The brief was for a simple brick-built asylum that would hold 200 patients, with accommodation for the superintendent and other officers, and plans were to be submitted by 1st October 1847. After a series of meetings under Sir John to consider the plans, the committee agreed on 8th November to award the first prize to Hamilton & Medland of Gloucester, with Frederick John Francis second and Samuel Stinton Markham third. There were twenty seven other submissions. Hamilton & Medland was a practice founded by architect Samuel Daukes, who took into partnership John Hamilton and later, when Daukes opened a London office, James Medland.

Sir John was therefore able to report this progress at the Epiphany sessions in 1848, but as there was clearly a great deal of work to be done getting the project under way, he wrote to the February meeting of the committee of visitors (as they were now called) to say he no longer wished to be chairman due to his parliamentary engagements. His place was taken by his colleague Thomas Curtler, and at this meeting Hamilton & Medland's plans were formally accepted. It was agreed to pay them a fee of five percent on the building costs up to £20,000. During the rest of 1848 progress was halted by the Lunacy Commissioners' slowness in approving the plans. As it became clearer what the new asylums should be like the plans had to be altered, and the building's fire-resistance was queried. The plans were not finalised until the middle of 1849. Another problem had arisen: the committee had to find their own means of finance, and a request for a government loan had been turned down. So advertisements were placed for loans, causing further delay, but in September a loan of £30,000 from the London Life Assurance Company to be repaid over thirty years at four and a half percent interest was accepted. The asylum would receive income from the county unions for the lunatics placed there, which would enable them to pay the running expenses of the asylum and repay the loan.

The committee was now able to go out to tender, and on October 3rd 1849 these were opened. That of Thos Haines of Cheltenham at £23,500 was selected, and £3,000 worth of extras would be needed as well. Haines reported that there was good brick earth on site. The project could now advance at a more rapid pace, and at the 1850 sessions it was reported that the building 'was going on with great despatch'.

*An aerial view of Powick Asylum at his peak c. 1950s. The original buildings and detached chapel can still be seen at the front left, with considerable additions and staff accomodation at the rear. The asylum farm is at the lower right. Photo courtesy of the George Marshall Medical Museum.*

One of the architect partners, John Hamilton, had by now left to work in the USA, leaving Medland in sole charge, and the following year he suggested that the chapel, part of the main building, would make an excellent recreation room, and suggested building a separate chapel at a cost of £600. The committee agreed to add these and other extras, but the final bill, which much exceeded the original tender, forced them to raise another £10,000 on mortgage.

Although no longer chairman, Sir John attended several meetings of the committee in late 1851 and early 1852, when various matters had to be considered before the inmates could be admitted. The death of the contractor, Haines, did not help. The important appointment of the medical superintendent had to be made, and, after advertising, Dr John Grahamsley, almost inevitably a Scot from Edinburgh, was appointed at the quite generous salary of £350 per annum. He would start on 1st March 1852, and the first inmates would be admitted soon after. Grahamsley was keen to provide the inmates with work, so workshops would be built. He also proposed that an asylum farm of around 50 acres should be added with the requisite buildings, as he had found such work very beneficial.

Initially there were 175 inmates, mostly transferred from Ricketts' private asylum in Droitwich, and about half of those were fit to be employed, the males in cleaning the wards and on outside work, and the women on needle work, washing and ironing. Within twelve months the numbers had risen to 192, close to the asylum's maximum capacity. By October 1853 the report to the Michaelmas quarter sessions showed that numbers now exceeded 200, and that an extension would have to be considered. All who spoke at the session said the inmates appeared to be much better provided for than previously. There was some grumbling at the escalating cost – the land had cost £6,000 (including the farm), and the total expenditure on the asylum and its fitting out had been £54,000 to date, thus requiring even more mortgages.

Dr Grahamsley seems to have been well regarded – Berrows wrote 'we cannot speak in too high terms of the mode of treatment which Dr Grahamsley adopts in endeavouring to reinstate on a firm basis the wandering intellects of those unfortunate persons placed under his care'. But in the following year, 1854, tragedy struck when, on Sunday August 6th, he was found dead in the building where gas was made, having taken his own life by drinking prussic acid. At the inquest several references were made to differences between the matron, Mrs Piaget, to whom he was related by marriage, and himself, which had caused him to complain about her to the visiting committee. Soon afterwards she was dismissed for insubordination.

From this point Sir John ceased to be involved, either by way of the visiting committee or through quarter sessions, so we will just note that the asylum gradually expanded so that by 1871 there were over 600 patients, and in the 1930s over 1,000. However in the 1980s attitudes to these institutions changed and it was closed in 1989, and was replaced by new housing.

# Chapter 14
# The Year 1847

The year 1847 began, as 1846 had ended, with a rather heated meeting in which Sir John played a prominent part, but this one concerned the Worcester Infirmary, and which followed the controversy the previous June. At the heart of the dispute was the pride of the medical men employed at the Infirmary, and at the previous meeting they had persuaded the Infirmary guardians present to vote against Thomas Curtler's proposal to allow committees to be set up with limited membership.

Credit should go to Thomas Curtler for not giving up on the matter. He had found various financial irregularities in the accounts of the Infirmary, and felt these could not be properly investigated under the present rules, which, he claimed, allowed the medical men to swamp any committee if they so chose. This meeting, in the Shire Hall on January 1st, had been carefully prepared, and a compromise had been worked out that he hoped the meeting would adhere to. To give this weight the Bishop of Worcester had agreed to take the chair, and the Mayor of Worcester had also been involved in trying to get agreement. So when the meeting started Thomas Curtler rose to outline his proposal, which was that a new committee should be formed, consisting of nine guardians and two medical men, to deliberate on how the rules should be changed, and whose recommendations should be binding.

Dr Matthew Pierpoint, representing the medical men, replied saying that they agreed to the proposition in principle, but with one proviso: that they felt that Curtler had no power under the existing rules to propose a closed committee, and that it should therefore be an open one. This, of course, amounted to a repudiation of Curtler's proposal. Another medical man, Dr Jonas Malden, evidently one of the more loquacious people present, made an impassioned plea, or 'descant' as Berrows called it, on behalf of the founders of the institution, about the glorious principles on which it had been governed, and the superiority of the medical men to all sublunary considerations.... At this point the Rt Rev. Chairman called him to order, and asked for a simple answer to the proposition. Initial intransigence gave way to a desire for compromise, and Dr Pierpoint, the doctors' spokesman, went into a huddle with the mayor and Messrs Curtler and Pakington. They eventually proposed that it might be acceptable if the meeting were to agree that, in principle, all the medical men had the right to attend the committee, but that they would give their word that only two would ever actually attend. There was much further discussion, but it seems that this rather contrived compromise satisfied most people, and it was agreed. Sir John was pleased – he wrote that 'doctors were obliged reluctantly to give way & Curtler's proposal was virtually carried'.

The controversy following the Worcestershire Conservative association meeting on 11th December continued, at which it had been decided to invite the potential Whig candidate for the by-election caused by John Barneby's death to withdraw if he could replace the retiring Tory MP, James Arthur Taylor, at the forthcoming general election unopposed. This would mean that East Worcestershire would then have one Tory (Capt. Rushout) and one Whig member (John Hodgetts-Foley). The Tory-supporting Berrows had already complained that this would deprive the division of the chance of having two Tory MPs, as it had had till the death of Barneby. On 26th December the Worcestershire Herald published letters from James Taylor, the father of the sitting Tory MP, and Horace St Paul, who had served as Tory MP for the division from 1837 till 1841, both of which expressed opposition to the 'Droitwich Agreement'. St Paul wrote that he had attended the meeting on 11th December, but it had been poorly attended, and he was one of only four who voted against the proposition.

The following week, 1st January 1847, a letter from James Arthur Taylor himself was published, stating that although it was true that he had privately said that he might not be able to stand at the next general election for 'private reasons', he had never made any formal announcement on the matter, and he regarded himself as free to make a final decision up until when the election was called. (If, of course, he decided to stand, the promise made to John Hodgetts-Foley not to oppose him would be broken.) In the same edition, Sir John also had a long letter published seeking to justify himself, saying that Taylor 'must have forgotten the repeated and decided intimations which he has given of his determination not again to come forward'. He also said that the Worcestershire Protection Society (see page 215) had pressed Taylor to make a decision, 'and after some negotiation, his ultimate desire to retire from parliament ... was final and conclusive, not conditional'. Sir John then paid tribute (perhaps faint praise might be more apposite) to Taylor, and claimed 'that in the present state of politics, such an arrangement is, in this division, the fairest and most prudent for both parties'. It may be noted that there is no record of Taylor ever having spoken during his time in parliament from 1841 when he was first elected.

The controversy continued for another two weeks, as on 8th January Taylor published another denial, saying the private reasons that may have led to him having to retire 'were capable of change'. Sir John clearly found this something of a slur on his honour, and the following day a hurriedly called meeting of the committee of the Protection Society was held, and passed the following resolution:

> That on being applied to by them, Mr Taylor expressed his willingness to become a candidate [at the next election] providing certain existing objections beyond his control should be removed, but not otherwise. That subsequently it was found, upon reference to another quarter, that those objections would not be removed, and therefore that Mr Taylor would not again consent to be put in nomination as a candidate for East Worcestershire…

This resolution was published in another letter from Sir John, and below this was yet another one from Taylor, again denying that he had ever formally said he would not stand. In former years the contending parties might have felt justified in resorting to Kempsey Ham, but on this occasion wiser counsels prevailed, and that was the end of the matter. In the event Taylor did not stand.

Quarter sessions occupied much of the next week, then on Monday 11th January came the nomination of Capt. Rushout to represent East Worcestershire in place of the late John Barneby. As we have seen, Rushout was unopposed, and a cold wind was blowing, so the nomination and election at the hustings, which were by the Worcester Road in Droitwich, was a relatively low-key event attended by less than the usual large crowd. Berrows recorded about 150 as being present, but only including about a dozen electors, so most were there just for the spectacle. Sir John opened proceedings by first paying tribute to the late member. He then nominated Rushout, who, he said, had long-standing ties to the county by reason of family and descent. He had also had previous parliamentary experience and had proved his devotion to discharging his public duties. (Rushout had represented Evesham from 1837 to 1841; his fellow MP, Peter Borthwick, had also been elected in 1837, but later unseated on petition in favour of the Whig candidate. The controversy over this led to Rushout and Borthwick, both Tories, fighting a duel at Wormwood Scrubs.) Sir John referred to the recent divisions in the Tory party, but said the present lack of inter-party rivalry would help when it came to dealing with the "alarming – I will say the frightful – state of Ireland".

James Taylor, the father of James Arthur Taylor the MP who had created the recent controversy, seconded the nomination, and drew the attention of the crowd to the support in Rushout's address of the Protestant religion 'a true palladium of English liberty, and safeguard of our happy land'. Rushout said he only wished that those principles travelled throughout the whole of her Majesty's dominions, and, he added somewhat optimistically, he hoped that the present distress and famine in Ireland would lead to the spread of those principles in that country. Both he and Sir John referred only very briefly to the recent controversy, not wishing to sully the present occasion, then, when the High Sheriff declared Rushout elected, he made his own speech. He referred to his feelings on Protestantism, and said that while he was in favour of religious tolerance, he was determined to resist the sapping and undermining by sidelong attacks on the fabric of the Protestant church. Coming to the great question of the Corn Laws, Rushout confirmed that he was a protectionist, saying: "nothing, in my opinion, can compensate a nation for a dependence upon strangers for the bread which we eat...". Peel's promise of cheaper bread, and hope that other nations would lower their tariff barriers just as we had done, had not been borne out in practice. Finally, he said he had been asked whom he would support as leader now the Tory party had split, and he said he would follow that 'nobleman, whose great capacity of mind, indomitable energy of mind, powerful eloquence and upright honesty of purpose must ever endear him to the minds of Englishmen – Lord Stanley'.

Thereafter the party partook of a cold collation at The George Hotel in Droitwich at which Sir John presided, and, although it was only a lunch rather than a dinner, the usual toasts were drunk all round.

Johnny had been spending Christmas with his parents, and his father must have been concerned about his relationship with his step-mother's sister. On 14th January he 'talked to Johnny about Eleanor, and received his astounding announcement of his engagement to her!' Sir John's concern over their relationship went back three years to 1844, when he cautioned Johnny about it, but evidently the affair had blossomed, and Johnny, still only 20 and at Oxford, believed he was to marry his father's 18 year old sister-in-law. Afterwards Sir John's diary simply records that 'we shot, and all dined at Perdiswell [Sir Offley Wakeman's] and attended Hunt Ball'. The next day Johnny returned to Oxford, and only after he had left did Sir John give his wife the news. Her reaction is not recorded.

On Monday 18th Sir John had to attend a lunatic asylum committee, then after dinner he and Augusta left for London by express train (it was now possible to leave Worcester at 5.50 p.m. for Birmingham, and be in London at 11.00 p.m.), and slept with her parents in Eaton Place. Parliament opened next day, and Sir John introduced Capt. Rushout, the new member. Sir John's new house in Eaton Square was nearing completion, and they had to spend time arranging for the furniture, but between this and attending the House, Sir John still found time to see Mrs Milner. On Friday there was a proposal by Lord John Russell, the prime minister, to appoint a committee to investigate the Poor Removal Act, which had been passed last session and already found to be needing revision. Sir John made a short contribution. He welcomed the idea of making the Poor Law Commission more accountable to parliament. He felt the report of the Andover committee, on which he had served the previous year, was unduly critical of the commissioners in some respects, as he believed they had always acted from the best of motives. As to the law of settlement he would welcome any enquiry into this, as he would support any proposal to lessen its impact, possibly even do away with it altogether. In saying this, Sir John was showing the more practical and humanitarian side of his character, using the experience he had gained in chairing the Droitwich Board of Guardians.

Their stay in London only lasted five days. After attending to local business during the following week, Sir John had tickets to attend the Worcester Ball on 28th January (tickets including tea, supper and wine, were half a guinea each), but Lady Augusta was unwell and he went alone, returning early. On 4th February they returned to London and stayed again at Eaton Place, where they were greeted by the news that Augusta's sister Mary was to marry Rev. Jermyn Pratt. Despite having the same surname as Lord Camden, Mary's elder sister Harriet's husband, no relationship has been found between them. Jermyn Pratt was the younger son of Edward Roger Pratt of Ryston Hall, Norfolk, and a descendent of the seventeenth century architect Sir Roger Pratt, who built Ryston Hall.

Two days after their arrival they had the chance to discuss Johnny and Eleanor with the Bishop, Lady Sarah and their eldest son George. 'We agreed generally,' Sir John wrote, presumably that the relationship had to be stopped, and it was left to his father to write to Johnny. Sunday intervened, then on Monday more discussions were held, in which 'I pressed in vain that Eleanor should know truth about future possibilities'. Quite what this means is not clear. Whether Sir John wanted to explain that his own financial position was less than rosy, which would ultimately impact on Johnny, or whether Sir John had already sowed the seeds of Johnny's future marriage to Diana Boyle, then only two years away, or whether there was some other unknown impediment, we can only guess. Sir John wrote to Johnny requesting his presence the following day. Johnny dutifully came, and his father had a 'distressing conversation with him in which he showed deep feeling', but that is not quite the last we hear of this affair. Two years later Johnny married Diana Boyle, and Eleanor was to marry John Tufnel in 1853 and have nine children by him, so it seems that this teenage infatuation did eventually end.

The day of the 'distressing conversation' was the day Sir John's servants came from Westwood to move into the new house in 41 Eaton Square, where they were joined two days later, 11th February 1847, by their master and mistress. There was still much to do for the new house, including hanging pictures and laying down a cellar of wines. Commons business took much of Sir John's time, with attendances at the Railways Classification Committee, and late night sittings on the Ten Hours Factory Bill and public works for Ireland, to mention just three. Sir John had also been preparing for the introduction of a Juvenile Offenders Bill into the House of Commons, and on Tuesday 23rd February he rose to ask for leave to introduce his bill.

He started by saying there were three aspects to the subject on which he was addressing the house – the lamentable state of education which characterised nearly all criminals; the way in which justice was dealt out to juvenile offenders; and lastly the way in which juvenile offenders were punished after conviction. He said the subject of national education was one on which he held strong views, but this was not the subject of the present bill; and the last was one on which the government and the home secretary, Sir George Grey, were currently working. It was the second aspect that he wished to speak about, drawing on his experience as a magistrate. At present, anyone over seven years old accused of an indictable offence had to go through the same machinery of an indictment, imprisonment awaiting the next sessions, a grand jury, and a petty jury, before sentence could be passed. This applied to any crime that was a felony, which included the theft of a sum as small as twopence (to quote one recent example from Worcestershire), and while he was appreciative of the value of the long established system of trial by jury, he felt that in these cases it was outweighed by its disadvantages. These were principally that awaiting trial the young prisoner had to be held for up to several weeks in prison, and that during this time was subject to all the evil and immoral influences to be found there. Another evil was that judges, appreciative of the fact that offenders may already have spent some time in prison awaiting trial for a petty offence, sometimes gave very short sentences or even no sentence at all, thus introducing arbitrariness into the system. His proposal was therefore that, subject to various safeguards, juvenile offenders should be dealt with by magistrates in petty sessions, thus very much speeding up the process of justice, and that appeals should be referred to quarter sessions.

To strengthen his case, Sir John quoted from reports issued by committees chaired by Sir Robert Peel in 1837, and the report of the Criminal Law Commissioners in the same year. He had even gone a few days before to see the present head of the Commission, Sir Edward Ryan, to seek his views, and they were entirely in accordance with the provisions of the bill.

*No. 41, Eaton Square, which Sir John and Lady Pakington occupied from 1847.*

A few speeches followed, including one by the home secretary, and all congratulated Sir John on introducing the subject to the House, although several expressed doubts about some of the details. Sir John had booked places in the visitors' gallery for Augusta, but she had gone down with 'flue on Sunday and was not well enough to go.

The next day, Wednesday, Sir John attended a levée, and was presented on the occasion of his baronetcy by Lord Camden, after which he travelled to Worcester for the adjourned quarter sessions, and slept in accommodation in the courts. They did not start till Friday, so he spent the next day doing business at Westwood, returning to the courts in the evening ready for the trials the next day – there were sixty trials spread over two courts. These were all dealt with by Saturday midday, after which he returned to London, finding Augusta better, but feeling poorly himself with a cold.

Two weeks later Sir John went to visit Johnny at Oxford, and there is no mention of Eleanor in his diary. After dining in hall Johnny and his father went to a performance of the Messiah. Among those who accompanied him was Boyle – this is the second time the brother of Johnny's future wife is mentioned. Back in town, Sir John notes a 'fine speech' by Lord John Russell in a debate on the new Irish Poor Law Bill. He explained how government money was enabling over 700,000 Irishmen to be employed on public works. This new measure would establish a new Poor Law for Ireland, which Russell felt was essential if poverty and starvation were to be avoided. It had been claimed that private charity alone would be sufficient; but he regretted to note that, although resident landlords were often generous, non-resident landlords often gave little or nothing to relieve their tenants. He finished by calling on all members of the Irish community, Catholics and Protestants, Whigs and Tories, resident and non-resident, to forget their differences and work together to overcome the tragedy that was engulfing the country.

Living in Eaton Square, the Pakingtons had the choice of two nearby Anglican churches – St Peter's, which was at the east end of the

*St. Peter's, Eaton Square. Built in 1827 to the designs of Henry Hakewill, it was rebuilt to his original designs after a fire later in the century. However, in 1987 it was yet again engulfed in fire, and although the exterior was largely saved, the interior was totally remade, and it was re-opened in 1991. Image courtesy of City of Westminster Archives Centre.*

square, near no. 41, and St Michael's, which was at the other end. The former, with its grand Grecian entry, had been opened in 1827, and the latter, described as more 'low church' in design, was newly finished. Sir John had previously mainly attended St Peter's, but on 14th March went to St Michael's for the first time, and was greatly pleased with the preaching of the first vicar, Rev Harrison, so he must have improved since Sir John wrote that he was 'not quite satisfied' with him the year before. Thereafter that year he mainly attended St Michael's when in London.

Moving house did not interrupt his House of Commons work. As well as the Railway Bills Classification Committee he had joined the new Scotch Sites Committee. This was set up to enquire into the difficulty the New Free Church of Scotland was having in finding sites for new churches because certain large landlords who had opposed the split of 1843 would not co-operate. He still found time to go to the Ethiopian Serenaders yet again, and see Donizetti's 'Lucia di Lammermoor' on 16th March. This apparently finished in time to allow him to attend a foreign affairs debate, which concluded at 1.15 a.m., in the House of Commons. The following day his Juvenile Offenders Bill was due to have its second reading, but, with the Easter recess coming up, the House wished to debate the Factories Bill instead. There was a division on the motion that debate on Sir John's Bill be adjourned, which was carried by a large majority, so he was disappointed. But at least the Factories Bill, limiting the hours of work of children in factories to ten hours from 1849, went through committee. The House adjourned at 6.00 p.m., and this still left time for Sir John to host a dinner party – the first in his new house. Two days later there was another 'first' to celebrate – the House of Lords chamber

*The new chamber of the House of Lords, opened in 1847, from the Illustrated London News. The throne and the woolsack are at the far end; William Dyce's fresco 'the Baptism of St Ethelbert' is above the throne.*

was the first part of the rebuilt Palace of Westminster to be completed, and Sir John took a party including Augusta and Johnny, down on a visit from Oxford, to see the 'splendid new House of Lords'. The first sitting there was to be immediately after Easter.

Sir John's interest in prisons has been noted before, and on Saturday 20th March he went with some others to see Reading gaol. This had been built a few years before based on the design of Pentonville prison, which Sir John had also seen, and used the separate system of rigid solitary confinement that he had expressed himself as being opposed to. In the evening he hosted the second dinner party of the week in Eaton Square.

The nation had been shocked by the Irish famine, and Wednesday 24th March 1847 was designated a fasting day and churches held services to pray for the Irish. The houses of parliament were closed, and Sir John wrote that it was well observed, and attended St Michael's twice.

Mrs Milner made yet another appearance at this time in Sir John's diary. She was now in London, and Sir John was trying to find her new lodgings. She had been staying in Ulster Terrace, and new lodgings they had found for her were not ready, so she was to stay with the Pakingtons in Eaton Square till they were. The following Friday was Good Friday, and on Wednesday they took their grey horses and the under-butler back to Droitwich – work was evidently still going on at Westwood, and Sir John remarks that he is 'well pleased with progress of paint' there.

While back in Worcestershire Sir John attended as many of his local committees as he could – the Lunatic Asylum committee (twice), Droitwich Board of Guardians, and, of course, quarter sessions. They needed to choose papers and carpets for Westwood, which they did in Worcester, and there were also alterations in the gardens to supervise. Their stay in Worcester lasted less than two weeks, and on Monday 12th April they returned to London, leaving home at 6.00 p.m. and getting to Eaton Square before midnight. Later in the week Augusta was presented to the Queen by her mother at a 'drawing room', mirroring Sir John's presentation at a levée in February. Then on Saturday, apparently on his own, Sir John went to the newly reopened Royal Italian Opera at Covent Garden to one of those curiously eclectic nineteenth century evenings when the first act of Semiramide was followed by the second act of La Sonnambula, the evening concluding with 'a new grand ballet' La Reine des Fees.

At this time the Scotch Sites Committee was taking much of Sir John's time, but he was never to forget the question of national education, which he had always entertained ambitions of being able to improve. In April a debate lasting three days was held on the government proposal to increase to £100,000 and widen in scope the grant given to the education committee of the Privy Council so that religious groups other than the Church of England would benefit from it. On the final day, 22nd April,

Sir John managed to speak, and referred to the letter he had received from King Edward VI's school in Birmingham in 1843. About seventy percent of the pupils there were Church of England, the rest from a wide variety of other sects and faiths, and the letter described how the school managed to accommodate all these by allowing children to opt out of some particular religious part of the curriculum, and how by making these small adjustments everyone's interests were accommodated.

The increased grant was approved by a large majority, with only a small number of mainly non-conformist members such as John Bright objecting. Dissenters would not on principle take government money to teach religion, and they therefore thought that government money was favouring the established church. The debate went into a fourth night when it was proposed to make it compulsory for schools thus aided to take steps to admit children of a multiplicity of faiths; but, while being in favour of the principle, Sir John again spoke and thought that to make it compulsory was premature. Again he was with the majority when it came to a division.

The following week Sir John's Juvenile Offenders Bill came up for its second reading. As the home secretary, Sir George Grey, had said he favoured it in principle, Sir John had high hopes. But the debate got off to a bad start when the first speaker, the radical John Roebuck, attacked various measures proposed by the bill, particularly the proposal that magistrates could hear the cases in private, and still send the young offenders to prison. He thought one of the objectives of the bill was to keep them out of prison. Then the home secretary spoke. He had obviously had something of a change of mind since he first welcomed the bill, and said that this was a complex subject covering more areas than the bill did, including how young offenders should be punished. He therefore requested Sir John to withdraw his bill. Grey said that the principle had been accepted by most speakers, but it would now be better to leave it to the government to come up with more comprehensive and carefully thought out proposals. The attorney general spoke next, and broadly re-iterated what his colleague had said. Sir John must have been disappointed, since he had invited the attorney general Sir John Jervis and his wife to dinner in March, when no doubt he tried to enlist his support.

Other speakers supported the home secretary, but Sir John made a forceful speech and declined to withdraw his bill. The government were fond of saying they had proposals of their own to bring forward, but he did not believe anything imminent was proposed, and he pointed out again that the initial reaction of the home secretary had been positive. He had carefully researched his proposals which had the support of many outside parliament. If the government wanted to propose some detailed changes he was quite ready to discuss these, but none had been proposed, so he would press his bill to a second reading. Perhaps rather surprisingly, when the division was held there was a majority of 75 to 23 in favour. 'I spoke well & carried 2nd reading by large majority', he wrote.

Over the weekend Sir John took Johnny for one of his lightning visits to Droitwich, where they went to inspect progress on the renovations at Westwood.

Tuesday 4th May saw Mary Murray's marriage to Rev. Jermyn Pratt at St George's, Hanover Square, but Sir John notes that 'Johnny was upset and returned to Oxford' – perhaps his feelings for Eleanor had not yet been extinguished. Sir John attended the service and wedding breakfast, and still had time to attend the Commons, where a preliminary meeting of the Juvenile Offenders Bill committee was held. There were two more meetings of the committee in May, through which the bill passed.

Sir John maintained a long-standing interest in singing and opera, and was naturally keen to hear Jenny Lind, already famous and then enjoying her first season in London. On Saturday 15th May she sang the role of Anima in Bellini's opera 'Sonnambula' at Her Majesty's Theatre in the presence of the Queen, and the following Tuesday Sir John went to another performance with the Hanbury Williams's. The week before Sir John noted his 'first lesson from Marras' – this would be Giacinto Marras, the Italian tenor who had settled in London the year before. Sir John also mentioned at this time two sittings for Pickersgill, the artist they had chosen for the portrait of Robert Henry Clive, but no portrait of Sir John by this artist is known to have survived.

Sir John returned to Westwood for the Whitsun weekend mainly, it seems, to have a long conversation with Curtler. Back in London he talked to the Bishop about Johnny, then again two days later Johnny came to town from Oxford, and his father talked to him and again to the Bishop and his wife about him – perhaps Johnny's time at the Inner Temple was not proving very fruitful, and his father was trying to plan something more positive. It seems that something had been proposed to the Bishop, but whatever it was must have been turned down as the next day 'Bishop called & gave me their decision about Johnny &c'. Sir John's sister Elizabeth also seems to have been having some problems, as on 28th May 'I had a disturbing communication about Elizabeth', and the following day 'I had a painful interview with Elizabeth', but again we are given no more information.

Thursday 27th May was the Queen's birthday, and as usual there were great celebrations in London. In the morning Prince Albert and the

*Giacinto Marras (1810-83) was born in Naples, and led a successful international career as an opera singer, settling in London in 1846. He was also a composer, and wrote important treatises on singing.*

Duke of Wellington inspected the household troops, and the Queen held a 'drawing room' at St James' Palace, which the Pakingtons attended. The Times reported that carriages of those invited started arriving at 1.00 p.m. and formed a continuous stream setting down for two hours. Several members of the Royal family were there and some foreign royals, including Grand Duke Constantine of Russia. The list of those present, headed by three archbishops and seventeen bishops, filled two closely spaced columns in The Times. The occasion opened with an address from the Archbishop of Canterbury congratulating the Queen 'on the auspicious return of her natal day'. Prince Albert wore the uniform of a Field Marshall, and the Queen must have looked splendid in 'a train of gold embroidered satin (of British manufacture), trimmed with honeysuckles and tulle, and ornamented with diamonds. The petticoat was of white satin trimmed with honeysuckle and tulle. Her Majesty's head dress was formed of black velvet and feathers with point lace lappets, and a superb tiara of diamonds'. It was also the custom of ministers of state to give celebratory dinners in the evening, and Sir John records that he attended one given by Sir Robert Peel. The celebrations continued the following evening when the Queen gave a concert followed by a 'sumptuous supper' in Buckingham Palace, and again Sir John was invited.

At the beginning of June there was a debate lasting three nights on the government's radical proposals for altering the way criminals were punished. The home secretary, Sir George Grey, opened the debate describing how he felt the system of transportation had failed, despite the various changes made to it. One of the great evils was the keeping of prisoners together, as was currently the case in Tasmania, which merely led to the worst aspects of the prisoners' characters spreading among them all. He praised the separate system of solitary confinement, then being used on a wide scale in England, although he stressed the importance of proper medical and general supervision of the prisoners. The government's proposals were that in future men who were sentenced to transportation should first spend a period of detention under the solitary system here, which would last from six to eighteen months. Afterwards they should be sent to somewhere such as Gibraltar or Bermuda where they would be employed on public works, and finally they would be sent to New South Wales, where they would be regarded as being conditionally pardoned, for the rest of their sentence.

The plan came under attack from the Tory opposition, and on the second evening Sir John 'gave up Sir E Hartopp's party and spoke on transportation question with great success'. He first criticised the government for introducing this major change under the Royal prerogative, without the sanction of parliament, and secondly he questioned their figures. Grey had stated that the first stage of the punishment would be in a British prison under solitary confinement; but Sir John had done some research and could not see, even taking account of all the recent new and enlarged prisons, that there would be enough accommodation. He went on to say that, although the government were showing great concern for the welfare and moral improvement of the prisoner, they were discounting the deterrent effect of the more severe aspects of transportation.

> Whatever might be the faults of the transportation system, whatever doubts might be entertained as to its effects upon the individual himself, I have no hesitation in saying – and I have often witnessed it in my own experience – that it has the greatest possible effect in deterring others; and I do not believe that the plan which the Government now proposes can possibly exercise a terror over the class that are in danger of becoming criminals, equal to that of transportation.

Furthermore, he disliked the idea of making a sentence of transportation mean something different:

> What will be the meaning of a sentence of transportation under the proposed system but an idle form of words? Those unfortunate classes who are exposed to it would soon come to know that its real meaning was that they should either be kept at home, with a prospect of free pardon after a limited period, or, as the other alternative, that they should be sent out to the colonies, where their families would follow them, and where they would be placed, I fear, in a better condition than that of the honest labourer who remained at home.

But Sir John may had have mixed feelings about the whole question, as he noted that on the final evening of the debate 'I would not vote in division'.

The following Monday, transportation came up again in another connection, and Sir John would have been in the House as the Juvenile Offenders Bill was given its third reading. The case of the late Sir John Eardley-Wilmot came up, which Sir John would have been interested in and noted in his diary, as Eardley-Wilmot had been a Warwickshire MP and chairman of the quarter sessions there. In February 1843 he had been appointed governor of Van Diemen's Land (now Tasmania). As was noted above, Sir John himself had been offered that post, and was probably now glad he had refused it. Eardley-Wilmot's tenure had been most unhappy, and,

*Sir John Eardley-Wilmot, 1783-1847. He was the son of a barrister and grandson of a judge, and was called to the bar himself. He opposed slavery and went into politics, and his career ended after he died in Hobart after a controversial time as govenor of Tasmania.*

under the strain of the events, he had suddenly died. At that time it was mainly a penal colony, and the prisoners were inadequately controlled, and sometimes ran riot. Immorality was rife, some blamed the governor for the lax state of affairs, and the colony's finances were in a mess. There was much factionalism, and some of the governor's enemies started to spread rumours about his private life, saying no woman was safe in government house. William Gladstone, at that time secretary of state for the colonies, decided that the Eardley-Wilmot should be recalled. Officially, this was because of Eardley-Wilmot's 'insensibility to the vast importance of the moral and religious state of the convicts', but in a second 'private' letter to the governor, Gladstone said that rumours about his private life made it impossible for him to continue. There may have been some grounds for these rumours. Eardley-Wilmot had left his family at home and may have taken a mistress, but they were certainly grossly exaggerated, and, outraged, he made the accusations public and put them before the executive committee of the colony. Letters and testimonials in his complete support were forthcoming. But Gladstone was then replaced by Earl Grey, and Eardley-Wilmot died, still in office, so nothing more came of the affair.

In the House that day Richard Spooner, MP for Birmingham, made a strong statement in complete support of Eardley-Wilmot. There was some debate about the government's handling of the affair, and whether he should have been given official recognition by the award of an honour, but all who spoke felt Eardley-Wilmot's character and honour were impeccable.

Sir John's wife Augusta had given birth to a female baby in April 1845, who was buried shortly after, and in May the following year she had miscarried. Now in June 1847 she was 'in the family way' again, and her husband was extra-careful to ensure a successful pregnancy. On June 12th he found the phaeton too rough for her when driving to Kensington Gardens, and sent for the barouche instead, and she stayed at home rather than attend a dinner that night.

The day after the debate on transportation concluded another one started which caught the attention of Sir John. In Portugal the previous October the respected and ageing Duke of Palmella had been removed from office and exiled by a more extremist and right-wing faction led by the Duke of Saldanha. This had led to an insurgency by those wishing to return the country to a more constitutional monarchy. Concerned at the bloodshed and civil unrest that was leading to inflation and shortages in Britain's oldest ally, the government had despatched a Col Wylde at the beginning of April to put peace proposals to both sides. The Queen, Maria II, seemed ready to accede, but her ministers were against any compromise with the rebels, so the mission failed. It was then announced that, under the terms of an earlier treaty, Britain, France and Spain would intervene to uphold the monarchy.

On 11th June Joseph Hume, member for Montrose, opened a debate on his motion deploring British intervention. Sir John seems to have attended all three days of the debate, and on the third night he noted that Peel's speech had an 'extraordinary effect'. Many Tories had supported Hume's motion, but Peel, as always rational and dispassionate in his assessment, sympathised with the government's dilemma when the decision to send Col Wylde out had been made two months before. There was then every chance that peace could be restored, in which case no-one could have criticised their action. He felt the decision then had been right, and he went into some detail about what might have happened in different scenarios, none of which would have been favourable to British interests. When Peel sat down Sir John was found to be one of only 31 members present, and the debate was forcibly concluded as the House was counted out.

On 18th June he was pleased to note that the Juvenile Offenders Bill passed through committee in the House of Lords. He also records a 'painful interview with Bp, Lady S and George' (Rev George Murray, Augusta's eldest brother). We are left to guess what problem had arisen, but perhaps it again related to Johnny, and his relationship with Eleanor. George was present at the earlier discussion, so perhaps the couple were still seeing each other in contravention of a promise.

The following week Sir John spoke in the House on the subject of the settlement of paupers. The parish of a pauper's settlement was responsible for relieving him; and for a long time this had been the parish of his or her birth. But all sorts of situations arose when it was desirable to make exceptions to this. In the previous session parliament had passed an act, the Poor Removal Act, making a parish in which a man had been living and working for a minimum of five years responsible for his relief. One effect was to allow factory workers to stay in their homes if they became unemployed rather than being removed to the rural parish whence they came; but some people felt this put an unfair burden on certain parishes. So in 1847 William Bankes introduced a bill to repeal part of that act, which was debated that evening. Sir John was the third to speak, and opposed repeal, suggesting that on the whole the Poor Removal Act had worked well. The home secretary agreed with Sir John, so did an earlier home secretary, Sir James Graham, and when the House divided the Bill was defeated by 107 votes to 104.

Sir John was friendly with Richard Spooner, MP for Birmingham, who had introduced a bill, the Prostitution and Seduction Bill, to increase the penalties attached to procuring for the purpose of prostitution, brothel keeping, and other immoralities. The bill was in its committee stage that night, and Sir John made the rather convoluted comment that "I compliment the gentlemen through whose instrumentality an account of what passed in that House is usually conveyed to the public upon the discretion they have shown in refraining from entering at any length into this subject when it was last under the consideration of the House" (general approbation) "and I hope they will pursue a similar course on the present occasion". The report on the debate in Hansard was consequently kept quite brief.

The very next evening, 24th June, the Poor Law came up again for debate in the House, this time the third reading of the Poor Law Administration Bill. The Poor Law Commission's latest five year term would terminate at the end of that year. This bill, which was strongly influenced by the Andover scandal and select committee report, was to replace the Poor Law Commission with a Poor Law Board, the main difference being that two of its members would members of parliament to make it more directly accountable. The debate on the 24th brought out, as had the previous ones, the well-known enemies of the Commission and the whole poor law structure. One of them, Thomas Wakley, MP for Finsbury, spoke first that night, attacking the whole working of the poor law, and was followed soon after by William Ferrand, MP for Knaresborough.

Despite these attacks the government survived the first two divisions with comfortable majorities. An amendment was then proposed by Peter Borthwick, MP for Evesham. One of the unpopular features of workhouses was that the inmates were strictly segregated by sex, so pauper families did not live together. Indeed the prospect of being separated was a powerful disincentive from seeking relief. This was felt particularly hard with elderly couples, past the age when they could gain employment, so Borthwick moved an amendment 'That when any two persons, being husband and wife, both of whom shall be above the age of 60 years, shall be received into any workhouse..., such two persons shall not be compelled to live separate and

*Peter Borthwick was born in Edinburgh in 1804. He served for a period as Tory MP for Evesham, and his opposition to the immediate, rather than gradual, abolition of slavery endeared him to West Indian interests and right-wing Tories. But 'Borthwick's clause', referred to in the text, showed a more humanitarian side of his character. A critical article in the Illustrated London News in 1843 described him as* 'fluent enough... but as to ideas they are the most perfect commonplace... His rising is the signal for members to lean back in all the repose of inattention'. *He lost he seat in 1847, and later became editor of The Morning Post. After his early death in 1852 his son took over at the Morning Post, and was later created Lord Glanesk.*

apart from each other in such workhouse'. Sir George Grey, the home secretary, said the government opposed this clause, as in any case, where circumstances permitted and the Poor Law Commissioners gave permission, couples could live together, and indeed some unions had constructed special cottages for this purpose. But to make it obligatory would raise all sorts of practical difficulties.

Sir John, who had been attending the debate throughout, missing Lady Jane Downe's party and Miss Hallifax's ball, spoke to oppose the clause, and said 'that every one acquainted with the practical administration of the Poor Law must know that it was absolutely impossible, with any regard to decency, that any such regulation could be carried into effect'. If, he said, this was a way to force guardians to give more outdoor relief (because it would not be practical to accommodate couples together inside) then that should be legislated for openly. But Borthwick's clause was approved by 71 votes to 35. After several divisions the sitting ended at 2.30 a.m. – 'bad night – government obliged to give way', Sir John noted.

The following week he had to attend quarter sessions in Worcester, and on the way stopped overnight in Oxford and met Johnny, where there was a grand dinner in hall of 'scientifics'. Afterwards they attended a lecture given by Michael Faraday in the Radcliffe Camera. Although then 56, Faraday was still developing his theories of magnetism, and a lecture he gave the year before laid, according to the Dictionary of National Biography, 'the foundations of the field theory of electromagnetism' which became one of the fundamental concepts of modern physics. The next day Sir John went with Johnny and his friends to see Blenheim Palace before catching a train to Droitwich, which, as the Oxford, Worcester and Wolverhampton Railway had not yet been built, would have involved a rather circuitous journey probably via Swindon and Bristol.

Quarter sessions seem to have passed off routinely, and Sir John was pleased to note that no general rate would be required in the county, on account of the government meeting the costs of prosecutions since last Michaelmas. There would be a farthing rate for the police. He was less pleased by the fact that attendance on the grand jury was thin – only 18 were present against a quota of about 24, which was particularly regrettable as there were 113 prisoners awaiting trial. Sir John said that if this occurred again he would feel obliged to impose the penalty for non-attendance that the law allowed. As soon as sessions were finished he returned to London, and the next day met Johnny and took him to see, yet again, the Ethiopians. Back at his home afterwards, he had some bad news. At the forthcoming election he would be opposed at Droitwich. This seems to have started something of a panic, as the next morning he returned to Droitwich, and met his friends Martin Rickets and the Curtler brothers. He issued his election address the following day, then rushed back to London, where he found his wife and Johnny at the opera. On Monday the Scotch Sites Committee finished its report, and he still had time to attend Vauxhall Gardens in the evening with Johnny, where a variety of entertainment was provided – he was 'much amused'.

The parliamentary session was coming to an end. It was to be dissolved prior to a general election at the end of July, and there was much business still to do. The Juvenile Offenders Bill had run into trouble in the Lords, and Sir John did not agree with some amendments passed there, but after meetings with the business managers in the Lords the matter was satisfactorily resolved, and it received the Royal assent. As will be described in chapter 16, the Juvenile Offenders Bill was later extended to cover children up to the age of 16, but it was to be a long time before any further changes to the treatment of juvenile offenders were made. Not everyone agreed that the Act was successful. Some claimed that it led to more children being sent to prison, where they became more criminalised, and frequently re-offended thereafter. But special children's courts and penal institutions were a long way off.

At the end of the week, on 10th July, the Pakingtons started to prepare to leave for Droitwich, and the servants' carriages left first. That night he went to hear Jenny Lind again, singing in Donizetti's 'La Figlia del Reggimento'. After dining with Mrs Milner on Saturday, he sat with her a long time to take leave on Sunday. Monday 12th July marked the end of his London season, and the Pakingtons caught an early train, and his remaining servants, horses and carriage followed later. They had time for a rest in Birmingham, then the whole party left at 4.15 p.m. arriving home in time for dinner.

His opponent at Droitwich was now known to be a Mr C. Lloyd, and Sir John immediately started his canvass, but complained that it was so hot he could hardly ride. But after two days'

*Jenny Lind (1820-87), 'The Swedish Nightingale'. Her first big success as an opera singer was in Sweden in 1838, after which she visited many European countries, including Britain in 1847, '48 and '49. In 1850 she contracted with B. T. Barnum to give concerts in America for $1,000 per night, which, after 93 performances, made her very rich. But she gave much of her earnings away to charity. She settled in London after her singing career ended, and was appointed a professor of singing at the Royal Academy of Music.*

canvassing he had to attend the grand jury of the assizes which were starting in Worcester on Thursday, dining later with the judges. The following day he rode 45 miles canvassing, the weather being a little cooler. On that day he was accompanied by John Curtler and Henry Bearcroft. Bearcroft, a solicitor, was the younger brother of Edward Bearcroft of Mere Hall (where they lunched) and was later a friend and political agent for Harry Vernon of Hanbury Hall. As Vernon was a Liberal MP in the 1860s it seems that Bearcroft later changed his allegiance.

The following week saw more canvassing on Monday and Tuesday, and after hanging pictures on the Westwood stairs on Wednesday Sir John went to Hanbury Rectory for archery practise. The rector was Rev. William Vernon, younger brother of the late Thomas Tayler Vernon of Hanbury Hall, and uncle of the head of the family, Thomas Bowater Vernon, aged fourteen. Rev. William had a brother George Croft Vernon, a solicitor, who seems, like Rev. William and a third brother Edward Vernon of Shrawley, to have been a Tory supporter. The following day George Vernon saw Mr Lloyd, the erstwhile Liberal candidate, evidently on a mission to dissuade him from proceeding. Further meetings were held that day and the next, the result being that on Friday afternoon Sir John was told that 'Lloyd had resigned!'.

We do not know anything else about this Mr Lloyd. Berrows, a keen supporter of the Tories and Sir John, did not publish Lloyd's election addresses, although they appeared several times in the Worcester Herald – perhaps Sir John's influence was at work here. Lloyd's main address had explained at some length his policies on trade and tax, showing him to be a free-trader. After his initial canvass he published a further letter in which he said that 'the numerous promises of support accorded me, justify me in the hope that I will be placed in a considerable majority upon the poll…'. He then went home to London, and it was on his return that he saw George Vernon, and on withdrawing published a further rather peevish letter in the Herald:

> …my first canvass, which had undergone a rigid scrutiny by competent and impartial friends, was such as to justify me in entertaining the confident hope of being placed in a majority upon the poll. Since my return into your neighbourhood I have ascertained that several of the electors upon whose votes and others upon whose neutrality I had counted, in conformity with their pledges, have found it impossible to withstand the influence which has been used against them, and are unable in consequence to give me that continued assurance of their support with which an honourable victory could alone have been achieved. Under these altered circumstances and in conformity with the advice of some influential friends, I have decided upon withdrawing from a contest, the result of which would have been to place my opponent in a small majority…

The Droitwich election was due to take place the following Friday 30th July, and, not wanting to be far from the action during the week, Sir John sent Johnny to represent him at the funeral of a Slaney relative on Monday. On Wednesday he still had time to attend a meeting of the Droitwich Guardians, followed by some archery at The

Mount, Hanbury, the home of George Vernon. The following day Sir John discussed his nomination speech with the two Curtlers, the two Bearcrofts and Martin Ricketts, and whether to allude to Benbow. Benbow was probably the man of the same name who was the agent for Lord Ward. Sir John had had suspicions about him the previous week that were confirmed when he talked to George Vernon. Presumably he was something to do with the unwelcome intrusion of Mr Lloyd into the election, possibly on behalf of Lord Ward.

Berrows describes the colourful scene at the nomination thus:

> The nomination took place in a field at the south end of the town at 11 o'clock. A great number of electors met the honourable baronet on his way from his seat at Westwood; a number, in fact, sufficient, it is said, to have returned him alone even had there been any opposition. The cavalcade gave things more the appearance of a county than a borough election. Having alighted at the George Hotel, they walked in procession to the hustings, being headed by a band, and scarlet flags and banners. The salt women, tricked out in gaudy red handkerchiefs and dancing to the strain of the music, proved a very singular spectacle to those unaccustomed to a Droitwich election.

Sir John was nominated (for the third time) by Martin Ricketts, and seconded by Edward Bearcroft. He then made his acceptance speech, which, according to his diary, lasted for an hour and a quarter. After thanking the electors for their great kindness in electing him for the third time, he noted that on each occasion some opposition had been attempted, and on each occasion abandoned. He said that at the last election the party to which he belonged was 'triumphant', but now, after a parliament of unusually long duration, it was 'powerless, broken and scattered'. He then went on to mention, at some length, the attempted opposition of Mr Lloyd. Although Mr Lloyd had behaved towards him in an honourable and gentleman-like manner, he thought he had been misled as to his chances of success.

> When the truth, however, was developed, and Mr Lloyd was compelled to exchange a first-class position on the poll for a first-class ticket in a railway carriage (loud laughter) when he found himself in his unpleasant position I am sure he must have felt extremely annoyed at being obliged to back out, but I do say that I wish he had gone away from the town without abusing those whom he left behind him.

This referred to Lloyd's resignation letter, mentioned above. Lloyd's reference to the 'influence' being used against him particularly annoyed Sir John, who said "I emphatically deny that I hold my seat from any such disgraceful causes". But there were, no doubt, different ways for landlords to put pressure on tenants without the actual threat of eviction, and it is interesting to note that the previous week he wrote that he rode to call on two men, Mucklow and Williams of Berry Hill, and had an 'unsatisfactory interview with the latter'. These were probably his tenants, and it does sound as if he was using all means he had to secure support.

Sir John was not content to leave the matter there, and in continuing he exposed what was probably one of the less attractive sides of his character. He said:

> Every public man must look for and expect a fair opposition. I have no claim on the electors of Droitwich beyond that which I may derive from the approbation of my public conduct, and their kindness towards me as their friend and neighbour. If my public conduct should hereafter be such as to excite your displeasure, I must doubtless pay a penalty which is always hanging over the representatives of the people; but if I ever am displaced from that situation which I now hold, I do hope that it will be the result of a fair, open, straightforward, political opposition, and not the result of a vindictive intrigue (hear, hear, and cheers) organised in secret, and brought about by those to whom I had a right to look as my supporters and friends (hear, hear). But where, on this occasion, did the opposition arise? It did not come from ordinary local people who hold different political opinions from mine; nor did it come from the Whig government putting up a man in to oppose me.
>
> I'm sorry to tell you, but I have no hesitation in expressing my belief that that opposition was organised nearer home; and here I should observe that I have no charge to make against Mr Lloyd in connection with this matter, but I feel bound to refer to those subordinates of a noble lord whose name has been prominently mixed up with the late contest – if I might so call it and in a way which it ought not to have been. I have always regarded that noble lord with feelings of private and public approbation, and I should state in justice to the electors that I have the best reason for believing that that noble Lord had no knowledge of conduct which has been pursued by his subordinates in the matter of the late opposition. But, gentlemen, I have no hesitation in telling you that to the subordinates of that noble lord I owe this opposition. From feelings of delicacy toward that noble lord, I will not go into the nature and character of that opposition, but this I will say that so extraordinary has it been – so unlike what a gentleman ought to look for in the character of a political opposition have been the circumstances of this opposition, that I have made it my duty thoroughly to investigate them, and I have obtained a chain of evidence which leads to no doubt in my mind as to where that opposition originated. And this I will say, that if I am ever again attempted to be made the victim of secret intrigue, nothing shall deter me from exposing the parties to that indignation which must be felt by every honourable man in such a case.

As we have seen, Sir John was here most likely referring to Lord Ward of Witley Court and his agent Benbow. Probably Benbow had been covertly using his master's influence to promote the Whig candidate, Lloyd.

Sir John then went on to reflect on his ten years in parliament, and said his experiences had brought him to a conviction that there are two paramount subjects to which the attention of the legislature ought to be devoted:

> The first of these is that we are bound to take efficient measures for improving the condition of the working classes. (Cheers) When I consider our teeming and fast

> increasing population, when I consider the magnitude of our commercial and manufacturing interests, when I consider the blessings with which Providence has favoured this country, and the prosperity which we enjoy, I hold it to be our duty to endeavour to raise the working classes of the kingdom from their comparatively low condition, and to endeavour to give them a fair share of our national prosperity (hear, hear). My opinion is, that if we do not care to these things, our national prosperity will not be a lasting prosperity, and it is fit that it should not be so. This second point of paramount interest is, that we should strain every nerve to elevate the moral and social condition, and, if possible, win the affections, of the Irish people. Depend upon it that the darkest spot on our bright empire is the unhappily distracted and now famine-stricken Ireland. I believe that nothing more urgently calls the most earnest attention than the state of Ireland.

This led on, of course, to the subject of Maynooth, where Sir John had voted with the government, but against the inclinations of many Tories. He spoke at length justifying his vote, saying:

> I never gave a vote with a deeper conviction that I was right, or that, so far as that vote could have any effect upon the Protestant church, I was giving a vote favourable to that church rather than otherwise... But the deepest conviction which I entertain as a churchman, is that we ought to feel toleration for the opinions of others, and extend a feeling of charity to all (hear, hear), and here let me make you realise what is the real state of Ireland with regard to religious matters. The number of members of the established church in Ireland is 850,000, and they possess a property of £550,000; while the members of the Roman Catholic religion number six millions and a half, without a farthing to support their church, which is left entirely to the agency of voluntary support, under every combination of circumstances which makes it most objectionable and dangerous. What is the result of this? Why, that we have Ireland ignorant, uncivilised, wretched, and disaffected to the state. Do you think, as English churchmen, that this is a state of things which can be allowed to continue without danger to the Protestant established church – making her the subject of envy and irritation on every hand? If you would alter this state of things you must treat the sister country with conciliation and kindness. I fervently desire to see the day when the errors of Romanism shall be corrected, and when we shall all be united under one church: but if ever that day does arrive, its consummation must be accompanied by measures of conciliation and kindness, and not by harshness and severity.

He said the importance of Maynooth had been much exaggerated; it was already fifty years old, and we had supported similar Catholic institutions in Canada and other colonies. He then repeated the arguments used by those in favour of the increased Maynooth grant – that the system at Maynooth should not be left in its present mischievous condition, and, by adopting a more generous course, Maynooth should be enabled to do respectably and well what had been badly and inefficiently performed before. Still on the Irish question, he said there was also the question of the endowment of the Roman Catholic priesthood there, but he felt public opinion was not yet ready for that subject to be raised, and he would not yet give any pledges as to how he would view it; but one feels he might have been sympathetic to some change even on this front.

Sir John had spent some time discussing Maynooth as he knew that many electors would have had him vote differently; but on the question of the Corn Law repeal he was on surer ground. He certainly understood the need to adjust duties on corn in response to the desire for cheaper food for factory workers and to relieve the Irish famine;

> but I did not feel that either of those causes made out a case of wanting the removal of all protection from agriculture; and although the proposal emanated from the minister with whom I generally acted, I could not allow that consideration to cause me to swerve from my duty, and I thought it to be my duty to give my opposition to the proposed measure. (Hear, hear.)

But the subject had now 'gone by', and was entitled to a 'fair trial'. Again, one senses that Sir John was not so strongly protectionist as some of his colleagues.

He then spoke about the need for a scheme of national education, and hoped it would be possible to allow children of dissenters to participate in a secular education. He reviewed foreign affairs, and said the late Tory government had put right many of the international problems in India, China and elsewhere that beset the previous Whig government. He also pointed to the improved national finances achieved by Peel's administration. But then he alluded again to the split in the Tory party, and said that in the recent session there had been few matters in which he found himself in disagreement with Lord John Russell, who had replaced Peel as prime minister, and in particular thought that he had acted as best he could over the Irish famine. Lord Stanley was now leader of a faction of the Tory party; he thought highly of the honesty of Lord Stanley, but "at the same time I am bound to say that there were public men acting with his Lordship in whom he could not place confidence". Was he referring to Disraeli? The political future was uncertain, but Sir John summed up by saying that "I will only emphatically state that I have always acted, and shall continue to act upon essentially conservative principles" (hear, hear and cheers) "but at the same time on principles of moderation; because I believe that it is only by maintaining those principles that we can continue to enjoy an unexampled prosperity, and sustain our valued and time-honoured institutions".

As usual, the nomination was followed by luncheon in the large ballroom in The George Hotel, which was 'quite filled'. All the usual toasts were drunk, although it was noticed that Lady Pakington was not present due to 'delicate health'.

The following week, on Monday 2nd August, Johnny's coming of age was marked. After drilling in the park, his father had arranged for the Westwood Squadron of the Worcestershire Yeomanry Cavalry to be joined by that of Hanbury for a celebratory dinner in The George Hotel. Nearly one hundred in full dress uniform sat down at 3.00 p.m., and after the meal the Captains (Pakington, Galton and Emmot) made, according to Berrows, some 'fine speeches' and proposed the usual toasts.

The following day Sir John had an appointment with Hardwick to discuss the painted windows in the hall, and on Wednesday 4th August the first Archery Society meeting of the season took place at Hanbury Hall, attended by Sir John, Lady Augusta and Johnny. The occasion was somewhat spoilt by the weather, and Sir John noted that attendance was 'thin', but Berrows records eighty two members plus thirty eight visitors present, and a large number of county families were represented.

As well as the Droitwich nomination, Sir John also appeared at that for both the east and west divisions of Worcestershire. The nomination for the West Worcester–shire seat was held on 5th August at the Worcester racecourse grandstand, and Hon. Henry Lygon, by now a general, and Frederick Winn Knight, both Tories, were re-elected without opposition. After the usual speeches, the crowd called on Sir John to speak, and after a repeated clamour he stepped forward and made some remarks in favour of the candidates. Afterwards the new MPs paraded in the City before hosting a luncheon at The Star Hotel, where Sir John spoke again 'in his usual able manner'. Another of the speakers was Richard Spooner (see below).

The following day Sir John and some other members of the Severn Commissioners joined Lord Hatherton and other directors of the Staffordshire and Worcestershire Canal Co. to take a trip by steamer from Worcester to Gloucester. The main purpose of the excursion was to test the works. The summer having been very dry, it was found, as predicted, that the depth of six feet that should have been maintained all the way was deficient by up to two feet in places. On this lower section the depth had

*Edward John Littleton, 1st Baron Hatherton, 1791-1863. His great uncle, Sir Edward Littleton, had been a promotor of the Staffs & Worcs Canal when it was built in the 1760s, which passed close to their seat, Teddesley Hall, in Penkridge. Hatherton took a great interest in railways, but fell into conflict with the London and North Western when their proposals for new lines threatened the revenue of the Staffs & Worcs Canal, of which he was chairman. The Staffs & Worcs, which had been very profitable, provided much of the capital for the Severn Navigation improvements.*

been achieved by dredging, but as the dredged channel had had to be wide enough for two boats to pass, at times of low water dredging was simply not sufficient to maintain the six feet depth. Berrows commented, 'nevertheless, on the whole, we believe it must be admitted, in fairness, that the improvement has answered much better than was anticipated, and that the trade on the river must have received a considerable stimulus'. Tolls in the six months since the works were completed amounted to £7,000. At Gloucester a dinner was held in the Bell Hotel, and Berrows reported that the general feeling was 'let bygones be bygones', and the past opposition of Gloucester men to the project was now forgotten. It must have been a long day – Sir John left Holt by boat at 8.30 a.m., and returned by late train from Gloucester after the dinner.

On the Saturday of what had been a busy week the nomination for East Worcestershire was held in Droitwich, and there had been some nervousness that the 'Droitwich agreement' of the previous December was going to be broken. On 31st July Sir John noted that he heard a rumour that Richard Spooner, who the night before had lost his bid to be re-elected for Birmingham, might stand as a Tory for the county. Spooner had started as a radical, but, now in his 60s, had moved to the extreme right. He had been elected for Birmingham in 1844 rather by accident when the Whigs were split, but was defeated there at the poll held in July. Through the vagaries of the electoral system at the time, Spooner was able to transfer his candidature to another constituency where the poll had not yet been held, which was the case with East Worcestershire. But this would have involved a contested election, which the Droitwich agreement was intended to avoid, so Sir John met some of his colleagues in Worcestershire and communicated with Col Rushout, asking him to explain the situation to Richard Spooner. Spooner then transferred his nomination to North Warwickshire, where he was elected and which he continued to represent till 1864 when he was 81.

So after the East Worcestershire nomination, held on 7th August, Sir John was able to note that 'the compromise [was] quietly carried out'. But tensions between the different flavours of Toryism surfaced in the speeches that day. Sir John proposed the Tory Capt. George Rushout, who was not able to be present through illness, and his speech was routine. But the seconder, James Taylor, father of the retiring MP, proved himself to be not in accord with Sir John's views on Catholicism. He quoted remarks by Lord John Russell, who would inevitably continue as prime minister, showing that he was favourable not only to the Maynooth grant but also to endowing the Irish Catholic priesthood and the encouragement of Catholic schools. Taylor was much against these ideas, and said "I hope that the Protestants of our day will show a greater determination to uphold their religion than the Jews of old…". Judging by the report in Berrows, there was a strong Liberal contingent present, and these remarks were subject to much interruption and 'hisses and groans'.

John Hodgetts Hodgetts-Foley was the Liberal candidate. He had been MP for Droitwich from 1822 to 1835, when he had been narrowly defeated by John Barneby. Hodgetts-Foley was nominated by E. Holland, who also did not wish to court controversy as in any case there was no contest. So he paid tribute to Capt. Rushout, and said there were very few points on which he disagreed with what Sir John, his proposer, had said, but that he did not entirely concur with Mr Taylor's references to the Catholics and the Jews. Before proceedings were completed, Mr Baldwin, a Birmingham paper maker, stepped forward and asked if he might question the candidates. The sheriff agreed, so he asked Hodgetts-Foley whether he agreed with the principles of free trade. When he replied in the affirmative, Baldwin turned to Sir John and asked whether Capt. Rushout was of the same opinion. Sir John replied that he was all for the freedom to ask candidates questions, but he did not feel able to answer for Rushout. Perhaps it was just as well that he was not present, although one would have thought that his proposer would know the candidate's views on this important political topic. Baldwin's next question was whether the candidates favoured religious liberty, to which Hodgetts-Foley gave the somewhat evasive answer that he was for "supporting the established Church, which he thought ought never to be interfered with". Again, Rushout's absence saved him from having to answer.

When proceedings ended Rushout's supporters had a lunch in The George Hotel, while the Liberals gathered at a marquee in the garden of Rev. Topham's residence, The Herriots, nearby. Two hundred sat down in the ballroom of The George, and after the 'elegant repast' there were the usual toasts, and Sir John spoke about the present political situation. He was pleased to see that Lord Russell had seen the importance of opposing radicalism, and some of the measures recently put forward by him in parliament had been 'taking a leaf out of the Conservatives' book'.

The following week was to prove as busy as the last, and began on Monday when Sir John attended a special meeting of the Diocesan Board of Education. This was to consider establishing a Training Institution set up to nurture new school teachers, so as to render it eligible to receive money from the education committee of the Privy Council. On Tuesday he spent all day with a Mr Thomas, who was designing the garden at Westwood, part of the renovations. On Wednesday much time was taken by a meeting of the Droitwich Poor Law Guardians, and on Thursday was another celebration of Johnny's coming of age, when about thirty tenants were invited to dinner, followed by a ball for the wives and daughters. The following day it was the turn of the cottagers to have a celebratory dinner, followed by dancing on the lawn. As many as ninety dined, and sixty children had tea and cake afterwards.

The Bishop of Rochester and his family were due to stay next week, and most of the family went to archery at Hadzor on Wednesday, and finally left on Friday on the way to the Lake District. The last week of August saw more socialising in the newly restored Westwood House, which they must have re-occupied shortly before. There was sailing on the lake and an archery party was held on 25th. Although rain brought it to a premature end, 'music and dancing went off well, & beautiful moonlight effects at night'. Among the visitors was 'young Vernon' – this was Thomas Bowater Vernon, the young owner of the Vernon estates, who was being brought up by his uncle George Vernon as his father had died when he was only three. September 1st marked the first day of the shooting season, and Sir John and Johnny wasted no time in seeking partridges on the estate, but strong wind made for bad sport.

The Pakingtons attended the second meeting of the Worcestershire Archery Society held at Hagley Hall, the seat of the Lytteltons, on 7th September, but the event was interrupted by rain and eventually had to be abandoned. The guests, comprising 150 families, the élite of the county according to Berrows, were summoned by a bugle call to dinner in a marquee. As the rain still persisted, the house was thrown open, and the prizes were distributed by Lady Lyttelton in the picture gallery. These included a wooden spoon prize, but Berrows refrained from naming the winner! Tea was then served, and the gallery cleared for dancing – 'even the grim old portraits looking out from their gilded frames upon the moving and joyous forms below them smiled with satisfaction' wrote Berrow's correspondent.

Yeomanry week started soon after, and Pickersgill's picture of Col Clive arrived to be examined by the officers, and was later exhibited to the public in Shire Hall. The continuing bad weather stopped the regiment turning out at Kempsey on Monday, and on the same day Sir John presided over the AGM of the Severn Commissioners, at which the deficiencies of the navigation below Worcester were reported. A committee under Sir John was appointed to determine the best way of remedying this and raising the finance. On Tuesday the portrait was presented to Lady Harriet Clive in Shire Hall. It was a 'fine scene', and Augusta and Mrs Milner, who was staying, came into Worcester for the presentation. Sir John's main social event seems to have been during the week commencing 20th September, when a succession of the great and good came and went – lionizing Westwood and the park was the main activity, but there was sailing and visits to Claines, Ombersley and Hampton church, but no shooting was recorded. Sir John and Johnny made up for it the following week, shooting on every day except one.

*Hagley Hall and park, from Nash.*

The big event the following week on 31st October was the meeting at Dee's Hotel, Birmingham, to discuss the training school decided upon at the Diocesan Board of Education meeting in August. It was first addressed by the Bishop of Worcester, Dr Henry Pepys, who pointed to the importance of good teachers to meet the expanding demand as education increased, and said that at present teachers tended to be 'decayed carpenters and bankrupt tailors'. The intention was to encourage the brightest pupils to stay on at school instead of leaving at 13, who by the time they were 18 should make good teachers. The Bishop was followed by Lord Lyttelton who gave more details – a piece of land in Saltley near the centre of Birmingham had already been given by Bowyer Adderley MP. A series of resolutions was then proposed and seconded, the second of which was that the school should be for a minimum of forty scholars, and that it could later be enlarged at the discretion of the governing body. This was proposed by Lord Lifford, and seconded by Sir John who, as he often did, thought he 'spoke well'.

Later in the week more visitors came to Westwood. Lord Hatherton stayed while attending a Severn Commissioners' meeting, and enjoyed being shown round the house and park. On 11th October there was another big house party at Westwood – twenty sat down to dinner on Monday, and sixteen the next night. On Wednesday most guests left, leaving Sir John free to attend a Poor Law Guardians' meeting and another education committee meeting.

At Michaelmas quarter sessions there were 136 prisoners to deal with. Sir John notes with some pride that he and his fellow judge Thomas Curtler dealt with eighty in one day! After attending another training school meeting in Birmingham he went to London on Thursday, and made a few calls on Friday including Mrs Milner at her new house in Eaton Square, before travelling to Walton where Augusta was staying with her sister. During the next two weeks he attended the training school committee in Birmingham and the lunatic asylum committees several times, as well as fitting in a visit to Leicester to see the lunatic asylum and new gaol there, and visiting his nephew Capel Hanbury Williams at Rugby School. The Severn Commissioners needed new powers to improve the shallow draft between

*Detail from the presentation portrait of Robert Henry Clive, Colonel of the Worcestershire Yeomanry Cavalry. It now hangs in army barracks in Telford.*

Worcester and Gloucester, which was decided on at a meeting on 11th November, and Sir John also managed to attend meetings of the Droitwich Guardians more regularly at this period.

The Worcester Music Festival was due to be held in Worcester in 1848, and a preliminary meeting under the chairmanship of the Bishop Pepys was held on 15th November. Sir John took a prominent part, and started by suggesting that the Festival be held in late August rather than September, as the yeomanry week took place in September, and the start of partridge shooting on 1st September 'occupied the attention of many country gentlemen'. This was agreed, although in the event it was held in September as usual. The meeting then went on to discuss the finances. Recent festivals had lost money, which had to be made up from the guarantees offered by the stewards, and the Bishop proposed that sixteen stewards be appointed, each to guarantee £40 against loss. Sir John disagreed; he said that with so many stewards the number of eligible gentlemen in the county would become exhausted, and thought that twelve would be sufficient. Although the Bishop was doubtful that £40 would suffice in that case, the number would be limited to twelve for the time being.

Sir John then raised another point. He said the Birmingham Festival guarantees were only called upon after the charitable collections had been amalgamated with the ticket sales, whereas at Worcester the collections, in favour of the widows and orphans of the clergy, were earmarked for that purpose and the expenses were set only against ticket sales when calculating the guarantees. But this idea, which might have meant money donated to charity being used to pay festival expenses, was not popular, and the Bishop called it 'hazardous'. The Bishop then raised the vexatious question of the ball. He had received a long letter saying that this was inappropriate after a festival of religious music, and also that professional singers should not be engaged. No doubt this was from the same person who had raised the same questions at the previous, 1845, festival. The bishop saw no objection to having a ball, but perhaps it would be better if it was held as a distinctly separate entity. But Sir John said he thought this would not meet the 'overstrained scruples' of the writer, and if they also followed the request not to have professional singers, the festival could not possibly succeed. He proposed that the subject of the ball be referred to the committee. The Bishop agreed, saying that although he had given up dancing himself, 'I cannot see the slightest objection to it – I think it is a harmless recreation'!

A short time afterwards a letter from the anti-ball campaigner, who styled himself Philoprepes, appeared in Berrows, saying he had been misrepresented at the meeting by the Bishop and by Sir John. He did not object to professional singers, but to those who were operatic and theatrical. As to the ball, taking the mention of it off the Festival placards would be like 'taking the label off nauseous medicine, but still compelling the patient to swallow the draught'! His point was not that there was anything wrong with dancing *per se*; 'but is it decorous and consistent for the high solemnities of a morning service at a cathedral to be closely coupled with the midnight gaieties of a grand ball, or giddy dance'?

As the meeting concluded, Sir John said that as Westwood had never contributed a steward to the Festival (he had been a steward in 1824, but that was before he had inherited Westwood) he would be happy to act as one in 1848. Sir John's interest in music had clearly not diminished, as at the same time he was rehearsing for a concert to be given at the Deanery, where Dr John Peel had replaced Rt Rev. Murray as Dean, on 20th November. Augusta was unable to perform due to a cold.

The following week the new parliament opened, and Sir John travelled down to hear the Queen's speech, delivered by commission in her absence. Johnny had come down to London from Oxford for a few days, and after he left Sir John spent some time with Mrs Milner, before returning to Worcestershire on Saturday. On Sunday, as was routine at this period, he attended church and held prayers at Westwood, and on this occasion, as the servants were unable to attend church for some reason, he gave them a sermon as well.

Sir John was kept in Worcestershire on Monday 29th November by Lunatic Asylum and Severn Commission meetings, but travelled to London the next day to attend the House of Commons, where he heard a 'clear and able speech by the chancellor of the exchequer' (Charles Wood). The Bank Act of 1844 had regulated the issue of paper currency by the Bank of England in order to maintain the gold standard, and in April there had been a crisis when the Bank had had to restrict the issue of paper. In early October a worse crisis developed, with the failure of several trading houses and even banks, and the government had had to step in to authorise the issue of paper currency beyond that allowed by the 1844 Act. Wood gave a long and detailed description of the crisis as he saw it. Banks and trading houses over-extended themselves and there was a crisis of confidence and sudden shortage of credit, caused partly by overtrading in corn, the price of which had collapsed, and partly by the extraordinary need of capital by the railway boom. Wood claimed that the authority to issue extra currency relieved the panic, and that trading was now getting back to normal again.

Sir John stayed two more days in London, and on Wednesday went to the Lyceum to see Kathleen Fitzwilliam, daughter of the celebrated actress Fanny Fitzwilliam, in her débût in a farce 'Peggy Green' at the Lyceum. He went with Hallifax, who found the heat too much and left. Perhaps he agreed with The Times that the piece was 'the merest trifle in the world', and felt he had had enough! Returning to Droitwich on Friday, Sir John missed Peel's speech in the debate on commercial distress, but was able to take his sister-in-law Caroline to Hanbury to see Mere Hall, residence of the Bearcrofts, and Hanbury Hall, the seat of the Vernons. The following week Sir John felt he had no need to attend parliament as the vote against the Irish Coercion Bill was very small, and on Sunday 12th December, for the third week running there were prayers and a sermon at Westwood.

On Monday 13th December there was a meeting of the Severn Commissioners under Sir John's chairmanship to discuss a report from the committee appointed at the AGM to look into the best way of improving the navigation from Worcester to Gloucester. The report recommended that the proposals of the consulting engineer, William Cubitt, should be adopted. These involved a new weir and locks near Tewkesbury to raise the level of the river above it, further works in Gloucester, and below Gloucester to the beginning of the Gloucester and Berkeley Canal. The committee had also looked carefully at the Commissioners' finances; at present the income was insufficient by nearly £3,000 a year to cover expenses, as tolls were below expectations, and the capital expended had had to be increased to £210,000. But there would be a saving of £2,000 a year on dredging if the new works went ahead, which would be sufficient to cover the extra interest on the new capital needed of £50,000. The committee had concluded that the tolls authorised by the act were not sufficient to cover the costs of maintaining the works, and recommended increasing these by one half a farthing per ton per mile. Furthermore, the committee felt that the present exemption from tolls of traffic that originated above than Stourport was unjustified, and should be stopped. These two measures should increase the revenue by £5,500.

Clearly the increase in the tolls and the removal of the exemption from traffic coming from Shropshire did not go down well with many of those present. Some felt that these impositions would just serve to drive even more traffic to the railways. Thus the increase in revenue forecast by the committee might not happen. Someone remarked that it was possible to 'pay too dear for the whistle'. Perhaps after all a depth of six feet was not really needed – maybe four feet would be enough. In any case, the engineer's predictions had already been proved wrong once, and who could guarantee that they would be right this time? Others objected to the proposed extension of the Commissioners' powers further down-stream, and felt that landowners' interests there would be affected. One of those, Mr Fulljames, proposed that that part of the report referring to these down-stream powers be deleted.

The meeting was starting to get bad-tempered, and Sir John tried to calm things down by going into all the objections that had been raised to show why they were wrong. Mr Fulljames pressed his amendment to a vote, but then another point was raised that caused consternation. Someone claimed that shareholders in the Staffordshire & Worcestershire Canal were not entitled to vote as they were interested parties, and were barred by a clause in the Act. Sir John immediately admitted to being a shareholder, but said he had never seen the clause referred to interpreted in that way. If that was correct, he would have to vacate the chair. Some further argument took place, and the chairman said he regretted, not for the first time, that the Commissioners had more regard to local interests than the furtherance of these important public works. A legal gentleman, Mr Williams, who had been leading the opposition, contended that Sir John did not have the right to be in the chair, whereupon 'Sir John left the chair and retired from the room amid increasing confusion'.

After this, personal arguments continued for some time before order was restored and the clerk, Mr Waters, proposed that Sir John should be invited to return to the chair, and Williams agreed to waive his objection as long as the votes were taken 'under protest'. Three gentlemen left the room and found the chairman in the street, but he agreed to return. Eventually the meeting agreed to vote on the resolution that the report be adopted, omitting the amendment that the section relating to the lowest part of the river; the result was seven votes for the amendment against four for adopting the whole report, and the meeting eventually broke up at five o'clock, after four hours.

Later in the week Sir John returned to London by the Great Western route, via Gloucester into Paddington. That day saw the first of the two day debate on a bill to allow Jews to enter the House of Commons, prompted by the election of Lionel de Rothschild to represent the City of London in the recent election. Sir John attended both days. It is interesting now to read the arguments put forward for and against the proposition. Lord John Russell, the prime minister who spoke first for the bill, based his argument mainly on the fact that the past exclusions of certain classes of person, in particular Catholics, had not been aimed at Jews, but at people who might owe allegiance to a power outside England, in Rome. He did not think those acts were intended to exclude Jews, whose virtues Lord Russell was keen to elucidate.

The two members for Oxford University were among the next speakers. Sir Robert Inglis opposed the bill. He implied that it was somehow unfair for the prime minister himself to introduce the bill, putting the full weight of the government behind it. On previous similar occasions private members had brought in the measure. And if it was true, as the prime minister alleged, that all British citizens should enjoy equal rights under the law, what about the very large numbers of people who could not enter parliament, or could not even vote, as they did not meet the property qualification? The other Oxford University MP, William Gladstone, took the opposite and more liberal view, which he did reluctantly as Inglis had brought in a petition from members of the University opposing the measure. Then Lord Ashley spoke – he could not speak too highly of the culture and art of the Jews, and praised their many other attributes. But as a true Christian his beliefs did not allow for compromise. He believed in England being a Christian country, and if Jews were admitted now, where would it end? Perhaps – heaven forbid – we would be saying goodbye to a white parliament, or even an all-male one, if the liberal argument was allowed to prevail. He quoted Dr Arnold:

> The Jews are voluntary strangers here, and have no claims to become citizens but by conforming to our moral law, which is the Gospel… I would give the Jews the honorary citizenship which was so often given by the Romans – they had the private rights

> of citizens but not the public rights. Every member of Christ's catholic church is one with whom I may lawfully join in legislation... but a Jew, or a heathen, I cannot apply to voluntarily, but only obey him passively, if he was to rule over me.

Not for the first time, Ashley the reformer is not always easy to equate with Ashley the strict Christian.

Ashley was followed by Benjamin Disraeli, who, as he was of Jewish origin, must have been listened to with particular interest. He took the rather novel line of arguing that, unlike more distant religions such as Islam, Judaism was the origin of Christianity, therefore to that extent Christianity was just a development of Judaism. Many of the things Christians believed were of Jewish origin. For that reason to admit Jews into parliament would be entirely consistent with keeping England a Christian country. He also pointed out (with dubious accuracy) that there were those who said that Jews should be condemned for crucifying Our Lord. But these Jews were not necessarily the ancestors of Jews in Britain today – many Jews had dispersed out of Palestine well before the time of Our Lord, and therefore their descendants could not be blamed.

The debate continued in a similar vein on the following day, at the end of which the House divided. Many traditional Tories voted against the bill, but some of its more prominent members including Lord Bentinck, Peel, Graham and Disraeli voted in favour, and with most Liberals voting in favour the measure was carried by a good majority. Sir John voted against; in view of his oft-expressed views on the need for religious toleration he might have been in favour, but perhaps he felt that toleration was one thing, and allowing Jews into parliament something else. In fact although it passed the Commons the bill was thrown out by the Lords, and this happened again in

*Anthony Ashley Cooper, Lord Ashley, later 7th Earl of Shaftsbury, 1801-85. Among many other causes, he was an early proponent of the return of the Jews to Palestine.*

1851. It was not until 1858 that Rothschild was allowed to take his seat, after a compromise act allowed each house to choose its own oath.

Sir John returned home on Saturday 18th for Christmas, and the following week had another large party with some shooting, and he noted that Johnny had a 'long ride with Miss Childe'. Perhaps his father was concerned that Johnny might be starting another unapproved romance.

As usual Sir John summed up the year at the end of his diary, and this is what he wrote about 1847:

> I thank God for the great blessings, happiness & prosperity which I have enjoyed throughout the past year. Domestic happiness – Augusta once more likely to increase her family – Johnny of age with charming character – house in London complete – Westwood renovated & complete – iron ore discovered on my Welsh property – parliamentary success – my own health uninterruptedly good – these are only a portion of the manifold blessings which have been vouchsafed to me – I feel how little I deserve them – I hope I receive them with gratitude & submission & that they may have some effect on my future life & conduct – may God be merciful to me & those dear to me through the year which now begins.

## Chapter 15
## The Years 1848 and 1849

Although Augusta was nearing the end of her pregnancy, the year 1848 began normally with quarter sessions occupying much of the first week, and there were meetings to discuss fund raising for the proposed new training school, and the Hunt Club ball attended by Sir John and his son.

As soon as these events were over, Sir John and Lady Augusta went to London for her confinement. At the new session of parliament, which opened on 3rd February, Sir John congratulated the Attorney General on his proposals to bring forward some bills to do with the magistracy, and he was appointed to serve on the committee looking into the sugar and coffee plantations in the West Indies. Lady Sarah Murray joined them in Eaton Square, and, as Sir John later wrote, 'we passed a most happy month in London of unqualified domestic comfort... With what depth of feeling shall I ever remember our extreme mutual tenderness during the 'precious moments' (as Lady Sarah one day called them) of that month, both of us influenced by the dread that a time of danger was at hand...'. Then, he wrote, 'on 12th February at 9.00 a.m., after a short and favourable labour, my beloved Augusta gave birth to a fine, healthy boy. She bore her suffering with characteristic fortitude, and I can never forget the look of intense delight which she gave me as I stood by the bed-side holding her hand in mine, when the first strong cry of the child assured her of its life. The joy of that moment was in proportion to the length of time and the anxious desire with which she had awaited it...'.

But after such a propitious start to the year, events soon started to take a tragic turn. 'Throughout the day of the confinement she was apparently going on well, but at night the first bad symptoms appeared, though unheeded at the time, in her not having the sleep which she required...'. Then there was some improvement, and on Wednesday 16th Sir John felt confident enough to leave the house to have dinner with the Tatton Egertons, who were relations of Mrs Milner's. About this occasion, Sir John wrote 'I sat next to Mrs Dugdale during dinner, and discussed with her the perfections of my darling Augusta's character – a favourite topic with her as well as with me. But though I reported favourably of her progress to our friends, I was out of spirits, and throughout the evening could not overcome a feeling of dejection. When I returned, the feverish symptoms were again strong, and the night was not satisfactory…'.

On the following day the illness took a more alarming turn, and Sir John suggested that it might be a case of puerperal fever. Her physician, Dr Laycock, denied that this was so, but was obliged to admit that anxiety was justified. On Friday 18th Sir John wrote: 'This was the last day on which I was permitted to enjoy any portion of that intense happiness for which I was indebted to the affection of my beloved Augusta… When Dr Laycock came at breakfast time he found her much better. He laughed at our alarm about puerperal fever; and throughout the morning her symptoms had so much subsided that I fondly persuaded myself that her illness was at an end…'.

Sir John continued 'when I was with her in the afternoon before I went out, she greeted me with some of her usual little cheerful jokes, and afterwards, in her accustomed affectionate manner, called me to the bedside that she might kiss me… I dined at the House, and did not return home till between 9 and 10 p.m. During this interval I reported to my friends the decided improvement at home; and during this interval, when my mind was full of thankfulness and joyful hope, that fatal change took place which crushed such hopes for ever…'. During that night Augusta began to say that she thought she might not recover and that she did not want to die unprepared. Sunday was Sir John's birthday, and he wrote 'I thank God that He enabled me to bear the accumulated misery and misfortune – beyond the ordinary extent of human suffering – which it was His will, for His own inscrutable purposes, before the close of this memorable day to inflict upon me…' Augusta's sister Caroline and Johnny arrived, and Sir John went to evening service at St Michael's, Chester Square.

On his return from church, it was discovered that Augusta's arm and shoulder were greatly swollen. Dr Laycock diagnosed erysipelas, and thought the illness had become scarlet fever, which Augusta's maid Barratt was thought to have. Laycock also attended the Queen, and had promised not to come into contact with any infectious diseases. He advised his assistant Mr Sampson and Johnny to leave the house, and Sir John wrote:

> Never before did I so intensely feel how utterly dependent we are on Divine support and comfort, where each medical man had deserted their charge in a time of extreme need, and I could not feel confident who might be found faithful in such danger, my only resource and consolation was deep and earnest prayer… When I returned from Johnny's room I found Dr Laycock fainting away. The fit was no doubt caused by fatigue and conflicting feelings. When he recovered he so far arranged for the morrow as to determine that he should write in the morning to Dr Watson to take his place, and he and Mr Sampson then both left us to carry out their instructions during the weary night as best we could. I again sat up through-

> out the night. Lady Sarah, exhausted by long watching and her unremitting care, had fortunately obtained several hours sleep during the time of which I have been writing, but when, at an early hour, she returned to the sick room, I had to inform her of all that had occurred during her absence.

It was soon realised that the diagnosis of scarlet fever was incorrect, and Mr Sampson was able to resume his attendance, but by Tuesday evening it was clear that Augusta was sinking. On Wednesday she was very restless, and morphine was proposed, but Sir John felt that by giving his consent 'he might be promoting that very fate of being taken in her sleep, of which she had more than once expressed a dread'. He eventually agreed to this treatment and, as a result, the restlessness was cured. She gladly agreed that her brother George and Johnny should be godfathers. After giving her husband her blessing, she remarked 'what a happy hour is this to pass through'. By this time her parents, other members of the family, and Johnny were present, and she bade farewell to her monthly nurse and her maids. She lingered for some time, but died on the afternoon of Wednesday 23rd February, 'strong in Christian faith, and supported by that deep and trustful piety which had marked her life'.

This account of Augusta's last days is based on an account her husband wrote dated April 1848, running to twenty four pages, of which at least twelve copies were produced. Unfortunately none of those seem to exist now, but it was available to Richard and Humphrey Pakington when they wrote 'The Pakingtons of Westwood'. The cause of Augusta's death must remain a little uncertain, but it was most likely caused by septicaemia, which, in those pre-antibiotic days, was impossible to control once it took a hold. Augusta's remains were taken back to Westwood, and the well-attended funeral took place at Hampton Lovett on 3rd March, and an obelisk to her memory was erected in the graveyard, which still stands.

The baby boy was baptised Herbert Perrott Murray Pakington. From a letter from Augusta's sister Caroline Mordaunt we know that the baby was taken into the Murray family at Danbury to be looked after. Caroline wrote 'I have just been seeing him in his bath, which he seems to enjoy greatly. It was the first time I had seen him undressed, and I was more struck than ever with his beautiful limbs and well formed chest…'.

Immediately after Augusta's confinement Sir John had continued his parliamentary duties. On 16th and 17th February he chaired a committee looking into allegations of bribery at the Great Marlow election, and again on the 16th he spoke against the Roman Catholic Relief Bill, similar to the one that had been introduced two years before. This repealed certain old and obsolete anti-Catholic legislation, and also liberalised some of the restrictions, for example, on Catholic monasteries, that still existed. Nothing was more guaranteed to excite some of the more Conservative members of parliament than measures that seemed to undermine the status of England as a Protestant nation, or introduce any suggestion that Catholics might owe as much or more allegiance to the Pope as to the British monarch. Several speakers that day opposed the bill going into committee. Sir John, while sounding more moderate than some other speakers, nevertheless also opposed it. He said he was all in favour of relieving 'his Roman Catholic fellow-subjects from every disability which could possibly hurt them, and to extend to them every concession consistent with a fair and just support of Protestantism'. He saw no objection to repealing old and outdated legislation, but he was not in favour of removing the 'securities' introduced in the 1829 Catholic Emancipation Act, for example insisting that Catholic monks should register their names.

After returning to Worcester for the funeral, Sir John took leave from business. He was absent from the adjourned Epiphany quarter sessions just before the funeral, and was absent again from the Easter sessions held on 3rd April. He was present at the re-opening of the new Wellesbourne church on 13th April, so we may presume that baby Herbert ('Herby') had been transferred to Walton from Danbury and that Sir John was staying there with his widowed sister-in-law Caroline.

Sir John resumed his attendance on the select committee on sugar and coffee planting on 22nd May, and on the same day he was appointed to join yet another committee investigating a challenged election, this time in Stamford, where it was alleged that the Marquis of Exeter, in nearby Burghley House, had interfered. He was first recorded in the House on 7th June when he voted on the Game Certificates for Killing Hares Bill. On Friday 16th June a debate was held on a matter arising from the Select Committee on Sugar and Coffee, which had just published its eighth and final report. This concerned the duties on sugar imported from the tropics on the other side of the Atlantic. Slavery had been abolished by the Emancipation Act of 1833, but many other sugar producing countries such as Cuba and Brazil still had slavery, and plantations in the British West Indian colonies had experienced depression in recent years. In 1846, in order to free-up trade and provide the British worker with cheaper food, duties had been reduced on sugar both from British colonies and other countries which still had slavery. Now, for the government, Earl Grey proposed that loans should be offered to the British colonies to help finance the introduction of new labour, the shortage of which was one of the problems, and he proposed a new somewhat increased protectionist duty with a series of reductions that would equalise them all at a new lower level of ten shillings a hundredweight in 1854, thus offering no further protection for British colonial sugar after that year.

Sir John was next to speak after Earl Grey had sat down, and said that, while he agreed with the government that there was to be no going back on the Emancipation Act, he could not agree with the lowering of duties on slave sugar. This would surely have the effect of encouraging slavery there and making life even harder for British plantation owners. The introduction of cheap sugar for the British consumer was all very well, but priority should be given to encouraging British plantation owners, and discouraging those that used slaves. In 1833 it had been clearly understood that in return for the abolition of slavery the West Indian colonists would be offered permanent protection against slave grown sugar.

When the debate continued on the following Monday Sir John put down a resolution saying that the remedies proposed by the government would neither effect the relief the growers needed, nor check the slave trade. The debate on Sir John's motion continued over five nights, and he took a prominent part, quoting figures for the export of machinery and the import of sugar which he alleged illustrated the decline of British colonial sugar production and the increase of that in slave states. The debate did not conclude until 29th June, when in the division his motion was defeated by a small majority.

The well known liberal John Bright then moved an amendment that the government's proposals were not needed at all and that the duties imposed in 1846 should stand unaltered, thus giving cheaper sugar to the mass of British people who, he said, had hardly been mentioned in the debate. He quoted Sir John's figures but claimed that he had drawn the wrong conclusions from them and that the act of 1846 had not led, as Sir John had alleged, to a large increase in the importation of slaves from Africa. But this more radical proposal was heavily defeated. Despite the defeat of his general motion Sir John did not give up, and on 3rd July made a more specific proposition: that the duty on British sugar should be immediately reduced to ten shillings per hundredweight instead of the thirteen shillings under the government proposals, and that on slave sugar should be increased to twenty shillings – the ten shilling differential would be the same as that introduced by Peel's government in 1845, before it was lowered by the present government in 1846. There followed another lengthy debate, in which the chancellor of the exchequer disputed many of the propositions made by Sir John in his speech, and said the government were not prepared to give the interests of the West Indies proprietors priority over those of the vast mass of the British population, especially as it was generally admitted that many of the British sugar plantations were inefficiently run. In the division Sir John's motion was defeated by 231 votes to 169.

The debate continued over several more nights until 10th July, nearly four weeks after it had started, when the government finally got their way.

Once this marathon debate was over, Sir John does not seem to have attended the House of Commons again that year, even though the session lasted until 5th September. Perhaps, having lost his battle over the sugar duties, he decided to make a clean break from English affairs and take a foreign tour. September 5th was also the first day of the Worcester Music Festival, of which it will be recalled that Sir John was a steward. It had been heavily advertised locally, and was, it was claimed, to include the biggest and best band and chorus ever, totalling 350. The choir had been selected from those of Worcester, Birmingham and Gloucester, and would include 100 professional singers from London. A long list of celebrated soloists would perform, although an attempt to engage Jenny Lind had failed. The Festival would open with the usual service with a sermon by the Dean, Dr Peel, and a performance of Handel's Dettingham Te Deum. Wednesday would feature music by Purcell; Mendelssohn's Elijah would be performed on Thursday; and on the last day, as usual, Messiah would be performed. There would be evening concerts on the first three days, and on Friday would be held the Grand Ball, so it seems that the earlier intention of the committee to disassociate the ball from the Festival had been forgotten.

Although Berrows lists those attending some of the functions, Sir John's name is not included, although Johnny's name does feature, so it is possible that Sir John thought it inappropriate to attend these festivities. But he was in Worcester the following month for the quarter sessions which began on 16th October, and chaired a bench of over forty mag-

*The advertisement for the 1848 Festival as it appeared in Berrows Worcester Journal.*

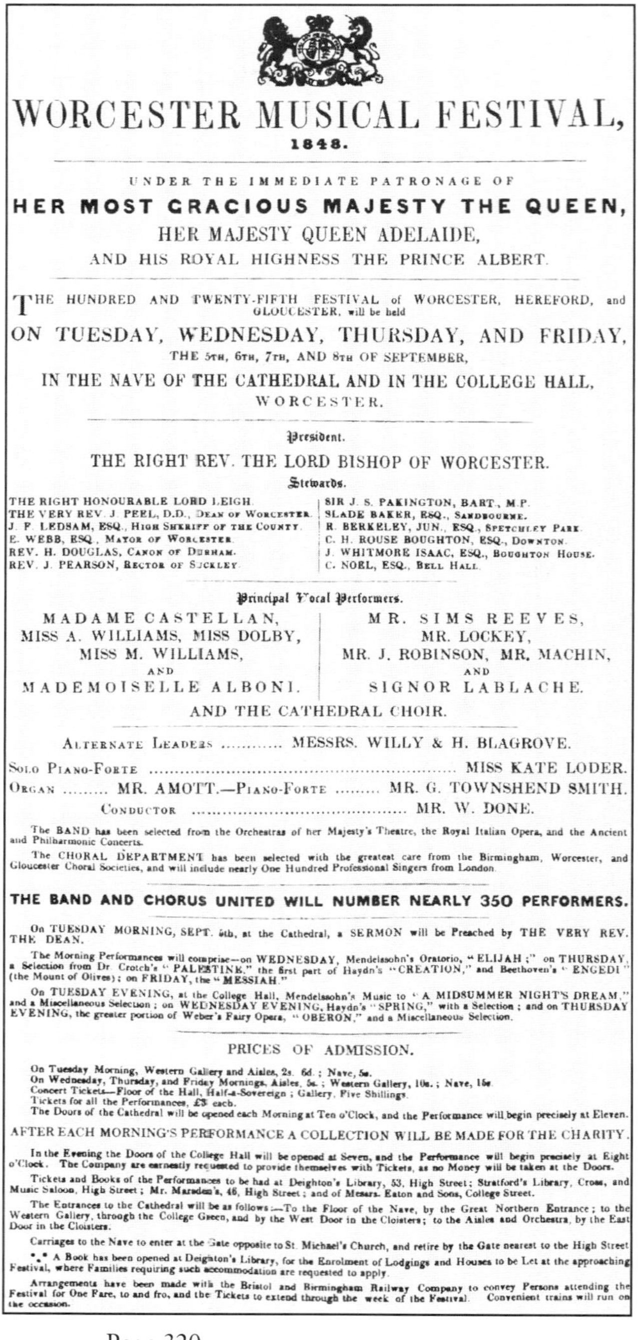

WORCESTER MUSICAL FESTIVAL,
1848.

UNDER THE IMMEDIATE PATRONAGE OF
**HER MOST GRACIOUS MAJESTY THE QUEEN,**
HER MAJESTY QUEEN ADELAIDE,
AND HIS ROYAL HIGHNESS THE PRINCE ALBERT.

THE HUNDRED AND TWENTY-FIFTH FESTIVAL of WORCESTER, HEREFORD, and GLOUCESTER, will be held
ON TUESDAY, WEDNESDAY, THURSDAY, AND FRIDAY,
THE 5TH, 6TH, 7TH, AND 8TH OF SEPTEMBER,
IN THE NAVE OF THE CATHEDRAL AND IN THE COLLEGE HALL,
WORCESTER.

President.
THE RIGHT REV. THE LORD BISHOP OF WORCESTER.

Stewards.

| | |
|---|---|
| THE RIGHT HONOURABLE LORD LEIGH. | SIR J. S. PAKINGTON, BART., M.P. |
| THE VERY REV. J. PEEL, D.D., DEAN OF WORCESTER. | SLADE BAKER, ESQ., SANDBOURNE. |
| J. F. LEDSAM, ESQ., HIGH SHERIFF OF THE COUNTY. | R. BERKELEY, JUN., ESQ., SPETCHLEY PARK. |
| E. WEBB, ESQ., MAYOR OF WORCESTER. | C. H. ROUSE BOUGHTON, ESQ., DOWNTON. |
| REV. H. DOUGLAS, CANON OF DURHAM. | J. WHITMORE ISAAC, ESQ., BOUGHTON HOUSE. |
| REV. J. PEARSON, RECTOR OF SUCKLEY. | C. NOEL, ESQ., BELL HALL. |

Principal Vocal Performers.

| | |
|---|---|
| MADAME CASTELLAN, | MR. SIMS REEVES, |
| MISS A. WILLIAMS, MISS DOLBY, | MR. LOCKEY, |
| MISS M. WILLIAMS, | MR. J. ROBINSON, MR. MACHIN, |
| AND | AND |
| MADEMOISELLE ALBONI. | SIGNOR LABLACHE. |

AND THE CATHEDRAL CHOIR.

ALTERNATE LEADERS ........... MESSRS. WILLY & H. BLAGROVE.
SOLO PIANO-FORTE ........................................................ MISS KATE LODER.
ORGAN ......... MR. AMOTT.—PIANO-FORTE ......... MR. G. TOWNSHEND SMITH.
CONDUCTOR ............................................ MR. W. DONE.

The BAND has been selected from the Orchestras of her Majesty's Theatre, the Royal Italian Opera, and the Ancient and Philharmonic Concerts.

The CHORAL DEPARTMENT has been selected with the greatest care from the Birmingham, Worcester, and Gloucester Choral Societies, and will include nearly One Hundred Professional Singers from London.

**THE BAND AND CHORUS UNITED WILL NUMBER NEARLY 350 PERFORMERS.**

On TUESDAY MORNING, SEPT. 5th, at the Cathedral, a SERMON will be Preached by THE VERY REV. THE DEAN.

The Morning Performances will comprise—on WEDNESDAY, Mendelssohn's Oratorio, "ELIJAH;" on THURSDAY, a Selection from Dr. Crotch's "PALESTINE," the first part of Haydn's "CREATION," and Beethoven's "ENGEDI" (the Mount of Olives); on FRIDAY, the "MESSIAH."

On TUESDAY EVENING, at the College Hall, Mendelssohn's Music to "A MIDSUMMER NIGHT'S DREAM," and a Miscellaneous Selection; on WEDNESDAY EVENING, Haydn's "SPRING," with a Selection; and on THURSDAY EVENING, the greater portion of Weber's Fairy Opera, "OBERON," and a Miscellaneous Selection.

PRICES OF ADMISSION.

On Tuesday Morning, Western Gallery and Aisles, 2s. 6d.; Nave, 5s.
On Wednesday, Thursday, and Friday Mornings, Aisles, 5s.; Western Gallery, 10s.; Nave, 15s.
Concert Tickets—Floor of the Hall, Half-a-Sovereign; Gallery, Five Shillings.
Tickets for all the Performances, £3 each.
The Doors of the Cathedral will be opened each Morning at Ten o'Clock, and the Performance will begin precisely at Eleven.

AFTER EACH MORNING'S PERFORMANCE A COLLECTION WILL BE MADE FOR THE CHARITY.

In the Evening the Doors of the College Hall will be opened at Seven, and the Performance will begin precisely at Eight o'Clock. The Company are earnestly requested to provide themselves with Tickets, as no Money will be taken at the Doors.

Tickets and Books of the Performances to be had at Deighton's Library, 53, High Street; Stratford's Library, Cross, and Music Saloon, High Street; Mr. Marsden's, 46, High Street; and of Messrs. Eaton and Sons, College Street.

The Entrances to the Cathedral will be as follows:—To the Floor of the Nave, by the Great Northern Entrance; to the Western Gallery, through the College Green, and by the West Door in the Cloisters; to the Aisles and Orchestra, by the East Door in the Cloisters.

Carriages to the Nave to enter at the Gate opposite to St. Michael's Church, and retire by the Gate nearest to the High Street.

*.* A Book has been opened at Deighton's Library, for the Enrolment of Lodgings and Houses to be Let at the approaching Festival, where Families requiring such accommodation are requested to apply.

Arrangements have been made with the Bristol and Birmingham Railway Company to convey Persons attending the Festival for One Fare, to and fro, and the Tickets to extend through the week of the Festival. Convenient trains will run on the occasion.

istrates. As was traditional, he addressed the grand jury on various subjects, and explained at some length the various acts of parliament passed that year that would impact on the criminal justice system. One wonders what all that had to do with their duties in examining the charges against the prisoners. On Friday of the same week he presided over another meeting of the Severn Commissioners. As on previous occasions the meeting was strongly divided. Some wanted to seek parliamentary powers to build a weir and locks somewhere south of Diglis in order to achieve the originally intended depth of six feet throughout; others opposed any further expenditure and increase in tolls. Sir John was known to favour the proposed new works, and the meeting got off to a controversial start when an alternative chairman, who was against the proposals, was proposed, but on a vote Sir John was elected by 13 votes to 11.

A bill for the new lock and weir had been submitted to parliament in the last session, but had met opposition and had not succeeded. Sir John said he thought that as matters were presently arranged in parliament, the bill would probably succeed next time. The opponents of the scheme had commissioned a report from a Mr Cockburn Curtis which predicted all sorts of dire consequences if the new weir was built, but the project engineer William Cubitt and another engineer Mr Randall were present to give opinions backed by more experience and knowledge than the young Mr Curtis. Berrows commented that his report 'was not worth the paper it was written on'. To begin with there was a lot of wrangling over the precise form of the resolution to be put to the meeting, during which it was clear that there was a wide divergence of opinion. As at the previous meeting the proposed increase in tolls was the focus of many objections; some alleged that the present shallower draught was perfectly adequate for most of the small boats using the river, so what was the purpose of deepening it? Eventually a vote was taken on the proposition that a new application should be made to parliament for the necessary powers, and when the votes were counted it was found that 13 commissioners had supported the resolution, and 13 opposed it. By the original act of parliament the chairman had the casting vote, and Sir John used it to support the proposal. Then there was a similar result when a proposition was put to limit the powers of the proposed new committee; again the commissioners divided equally, and the chairman used his vote to negative the proposal.

Berrows reported that the meeting lasted over five hours, and eventually a committee of sixteen to include Sir John was appointed to arrange the necessary steps for a bill to be prepared. 'At the close of the meeting many of the honourable commissioners appeared to be completely exhausted', Berrows reported.

The only other recorded appearance of Sir John at a public meeting in 1848 was on December 11th, when a special meeting of the Worcester guardians was held to discuss proposals for moving away from parish rating, under which each parish was rated according to its actual expenditure on poor relief, to union or even national rating, and also the possibility of establishing district industrial schools. As these topics concerned all unions, representatives from other Worcestershire unions had been invited, and Sir John was there representing Droitwich. The discussion about rating concluded with the meeting passing a resolution that national rating would be much preferable to the present system, as not only would it mean that richer parishes would contribute a fairer share of the poor rates, but would also do away with the system of settlement, which currently meant that considerable time and money was spent disputing the correct settlement of a pauper, then removing him or her there. The whole question of settlement would become irrelevant under national rating.

Sir John was not recorded as contributing to that part of the discussion, but showed great interest when the question of district schools came up. In 1844 an act had been passed allowing the formation of 'district schools' for workhouse children from several local unions, which would give them some manual training to further their prospects of obtaining employment. This act had proved a dead letter for various reasons, but now the Poor Law Board were campaigning to establish district schools that would train boys in agricultural work. The speaker was Jelinger Symons, the regional workhouse schools inspector and a well-known advocate of these proposed 'model farms'. He said that at present workhouse education consisted of teaching reading, writing, arithmetic and religion, which the guardians were obliged to provide by law. That was fine as far as it went, but did it prepare children for employment? In the case of the boys, it did not:

> The general rule in workhouses is to bring up the boys more like girls than boys – in physical idleness. (Hear, hear.) There was no development of muscular energy, strength or activity… Under the present system they were literally bringing up children in workhouses for future pauperism. They were turned out so flaccid in limb and inert in mind, that even when they did get employment in after life they frequently returned to the unions, and perpetuated a race of paupers'.

This was a time when many people believed that 'hereditary pauperism' was tending to perpetuate pauperism. Children who had only known the security offered by the workhouse tended to revert to it in later life. Furthermore, they were under the influence of their parents in the workhouse – often they were the 'worst sort of people', and the children would tend to absorb the culture of dependency from them.

Symons then described in detail the proposals for agricultural schools based on small farms specially bought and equipped for the purpose. Not only would the boys be instructed in the rudiments of agricultural work, but would be kept apart from the bad influence of their parents and other workhouse inmates. A farm of fifty acres would be needed for a school of forty boys, and the land would be worked using spade cultivation and liquid manure. Milking cows and raising pigs would be the main activity. He urged the guardians to visit the school at Quatt in Shropshire, which was operating very successfully on these principals. Symons then went into some details of the economics, and his figures showed that such a school would need a subsidy of about £2,250 per year.

Sir John made a short contribution, and seems to have been somewhat sceptical about the proposals. He said he had a great interest in education and the administration of the Poor Law, and had already considered the proposal for a district school. The question of expense was the main problem. He doubted that a farmhouse could be found large enough to hold the forty boys and the staff, in which case one would have to be built, which would cost a great deal. And with great respect to Mr Symons, he wondered whether his estimates of expense were accurate. But there was a bigger question:

> How far were they justified in giving to pauper children that education which the children of independent labourers were unable to obtain?... The independent labourer would feel that if he wanted to place his son in such a position that by his superior education would fit him for getting on in the world, the best means to effect that object would be to become a pauper, and so to give his offspring the benefit of this excellent education; thus putting a premium upon poverty.

But he would welcome the views of other Boards, and if they disagreed then he would not want the Droitwich Guardians to stand alone.

Lord Lyttelton, chairman of the Bromsgrove guardians, said in answer to Sir John's latter comment that that question had been long ago settled by the legislature, insofar as providing a basic education for pauper children was compulsory. Mr Hudson, representing the Pershore guardians, thought that, rather than establish a special school, it might be easier and cheaper for the guardians to pay a premium to farmers to take the boys of twelve or thirteen, and to subsidise their maintenance for the first year; thereafter the boys would be able to earn their own keep. Mr Symons said that doubters should go and see the Quatt school, which was working very well. As to Sir John's suggestion that parents would actually pauperise themselves to provide an education for their children, he doubted whether this had ever actually happened. As the meeting broke up, Lord Lyttelton seemed interested, but others wanted to take a more detailed look at Symons' figures before committing themselves any further.

Although Symons' ideas were initially taken up by the Droitwich guardians, the project, as was described in an earlier chapter, eventually came to nought.

Back in London in the new year 1849, Sir John was present at the opening of parliament on 1st February, when he voted with the great majority against an Irish amendment objecting to a passage on Ireland in the Queen's speech. Sir John had planned a project for the session – it was to introduce a bill against bribery at elections. He had been planning it since at least the previous December, when he consulted Lord Brougham about it, and on 13th February rose to seek leave to bring in his bill. "The importance of this bill, which I have prepared with some degree of care," he said, "will be generally admitted. I have learned since I entered the House that the gross and notorious extent of bribery and corruption at the last two general elections is so generally acknowledged, that there is not likely to be any opposition to my motion to bring in the bill". He therefore reserved detailed comment until the second reading.

Inevitably there was some opposition when the bill was brought before the House for its second reading on 21st February. Sir John opened the debate by referring to the 'notorious corruption that had taken place at the elections of 1841 and 1847, which had been evidenced by the large number of petitions that had been brought before the House'. He continued with a comprehensive review of present legislation, the most recent of which only dated from 1842. Although the penalties were severe, they depended on petitions being got up for parliament's attention, and there were plenty of reasons why people would not want to go to the trouble, expense and the possibility of odium being heaped on all parties. Even when petitions were presented, they were often withdrawn at the last moment when the parties involved came to an agreement. An earlier act of George II had made it possible to administer an oath to electors that they had not been bribed. But this had proved ineffectual, even impractical, and in any case should not it be the tempter rather than the tempted who were punished? He also made reference to a bill then in the House of Lords which provided for a commission to go to places whence petitions had emanated; but this was still open to the objection that a petition would have to be got up first.

To strengthen his case for change he referred to two boroughs, which for obvious reasons he would not name, but he assured the House on his honour that the facts he would give them were true. In borough 'A', nearly all the electors except the banker, the clergymen, some lawyers, and a few respectable tradesmen, were susceptible to corruption, and had openly asked the candidates in advance what terms they were offering. The usual bribe was £4 or £5, and the voters were told to go to a certain place after the election to receive their money. Six hundred and fifty out of the 700 voters, Sir John alleged, had received a bribe. In 1841 £7,000, and in 1847 £8,000, had been spent on election expenses in that place. In borough 'B' the rate of bribe was even higher.

> The sums given ranged at £10, £12, and £15, as the usual price per head in the earlier portion of the election. But later in the day, the prices rose to £50; and before the close of the day, one or two voters received £100 for their votes. And to show the contaminating and demoralising influence of this system of corruption, where it obtained so extensively, I am sorry to add, that in this case master tradesmen and professional gentlemen were not above taking prices for their votes. In the aggregate a sum of no less than £13,000 was spent at that place in the direct purchase of

> votes... Was that vile system of bribery to be allowed to continue unchecked and uncontrolled? In not one of those cases which I have detailed to the House, has a petition been presented, or the matter brought before the House. How could it? The losing candidate dare not; he would be himself involved in the punishment he sought to draw upon others. The electors could not petition, because they had a common interest in continuing the corruption.

Parliament had decided on mass disenfranchisement as a punishment when corruption was proved, but this was punishing the innocent for the sins of a few, and did not act as a deterrent. In Great Yarmouth one thousand electors had been disenfranchised when sixteen were proved to have been guilty; yet not long before the nearby borough of Sudbury had been disenfranchised. Again, it was the voters rather than the candidates who were punished. His first and foremost proposal was that all MPs, on first taking their seat, should swear an oath that they had not, as far as their knowledge went, indulged in any corrupt practises. He also proposed that if two electors suspected corrupt practices, then they could require the candidate to take a similar oath upon the hustings. By making corruption a matter of honour, Sir John thought that no member would risk the disapprobation that would ensue if an MP was shown to have sworn a false oath.

His second proposal was to make all MPs shown to have been guilty of corrupt practices ineligible for life to stand for parliament again. He went on to say that he knew there would be objections to some aspects of his bill. Some might say that large constituencies or an extension of the franchise would be the answer. But he quoted examples of large constituencies where bribery had still taken place, and although he was not against changes like these, it was not the answer to bribery.

In the debate that followed, all speakers said they agreed with the aim of the bill, to stop bribery, but what else could they say? Most said that detail would have to be gone into in committee, but a number of speakers thought more radical alterations to the bill would be needed; and many had their own ideas of how to stop the evil. One objection was that men with tender consciences might hesitate to take the proposed oath, even if they thought themselves innocent. Perhaps, unknown to them, their agent had offered a voter some small favour, or what if the MP thought he might be asked in future by a supporter to do him or a relation a favour? Another was that giving a select committee the power to permanently ban a man from the Commons was going too far. The committee might be subject to party influence, particularly at times when party feelings ran high. It was therefore preferable to leave matters in the hands of the ordinary courts of the land.

The home secretary, Sir George Grey, spoke for the government, and said it was not good enough to say that changes could be made in committee; this process was intended to look into the detail of the bill, not the main principles. Those MPs who felt dubious about the principles should vote against the second reading, as he intended to do, and he suggested that the appointment of a select committee to look into the whole subject might be a preferable way forward.

But when it came to the division 110 voted for the second reading and 80 against. Most MPs were probably keen not to be seen voting against this measure, even if they were doubtful about its principles.

Sir John was also involved in the very next item on the order paper: public roads and turnpikes. Leave to introduce a bill was being sought, the object of which was to abolish the 1,150 turnpike trusts and take the maintenance of the roads away from parishes and make them the responsibility of the county, by a new board to be elected at quarter sessions, with local responsibility in the hands of the poor law unions. Sir John spoke in favour of the bill. In addition to the committee he had served on in 1837 he had been chairman of a committee appointed in 1841 to examine a bill on turnpike trusts, and had come to similar conclusions to those in the present bill.

On 5th April Sir John's Bribery Bill came back to the House after undergoing 'material changes' in committee. Sir John again made a speech in favour of his measure, saying that, although objections had been raised that it would not cover all species of bribery, he nevertheless thought that the great evil of thousands of pounds being spent on bribing electors should be tackled, even if imperfectly. But he found little support among the other speakers, who all paid tribute to his attempt to stamp out bribery, but mostly felt that the proposed declaration would be liable to trap those with tender consciences, but not put off those who had already indulged in illegal practices. In other words, it might make bribery worse rather than better. One campaigning member, Joseph Hume, said he had proposed a similar measure twenty two years ago, but experience had taught him that such solutions rarely worked. He had a very simple solution, which was to introduce the [secret] ballot. It had now been tried in the USA and in France and found to work perfectly well, and had got rid of all the 'riots, debauchery, bribery and corruption which disgraced our elections'. Hume, of course, was quite right, but ahead of his time; no-one else mentioned this, and it was to be twenty five years before the secret ballot was adopted.

In the debate the Whig leaders Sir George Grey and Lord John Russell both opposed the bill, as did Sir Robert Peel, after which Sir John said he realised that as the leaders of both parties had opposed the bill it stood little chance of success. But the House divided nonetheless, and only 54 MPs could be found to support his bill, while 146 voted against. This debate, however, mainly concerned the first part of the bill requiring MPs to make a declaration before taking their seat, and on a motion the next day for the bill to be considered in committee Sir John announced that there was still a feeling among 'some influential members of the House' that the rest of the Bill be proceeded with. At this point Col Charles Sibthorp, a well-known ultra-Tory, intervened to complain about the introduction of this subject late at night, when he had understood that the Bill was being withdrawn in its entirety. He continued,

"There is an old saying, 'catch a weasel asleep', and I will not be caught asleep again. I will trust to no one at all; I would say to the hon. gentlemen – be on your guard, for there was so much chicanery going on it is impossible to know what to believe. I shall in future watch the hon. baronet as a cat watches a mouse, and oppose him in every measure of a similar nature". Probably everyone smiled, but it was agreed to strike out the clauses dealing with the declaration, and continue with the rest of the bill in a later committee.

In passing, it is interesting to note that on 24th May Henry Berkeley sought leave to bring in a bill to use the secret ballot at elections. Although there was considerable support for the motion, when Grey, Russell and Peel all opposed it leave was denied by 136 votes to 85. Sir John was not present on that occasion, but Osman Ricardo, MP for Worcester, did support it. Berkeley was a son of the rather unconventional union between Frederick, 5th Earl Berkeley and a butcher's daughter Mary Cole, and presented a motion in favour of the ballot every year for over twenty years. In the end this became something of a joke, although MPs enjoyed his witty speeches.

The remainder of Sir John's Bribery Bill did have its third reading in the Commons on 13th July, but the Lords did not think much of its contents, and it failed to make any progress there, so it never passed into law.

Earlier in July had been the big event of Sir John's son Johnny's marriage with Diana Boyle. Mention was made earlier of the fact that her brother George Frederick Boyle, younger son of George Boyle 4th Earl of Glasgow, was a contemporary of John Slaney Pakington at Christ Church, and a fellow member of the Oxford Union. This is the only known connection between Sir John and the Boyles. The 4th Earl was born in 1765, and had three children by his first wife Augusta, who had died in 1822, and two by his second, Julia. He had died in 1843, and the eldest son of the first marriage, James, was now the 5th Earl, but although he had married in 1821 the marriage had been childless, leaving the George Frederick, born in 1825, as heir to the Earldom, which he was to inherit in 1869.

Sir John must have welcomed the union with Diana, who was descended from David Boyle, 1st Earl Glasgow (1666-1733), who had been a commissioner of the Union with England in 1707. The marriage took place on 4th July at St Paul's, Knightsbridge. This church, situated near Hyde Park Corner, had been consecrated in 1843, and was the first London church to champion the ideals of the Oxford Movement. George Frederick Boyle was a strong supporter of the tractarian or Oxford movement, and at this time was just starting to build the Cathedral of the Isles on his property on Great Cumbrae, an island in the Firth of Clyde. According to newspaper reports, over one hundred guests were present at the wedding breakfast, after which the newly married couple went to Westwood.

Mention has already been made of one of Worcester's most famous sons, Charles, after 1850 Sir Charles, Hastings (page 266). On 1st and 2nd August 1849 the annual conference of the Provincial Medical and Surgical Association was held in the Worcester Shire Hall. A grand dinner was part of the proceedings, and Dr Hastings presided, with the Mayor, High Sheriff, Lord Lyttelton, the Hon. William Coventry, Sir John Pakington, Osman Ricardo MP and other notables also on the high table. Among the usual toasts, Dr Hastings proposed 'the health of Sir John and the rest of the county magistracy'. He was particularly grateful for the use of the Shire Hall, and said that although Sir John may be best known for his public duties, 'he also had a particular claim upon the Association from the fact that he derived his origin from one of the greatest ornaments to surgery that ever lived'. This was William Russell, 'so well known for his distinguished ability, generosity and talents'. In his reply, Sir John paid tribute to Dr Hastings, the PMSA and their publications, and said how valuable were 'periodical meetings like the present, where the members of the Association from the most eminent down to the most humble individual of the profession might meet together as brethren, and talk over results of their past experience...'.

The following week the first of the late summer meetings of the Worcestershire Archery Society was held at The Nash, the home of Richard Temple, just south of Kempsey. For a change the weather was fine, and Sir John, his son and daughter-in-law joined over 100 of the county gentry for the archery, followed by dinner and dancing in the marquee.

The Music Festival not being in Worcester in 1849, Sir John turned his attention to the other great triennial music festival, that of Birmingham. Founded in 1768 to raise money for the general hospital, it was first held in the newly built town hall in 1834. It developed an association with Mendelssohn, whose Elijah was first performed there in 1846. Sir John was in Cowes on that occasion, but was a vice-president at the next festival in 1849, and was a regular attender. The programme followed a similar pattern to that of the Worcester Festival, with three morning concerts of choral music, and three miscellaneous evening concerts, with balls afterwards. As at Worcester, foreign sing-

*The Nash, the seat of Richard Temple. Supposed to date originally from 1600, the house was owned by the Temple family from 1738 to 1926. Many of the windows were replaced in the twentieth century.*

ers featured prominently, and the Messiah was performed every year, as was Elijah after 1846. A lesser known work by Mendelssohn, Athalia, was given its Birmingham première in 1849, as well as a piece by Prince Albert 'L'invocazione all Armonia', which The Times' critic thought 'highly creditable to the illustrious amateur'. The evening concerts started at 8.00 p.m., and as the audience demanded encore after encore, one did not finish till 12.30 a.m.

The following week on 10th September Sir John chaired the AGM of the Severn Commissioners. Their affairs were in a bad state. The income from tolls was below expectations, mainly due to the shallow draught of the river between Diglis and Gloucester. Mortgage payments were in arrears; and an attempt to seek new powers in parliament had been unsuccessful when a report from an Admiralty inspector had cast doubt on some of the proposals. Now they were waiting upon a survey of the whole river as far upstream as Diglis. The engineer's report stated that dredging had proved totally unsuccessful as no sooner had the river been dredged than the current deposited new material. The only good thing to report was that the improvement in the navigation of the river was recognised in the debate in the House of Commons as a matter of national importance. The meeting closed with the appointment of a committee, again to be chaired by Sir John, to advance the interests of the Commission in parliament. They would first

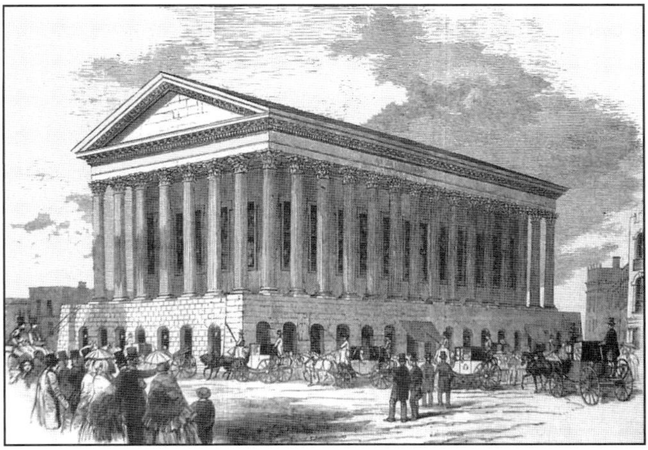

*Illustrations from the Illustrated London News showing arrivals at the Town Hall for the 1852 Birmingham Music Festival (left) and the interior during a concert (above).*

approach the Admiralty to see if the cost of the further improvements could be met by the nation, and if not to suggest an alternative approach.

The Royal family had been staying as usual at Balmoral, and at the end of September progressed back south in the royal train. After staying at Howick and Derby, the train passed through Birmingham on Saturday 29th September, whence it took the Birmingham and Gloucester line, which passed through Bromsgrove. Berrows reported:

> All the bridges on the line, and every available field or bank from which a view of the royal carriage could be obtained, were partially occupied by the occupants of the various localities, anxious to catch a glimpse of the royal party... Bromsgrove station was most tastefully decorated with a profusion of evergreens, dahlias and other choice flowers, which were liberally supplied from the gardens of Col Clive at Hewell Grange.

On the platforms the letters 'V.A.' and 'V.R.' were formed in flowers, and the carriage and engine sheds were also decorated. As the train was to stop briefly, Col Clive's party was stationed on the platform, and a large number of tickets had been issued to local people to occupy the other platforms. According to Berrows, some chose 'the roof of the building, the less fortunate being obliged to avail themselves of the goods' shedding and every other spot from which a view of the train could be obtained'. The Lord Lieutenant, Lord Lyttelton, was there of course, as was Lord Ward (now the occupant of Witley Court), who was Lt Col of the Worcestershire Yeomanry Cavalry. To complete the welcoming party two squadrons of cavalry were drawn up under the command of Col Clive, Capt. Clive (Col Clive's son), Capt. Pakington and the other commanders.

As soon as the royal train was sighted at the top of the incline the royal salute was fired from some ordnance stationed nearby, and as the train pulled up at the platform the national anthem was played by a band 'amid the cheers of the assembled multitude'. Lady Clive welcomed the Queen and presented her with a bouquet on a silver salver. Then the other notables dismounted and,

> uncovered, paid their respects to Her Majesty and Prince Albert. Her Majesty expressed herself highly pleased with her reception at Bromsgrove; after which the signal for departure was given, and presently the royal party were on their way for Gloucester amidst the roar of artillery and the hearty cheers of those assembled, too many of whom retired home deeply mortified at having been disappointed at not having had the opportunity of seeing the Queen's countenance, or those of her Royal Consort and children.

The royal party proceeded in like manner through Gloucester, Swindon, Reading and Basingstoke to Gosport, whence they were conveyed by the Royal Steam Yacht 'Fairy' to Cowes, and finally to Osborne House.

The autumn continued with Sir John attending the usual round of meetings, including the Worcestershire Natural History Society, founded by Charles Hastings, and the Worcestershire Agricultural Society annual meeting on 5th October. The latter was badly attended owing to the depressed state of agriculture, and Berrows' report started by lamenting the death of two secretaries of the Society within the last twelve months. Sir John spoke at the dinner, and also regretted the poor attendance, as he felt such meetings were valuable for the dissemination of knowledge. Although the rules of the Society prevented him from making political remarks, his reputation as a doubtful protectionist was reinforced when a letter appeared shortly afterwards in Berrows from an anonymous farmer, disagreeing with what he said were the views of Sir John and John Hodgetts-Foley (who had been in the chair). He said that the answer of those two gentlemen to the agricultural depression was to invest more capital (if they still had any) into the land by drainage and other means to increase production and thereby lower costs. But if that happened what would be the result? It would merely dump increased quantities of produce on the market, thereby lowering prices still further. And then 'the foreigner would turn his attention to the improvement of his land, and would then still have the advantage over us of paying no tithes, no poor rate, very moderate rents, taxes scarcely deserving the name, and labour fifty per cent cheaper'.

Quarter sessions took place as usual in October, then on 20th a meeting was held about the Great Exhibition that it was proposed should take place in 1851. This had been arranged by the Society of Arts, and all the 'nobility and gentry' of the county were invited. Sir John was there, of course, and listened to Mr Fuller of the Society of Arts explain that nothing was yet settled. Prince Albert, one of the movers behind the proposals, was asking for support from all over the country, and Fuller hoped the gentlemen present would form themselves into a committee to assist the grand objects of the exhibition. These were to form a great collection of the works of industry and arts 'for the purposes of exhibiting products of various countries and inducing a competition between them, and so encourage the progress of art and manufactures throughout the world'. The Prince was a very active and energetic president of the Society of Arts, which had already expended £100,000 of privately donated funds on rewarding works of merit. It was proposed that, firstly, raw materials from all over the world would be shown; then, with regard to manufacturing, deputations should be formed in manufacturing districts to ascertain the degree of interest there, and whether there was any fear of increased foreign competition. The general reaction so far had been "give the British manufacturer the opportunity, and he can produce the best article at the lowest possible price". Fine arts would form another category for the exhibition; His Royal Highness thought that sculpture had not been given enough importance, and also hoped that local committees such as that in Worcestershire would suggest other branches of art that might be given prominence.

As to location, after considering that Somerset House would not be big enough, it was proposed that a new building should be erected in Hyde Park. Finally, it had been decided that the exhibition would not be limited to British goods; and that by offering large money prizes, the best produce from all over the world would be shown. First prizes of £5,000 were to be offered in each section, with additional ones of £1,000, and he thought a prize fund of £50,000 would be sufficient. In total, it was thought that £100,000 would be sufficient to finance the whole project, and still leave something over for a repeat, which it was proposed every five years. This would be raised by national subscription.

The only cautionary note was introduced by Alderman Webb, who observed that the exhibition would expose our manufactures to comparison with those of France and Germany. In those countries, he said, design was taught in every school. But he was sorry to say that 'our manufacturers are mere copyists, and in that department they are very excellent, but they want originality. He hoped the exhibition would be a stimulus to fulfil a want which has been long and deeply felt in this country, the establishment of schools of design in every manufacturing town in the country'.

Various supporting resolutions were passed, the first being that 'it is the opinion of this meeting that exhibitions of skill and industry of nations must prove highly beneficial, and are calculated to develop the energy of individuals, without which no nation can become permanently prosperous; and that the proposed exhibition to take place in London in 1851, suggested by His Royal Highness Prince Albert, is eminently deserving of support of the City and County of Worcester'. This was proposed by the High Sheriff, John Dent, and seconded by Sir John Pakington. The question of how far the exhibition should be an international one had clearly been somewhat controversial, and the dreaded word 'protection' had been mentioned more than once. Sir John not only said how much these undertakings were valuable, citing the recent exhibition in Birmingham, but underlined the importance of the international nature of the project. Finally, 'in order to co-operate with His Royal Highness in so laudable an undertaking' a committee of noblemen and gentlemen was appointed, consisting initially of over thirty, including all the principal civil and religious dignitaries, the chairman of the quarter sessions, and leading land owners.

## Chapter 16
## The Years 1850 and 1851

Sir John may have been absent from Worcestershire in January 1850 as his presence is neither recorded at the Worcestershire Dispensary Ball nor the Droitwich Ball, although his son and daughter-in-law were there. He also missed a Protection Society meeting in Worcester organised on 19th and attended by over 2,000, which was perhaps fortunate, as his commitment to protection was regarded by some locally as rather unsure. Had he been there, he would have witnessed a great deal of disruption by free traders, which was reported disapprovingly and at length by Berrows. But undeniably farmers were finding things difficult – he himself had made a ten percent reduction in the rents to be charged to his tenants on Lady Day.

Parliament opened on 31st January, and Sir John was present. The main matter that he became involved with in the early part of the session was the County Rates and Expenditure Bill, which he disliked and eventually helped to kill. This was not the first time this matter had been brought before parliament, but no bill had found its way into law yet. Boroughs were now governed by elected councillors, who therefore controlled their expenditure, but county expenditure, and therefore the rates, were still governed by magistrates in quarter sessions. Some reforming MPs not unreasonably thought there should be more democracy, which was completely lacking in quarter sessions, except that they now had to be held in public. 'No taxation without representation' was a powerful rallying cry. On 13th February 1850 Thomas Milner Gibson, the reforming MP for Manchester, introduced a bill which proposed in future that county expenditure should be controlled by a county expenditure board, consisting of one member and one magistrate elected by each poor law union. This was perhaps rather a cumbersome arrangement, but hardly radical. Nevertheless it drew opposition from the start. The first debate was quite short, with MPs complaining that the bill had only been printed three days before. Sir John was one of those who spoke, and said that he did not oppose the bill outright; but we may be permitted to take that statement with a pinch of salt. He wanted time to go into the effects in his own county before deciding whether to support it.

The debate was adjourned till 13th March, when Sir John himself was first to speak. He proposed that the bill not be read a second time, but that a select committee be appointed to enquire into the whole subject first.

> It is my wish to approach the discussion of the bill in the fairest spirit. I admit that a great many petitions have been presented in favour of it; but what I feel is, that a bona fide inquiry into the subject is an essential preliminary in dealing with so difficult a matter. If it can be shown that the financial business of the counties, as conducted by English gentlemen, can be better managed by a board more popularly constituted, I should be most happy to give my consent to a change of this kind; but I am not prepared to assent to a bill which is most objectionable, not only in all its details, but, as I conceive, in its principle also.

So, having starting by saying that he was all in favour of sensible reform, he went on to list the objections he had to the principle of the measure. The bill, he said, had its origins in what was a local squabble in Lancashire, where there had been a dispute about the costs of the new lunatic asylum. The magistrates there were only doing their legal duty, so was it right they should be blamed? He then referred to Worcestershire, and quoted figures for the various heads of expenditure, pointing out that the magistrates had little or no control over most of these, their being required by act of parliament. A large item related to the police;

> but nothing could be more injudicious than to give control of the police to any varying and elected board. I have shown therefore, I trust, that as far as I have so far argued, that due economy is exercised by the existing machinery; that no grievances exist, and even if they did the bill, if passed, would not remedy them.

He then went on to point out that there were three Worcestershire parishes that

*Thomas Milner Gibson, 1806-84. Returned initially as a Tory in 1837, he later became an ardent free trader and ally of John Cobden, and joined the Whigs. He served as vice-president, and later president, of the Board of Trade under Russell before retiring from politics in 1868. Through a relationship with a servant, Susanna Bowles, he was an ancestor of the Mitford sisters.*

belonged to unions in other counties, which would make the elections unfair; but a more serious point was that in a certain union in Worcestershire there were four magistrates

> who from their abilities and habits ought not to be off any county board; they could not be well dispensed with, and it would be an injustice to deprive the county of their services; but under this Bill it would be impossible to choose more than one of them, and the others must be set aside, and magistrates elected from a different part of the county, who from habits and qualifications were not so fit to be members of the board.

In any case, he asked, is it right that in a county of 170 or more magistrates, only twelve of them should sit on the board, even though they are by far the largest rate-payers, along with twelve members elected from the boards of guardians, who are only small rate payers? He concluded 'the duties of the magistrates of England were never discharged with more care and economy than now: there is a finance committee in every county, and every transaction regarding the public expenditure is carried on under act of parliament in open court'. Thus spoke the chairman of the Worcestershire quarter sessions.

Various views were expressed in the debate, and the ex-home secretary, Sir James Graham, nominally a Conservative, poured scorn of some of Sir John's points. Yes, he said, it was a major reform, but many other reforms had passed in recent years. As to the point that magistrates were the largest proprietors and therefore had an incentive to keep down rates,

> why, on the very same ground they might entrust the taxation of the whole country to the House of Lords without any interference from the representatives of the people. The House of Lords consisted generally of the large landed proprietors of the country. They, therefore, it might be said, had an interest in keeping down taxation, yet it was found necessary to have the check and control of this elective assembly.

Sir James was in favour of giving the bill a second reading. Most other speakers, including Sir George Grey and Sir Robert Peel, were in favour of introducing some democracy into the management of county expenditure, and eventually Sir John agreed to withdraw his amendment to appoint a committee of enquiry before the bill proceeded further, and it was given a second reading.

There was an argument about the membership of the select committee, and Sir John pushed for more experienced men, including magistrates and lawyers. Sir John himself was, of course, a member, and the committee spent several weeks taking evidence. Its report was published on 20th June, and reads rather like a repeat of the speech Sir John made on 13th March. Sir John had attended most of its twenty five meetings, and, although the chairman was Thomas Gibson, Sir John put many of the resolutions to the committee which appeared in the final report. The committee was evidently split on many of its conclusions, but only three of the eleven members voted against most of them. The report came out completely against the bill, and started by stating 'that the financial affairs of the counties have been conducted by the courts of quarter sessions, generally, with proper attention to economy, with just regard to the public interests, and with all publicity required by law'. Secondly, it said that the 'dissatisfaction' (referring no doubt to Lancashire) has arisen from the adoption of the rural police, but that further experience of this will mitigate these feelings, and the building of gaols and lunatic asylums, which were in any case required by law. Thirdly, the committee felt that the number of petitions on the subject to parliament 'does not appear to have been such as to prove that any general desire prevails in the country for this measure'. Fourthly, as only one magistrate could be elected from every poor law union, the bill

> excluded a numerous body of gentlemen in every county in England from the transaction of financial business in which, as magistrates and proprietors, they have immediate and extensive interest and which they and their predecessors have conducted for a long period of time to the advantage and generally to the satisfaction of the public and to substitute for them a small and fluctuating body of men who would in many cases be less fitted for the discharge of such duties...
>
> ... in conclusion this committee cannot recommend the House to adopt a bill which they consider to be open to such grave objections.

So the bill was completely killed by the select committee, and chairmen of quarter sessions such as Sir John were given a clean bill of health. It was to be nearly forty years before elected county councils were created.

The other parliamentary campaign conducted by Sir John in 1850 was to extend his Juvenile Crime Act that had been passed in 1847. He felt this had been a success and wished to extend it to cover juveniles up to age 16 (rather than 14), and, more controversially, to any person committing a petty larceny in which, in the opinion of the magistrates, the articles stolen did not amount to more than one shilling in value. Sir John moved the second reading of his bill on 20th February, and said that apart from the raising of the age for summary conviction to sixteen, he felt the other change he proposed was important. In many cases now it was not thought worth committing someone for trial at quarter sessions for trivial offences, so the offenders got away scot-free. He pointed to the frequent offences committed in the Dudley area of coal stealing. He said a coal owner had told him that several tons of coal per week were stolen; but due to the delay, difficulty and expense of bringing a prosecution in a city 26 miles away, the culprits were often not prosecuted. Sir John then made reference to the costs of prosecution; he believed that these costs under his earlier act had usually not exceeded forty shillings. Cases at quarter sessions cost between five and eight pounds each, and in addition there would be a saving of costs in maintaining the prisoners awaiting trial.

In the short debate most MPs were sympathetic to the objects of the bill, and in particular the attorney general was favourably inclined. The bill was given its second reading, but when it started in committee on 20th March it met more opposition. The second part extending summary justice to crimes of larceny of items of less than one shilling in value was particularly contentious. Sir James Graham objected not only to this but the raising of the age of juveniles to 16. 'From the time of Edward III till now, the law made the age of fourteen the limit between the period during which a man was responsible for his actions, and that during which he was irresponsible. He was not prepared to alter a rule of law which was reasonable and had worked well'.

When the committee stage came up again on 18th April, the Bill met even more opposition from some noted reformers. The long debate started with Torrens McCullagh attempting to ditch the bill altogether, seconded by another reformer Sir George Strickland. Sir John replied that the time for a debate on the general principles of the bill had passed, as the House had approved these when it was sent into committee. When the House divided McCullagh's proposal was lost. However, the House had also on a previous occasion expressed the view that the Bill was really two: one to extend the age for summary justice from 14 to 16; and secondly to do the same for adults guilty of larceny of items up to one shilling in value. Sir John resisted this division, insisting that both parts were equally important, but after the home secretary had said it would be best to consider both parts separately this was agreed by a substantial majority.

So the House now considered the first part of the bill concerning juvenile offenders, and now for the first time in the debate the member for Sheffield, John Roebuck, spoke. Roebuck was another well-known radical, and immediately set about attacking magistrates in general, and Sir John in particular:

> The question which the Committee has to decide is whether it is advisable to give justices at petty sessions the power of flogging and imprisoning children of sixteen years of age summarily. The whole bill is confined to giving the magistrates the opportunity of enjoying this pleasure. Every step of the proceeding goes towards depriving the people of this country of trial by jury. By whom is this bill brought in? By a chairman of quarter sessions, one of a class for whom, abstractedly speaking I have great respect, but nothing beyond, and whom I am not disposed to indulge with any more power over the poor of this country. They first asked for, and got, jurisdiction up to fourteen years. They now asked for a further extension to sixteen years; and, in fact, by a sly artifice, they sought to extend it to persons of any age where the property stolen was under one shilling. This would, no doubt, be a very easy mode of dealing with poachers who stole pheasants' eggs, and such offenders. Let the committee understand in what way justice was administered to the poor of this country. The offender was brought into a back parlour in the squire's house by the constable of the parish. The squire had another squire to aid him, neither the one nor the other knowing the least of the law, but both having strong prejudices

> in the case. There was no bar; and, though a member of the profession, I will not hesitate to say that the presence of the bar on such occasions is a great safeguard for the freedom of the subject. There is not even a reporter of a newspaper present; and even if the county newspaper had a representative at the proceedings, it was not very likely that any account detrimental to the character of a patron would be published. The fact was, a trial under such circumstances was a denial of justice to the poor man. It would be a mockery and a shame, and I hope the people of this country will stand up against this attack on the palladium of their liberty, as trial by jury had been called. I wish to see the honest man, the attorney, the barrister, and, above all, the newspaper reporter watching these proceedings.

The next speaker, the Whig Henry Aglionby, took exception to some of the more extreme sentiments coming from John Roebuck: despite never having been a chairman of quarter sessions

> I will never admit that magistrates in petty sessions are guilty of the injustice which the hon. and learned member imputed to them; and I strongly protest against the proposition that they took any pleasure in flogging people; I cannot conceive, indeed, what pleasure there could be enjoyed by any man, on or off the bench, in flogging people, and my conviction is that flogging, when ordered, is only ordered in fulfilment of what was always felt to be, on the contrary, a most painful duty.

Roebuck was also out of date in contending that petty sessions took place in magistrates' back parlours, and the next speaker, Charles Packe, said that in his district of Leicestershire the press attended petty sessions as much as quarter sessions.

Sir John was understandably put out by the attack from Roebuck, who, he said:

> is so accustomed to indulge his sarcasm, and seems to think it so necessary that he should give point to his speeches by attacking somebody, and the more sneeringly and ill-natured the better, that I feel no surprise that that hon. and learned gentleman has selected me tonight as the object of his sneers. I am very happy to find, however, that the only ground on which he sneers at me is because I happen to be chairman of the quarter sessions. I can tell him that I feel the fact of my having enjoyed the confidence of my brother magistrates for a period of sixteen years is no matter of shame to me, and I am quite willing to submit to any sneer in which he chooses to indulge on that subject. When he indulges in sneers and sarcasms at my expense, I think, however, that I have some right to expect that the hon. and learned gentleman should be accurate in his facts; and when he alludes to the measure of 1847, to which I was a party, and complains that persons of wealth dealt with the poor in their back parlours, the hon. and learned member only showed his own utter ignorance. I think it would be better for his character and credit if he contrived to be somewhat better informed on the subjects upon which he speaks; for, if the hon. and learned member referred to the Act in question, he would find that it gave certain powers to justices of the peace in petty sessions assembled, at the usual place, and in open court.

The home secretary, Sir George Grey, attempted to calm things down by pointing out that magistrates already had powers to deal with many offences in petty sessions, and that 16 was recognised as the age of responsibility in many areas. The 1847 act had been in operation for over two years, and he had not had a single objection to its operation, so he would support the extension of it to persons aged up to 16, although, as the next speaker, pointed out "was it likely that a boy of fourteen would make a complaint to the secretary of state?".

The debate continued for some time, and other reformers including John Bright, MP for Manchester, and George Muntz, MP for Birmingham, rose to speak against the bill. It resolved into an argument about two issues: were magistrates as capable and unbiased as they maintained when administering summary justice, and was it right to give them the power to order a flogging for boys 16 years old as opposed to 14? Class came into the debate, of course, and some radical MPs pointed out that those who would be affected by this bill would always be of the lower classes. The administration of summary justice by magistrates, nearly all of whom belonged to the highest stratum of society, would cause resentment and dislike among the lower classes. As to flogging, some MPs felt there was a very great difference between a child of 14 and a boy of 16, and that the latter might feel degraded for life if he was flogged on the verge of manhood. Although it was true that magistrates in quarter sessions could order anyone to be flogged now, this was after counsel and a jury had adjudicated on the guilt of the accused. The jury had no say in the punishment; this was left to the presiding magistrate.

The question of flogging came to be the main issue of contention, and Sir Robert Peel probably influenced the debate when he spoke in measured tones at its conclusion. He said the extension of magistrates' powers to order a flogging

> would be at variance with the principle which of late years dictated a milder policy in their criminal code... I apprehend that there is a growing conviction that corporal punishment ought not to be inflicted except in cases of grave necessity; and although adults are subject to corporal punishment, yet, upon their conviction, the judges generally act on the principle of selecting some other punishment than that degrading one...

Finally the House divided on a proposal that magistrates would not be permitted to order a flogging for anyone over the age of 14, and this was carried by a majority of almost two to one. After the vote had been taken John Roebuck suggested that Sir John should withdraw his bill altogether now so much had been lost. However, Sir George Grey thought the extension of summary jurisdiction to persons up to 16 was a worthwhile measure, and Sir John refused to withdraw. It was in this form that it was eventually passed into law, except that a last minute addition, adopted at the third reading, required magistrates to read a form of words to offenders stating that they could opt for a trial by jury if they wished. The other part of the bill dealing with petty larceny was not proceeded with.

The only other occasion when Sir John is recorded as having made a substantial contribution to a debate was on the question of sugar duties. On 31st May there was a debate on a motion on the injustice of exposing the 'free-grown sugar grown in the British colonies to unrestricted competition with the sugar of foreign slave-trading countries'. Sir John had spoken on this subject before, and in this debate made a speech again attacking imported slave sugar into the country at a decreasing rate of duty. Anyone who bought such sugar was supporting the institution of slavery that we were committed to ending. It was true that our West Indies possessions had done rather better since the introduction of temporary protection by Sir Robert Peel, but appearances belied the fact that underneath there was great economic depression that was bound to get worse as the protection was removed. But the government opposed the motion, and the chancellor of the exchequer attacked some of Sir John's arguments as being inconsistent. At the end of the well-attended debate the government won, but only by 275 votes to 234.

In 1850 Sir John sat on a select committee appointed to examine prison discipline. It met thirty one times under the chairmanship of Edmund Denison, the Conservative MP for West Yorkshire, and included home secretary Sir George Grey. Sir John attended twenty two of its meetings, and clearly took a great interest in its proceedings, and its final report is based largely on motions introduced by him. Much of the proceedings concerned the separate system of imprisonment, in which, as we have seen, prisoners were kept strictly solitary, with no intercourse of any sort with other inmates. It was clear from the evidence given to the committee that the implementation of the system, and other aspects of prison discipline, varied much from gaol to gaol, and one of the committee's recommendations was the desirability of introducing more uniform standards throughout the country. For example, in some prisons men on solitary confinement were kept in the dark day and night, in others not. The committee recommended some light for sixteen hours a day.

Although there was some difference of opinion as to the detail, the committee strongly supported the principal of the separate system. Part of its report, published at the end of July, read:

> ...the entire separation, except during the hours of labour and religious worship and instruction, is absolutely necessary for preventing contamination, and for securing a proper system of prison discipline; and this committee is of opinion that, with this view, every prison ought to contain such a number of cells as would enable each prisoner to be kept separate, by day as well as by night, both before and after trial. ...this committee is of opinion that if conducted under proper regulations and control separate confinement is more efficient than any other system yet tried, both in deterring from crime and in promoting reformation.

In view of the misgivings he had earlier expressed about the separate system, it is surprising that Sir John did not try and qualify the report more than he did. But on a few issues, for example on whether strict separation should last for the first six or twelve months of a sentence, he took the more liberal view, although he was sometimes defeated, as he was on that issue.

Sir John now suffered another personal loss. On 30th April his sister Elizabeth died, just short of her 48th birthday. Her death certificate lists chronic hepatitis with its complication ascites as the cause. She left three children Mary (23), Annette Georgina (18) and Ferdinand Capel (16). In December 1853 Elizabeth's husband Ferdinand, now 54, married again. His new bride was Elizabeth Jane McRobert, and the couple lived some years in Boulogne. By her he had four more children, but we hear little more of the Hanbury Williams family in Sir John's later life. The only surviving correspondence concerning the family is from Mary, Hanbury Williams' eldest daughter. She had married a Lt Col James Davies of The Garth, Monmouthshire in 1849, by whom she had two children. She wrote in November 1854 that her sister Annette was in some sort of serious trouble, only a year after marrying Capt. Henry Gratton Bushe. When the letter was written, Annette was in Dawlish trying to get away to meet her husband in Dublin. But she was desperately short of money, with rent unpaid, and Mary wrote to her uncle Sir John to ask for advice, and Annette wrote asking him to come to see her urgently. What kind of disaster had befallen Annette is not known, but all was not well between Annette and her husband as in 1881 he was living on his own in rented premises, and very shortly after he died in 1888 Annette married again. She died in 1905 aged 73. As for Mary herself, she was said to be of a 'restless and discontented disposition', and had an affair with and ran off with a local bandmaster, a Mr McCarthy, in 1865, after which she was divorced.

Midsummer quarter sessions took place as usual on 1st July, and Sir John complained that only fifteen men had come for grand jury service. Those who did not answer the summons were fined £1 each, as Sir John had threatened on a previous occasion. Once the parliamentary session had finished he stayed in Worcestershire and

*Stanford Court, the seat of the Winningtons who had inherited it from the Salweys, from Nash. The house shown here is the one Pakington would have seen; it was burnt down in 1872 and rebuilt.*

attended the usual round of meetings. The Archery Society was still active, and on 5th September a contest was arranged between the Worcestershire and Herefordshire societies, which took place at Stanford Court, the seat of Sir Thomas Winnington. The Worcestershire gentlemen were paired with the Herefordshire ladies, and vice versa. John Slaney Pakington was paired with Miss Domvile, one of the daughters of Sir John's half sister Mary and her husband Rev. Domvile, rector of Pencombe, Herefordshire. They scored 36 hits which was rather below average. At the end Worcestershire had won by 1,110 hits to 791 – each archer shot 108 arrows. The Worcestershire ladies were dressed in their county uniform – a dark green bodice with white muslin skirt, with a white spreading chapeau with green ribbons. Sir John was present, although he seems to have only been a spectator. Most of Worcestershire and Herefordshire society were there.

A few days later there was a meeting of the Severn Commissioners in the Guildhall, chaired by Sir John. He only had bad news to report. The commissioners' financial position was serious, with a deficit last year of £2,637, and interest payments were in arrears. An approach to the admiralty for financial assistance towards the further works required below Diglis had failed. The engineer's report emphasised the contrast between the good navigation above Diglis, and the poor state below. The Admiralty were surveying the whole river. A committee including Sir John would investigate the further necessary works downstream. Some objected that the engineer's salary at £600 p.a. was too high; but the engineer countered that he had drawn up plans for parliament without charge, and also had to pay two assistants out of his salary.

The following day, 10th September, Sir John and his family attended the Music Festival at Gloucester. The next week he spoke at the annual meeting of the Worcestershire Agricultural Society. It had been an indifferent show, and the dinner at The Crown was overcrowded and the room hot. In his speech Sir John conceded that agriculture was depressed, but he still had confidence that the British farmer, using all his skill, capital and enterprise, would be able to emerge from the present difficulties stronger. On 10th October Sir John attended the laying of the foundation

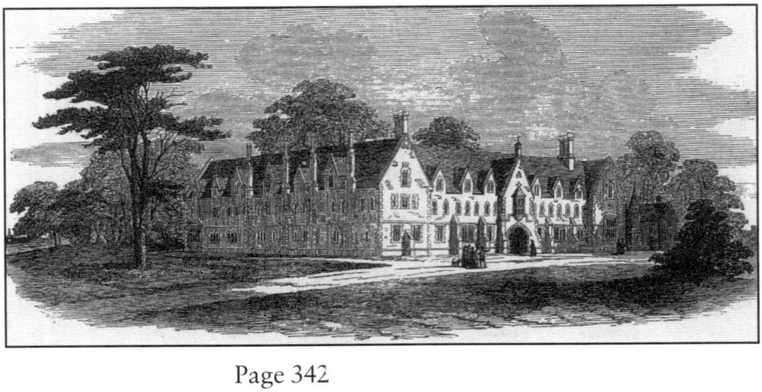

*The Worcestershire Diocesan Training School at Saltley, Birmingham. It was finally opened in 1852.*

stone of the Saltley Training School, first proposed in 1847, and Sir John took the place of Lord Lyttelton, whose sister had recently died. In his speech Sir John said:

> If prejudices still exist in any quarter on the great question of education; if there are some who think that the humbler classes of their fellow men can be better fitted for their duties on their station in life by being kept in ignorance of all that is requisite for them to know, if they think that the cup of life can be sweetened by depriving men of all intellectual resources which form the best solace under the afflictions and in the vicissitudes of human existence, I am glad to perceive that such prejudices and misconceptions are fast loosing ground before a better and more enlightened counsel.

Sir John regretted that shortage of funds had meant the building could not be built as first proposed; the clergy had given generously, but the laity had not, and he pointed out that Worcestershire and Warwickshire had been rated very poorly in criminality in a recent report; "the inhabitants of both counties should ponder and reflect on that statement".

Michaelmas sessions began on October 14th. Sir John's fellow magistrates had clubbed together to commission a portrait of him by Sir John Watson Gordon as a mark of their esteem, and would present it to him at a dinner the following week. Rev. Thomas Pearson was chairman and Thomas Gale Curtler the vice chairman of the testimonial committee. The portrait was inscribed:

> Sir John S Pakington bart MP
> To mark their sense of his eminent service for 16 years as chairman of the quarter sessions, and in proof of their personal respect this portrait was painted at the request and by general subscription of the magistrates of the county of Worcester.

*This portrait of Sir John Pakington for many years hung in the entrance of the county council headquarters, but has now been returned to a member of the family.*

Berrows considered the portrait 'a likeness but not a flattering likeness'. It was exhibited for a time at the Athenaeum in London.

A few days later Berrows reported that Sir John, his son and his daughter-in-law were leaving shortly for Rome, where they would be spending the winter. Sir John's diary for the following year, 1851, revealed that he was in Italy until he arrived back in London on 4th March, having spent 7½ days travelling from Naples after a 'rapid journey'. He wrote a separate account of his travels, but sadly this is lost. Sir John's first action on his return was to go and see little Herbert, just two years old, who had been left at Danbury in the Bishop's household. He 'had, thank God, the blessing & happiness of finding dear little Herby well'. After two nights at Danbury they all returned to London, where Sir John made his first appearance in the House of Commons that session, which had been adjourned the previous Monday after a political crisis. In February the Whig government under Lord John Russell had survived an important vote on a budget measure by only a small majority; on 20th February there was a debate on a motion to equalise the county and borough franchises, which would have greatly extended the county franchise. Russell had spoken at length against this, arguing that the constitution was delicately balanced between all the different franchises, and it would be unwise to upset this balance without very good reason. As an architect of the 1832 Reform Act Russell's attitude was perhaps understandable, but he did promise a new Reform Bill in 1852 if the present motion was withdrawn.

In a thin house the reformers unexpectedly won by a majority of almost two to one. Soon afterwards Russell announced he was to resign, because although this defeat may not have been too significant, he could see that the government were becoming vulnerable. The Tory opposition were still split. After Peel's death in 1851 from a riding accident the Peelites were now represented by Sir James Graham and Lord Aberdeen, and the protectionists by Lord Stanley. The Queen, faced with a somewhat difficult situation, decided to call on the leader of the next largest opposition group, Stanley, to form a government, but Stanley declined. Then the Queen had the idea of seeing if the Peelites would join Russell in a form of coalition, and Graham and Aberdeen spent time with Russell to see if there was enough common ground to form a government.

On most matters of major importance, including free trade and parliamentary reform, there was much common ground, but there was one issue that had only recently come to the fore that caused a problem. This was the fact that the Pope had, the year before, created twelve English Catholic bishops, and, understandably, they were to be named after the town or city where their cathedral was. This caused many staunch Protestants to be up in arms, as in some cases these duplicated the titles of existing Anglican bishops, for example in London. This matter raised again the whole question of the Catholic church, and whether its adherents owed more allegiance to Rome than to the British crown, and how far the crown alone had the right to appoint bishops. Russell's government had been against allowing these titles to be used, and had drafted an Ecclesiastical Titles Assumption Bill (henceforth the ETA Bill) to prevent it, but Graham and Aberdeen thought the measure unnecessary and an insult to British Catholics. So this bill was the insurmountable obstacle to forming a coalition, and the Queen was informed. Not sure what to do next she sent for the Duke of Wellington, then in his 80s and near the end of his life but still regarded as 'an elder statesman', and he advised her to send for Russell again and see if he could reform the previous ministry. This is what happened, and on 7th March parliament reassembled under the new/old ministry. Russell explained the alterations they were proposing to make in the ETA Bill, which had proved something of a legal minefield, and Sir John was in attendance.

The following day, Saturday, Sir John went by train to Walton to see Caroline Mordaunt, still alone after her husband's tragic death, and on Monday progressed to nearby Leamington, where Mrs Davies was staying.

Although there are many references to Augusta Davies, widow of Col Thomas Henry Davies of Elmley Park, in Sir John's earlier diaries before his second wife died in 1848, there are none in 1847 after Col Davies had died, and there are no diaries for 1848-1850. So it is uncertain how the relationship between the widow and the widower, both 52, was progressing. Now, it seems, he had determined to make her his third wife, and he stayed talking to her in Leamington and they went visiting together before he returned to London.

Augusta Davies was born Augusta Ann de Crespigny, the daughter of Thomas Champion de Crespigny and Augusta Charlotte Thellusson in 1799. Her mother was the granddaughter of Isaac de Thellusson from Switzerland, and her father's father was Philip Champion de Crespigny of Hintelsham Hall in Suffolk. Presumably his ancestors were foreign as well.

Back in London, Sir John was able to move back into his house in Eaton Square. It was at this time that he took the important decision to join Lord Stanley's adherents. Since the Tory party split in 1846, Stanley had been the acknowledged leader of the protectionist wing. He was more moderate than many and preferred to call the party 'Conservative' rather than 'Protectionist'. Since 1844 Stanley had been in the Lords, and since the fall of Peel and the early death of Lord Bentinck he had been forced to acknowledge the pre-eminence of Disraeli in the Commons in view of his debating skills, but they were never close. After the ministerial crisis of February Sir John would have felt that loyalties were hardening, and, recognising that Stanley was no extremist when it came to questions like free trade or Catholicism, Sir John found their views quite similar. He would also have recognised Stanley as a likely successor to Lord John Russell, should the government fall. He would have felt a government post was not too far from his grasp, and decided to nail his colours firmly to Stanley's mast. He must have written to Lord Stanley, as on 12th March he received 'long & interesting reply', which a few days later he showed to a Mr C and Admiral B in the House and had a 'long interview', but unfortunately we do not know who these people were. It is said that Stanley commented after declining to form a government in 1851 'it is a bungling fisherman who strikes at the first nibble, I shall wait till my fish has gorged the bait and then I am sure to land him'. Perhaps similar remarks were in his letter to Sir John, which would have raised his hopes of one day serving with Stanley in office.

The debate on the second reading of the ETA Bill started on 14th March and lasted no less than seven nights. Feeling was strongly in favour of it and when the division was finally held on 25th March it was given its second reading by 438 votes to 95, the noes including the Peelite notables of W. E. Gladstone and Sir James Graham. Sir John did not speak in the debate, but trooped into the aye lobby with the majority.

Another matter of interest to Sir John came again before the House at this time. This was another attempt to legislate for county financial boards that would have an overview of county expenditure. The bill came up for its second reading on 12th March, and after its promoter, Thomas Milner Gibson, had spoken, Sir John was quickly on his feet opposing it. Although Milner Gibson had claimed that it was similar to last year's bill, Sir John said the alterations 'made it more objectionable and more dangerous than ever'. He 'spoke strongly & at length', and reviewed some of the evidence given to the select committee the previous year. Those who supported

*Edward Stanley, 14th Earl of Derby, 1799-1867. Brought up at the family seat at Knowsley, Stanley entered parliament in 1822 as a moderate Whig, and in the 1830s held office as colonial secretary and Irish secretary. In 1835 he crossed the floor of the House to support Peel, and held office under him as colonial secretary, 1841-46, during which time he was raised to the peerage. Although still a moderate, he felt Peel had gone too far in ignoring the feelings of his party in 1846, and became the leader of the protectionist Tories. He served brief terms as prime minister in 1852, 1858-59, and 1866-68.*

the bill had been unfamiliar with county matters, whereas evidence against the bill, for example from the Earl of Stradbroke, was very strong. Winding himself to give a strong peroration, he asked the House whether they would

> take away one of the most delicate and peculiar, but I believe one of the most valuable, institutions of England – the duties which were now exercised by the unpaid magistracy of England? Let me warn the House to beware how you tamper with one of the most valuable institutions of the country. At all events, I will be no party to such meddling legislation. ...the bill is unjust, uncalled for, and mischievous, and even if I stand alone, I will protest against it.

Sir John was followed by Sir George Grey, the home secretary, who spoke in more measured tones, and felt that some of Sir John's claims were exaggerated. However, he did have some grave reservations about the details of the bill, and said that, if the House gave it a second reading, he would sit upon a select committee to try and bring the bill to a shape that would satisfy all parties.

On 20th March Sir John again went to Walton, where he had hoped to meet Mrs Davies, but she was indisposed. But she came to Walton the following day, staying two hours before Sir John had to leave. Back in town, he was able to relax by singing at two of Mrs Craddocks' musical parties, and taking Herby out shopping and visiting a clockwork farm on Saturday. Later he dined with the Bishop, after which they played chess, the result being '1 & 1'.

The following week Sir John attended a grand dinner for the supporters of Lord Stanley at the Merchant Taylors' Hall, chaired by Thomas Baring MP. Stanley gave a long speech, recounting the political history of recent years, and paying tribute to Lord Bentinck, the leader of the protectionists in the Commons until his early death in 1848. He tried to sound moderate on free trade, but pointed to the growth of imports in the cotton and other trades since 1846, and said that free traders

> are in the vain pursuit of cheapness, nothing but cheapness; and you forget that just in proportion that you make articles cheap and diminish the value of all articles to producers at large so you benefit one class, and one class only – those consumers who are not producers in their turn.

He referred to the ETA Bill, and said 'never was there so great a majority over so little a measure!'. He would have preferred to pass parliamentary resolutions deprecating what people saw as 'papal aggression', and have a lengthy enquiry rather than rush into precipitate and ill-considered legislation as the government had done.

Stanley's speech was followed by a much shorter one from Disraeli. He said that although the party did not have a parliamentary majority, they occupied the moral high ground, which surely would eventually give them power. The meeting lasted till midnight, which stopped Sir John attending Lady Harriet Clive's party, but he must have felt buoyed by the sight of the Conservative leadership making powerful speeches that night. The Times, however, pointed to Stanley's vagueness when it came to details of what his protectionist policy might be; and said it seemed unlikely that any politician could command general adherence with the millstone of protectionism round his neck.

The day after the grand dinner there was a further consideration of the oath Jews should sign before taking their seats, and the House agreed by a large majority to further the matter by appointing a committee to consider how best to change the oath. Perhaps surprisingly Sir John sided with the minority, even though his leader in the House, Disraeli, voted in favour. As Easter quarter sessions were coming up Sir John travelled to Droitwich on 4th April. He travelled with and then dined twice with Theodore Galton of Hadzor House, where he 'talked over travels'. On Monday he presided over the commencement of quarter sessions, but then hurriedly left to take the express train to London to vote on income tax. This had first been imposed during the Napoleonic wars, and afterwards withdrawn; but Peel in 1841 was forced to reintroduce it 'for a limited period' to deal with the poor state of the nation's finances after the Whig administration of the late 1830s. It had been further extended, but now the Conservatives felt it was no longer necessary, and had put down a motion for its further restriction. In proposing the motion, John Herries, MP for Stamford, quoted remarks by Lord John Russell and the present chancellor of the exchequer, Charles Wood, strongly opposing it when they were in opposition.

When Charles Wood rose to reply, he said, of course, that he had no objection to Herries searching through Hansard for this purpose; but did object to his remarks being taken out of context. Although the debate was a long one, it was not quite long enough for Sir John. He records that he arrived just as the House was dividing, but as his name does not appear in the voting lists one assumes he was too late to enter the lobbies – the government won by 278 to 230.

Sir John met Mrs Davies again at Walton on Thursday evening. He passed Friday morning with her 'and during walk our engagement was formed'. Sadly he had little time to celebrate. He had to return to London again that evening to vote on two matters to do with Smithfield market – never did a man take his parliamentary duties so seriously! The following day he wrote to Johnny and others with the announcement of his engagement, and his diary reads:

> This eventful week has decided that I shall again enter into the married state – God grant that my future wife & I may both find in our approaching union the comfort which we both require! – and that the happiness & welfare of my two dear children may be promoted by the step I have taken.

Remaining in London on parliamentary business till Tuesday, he hurried back to Westwood in the evening, and on Wednesday had a 'rather memorable day'. It started with a nice letter from Mrs Davies, then attendance at the weekly meeting of the

Droitwich Poor Law Guardians, at which he was unanimously re-elected chairman, although he had expected to be opposed. Young Herby arrived safely from London, and at a drill of the yeomanry cavalry squadron Sir John's horse Princess tried to throw him but failed! On Friday he left to stay at Elmley Park with Augusta for the Easter weekend, and on Sunday attended Elmley church twice. In the morning Rev. Park administered holy communion – 'a morning of deep feeling to us both'. His stay finished on Tuesday evening with a dinner 'tête à tête', after which he returned to Westwood. A note on the same day indicates that Johnny was in Florence – he had probably remained in Italy after his father left in February. A few days later he was in Milan.

Before returning to London Sir John had to 'spruce up' Westwood, and ordered new furniture for the private rooms. On Monday 28th April he returned with Herby and the servants to Eaton Square. He dined with Lady Sarah and the Murrays – in contrast with 1843 they could not feel uncomfortable with the timing of the engagement. The following day he had a 'distressing interview' with Mrs Milner – perhaps she had hoped to be the next Lady Pakington.

Thursday 1st May saw the opening by the Queen of the Great Exhibition of the Industries of All Nations, to give it its full name. Sir John was there, and noted 'attended opening of grand exhibition of all nations – fine sight – Royal group of parents & children very interesting – but above all interesting to see Waterloo veterans (Wellington & Anglesey) walking together'.

Mrs Davies' father Thomas Champion de Crespigny had died about the time that Augusta was born in 1799 aged only 36, and in 1827 her mother had married again. Her second husband was Sir Joseph Whatley, groom of the bedchamber to George IV and William IV. He had died in 1844, leaving his widow, Lady Whatley, living at Englefield Lodge, Surrey. After his meeting with Mrs Milner Sir John went down to Englefield Lodge to meet his future mother-in-law, then 75, who received him kindly. He had a 'happy walk & evening' with his fiancée, then returned to town next day for a meeting of the County Rates Bill committee. He received a 'delightful letter' from Johnny in reply to his announcement, and the following day Mrs Davies herself came to town, and Sir John met her at the station. They went to Eaton Square where she 'embraced' Herby, and his late wife's sister-in-law Caroline came and introduced Mrs Davies to Lady Sarah. That afternoon Sir John took Mrs Davies to see the Great Exhibition, then had a 'happy evening' dining with her in her hotel in Pont Street.

Mrs Davies returned to Englefield Lodge the next day, and Sir John had House of Commons business that day and the next when the ETA Bill was being debated again, but on Saturday he returned to Englefield Lodge. Back in town on Monday he discussed the marriage settlement with the lawyers, and invited Caroline Mordaunt and Francis Murray for dinner. The following day, Wednesday, the Convent Inspection Bill was being given its second reading, and Sir John made a short speech. The proposer of the bill, Henry Lacy, was concerned about stories that girls could be introduced to convents at a young and impressionable age, and once there it could be difficult, due to the strict and exclusive regime of many orders, for them to leave. Lacy gave a number of examples of females who had difficulty leaving a convent, and his bill provided for inspections by magistrates to make sure all was well and that everyone there was staying of their own free will. But most speakers, including the home secretary, Sir George Grey, and Lord Ashley, were against the idea, some suggesting that the

*The opening of the Great Exhibition, a day when 25,000 are said to have visited. The royal party arrived at midday, and the Queen can be seen seated on the throne, with the Princess Royal, Prince of Wales (in highland dress) and Princess Alice on her left. Prince Albert stands in front of her. Large equestrian statues of the Queen and Prince Albert can be seen behind the dais. Prince Albert described how the commission appointed by Her Majesty had fulfilled its objects, and the Queen responded. The Archbishop of Canterbury gave a lengthy blessing, and a large choir assembled in the gallery sang the Hallelujah Chorus. Then a long procession, including courtiers, ministers, and diplomats, proceeded round the exhibition. Paxton's building, 1,851 feet long, had a central transept, to the west of which were exhibits from Britain and her empire, and to the east from other countries. Initially tickets cost 3 guineas, but later (it closed on October 15th) this was reduced to 1 shilling. Over six million people are said to have visited it, almost one quarter of the population of the United Kingdom at that time.*

House would spend its time more profitably running the country. Sir John had some sympathy with the bill; he said the opponents were greatly under-rating the feelings on this subject in the country. He thought the present state of the law on this subject most unsatisfactory, and felt that the government should come forward with some other proposals. In the division the bill was defeated by 123 votes to 91, even though the government had no proposals to bring forward on the topic.

Parliamentary business prevented Sir John from attending another Great Protectionist Dinner in Worcester on 14th May, attended by 870. To remind them of his protectionist credentials, he had written a letter to the chairman, Thomas Curtler, who tried to read it out. But according to Berrows:

> he was greeted by groans, hisses and uproar, which continued for some time. After striving ineffectually to obtain a hearing, the chairman resumed his seat. On order being restored he again rose – and observed that he would appeal that their good sense, their love of justice and fairness in the matter would allow him to proceed. He thought that equal justice should be given to every man, and only wished they could hear Sir John speak for himself. He held in his hand (loud cries of no, no, order, and hisses) a letter and begged to tell them that Sir John Pakington had determined to have been present that day, but that his duties in the House on a committee which will sit on Thursday morning and from which it will be most inconvenient for him to be absent will prevent him attending.

Sir John had written:

> The apprehensions which induced me to oppose the repeal of the Corn Laws have been too fully realised. We have now the public admission of the statesman who promoted that dangerous experiment (for such I shall continue to consider it) that their anticipations have not proved correct. I should have been glad of an opportunity distinctly to assure my agricultural neighbours in Worcestershire that I partake in their alarm and sympathise in their distress, and that I am prepared to act with them and with their advocates in parliament in every effort to obtain relief for that great and injured interest to which we belong.

The Rev. John Pearson then rose and said:

> I cannot refrain from making a remark or two about the way in which Sir John's note has been received. Now Sir John Pakington, it should be remembered, voted against the repeal of the corn laws (cries of Oh Oh, we won't have it, and cheers).

The chairman intervened and said that the company might be assured that if any gentleman in addressing them made an incorrect statement he would himself interfere and set him right (cheers). His Reverend friend, however, had stated what was perfectly right and correct, and consequently he had not interfered (hear, hear). Mr Pearson resumed:

> I am sorry I have been met with interruption, but no-one cares less about being interrupted than I do. Sir John voted against the repeal of the corn laws but, after that measure had been carried, he, in common with many other gentlemen, had thought it right that it should have a fair trial. He had now, however, found out his error, and felt convinced that some protection was necessary, and he conducted himself on that as on all occasions as an honourable man (no, no, and cheers).

Next weekend it was Mrs Davies's turn to come up to town, and on Saturday they paid their second visit to the Great Exhibition. She stayed in town and they dined with various members of the Murray family, also Lady Glasgow – she was the widowed mother of Johnny's wife Diana. Later the same evening Sir John attended the House of Commons, where there was a debate on an education motion. This was proposed by radical MP William Johnson Fox, who, despite (or possibly because of) being a non-conformist minster, had brought forward a bill the previous year to establish a national system of secular education, independent of the teachings of the various sects. Such a proposal was too radical for most MPs and was heavily defeated, but, nothing daunted, on 22nd May Fox brought forward a motion 'that it is expedient to promote the education of the people, in England and Wales, by the establishment of free schools for secular instruction, to be supported by local rates, and managed by Committees, elected specially for that purpose by the ratepayers'. He pointed to the poor state of education in the country and the different opinions as to how far education and religion should be combined, and said that it would be best to cut a path through all these rivalries by leaving religious instruction to the clergy, and to establish schools which would concentrate simply on education.

Although backed by indisputable logic the idea was still too radical for MPs, who had long thought of religious instruction and education as inseparable. Most schools at this time were still church schools, and the home secretary, Sir George Grey, echoed these sentiments. He admitted that 'great deficiencies exist in the present system of education, and that there is a want of means to bring that system, defective as it was, into operation generally throughout the country'. But he denied that education for the poorer classes was getting worse, as Fox had alleged, and said there had been not only an increase in the number of schools but also in the improved qualifications of teachers. While he did not object to the general principle of funding education out of local rates, he could not agree with the idea that this funding should go exclusively to secular schools, thus disadvantaging religious ones. Grey concluded:

> If there is one thing upon which the opinion of the country has been clearly and distinctly expressed, it is this, that education should be based upon religion; that, instead of excluding that which is the most essential object of education, they ought to take especial care to see that all education included the instilling of religious principles, based upon the word of God, which is the only security for the discharge of those duties which man owes to his fellow-man, and still more for the discharge of his duty to God.

This seemed to be the general opinion amongst MPs, and Sir John joined the majority in the noe lobby which defeated Fox's resolution by 139 votes to 49.

The following night Sir John was back in the House, which was debating the ETA Bill yet again. Some legal pitfalls had been found in the bill, so various amendments had been proposed by the government. Although the bill was given large majorities at every division, it was taking a long time to get it through its various stages. On that evening the House sat till 01.30, and the debate had to be adjourned again till the following week, when it had two further lengthy sittings.

The same week there was a debate which lasted two nights on Ceylon (now Sri Lanka) in which the Tories thought they had a chance of embarrassing the government. In 1847 the thirty five year old Lord Torrington had been sent out as governor. The colony had previously been badly administered with a fiscal deficit and there had been an insurrection; Torrington had followed local advice, declared martial law and firmly restored order. He also improved the finances; but martial law had been maintained after the insurrection had been quelled and courts martial held without, it was alleged, proper form. Over one hundred summary executions were carried out and Torrington had been recalled in 1850. The debate became rather bad tempered at times as personal accusations and counter accusations flowed. On the second night the prime minister Lord John Russell and the leader of the opposition, Benjamin Disraeli, wound up. Russell pointed to Torrington's successful record having left the colony in a much better state than he had found it. Disraeli, in a clever speech, said it was all very well to say that Britain's interests had been safeguarded, but what about the natives? Not only had our normal standards of justice been abandoned in order to put fear and dread into the native population, but their property had been sequestered if they had left their village. The episode cast shame and dishonour on the mother country. He relied heavily on a report in a local newspaper, normally supportive of the governor, which described 'wholesale butchery', 'pillaging', and behaviour 'that was a disgrace to a civilized nation'. Sir John did not contribute to the debate but was there to cast his vote in support of the Tories, but the government won by 282 votes to 202.

That weekend Hanbury Williams and his daughters Annette and Mary came to meet Mrs Davies – the former on her own, the latter with her husband Col Davies. This was preparatory to Sir John's wedding which was to take place on Thursday 5th June, but on Tuesday and Wednesday his mind was much occupied by other matters. On Tuesday he worked hard all morning on a speech he was to give in the Commons on sugar duties, but only later did he discover that the House was not to sit that day, so his work was in vain. The following day he attended the AGM of the National Society for Promoting the Education of the Poor in the Principles of the Established Church in England and Wales. Its aim was 'that the national religion should be made the foundation of national education, and should be the first and chief thing taught to the poor, according to the excellent liturgy and catechism provided by our church'. The schools it founded were known as 'National Schools', as opposed to 'British Schools' founded by the British & Foreign Schools Society, in which education followed more secular principles.

On this occasion the Archbishop of Canterbury took the chair, and several other bishops, deans and clergymen were present and, judging by the interest in the proceedings, it was well attended. During the previous two years the National Society, as it was usually known, had been dogged by controversy, centred round its relationship with the Privy Council Education Committee which was responsible for distributing the government education grant. The Privy Council Committee had, not unreasonably, made rules about the schools that it supported, and four of these laid down how they were to be managed. Every school was to be managed by a committee, and in the case of Anglican schools the committee should consist only of members of the church. Some people thought this took the management out of the direct hands of the clergy and the Anglican hierarchy, and delivered it into the hands of laymen.

One of the leaders of the opposition to state interference (as he saw it) in Anglican schools was Rev. George Denison, a noted high churchman who at one time was friendly with Henry Manning and the tractarians, although he did not go as far as some in converting to Catholicism. He did not agree that the National Society should accept the four management articles of the Privy Council Committee, and had brought forward resolutions to that effect in the past. At the AGM in 1851 Denison again had a resolution to propose. Although in his opinion more moderate, it still condemned the government for refusing state assistance to schools run entirely by the clergy of the parish and the bishop of the diocese. Sir John had come to the meeting that day to oppose Denison and to try and restore peace to the National Society. It is evident from the reports of the meeting that Denison had vociferous adherents and opponents, and the Most Rev. Chairman would rather see the controversy subside.

After Denison had put his resolution Sir John proposed an amendment, which was

> that the cause of sound religious instruction and the interests of the church demand, at the present juncture, the friendly co-operation of the National Society and the Committee of the [Privy] Council; and this meeting, satisfied that such co-operation must be for the advantage of the National Society as well as for the church at large, desires to deprecate any renewal of the agitation which has threatened the recent meetings of the Society, and to express the earnest hope that the two bodies may act cordially together.

In concluding, Sir John offered to withdraw his resolution if Denison did the same, but his reported response was a rather unclerical 'catch me at it'. The meeting then continued some time with speakers from both sides, and frequent interruptions, and, despite several invitations, Denison refused to withdraw. Finally the Most Rev.

Chairman said he must put the question to the meeting. At this the Bishop of London said he much deprecated the whole discussion, and hoped both the resolution and the amendment would be negatived. Sir John accepted the suggestion of the Bishop, and withdrew his amendment, but Denison still refused. When Denison's motion was rejected by a large majority, the result was greeted by 'great cheering'. Sir John was obviously pleased, as he noted in his diary that he 'spoke well in opposition to Denison, and was much complimented'.

The following day, Thursday 5th June 1851:

> Married at 10 a.m. to dear Mrs Davies at St Michael's church – ceremony performed by George Murray – left London by 12 train & at 8 p.m. having posted from Birmingham we arrived at Westwood for dinner.

They stayed in Worcestershire for two weeks before returning to London, and on the first Sunday

> attended morning prayers in new chapel for first time – my dear wife went with me in little phaeton to Hampton church – we took communion – in afternoon service in chapel – we then went to lodges & round lake walking & on pony. Happy day! – and eventful week! May God bless this my third marriage and make it conducive to the happiness of my children, my dear wife & myself.

From this it appears that a private chapel had been built at Westwood – there is still a room there called the chapel. The following Saturday they went for a stay in Elmley Park; they walked about all afternoon and had a 'pleasing reception by villagers'. On Monday a Mr Parker came 'to discuss letting Elmley Park, & in afternoon I took a beautiful walk with him to top of Bredon Hill & round estate'. The next day was rent day, and Sir John was introduced to the tenants. Col Davies's estate in Elmley Castle in 1840 amounted to 834 acres, so these rents would have made a welcome addition to the family income now they were not encumbered by the expenses of running Elmley Park. Col Davies in his will had left his wife a life interest in his estate, and said that her income should be made up to £2,200, as specified in their marriage settlement, so she does seem to have been well provided for.

On 18th June they returned to Eaton Square where they had left Herby, who they found 'quite well, thank God', and dined with Johnny and Diana, who were also staying in London. The next day Sir John was back in the House of Commons, but during a debate on whether Universities should continue to impose a religious test on undergraduates, thus excluding non-Anglicans, the House was 'counted out', there being less than forty members present. So the debate on sugar duties and the West Indies which had prompted Sir John's attendance did not take place. Sir John went in a new barouche to see the Royal Academy exhibition before attending yet another debate on the committee stage of the ETA Bill, but after taking part in one division he felt unwell and did not return. The debate continued on Monday, and after travelling to Englefield Lodge for a night on Tuesday, Sir John and Lady Augusta held their first dinner party in Eaton Square. The guests included Johnny and his wife and mother-in-law Lady Glasgow, and 'A Thellusson', a relation of his wife's late uncle Peter Isaac Thellusson, 1st Lord Rendlesham.

On Friday 27th June the debate on the ETA Bill continued. Sir John noted with satisfaction that the government were defeated twice and the Bill thus improved. After viewing a Panorama 'Great Marvel of the World' on Saturday and on Sunday going to afternoon service at St Michael's, Sir John took the night train to Worcestershire, arriving at 4.00 a.m. After breakfast he met Thomas Curtler to view Worcester gaol, as Sir Offley Wakeman had put down a motion about it for consideration at quarter sessions, which opened that day. Wakeman was very concerned about the women's gaol, where convicted prisoners were allowed to associate with those awaiting trial. "A woman of most notorious character under sentence of transportation was now in the county gaol and a girl of tender years had been repeatedly seen sitting beside her…" he said. In such circumstances, moral contamination was inevitable. He was also concerned about the poor ventilation and heating in the gaol and proposed that £150 be spent on improving all these matters. The chairman however wished to keep expenditure down and 'thought very great caution should be exercised in raising the temperature'. In the end only £80 was voted.

Sessions finished in time for Sir John to take the express back to town on Wednesday afternoon, and after House of Commons business on Thursday he went on Friday with his wife, Johnny and Diana for yet another visit to the Crystal Palace. This diary entry is the first to call his wife 'Madre'. On Saturday it was Herby's turn to be entertained with a visit to the Zoo, and later Sir John and Lady Augusta saw Mlle Rachel in Racine's 'Phedre'.

*St Michael's, Chester Square, was opened in 1846, and was designed by Thomas Cundy jun. who was surveyor to the Grosvenor estates. The Marquess of Westminster contributed £5,000 to its building. It was only a short walk from the Pakingtons' residence at 41 Eaton Square, and they were regular attenders.*

On the following week his diary is, unusually, blank, but on Saturday 12th July he went with Herby to the Murrays at Danbury, but Augusta was too unwell to accompany them. On Monday he returned leaving Herby there, and on Tuesday he had an engagement with Prince Albert who was to visit the Royal Philanthropic Society's farm school at Redhill, Surrey. This society had been founded sixty years before by men concerned at the number of children on London's streets who earned their living by begging or stealing. An institution was set up at Southwark to take in such children, most of whom had already been in prison, and to teach them a trade. In 1848 a farm was purchased at Redhill and the boys accommodated in the farm house. Additional facilities were built – Prince Albert laid the foundation stone for the chapel on 30th April 1849. It is not known when Sir John first became involved, but he was chairman at a meeting in January 1850 when it was reported that sixty five boys had so far been taken into the school, most of whom had been in prison several times. Success had been patchy – some had already left to emigrate, some had been apprenticed, but a few had absconded or gone back to a life on the streets. In his address the previous year Sir John had said, no doubt with his Juvenile Offenders Bill in mind, that "no subject could be more fitting for the deep and anxious attention of the legislature than the reformation of juvenile offenders. The object of this institution is to divert the polluted stream into the purest channel, and redeem from crime those young creatures who have been led astray...". Sir John, not for the first time, said "their zeal in the cause should not lead them to the adoption of any general system which might have the effect of holding out a premium to vice, and thus present advantages to criminals, of which the innocents were deprived".

Sir John toured the farm school with the Prince, and returned with him in the royal train. The next day Sir John was again out in a train, this time to Windsor to see a cattle show at which he was 'much pleased' and afterwards he was still able to take his wife to see 'The Marriage of Figaro'. According to The Times, Her Majesty's Theatre was packed to see the opera stars Henriette Sontag, Sophie Cruvelli and Luigi Lablache. After the opera the evening was rounded by Carlotta Grisis, the ballet dancer, and a violin performance by Julian, a child prodigy of eleven. Sir John and Lady Augusta with Johnny and Diana went to more music on Friday when they heard seven bands play together at Fulham – 'very beautiful' – but they stayed too long, and he again missed his chance of bringing up the sugar duties question in the House.

He also missed the start of a little drama that concluded on Monday, when he says there was 'an unusual scene in HoC from Salomons attempting to take his seat'. David Salomons was a banker and leading member of the Jewish community. In 1835 he served (after the passing of an act of parliament) as Sheriff of London, and also as High Sheriff of Kent, and became an alderman of London. In 1851 he was elected as a Liberal MP for Greenwich, but when he attempted to take his seat he swore on the old testament rather than the new, and did not include the words 'as a Christian' in the oath of abjuration. The speaker accordingly told him he could not take his seat, but as the prime minister was not present, the matter was deferred to Monday.

Salomons wanted to be prosecuted so the matter could be tested in a court of law, but on Monday Lord John Russell said the government did not intend to take that course. But Salomons entered the House and took his seat, and an excited and lengthy debate ensued. His friends said that as he had sworn in a manner that he regarded as tying his conscience as much as the more usual oath did, so he should take his seat. Unfortunately the majority in the House that day did not accept this interpretation, and eventually voted by a large majority that he should leave. When he refused the Sergeant at Arms came and arrested him, and he was later fined £500. More time was spent debating the issue the following day, and again the following week, but it was to be another seven years until the law was changed, after which Salomons was at last able to serve as MP for Greenwich.

The 1851 parliamentary session was coming to an end, and on 23rd July Sir John spoke a number of times when the Administration of Justice Bill was in committee. He supported the main aim, which was to allow courts to amend the terms of an indictment if it proved technically wrong, but he regretted that the bill did not extend to giving magistrates power to deal with cases of petty larceny. He also noted that he 'gave up Beer Bill' – this was another attempt to extend the restrictions on beer shops. It stipulated that anyone applying for a licence should have a declaration signed by six persons not in the beer trade rated at least as highly as the applicant, and that the premises should be rated at least at £20 in London, £15 in other towns, and £10 elsewhere. To verify that their premises were correctly rated, a certificate had to be obtained from magistrates in petty sessions that the declared rateable value was correct. To discourage beer licensees from giving credit, it also provided that debts

*Luigi Lablache (left) sang Bartolo, 'as admirably weighty as ever' The Times ciritc wrote, and (centre) Henriette Sontag who sang Susanna. Her* Deh, Vieni *was 'a perfect gem of cantabile singing'. (Right) Carlotta Grisi, an Italian ballet dancer, performed a 'divertissement' after the opera.*

incurred in beer shops should not be recoverable at law. But when he realised that it stood no chance of passing, he withdrew it.

The following day Sir John wanted to raise the sugar duty question again, and at the end of a debate on the third reading of the Customs Bill, a free-trade government measure, he moved an adjournment of the debate to give him a chance to raise the matter when it was resumed. The sitting had been delayed by a experimental morning one in the newly built Commons chamber, so it was late and the bill had already been delayed, so the prime minister was not pleased at Sir John's intervention and said "I must complain that after the time of the House has been occupied in the fruitless discussion which had taken place, such a course is most unfair". But then Sir John found a supporter in Disraeli, who said:

> The noble Lord at the head of the Government says we are wasting time; but I want to know how an independent member of parliament is to bring forward any question, unless he takes some such opportunity. This is no insignificant question. It is one which deeply affects the mercantile classes in this country, and is eminently entitled to the consideration of the House. But, Sir, the first minister of the crown gets up and tells us the time of the House is not to be wasted. I protest against the tone of the minister. I want him to understand that this House has some other duties to perform than to pass government measures; and though I do not wish to occasion any angry feeling, I think the government has not taken the proper course, and that my hon. friend is entitled to have his case brought under the consideration of the House.

Sir John himself made a further appeal, but Lord John would have none of it. He said the bill had already been delayed a considerable time, and he would countenance no further delay. On a division, Sir John's adjournment motion was defeated by a considerable majority.

The following day 'Herby with servants, carriages & horses went home'. Sir John paid a farewell visit to Mrs Milner which was 'very satisfactory', then, after another attendance at the House, he and his wife went home by train on Saturday 26th July. This was her first stay in Droitwich as Lady Pakington, and Sir John drove her around the local parishes as well as attending a meeting of the Board of Guardians on Wednesday morning. Afterwards he lunched with Thomas Curtler and discussed the remaining part of his estate in Pembrokeshire – he had in mind some new arrangements for managing it. But another opportunity to raise the sugar question in the House had presented itself, so on Thursday he returned to town by Great Western express, presumably from Cheltenham, and he noted that the last 53 miles were covered in 53 minutes over the straight and level broad gauge main line from Paddington to Swindon so impressively engineered by Brunel.

The debate on sugar followed a petition presented by Henry Labouchere from a number of sugar refiners expressing the hope that the government would not change the present system of paying duty on imported raw sugar. Sir John made a speech in support of his motion that sugar refiners should be allowed to refine sugar in bond, i.e. before any duty had been paid on it. As raw sugar was refined there was some loss, the amount depending on the quality of the raw material. The duty imposed on poor quality raw sugar was effectively increased as it was refined, putting producers of good quality raw sugar at an advantage over those of poorer quality. A further point was that the duty on imported refined sugar was the same as that on imported raw sugar, which meant that sugar refined in, for example, Holland, had a duty advantage when imported into Britain.

West Indian sugar producers saw that the present system acted to their disadvantage both because their sugar was not of the highest quality, and because sugar entering Britain from other countries enjoyed a duty advantage as explained above. However, in replying to the motion Labouchere, who was President of the Board of Trade, spoke of the practical problems that stood in the way of change, and of the importance of protecting government revenue. After Labouchere sat down another member rose to support Sir John, but less than the necessary forty members were sufficiently interested to be present, and the debate was terminated without a division.

Sir John returned to Westwood on Saturday (but not before taking leave of Mrs Milner once again). The county gentry were now mostly back at home, and the archery season started again. There were meetings at Hanbury Hall and Hadzor House ('where the gay dresses of the ladies added in no small degree to the brilliancy of the scene', Berrows reported) as well as one at Westwood itself that week. Lady Augusta was still unfamiliar with the local area, and the day after the Hadzor meeting Sir John drove back with her to Hanbury and called on George Croft Vernon at Hanbury Mount, where she was shown the view. From this site at the southern end of a low ridge, there is a fine view towards the Clee Hills, Abberley, and the Malvern Hills, and it is said that on a clear day the Severn estuary can be picked out. They then drove to the nearby Dodderhill Common, to enjoy a similarly fine view, with Hanbury church on its hill in the foreground. The following day he drove Lady Pakington round to see some of his tenants and their farms.

The following week starting on Monday 11th August Sir John devoted to visiting the Pembrokeshire estate to put in hand some 'new arrangements'. On Monday he got as far as Bristol, then the following morning, leaving at 6.00 a.m., Job Taylor in his boat 'Osprey' took him to Tenby where they landed at 4.00 p.m., and they continued to Haverfordwest. The next morning they went to the estate at Little Milford where there was a colliery, and he spent three days examining books and accounts and inspecting the farm house and cottages, and 'completed new arrangements'. He returned by the same method, staying overnight at the 'very good' Royal Western Hotel in Bristol. He got back home on Sunday and 'had the blessing of finding wife and Herby very well'.

The next week he devoted to making further local calls introducing Lady Augusta. In the last week of August the Worcester Music Festival was held. As usual, he had invited a party of friends, including Johnny and Diana, to stay and attend the concerts. The Festival started on Tuesday and included the usual sermon, this time by Rev. E. H. Cradock, Canon of the Cathedral. Sir John described it as 'very grand & excellent'. The text was 'the night cometh when no man can work' (John, ch. 9). Berrows reported that Cradock's reflections were 'deeply impressive and eloquent, reminding his hearers that the night which had already closed upon so many young and old during the past three years was rapidly hastening onward for them and it was therefore their bounded duty to work while it was day'. Cradock was probably referring to the cholera epidemic of 1849, which caused substantial mortality throughout Britain. The Festival was as usual to raise money for the widows and orphans of the clergy, and Cradock ended his sermon with 'a warm appeal in favour of this excellent charity'. It seems to have been a tradition that leading local figures held the plates at strategic locations to receive the audience's donations at the end of the concerts, and they worked in pairs of a lady and a gentleman. Those noted by Berrows included Mrs Pepys (the Bishop's wife) and Sir John Pakington, Lord Henley and Lady Diana Pakington, Capt. Rushout and Lady Pakington, Mr. Pakington and Lady Essington. Their efforts seem to have been successful, and £302 was collected at the doors that day from the audience of 1,282. Overall over £1,000 was raised, but the Festival, as usual, made a net loss of over £700, and the stewards and the guarantee fund had to be called on.

'Elijah' was performed on Wednesday, 'Samson' on Thursday and Messiah on Friday. Sir John returned home to dinner every day, and did not attend the evening concerts, including the grand ball on Friday night, even though both his wife and Diana were patronesses.

Most of his house party dispersed on Saturday, but some of the Peel family, including Lady Peel, widow of the late prime minister, called, but Sir John regrettably missed them. The principal meeting of the archery society was held on 4th September – it was supposed to have been at Madresfield, but was transferred to Ombersley Court due to the illness of Lord Beauchamp. Richard Temple was the chairman, and Lady Pakington and Lady Harriet Clive were seated either side of him at dinner.

On Monday 8th September Sir John presided over the annual meeting of the Severn Commissioners. It will be recalled that the works below Worcester (mainly dredging) had not succeeded in maintaining a depth of six feet, and this had led to poor receipts from tolls. However, Sir John was able to report some improvement in the finances, although some interest payments were still in arrear. An interesting experiment was described in the engineer's report, when a screw steamer, taking advantage of the river being full, was able to take 150 tons of cargo, while at the same time towing two other boats making a total of 230 tons, from Gloucester to Worcester in six hours.

This cost only one penny halfpenny per ton. In shallower water it would have needed three traditional trows each pulled by two horses each, and cost one shilling and four pence, nearly ten times as much, to achieve the same result, and still have taken twice as long. The river had however been too shallow since April, and at one point fifty boats had been stranded on a shoal at Upton upon Severn. The Commissioners were still waiting for the Admiralty survey to be completed, and Sir John would then be on a committee to determine how to advance the much needed improvements.

Other local matters occupied him during October, including Michaelmas sessions, the annual Agricultural Society meeting, a Hartlebury school governors meeting, and, on 31st, a meeting in Birmingham about the Worcester diocesan training school which was due to open in the new year. The chairman, Lord Lyttelton, said no progress had been made on the proposed middle school, due to lack of funds. There was also the usual social round, including a stay at Elmley Park with Johnny and Diana, when they enjoyed walking on Bredon Hill and some shooting.

In October he went to London for a few days, mainly, it seems, to pay final visits to the Great Exhibition. Caroline Mordaunt was also there, and, leaving his wife, who was afraid of the crowds, at home, Sir John took Caroline, and noted that it was the largest attendance of any day – an incredible 110,000. Although they were able to move about freely inside, they got 'mobbed' coming home. While in town he saw the Bishop and Lady Sarah, also Mrs Milner with whom he had 'a distressing interview'. They also went to hear Beethoven's 'Fidelio', and after a second visit to the Crystal Palace Lady Augusta went to Englefield Lodge, and Sir John returned home, as the Michaelmas sessions were to be held the following week.

Sir John noted that 'sessions ended with a long & good trial for needle stealing'. The prisoner, James Shrimpton, had exchanged 4,000 needles for a parrot and a satin dress with a travelling hawker. The needles had found their way into the hands of a man who tried to sell them in Redditch, but, being offered only 6d a thousand, took them away again. As some of the needles were labelled 'Bartlett & Co' (Shrimpton's ex-employer), the man was reported to the police, and through him they were traced back to Shrimpton, who was arrested and charged with theft. Evidence was given that a women who worked for Bartlett & Co was seen in a public house with Shrimpton talking about labels, the accusation being that she had given him different labels to make him appear to be a genuine needle factor. Shrimpton's counsel put up a vigorous defence, claiming there was no definite link between the needles found and those missed by Bartlett & Co. According to Berrows, Sir John gave a 'very impartial' summing up. But the jury found Shrimpton guilty, and Sir John sentenced him to imprisonment for nine months.

One of Sir John's interests was chess, and he occasionally enjoyed an evening game with the Bishop. In October he mentioned a chess tournament, and one of his opponents was a man called Carder. After a tournament game they played another private game, in which 'he [Carder] behaved ill'. The dispute continued, as it appears that Sir John reported the incident to higher authority, and another game with Carder was put off, and then a third – all caused by an 'unpleasant difference about move'. It seems that chess replaced archery as an excuse for socialising as the winter approached. As usual there were visits to country houses, usually involving shooting, including Badger in Shropshire, the home of the Capel Cures, The Nash in Kempsey, home of the Temples, and Oakley Park, home of the Clives, from where he went to see Croft Castle – 'disappointed with castle', he wrote. He was always interested in matters agricultural, and attended a lecture on flax, and in December went to see the great poultry show in Birmingham, and stayed – where else? – at the Hen and Chickens! He made further visits to Birmingham in connection with the training school at Saltley, and attended several meetings of the Powick Asylum committee to choose the first superintendent. He was able to enjoy Christmas with all his family as well as a number of house guests, and the party was enlivened by Johnny, who had taken up conjuring as a hobby.

As usual, Sir John made a note in his diary at the year end:

> And so ends a year the first that I can call happy since the bright year of 1847 & in which I have experienced many & great blessings! Thanks to God for his manifold mercies to me & mine!

Towards the end of 1851 he noted that he was rehearsing for an amateur concert, which was held on 13th January 1852. It was very well attended by Worcestershire society, and Sir John sang in a Rossini quintet in the first half, and a trio by the same composer in the second, both of which were given special mention by the Morning Post, as well a solo 'Spanish Song to Liberty'. Two weeks later parliament was opened. The next day Sir John was one of those MPs, comprising the whole of the protectionist wing of the Tory party, who assembled at the house of their leader, Stanley, who had succeeded his father as 14th Earl of Derby the previous year. The previous day Derby had replied to the address in the House of Lords by going through and commenting on the topics mentioned in the Queen's speech, and he largely repeated what he had said to the loyal troops at his mansion in St James Square. Much of the speech concerned foreign affairs, and Derby made a few comments, in particular about the state of affairs in France, where a coup d'état had taken place bringing a somewhat dictatorial regime to power. It was important, Derby said, to ensure that our own defences were ready to counter any military aggression by the new regime.

There were only two major domestic topics to be commented on. The Queen's speech had pointed to an improvement in the prospects for agriculture, but Derby begged to disagree. The price of wheat was falling to ever lower levels, and the situation of the agriculturalist and the land-owner was bad. Derby implicitly blamed the lack of protection, but avoided the suggestion that protection be reintroduced. By now he had at least recognised that such a measure could never be carried through the House of Commons. Finally, Derby referred at some length to the promise in the speech to introduce a bill of parliamentary reform. Derby was clear that this was neither necessary nor advisable. He said it would be twenty years after the 1832 Reform Act had passed – did reform only last that long, like an agricultural lease? He did not know what the new measure was to contain; but he was against upsetting the present balance in our constitution, based as it still was on that sheet anchor of stability, the owners of land.

The contents of the new reform bill were soon revealed. On 9th February Lord John Russell set out his proposals. His speech was a mixture of good sense and rather convoluted logic. He spoke at some length about the history of reform, and about the principles that drove the Reform Act of 1832. Of, course there was no question of any universal franchise, and the possibility of a secret ballot did not get a mention. Most of what Russell said concerned the smaller boroughs. Many had been disenfranchised or reduced to one member in 1832, but many remained, some with an electorate of less than 300. He felt that it was important to keep the representation of these boroughs – if their MPs was transferred to the larger cities, it would unbalance the House. It was true that some smaller boroughs were still largely in the pocket of a local magnate, and also that bribery had been by no means stamped out. His answer to this was to join many of the smaller boroughs with a neighbouring town; in this way personal influence would be diluted, and many larger towns given more direct representation. (When the bill was published shortly afterwards, it proposed that Droitwich should be joined with Bromsgrove in a new constituency; it can be imagined that Sir John, who would remember his rather unfriendly reception in the latter town in 1832, would not have been at all keen on this idea.)

The other major proposals were to reduce the borough franchise from occupiers of houses worth £10 per annum to £5 per annum, and that in the counties from £40 to £20; to remove altogether the property qualification required of MPs; and to have a new uniform oath for all new MPs that would include Protestants, Catholics and Jews.

Having failed in his attempt to bring in a beer bill in 1851, Sir John was determined to try again, and on 10th February sought leave to bring in the same bill as had failed last year. Although some members commented that, if the aim of the hon. member for Droitwich was to raise the morals of the working classes, then it was doubtful if this could be achieved through an act of parliament, leave was given. Soon afterwards, Sir John had to fight another long-running battle, this time about county finance. It will be recalled that in 1850 Milner Gibson had introduced a County Rates and Expenditure Bill that aimed to democratise the control of county finance by establishing county finance boards on which would sit members nominated by Boards of Guardians. Sir John had vehemently opposed this, and was a member of the select committee set up to examine the proposals in the bill. The committee rejected the bill as it stood, but recommended a number of changes that would improve it.

The promoter of the bill, Thomas Milner Gibson, had ignored these recommendations, and last session had re-introduced the bill more or less in its original form. Again a select committee was set up, this time with the home secretary, Sir George Grey as a member, which again worked hard to recommend some improvements. Sir John was the principal speaker in the current debate. He assumed that the 1852 bill would be based on the 1851 bill with these changes. But now he was amazed to see that, despite all this committee work, Gibson had not only not adopted these recommendations, but had actually made his bill even more radical by not adopting the automatic membership of magistrates on the county finance boards, and making them fully elected by the boards of guardians. He thought such an idea was totally uncalled for and would never work, and it was ridiculous to imagine that the ordinary ratepayer had any idea about the management of gaols, or the police, or all the other matters presently managed by the experienced body of county magistrates in quarter sessions. He proposed that consideration of the bill be delayed this time six months.

In the ensuing debate, the bill got little support, and after Sir George Grey had spoken against it Sir John's motion was carried by a substantial majority.

But although Lord John Russell's government commanded in theory a good majority in the House of Commons, it had been weakened by the ETA Act, which many suggested would be a dead letter, by a dispute with Palmerston who now did what he could to undermine Russell, and by doubt among many of his colleagues about the wisdom of introducing the new reform bill.

So it was that, at only the third division of the session on 20th February, after a debate on a militia bill, in which Palmerston rounded on his former colleagues, the government were defeated by 136 votes to 125, Sir John voting with the majority. Shortly afterwards Russell announced his resignation. As Lord Derby was the leader of the only organised opposition, the Queen sent for him to form a government, and, thinking that his time had now at last come, Derby accepted. He soon announced a cabinet, which included, to a certain amount of surprise including his own, Sir John Pakington. The story of how he fared in his new role will be told in a subsequent volume.

# Appendix
## John Somerset Pakington's Parliamentary Career

| Year | Prime Minister | Party | John Pakington |
|---|---|---|---|
| 1832-34 | Earl Grey (Lords) | Whig | |
| 1834 | Viscount Melbourne (Lords) | Whig | |
| 1834 | Sir Robert Peel (Commons) | Tory | |
| 1834-41 | Viscount Melbourne (Lords) | Whig | |
| 1837 | Viscount Melbourne (Lords) | Whig | Elected for Droitwich |
| 1841 | Sir Robert Peel (Commons) | Tory | Re-elected for Droitwich |
| 1846-52 | Lord John Russell (Commons) | Whig | |
| 1847 | Lord John Russell (Commons) | Whig | Re-elected for Droitwich |
| 1852 | Earl of Derby (Lords) | Conservative | Re-elected for Droitwich Colonial Secretary |
| 1852-55 | Earl of Aberdeen (Lords) | Peelite Tory | |
| 1855-57 | Viscount Palmerston (Commons) | Liberal | |
| 1857-58 | Viscount Palmerston (Commons) | Liberal | Re-elected for Droitwich |
| 1858-59 | Earl of Derby (Lords) | Conservative | First Lord of the Admiralty |
| 1859 | Viscount Palmerston (Commons) | Liberal | Re-elected for Droitwich |
| 1859-65 | Viscount Palmerston (Commons) | Liberal | |
| 1865-66 | Earl Russell (Lords) | Liberal | Re-elected for Droitwich |
| 1866-68 | Earl of Derby (Lords) | Conservative | Secretary of State for War |
| 1868 | Benjamin Disraeli (Commons) | Conservative | Secretary of State for War |
| 1868 | William Gladstone (Commons) | Liberal | Defeated John Corbett at Droitwich election |
| 1868-74 | William Gladstone (Commons) | Liberal | |
| 1874 | Benjamin Disraeli (Commons) | Conservative | Lost Droitwich election to John Corbett |

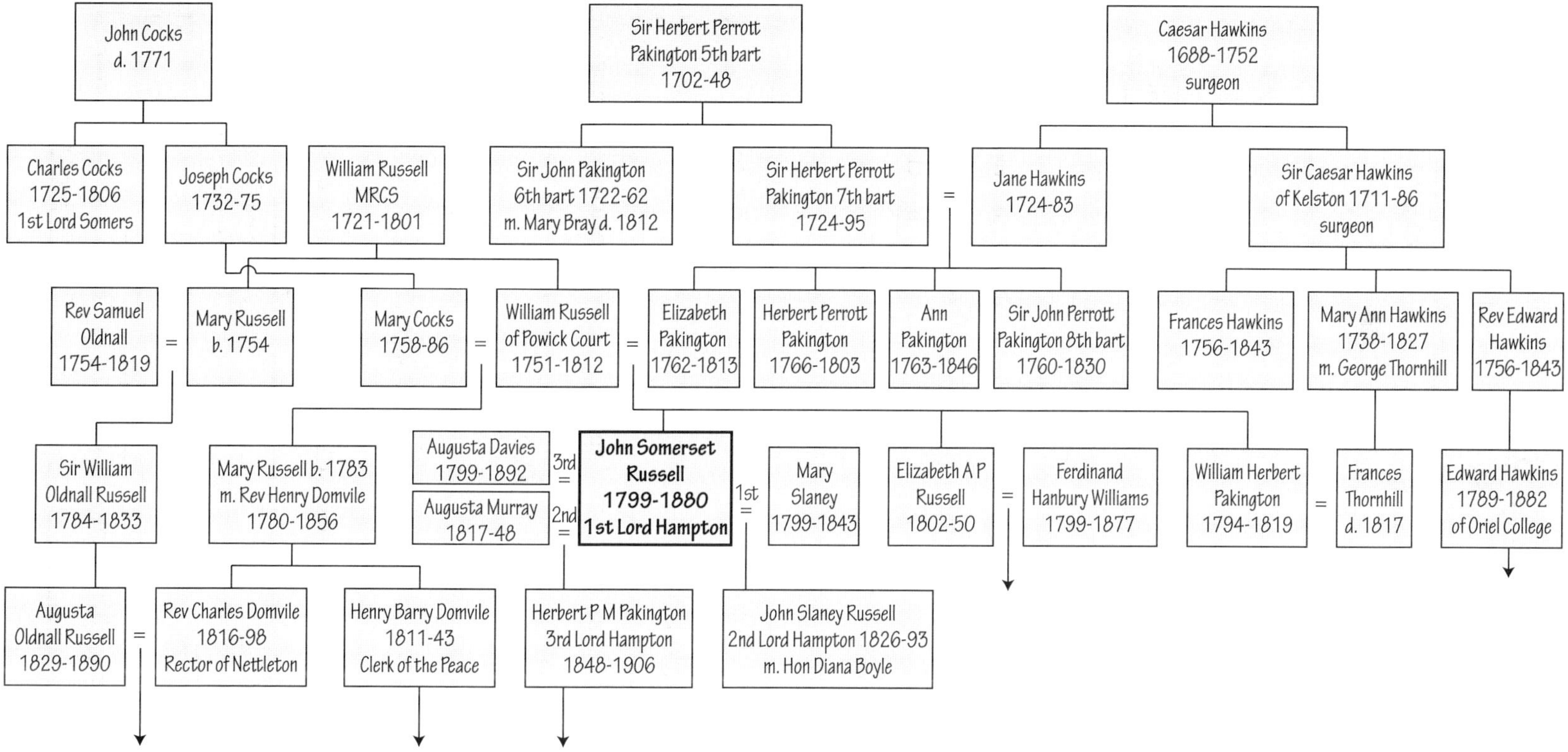


**Descendants of Sir Herbert Pakington 5th bart of Westwood Showing the relations of Sir John Somerset Pakington**

## Index

## Index of Illustrations